New

WITHDRAWN
Computers, Business, and Office

3

STACKS

Editorial Advisory Board

The Career Information Center includes:

- Agribusiness, Environment, and Natural Resources / 1
- Communications and the Arts / 2
- Computers, Business, and Office / 3
- Construction / 4
- Consumer, Homemaking, and Personal Services / 5
- Engineering, Science, Technology, and Social Science / 6
- Health / 7
- Hospitality and Recreation / 8
- Manufacturing / 9
- Marketing and Distribution / 10
- Public and Community Services / 11
- Transportation / 12
- Employment Trends and Master Index / 13

Computers, Business, and Office 3

Career Information Center

Ninth Edition

MACMILLAN REFERENCE USA

An imprint of Thomson Gale, a part of The Thomson Corporation

THOMSON

GALE

Detroit • New York • San Francisco • New Haven, Conn. • Waterville, Maine • London

Career Information Center, Ninth Edition

Paula Kepos, Series Editor

Project Editor
Mary Rose Bonk

Editorial
Jennifer Greve

Imaging
Lezlie Light, Daniel Newell, Christine O'Bryan

Permissions
Kelly A. Quin, Tim Sisler, Andrew Specht

Manufacturing
Rhonda Dover

For permission to use material from this product, submit your request via Web at http://www.gale-edit.com/permissions, or you may download our Permissions Request form and submit your request by fax or mail to:

Permissions
Thomson Gale
27500 Drake Rd.
Farmington Hills, MI 48331-3535
Permissions Hotline:
248-699-8006 or 800-877-4253 ext. 8006
Fax: 248-699-8074 or 800-762-4058

Since this page cannot legibly accommodate all copyright notices, the acknowledgments constitute an extension of the copyright notice.

While every effort has been made to ensure the reliability of the information presented in this publication, Thomson Gale does not guarantee the accuracy of the data contained herein. Thomson Gale accepts no payment for listing; and inclusion in the publication of any organization, agency, institution, publication, service, or individual does not imply endorsement of the editors or publisher. Errors brought to the attention of the publisher and verified to the satisfaction of the publisher will be corrected in future editions.

ISBN 0-02-866047-1 (set)
ISBN 0-02-866048-X (v.1)
ISBN 0-02-866049-8 (v.2)
ISBN 0-02-866050-1 (v.3)
ISBN 0-02-866051-X (v.4)
ISBN 0-02-866052-8 (v.5)
ISBN 0-02-866053-6 (v.6)
ISBN 0-02-866054-4 (v.7)
ISBN 0-02-866055-2 (v.8)
ISBN 0-02-866056-0 (v.9)
ISBN 0-02-866057-9 (v.10)
ISBN 0-02-866058-7 (v.11)
ISBN 0-02-866059-5 (v.12)
ISBN 0-02-866060-9 (v.13)
ISSN 1082-703X

This title is also available as an e-book.
ISBN 0-02-866099-4
Contact your Thomson Gale representative for ordering information.

Printed in the United States of America
10 9 8 7 6 5 4 3 2 1

Contents

Job Summary Chart

Job	Salary	Education/Training	Employment Outlook	Page
Job Profiles—No Specialized Training				
Bank Clerk	Median—$23,317 to $27,310 per year	High school	Poor	33
Bank Teller	Median—$21,120 per year	High school	Fair	34
Billing Clerk	Median—$27,040 per year	High school	Fair	37
Bookkeeper	Median—$28,570 per year	High school	Fair	38
Brokerage Clerk	Median—$35,235 per year	High school	Fair	40
Business Machine Operator	Varies—see profile	High school	Poor	42
Correspondence Clerk	Median—$29,340 per year	High school	Poor	44
Credit Authorizer, Checker, and Clerk	Median—$29,058 per year	High school	Poor	46
Credit Collector	Median—$27,456 per year	High school	Very good	48
Customer Service Representative	Median—$27,020 per year	High school	Very good	49
Data Entry Keyer	Median—$23,250 per year	High school	Poor	51
File Clerk	Median—$21,029 per year	High school	Poor	53
Human Resources Assistant	Median—$31,750 per year	High school	Good	55
Interviewer	Median—$23,670 to $33,114 per year	High school	Fair	56
Mail Clerk	Median—$23,650 per year	None	Poor	58
Mail Service Worker	Varies—see profile	High school	Fair	59
Messenger Service Worker	Median—$20,190 per year	None	Poor	61
Office Clerk	Median—$22,770 per year	High school	Fair	63
Payroll Clerk	Median—$30,350 per year	High school	Good	64
Receptionist	Median—$21,840 per year	High school	Very good	66
Statistical Assistant	Median—$31,390 per year	High school	Fair	68
Telephone Operator	Median—$28,392 per year	High school	Poor	70
Telephone Service Representative	Median—$27,020 per year	High school	Good	72
Word Processor	Median—$28,030 per year	High School	Poor	74
Job Profiles—Some Specialized Training/Experience				
Administrative Assistant	Median—$34,970 per year	High school plus training	Fair	76
Claims Adjuster	Median—$44,080 per year	High school; license	Good	78

★ High-growth job

★ High-growth job

Job	Salary	Education/ Training	Employment Outlook	Page
Employee Benefits Manager	Median—$66,530 per year	College	Very good	137
Employment Counselor	Median—$45,570 per year	College	Very good	139
⭐ Executive Search Recruiter	Median—$70,192 per year	College	Very good	140
Financial Analyst	Median—$61,910 per year	College	Good	142
Financial Planner	Median—$62,700 per year	Varies—see profile	Very good	144
General Manager	Median—$77,420 per year	College	Good	146
Human Resources Manager	Median—$81,810 per year	College	Very good	148
Insurance Underwriter	Median—$48,550 per year	College	Fair	150
Internet Entrepreneur	Varies—see profile	Varies—see profile	Varies—see profile	152
Investment Banker	Starting—$45,000 to $85,000 per year	Advanced degree plus training	Good	155
Management Analyst and Consultant	Median—$63,450 per year	Advanced degree plus experience	Good	156
⭐ Network Administrator	Median—$58,190 per year	Varies—see profile	Excellent	159
Office Manager	Median—$41,030 per year	College	Fair	161
Office Planner	Median—$40,670 per year	College	Good	163
Operations Research Analyst	Median—$60,190 per year	College	Fair	166
Organizational Developer	Median—$61,769 per year	College	Excellent	168
⭐ Outplacement Consultant	Median—$52,800 per year	College	Excellent	170
⭐ Recruiter	Median—$41,190 per year	College	Very good	171
Resume Writer	Varies—see profile	College	Fair	173
Securities Broker	Median—$69,200 per year	College plus training	Good	174
Software Trainer	Median—$44,570 per year	College	Very good	177
Statistician	Median—$58,620 per year	College	Fair	179
Training and Development Specialist	Median—$44,570 per year	College	Very good	181

⭐ High-growth job

Foreword

The ninth edition of the *Career Information Center* mirrors the ongoing changes in the job market caused by new technological and economic developments. These developments continue to change what Americans do in the workplace and how they do it. People have a critical need for up-to-date information to help them make career decisions.

The *Career Information Center* is an individualized resource for people of all ages and at all stages of career development. It has been recognized as an excellent reference for librarians, counselors, educators, and other providers of job information. It is ideally suited for use in libraries, career resource centers, and guidance offices, as well as in adult education centers and other facilities where people seek information about job opportunities, careers, and their own potential in the workforce.

This ninth edition updates many of the features that made the earlier editions so useful.

- A Job Summary Chart, a quick reference guide, appears in the front section of each volume to help readers get the basic facts and compare the jobs described in the volume. High-growth jobs are highlighted and identified with a star.

- Each volume of the *Career Information Center* begins with an overview of the job market in that field. These "Looking Into..." sections have been completely revised and updated. They also include new graphs, charts, and boxes providing information such as industry snapshots and the fastest-growing and top-dollar jobs in the field. The "Global View" feature tells how the new global economy is affecting jobs in the field.

- Each volume has a section called "Getting Into...," which contains useful information on entering the particular field. It offers self-evaluation tips and decision-making help; and it relates possible job choices to individual interests, abilities, and work characteristics. There is also practical information on job hunting, using the Internet and classified ads, preparing resumes, and handling interviews. "Getting Into..." also includes a section on employee rights.

- Each volume has a listing of all job profiles in the series and the volumes in which they appear, making access to profiles in other volumes easy.

- *Career Information Center* contains 694 job profiles. Each profile describes work characteristics, education and training requirements, getting the job, advancement and employment outlook, working conditions, and earnings and benefits.

- Job summaries, provided for each job profile, highlight the education or training required, salary range, and employment outlook.

- Volume 13 has been revised to reflect career concerns of the new century and employment trends through the year 2014. This volume includes updated articles on benefits, employment law, health in the workplace, job search strategies, job training, job opportunities at home, and identifying opportunities for retraining.

- More than 530 photographs provide a visual glimpse of life on the job. Photos have been selected to give the reader a sense of what it feels like to be in a specific field or job.

- Updated bibliographies in each volume include recommended readings and Web sites in specific job areas. Additional titles for the vocational counselor are included in Volume 13.

- Each volume also contains a comprehensive directory of accredited occupational education and vocational training facilities listed by occupational area and grouped by state. Directory materials are generated from the IPEDS (Integrated Postsecondary Education Data System) database of the U.S. Department of Education.

The *Career Information Center* recognizes the importance not only of job selection, but also of job holding, coping, and applying life skills. No other career information publication deals with work attitudes so comprehensively.

Using the Career Information Center

The *Career Information Center* is designed to meet the needs of many people—students, people just entering or reentering the job market, those dissatisfied with present jobs, those without jobs—anyone of any age who is not sure what to do for a living. The *Career Information Center* is for people who want help in making career choices. It combines the comprehensiveness of an encyclopedia with the format and readability of a magazine. Many professionals, including counselors, librarians, and teachers, will find it a useful guidance and reference tool.

The *Career Information Center* is organized by occupational interest area rather than in alphabetical order. Jobs that have something in common are grouped together. In that way people who do not know exactly what job they want can read about a number of related jobs. The *Career Information Center* classifies jobs that have something in common into clusters. The classification system is adapted from the cluster organization used by the U.S. Department of Labor. Each of the first twelve volumes of the *Career Information Center* explores one of twelve occupational clusters.

To use the *Career Information Center*, first select the volume that treats the occupational area that interests you most. Because there are many ways to group occupations, you may not find a particular job in the volume in which you look for it. In that case, check the central listing of all the profiles, which is located in the front of Volumes 1 through 12. This listing provides the names of all profiles and the volume number in which they appear. Volume 13 also includes a comprehensive index of all the jobs covered in the first twelve volumes.

After selecting a volume or volumes, investigate the sections that you feel would be most helpful. It isn't necessary to read these volumes from cover to cover. They are arranged so that you can go directly to the specific information you want. Here is a description of the sections included in each volume.

- **Job Summary Chart**—This chart presents in tabular form the basic data from all profiles in the volume: salary, education and training, employment outlook, and the page on which you can find the job profile. Jobs with a high growth potential are highlighted and starred.

- **Looking Into...**—This overview of the occupational cluster describes the opportunities, characteristics, and trends in that particular field.

- **Getting Into...**—This how-to guide can help you decide what jobs may be most satisfying to you and what strategies you can use to get the right job. You will learn, for example, how to write an effective resume, how to complete an application form, what to expect in an interview, how to use networking, and what to do if someone has discriminated against you.

- **Job Summary**—These summaries, located at the beginning of each profile, highlight the most important facts about the job: education and training, salary range, and employment outlook.

Education and Training indicates whether the job requires no education, high school, college, advanced degree, vocational/technical school, license, or training.

Salary Range provides median or average salaries that may vary significantly from region to region.

Employment Outlook is based on several factors, including the Bureau of Labor Statistics' projections through the year 2014. The ratings are defined as follows: *poor* means there is a projected employment decrease of any amount; *fair* means there is a projected employment increase of 0 to 8 percent; *good* means there is a projected employment increase of 9 to 17 percent; *very good* means there is a projected employment increase of 18 to 26 percent; and *excellent* means there is a projected employment increase of 27 percent or more. The outlook is then determined by looking at the ratings and other employment factors. For example, a job with excellent projected employment growth in which many more people are entering the field than there are jobs available will have an outlook that is good rather than excellent.

For all categories, the phrase *Varies—see profile* means the reader must consult the profile for the information, which is too extensive to include in the Job Summary.

- **Job Profiles**—The job profiles are divided into three categories based on the level of training required to get the job. Each profile explores the following topics: description of the job being profiled, the education and training requirements, ways to get the job, advancement possibilities and employment outlook, the working conditions, the earnings and benefits, and places to go for more information.

Job Profiles—No Specialized Training includes jobs that require no education or previous work experience beyond high school.

Job Profiles—Some Specialized Training/Experience includes jobs that require one, two, or three years of vocational training or college, or work experience beyond high school.

Job Profiles—Advanced Training/Experience includes jobs that require a bachelor's degree or advanced degree from a college or university and/or equivalent work experience in that field.

- **Resources—General Career Information** includes a selected bibliography of the most recent books and Web sites on general career information, including how-to books on such topics as resume writing and preparing for tests. In addition, there is a special guide to readings for the career counselor in Volume 13.

- **Resources**—Each volume also contains a bibliography of books and Web sites for specific fields covered in that volume.

- **Directory of Institutions Offering Career Training**—This listing, organized first by career area, then by state, includes the schools that offer occupational training beyond high school. For jobs requiring a bachelor's degree or an advanced degree, check a library for college catalogs and appropriate directories.

- **Index**—This index, which is located at the end of each volume, lists every job mentioned in that volume. It serves not only to cross-reference all the jobs in the volume but also to show related jobs in the field. For example, under the entry OCEANOG-RAPHER, you will find chemical oceanographer, marine biologist, and marine geophysicist.

- **Volume 13, Employment Trends and Master Index**—This volume includes several features that will help both the job seeker and the career counselor. A useful guide provides the *DOT (Dictionary of Occupational Titles)* number of most of the job profiles in the *Career Information Center*. There is also a special section on career information for Canada. The updated and revised "Employment Trends" section contains articles on health in the workplace; search strategies for finding your first job; employment trends for women, minorities, immigrants, older workers, and the physically challenged; employment demographics; benefit programs; training; employment opportunities at home; employment law; and identifying opportunities for retraining. The articles provide job seekers and career professionals with an overview of current employment issues, career opportunities, and outlooks. Finally, there is a master index to all the jobs included in all 13 volumes.

The *Career Information Center* is exactly what it says it is—a center of the most useful and pertinent information you need to explore and choose from the wide range of job and career possibilities. The *Career Information Center* provides you with a solid foundation of information for getting a satisfying job or rewarding career.

Comprehensive Job Profile List

The following list includes job profiles and corresponding volume numbers.

Accountant, Management, 3
Accountant, Public, 3
Actor, 2
Actuary, 3
Acupuncturist, 7
Administrative Assistant, 3
Admitting Interviewer, 7
Adult Education Worker, 11
Advertising Account Executive, 10
Advertising Copywriter, 2
Advertising Manager, 10
Aerospace Engineer, 6
Aerospace Engineering and Operations
    Technician, 6
Aerospace Industry, 9
Agricultural Engineer, 1
Agricultural Inspector, 1
Agricultural Technician, 1
Agronomist, 1
AIDS Counselor, 7
Air Pollution Control Technician, 1
Air Traffic Controller, 12
Air-Conditioning Engineer, 6
Air-Conditioning, Heating, and
    Refrigeration Mechanic and
    Installer, 4
Aircraft Dispatcher, 12
Aircraft Mechanic, 12
Airline Baggage and Freight Handler, 12
Airline Flight Attendant, 12
Airline Reservations Agent, 12
Airline Ticket Agent, 12
Airplane Pilot, 12
Airport Manager, 12
Airport Utility Worker, 12
Alternative Fuels Vehicle Technician, 6
Aluminum and Copper Industries, 9
Ambulance Driver, 7
Amusement and Recreation Attendant, 8
Anatomist, 6
Anesthesiologist, 7
Animal Caretaker, 8
Animal Scientist, 1
Animal Trainer, 1
Announcer, 2
Anthropologist, 6
Apparel Industry, 9
Apparel Workers, 9
Appliance Service Worker, 5
Appraiser, 5
Architect, 4
Architectural Drafter, 4
Architectural Model Maker, 4
Armed Services Career, 11
Art Director, 2
Artificial Intelligence Specialist, 6
Artist, 2
Assembler and Fabricator, 9

Astronomer, 6
Athletic Coach, 8
Athletic Trainer, 8
Auctioneer, 10
Audiologist, 7
Auditor, 3
Auto Body Repairer, 12
Auto Parts Counter Worker, 10
Auto Sales Worker, 10
Automobile Driving Instructor, 12
Automotive Exhaust Emissions
    Technician, 12
Automotive Industry, 9
Automotive Mechanic, 12
Avionics Technician, 12

Baker, 1
Bank Clerk, 3
Bank Officer and Manager, 3
Bank Teller, 3
Barber and Hairstylist, 5
Bartender, 8
Bicycle Mechanic, 12
Billing Clerk, 3
Biochemist, 6
Biological Technician, 6
Biologist, 6
Biomedical Engineer, 6
Biomedical Equipment Technician, 7
Boilermaker, 9
Bookbinder, 2
Bookkeeper, 3
Border Patrol Agent, 11
Botanist, 6
Bricklayer, 4
Bridge and Lock Tender, 12
Broadcast News Analyst, 2
Broadcast Technician, 2
Brokerage Clerk, 3
Building Custodian, 11
Building Inspector, 4
Bulldozer, Grader, or Paving Machine
    Operator, 4
Business Family and Consumer
    Scientist, 5
Business Machine Operator, 3

Cable Television and
    Telecommunications Technician, 6
Cable Television Engineer, 6
Cafeteria Attendant, 8
Camera Operator, 2
Candy Manufacturing Worker, 1
Car Rental or Leasing Agent, 12
Car Wash Worker, 12
Cardiac Monitor Technician, 7
Cardiac Perfusionist, 7
Cardiology Technologist, 7

Carpenter, 4
Cartographer, 1
Cartoonist and Animator, 2
Cashier, 10
Caterer, 8
Ceiling Tile Installer, 4
Cement Mason, 4
Ceramic Engineer, 6
Ceramics Industry, 9
Chauffeur, 5
Cheese Industry Worker, 1
Chemical Engineer, 6
Chemical Technician, 6
Chemist, 6
Child Care Worker, Private, 5
Chiropractor, 7
Choreographer, 2
City Manager, 11
Civil Engineer, 4
Civil Engineering Technician, 4
Claims Adjuster, 3
Claims Examiner, 3
Clinical Laboratory Technician, 7
Clinical Laboratory Technologist, 7
College Student Personnel Worker, 11
College/University Administrator, 3
Companion, 5
Comparison Shopper, 10
Compensation and Benefits Analyst, 3
Composer, 2
Computer and Information Systems
    Manager, 3
Computer and Office Machine Repairer, 3
Computer Consultant, 3
Computer Control Operator, 9
Computer Control Programmer, 9
Computer Database Administrator, 3
Computer Network Technician, 3
Computer Operator, 3
Computer Programmer, 3
Computer Security Specialist, 3
Computer Software Documentation
    Writer, 3
Computer Software Engineer, 3
Computer Support Specialist, 3
Computer Systems Analyst, 3
Conservation Scientist, 1
Construction Electrician, 4
Construction Equipment Dealer, 4
Construction Equipment Mechanic, 4
Construction Laborer, 4
Construction Millwright, 4
Construction Supervisor, 4
Consumer Advocate, 5
Consumer Credit Counselor, 5
Controller, 3
Cook and Chef, 8
Corporate Travel Manager, 8

Industrial Hygienist, 6
Industrial Machinery Maintenance
	Worker, 9
Industrial Production Manager, 9
Industrial Traffic Manager, 12
Industrial Truck Operator, 12
Inspector and Tester, 9
Institutional Child Care Worker, 11
Institutional Housekeeper, 11
Instructional Designer, 2
Insulation Worker, 4
Insurance Agent and Broker, 10
Insurance Underwriter, 3
Intercity Bus Driver, 12
Interior Designer, 5
Internal Revenue Service Worker, 11
Internet Entrepreneur, 3
Interviewer, 3
Investment Banker, 3

Jeweler, 5
Judge, 11

Labor Relations Specialist, 9
Laboratory Animal Care Worker, 7
Landscape Architect, 4
Lather, 4
Laundry Worker, 5
Lawyer, 11
Lawyer, Corporate, 11
Lawyer, Public Service, 11
Leather and Shoe Industries, 9
Legal Assistant, Corporate, 11
Librarian, Public, 11
Librarian, School, 11
Librarian, Special, 11
Licensed Practical Nurse, 7
Lifeguard, 8
Lighting Technician, 2
Linguist, 6
Literary or Theatrical Agent, 2
Lithographic Worker, 2
Local Transit Operator, 12
Local Truck Driver, 12
Locksmith, 5
Lodging Manager, 8
Logger, 1
Long-Haul Truck Driver, 12
Lumber Mill Worker, 1

Machine Operator and Tender, 9
Machine Setter, 9
Machinist, 9
Mail Clerk, 3
Mail Service Worker, 3
Maintenance Electrician, 4
Makeup Artist, 2
Manufactured Home Assembler, 4
Manufacturers' Sales Worker, 10
Marble, Tile, and Terrazzo Worker, 4
Marine Engineer, 1
Marine Technician, 12
Marketing Director, 10
Marketing Research Worker, 10
Marriage and Family Counselor, 11

Massage Therapist, 5
Mathematician, 6
Meat Packing Worker, 1
Mechanical Engineer, 6
Mechanical Engineering Technician, 6
Media Buyer, 10
Medical and Health Services Manager, 7
Medical Assistant, 7
Medical Illustrator, 7
Medical Physicist, 7
Medical Records and Health Information
	Technician, 7
Meeting and Convention Planner, 8
Meeting Planner, 3
Merchandise Displayer and Window
	Trimmer, 2
Merchant Marine Captain, 12
Merchant Marine Engineer, 12
Merchant Marine Purser, 12
Merchant Marine Radio Officer, 12
Merchant Marine Steward and Cook, 12
Messenger Service Worker, 3
Metallurgical Engineer, 6
Metallurgical Technician, 6
Meteorologist, 1
Microbiologist, 6
Microwave Engineer, 6
Miner, Coal, 1
Miner, Metal, 1
Mining Engineer, 1
Mining Technician, 1
Model, 2
Motion Picture Projectionist, 8
Motorboat Mechanic, 12
Motorcycle Mechanic, 12
Mover, 12
Multimedia Developer, 2
Museum Conservator, 8
Museum Curator, 8
Music Teacher, 2
Music Video Producer, 2
Musician, 2

Nanny, 5
Natural Science Manager, 1
Naval Architect, 1
Network Administrator, 3
News Reporter and Correspondent, 2
Nuclear Engineer, 6
Nuclear Medicine Technologist, 7
Nuclear Technician, 6
Nursery Worker, 1
Nursery/Greenhouse Manager, 1
Nursing Aide and Orderly, 7

Occupational Health and Safety
	Specialist, 1
Occupational Therapist Assistant, 7
Occupational Therapist, 7
Oceanographer, 1
Office Clerk, 3
Office Machine and Computer Industry, 9
Office Manager, 3
Office Planner, 3
Operations Research Analyst, 3

Ophthalmic Laboratory Technician, 7
Ophthalmologist, 7
Optometric Assistant, 7
Optometrist, 7
Organizational Developer, 3
Orthoptist, 7
Osteopathic Physician, 7
Outdoor Guide, 8
Outplacement Consultant, 3

Paint, Varnish, and Lacquer Industry, 9
Painter and Paperhanger, 4
Painting and Coating Worker, 9
Paper Industry, 9
Paralegal Aide, 11
Park Naturalist, 1
Park Ranger, 8
Parking Analyst, 12
Parking Attendant, 12
Parking Cashier, 12
Parole Officer, 11
Party Planner, 8
Pastry Chef and Baker, 8
Pathologist, 6
Payroll Clerk, 3
Personal Exercise Trainer, 5
Personal Service Worker, 5
Personal Shopper, 5
Pest Control Worker, 5
Pesticide Handler, Sprayer, and
	Applicator, Vegetation, 1
Pet Care Worker, 5
Petroleum and Natural Gas Exploration
	and Production Worker, 1
Petroleum Engineer, 1
Petroleum Refining Industry, 9
Pharmaceutical Industry, 9
Pharmaceutical Sales Representative, 7
Pharmaceutical Technician, 6
Pharmacist, 7
Pharmacologist, 7
Photo Researcher, 2
Photographer, 2
Photographic Processing Machine
	Operator, 2
Photonics Engineer, 6
Photonics Technician, 6
Physical Therapist Assistant, 7
Physical Therapist, 7
Physician Assistant, 7
Physician, 7
Physicist, 6
Piano and Organ Tuner and Technician, 5
Pile-Driver Operator, 4
Plasterer and Stucco Mason, 4
Plastics Industry, 9
Plumber and Pipe Fitter, 4
Podiatrist, 7
Police Officer, 11
Political Consultant, 11
Political Scientist, 6
Postal Service Worker, 11
Power Plant Worker, 11
Power Tool Repairer, 4
Prepress Worker, 2

Looking Into Computers, Business, and Office

Henry Ford revolutionized industry in 1913 when he constructed a factory in which each worker assembled just one part of a car before sending it down a production line to another worker. Up to that point, automobiles were made from the ground up by a team of highly paid workers. As a result, automobiles had been an expensive means of transportation, a toy for the wealthy. Ford's innovation became known as the assembly line method of production, and it proved to be much more efficient at producing complex machines. It dropped the price of cars radically and made them affordable for average working people. Ford's assembly line method and the subsequent growth of the automobile industry fundamentally changed the way people did business in America and around the world.

By the twenty-first century another technological revolution had changed American business as profoundly as Ford's assembly line changed manufacturing. Ford's assembly line was part of what historians call the "Age of Industry." Today Americans live in what many economists are calling the "Information Society," a phenomenon brought about by the development of computers, computer networks, the Internet, and digital technology. In the Information Society, many manufacturing jobs—which were the backbone of the industrial economy—are becoming obsolete in the United States. Indeed, during the last decades of the twentieth century, computer technology affected the jobs of most workers at every level of the American economy by making workers much more efficient. The changes were dramatic and will continue to transform the way we work.

What's more, economists state that the revolution in American business is really twofold—it is political as well as technological. The United States is part of an ever-expanding global economy brought about by the end of the Cold War and fueled by growth in newly formed nations seeking to build their own economies. Trade agreements such as the North American Free Trade Agreement (NAFTA) and the General Agreement on Tariffs and Trade (GATT) have already had a great impact on American business by shifting many manufacturing and data processing jobs to countries such as India and Mexico, where labor is cheap. Though many laborers in the United States have had to find new work,

the shift of jobs has led to an increase in commerce and profitability for U.S. companies.

This twofold revolution presents American business with great challenges—and opportunities. Historically, American business has shown a great ability to overcome and even profit by adversity. In the twentieth century alone, the American brand of capitalism survived the stock market crash of 1929, the Great Depression, a number of recessions, two world wars, the Cold War, great changes in family and society, and a reordering of the world political map.

The beginning of the twenty-first century brought new challenges, including high energy prices, corporate scandals, a new war in the Middle East, the Hurricane Katrina disaster, and resistance to the globalization of American business. The tragic terrorist events of September 11, 2001, and the continuing threat of more terrorist acts have taken a heavy toll on consumer confidence and American economic health in general. Despite periodic setbacks, however, business dominates American culture and remains immensely prosperous.

But what exactly is meant by the term "business"? The word has almost as many meanings as there are types of businesses, and in today's rapidly changing business environment, definitions are constantly

Workers use computers to quickly access information and relay it to clients and other workers. *(Photograph by Kelly A. Quin. Thomson Gale. Reproduced by permission.)*

evolving. In this article, "business" refers specifically to the management and administration of commercial enterprises. This volume discusses the people involved in staffing these enterprises and the jobs they do.

TODAY'S OFFICE

Every business or government agency that produces goods or services needs a variety of people to handle administrative and clerical responsibilities and to manage the operation. Most of these people work in offices. An office staff may range in size from one to thousands, but every organization—no matter what size or what type—requires office workers to deal with day-to-day tasks. Office workers handle many different aspects of a business, including bookkeeping, word processing, data processing, telecommunications, and others. They are needed in every sector of the economy—from manufacturing to transportation.

New technology has dramatically changed the way people do business. It has transformed many of the jobs traditionally performed in offices. In all cases, though, technology makes one basic contribution: it allows a greater amount of work to be done in a shorter period of time than would be possible without it.

The Early Development of the Modern Office

The modern office has its roots in the late nineteenth century. Following the Civil War, innovations such as the department store, the chain store, and the mail-order catalog business significantly increased the volume of manufacturers' and retailers' sales. As a result, more workers were needed to keep track of production, inventory, and sales. At the same time, the rise of large corporations required more sophisticated methods of running a business. This led to the development of more efficient procedures, which involved a high degree of administrative specialization.

Modern office procedures were made possible by inventions such as the telegraph, telephone, typewriter, and adding machine. These devices came into widespread use between the end of the Civil War in 1865 and the beginning of the twentieth century.

The Evolution of Office Equipment

Throughout the twentieth century new and innovative business machines were developed in quick succession. Each new generation of business machine made its predecessor obsolete. When a new piece of office equipment was first introduced, it was often greeted with skepticism. Eventually, however, the benefits of the equipment became obvious, workers' reluctance faded, and the equipment became standard. Such was the case with manual typewriters, which were commonly used in business offices in the early twentieth century. They were replaced by electric typewriters, which were then replaced by personal computers. In the same manner, photocopiers replaced carbon paper and calculators replaced adding machines.

In general, office equipment evolves to allow for increased automation. Office automation means using machines to do repetitive, time-consuming tasks formerly done by people. Machines also help workers get work done faster and more efficiently. Fax machines, for example, are used to send documents over telephone lines to offices within the United States or in other countries. The documents are received within minutes, instead of the days (or even weeks) once required to receive them via mail.

The Advent of Computers

The computer has revolutionized the modern office more than any other piece of equipment. Mainframe computers were introduced to the workplace in the 1960s and 1970s, but their very high cost and cumbersome size limited their use to large companies. By the 1980s, however, personal computers—smaller, less expensive, and more user friendly than mainframes—had become standard equipment in even the smallest offices. Today, most offices would be unable to function without computers, as evidenced by the blackout of August 2003. Without electrical power, most offices from Detroit to New York were forced to close for a few days.

Computers are changing and improving all the time, with faster, smaller, more versatile, and more powerful equipment introduced nearly every week. In the mid-1990s the notebook computer—with the dimensions of a notebook and an average weight of less than six pounds—became very popular, especially with business users who work away from the office. The notebook computer, and the even smaller sub-notebook, fits easily into a briefcase and can work on battery power, making it particularly useful for business travelers. Also available are even smaller palmtop computers and personal digital assistants (PDAs). Wireless components such as keyboards and mice, wireless networks, and high-speed Internet access (called broadband) have become common. Another recent innovation is the capability of computers to listen to and respond to handwritten or voice commands. Thus, for some tasks even the computer keyboard may become obsolete.

Information Processing

Technology has changed the way office work is conducted. The modern office is sometimes referred to as the "electronic office" because of the electronic circuitry within so much of its equipment, including computers, telephones, and copiers. It is hard to identify an office tool that has not been improved by electronics.

Global View: Computers, Business, and Office

U.S. and foreign companies have been doing more and more business in the international marketplace. International agreements, such as the General Agreement on Tariffs and Trade (GATT), the North American Free Trade Association (NAFTA), and the General Agreement on Trades and Services (GATS) have lowered trade barriers. Computer technology, including the Internet, has also made it easier for companies to access markets in different nations. The enormous growth of international business is opening new career and business opportunities to people everywhere.

Rapid advances in computer technology have gone hand in hand with the globalization of business. Computers have made it easier for people in different locations and time zones to communicate. Some banks in New York work around the clock to keep in touch with bankers in London, Tokyo, and other cities around the world. Better communications also help companies sell their products in multiple nations. Entrepreneurs have started many new "dot-com" businesses to take advantage of the international markets that are conveniently accessed via the Internet. Though many of these new Internet companies were folding when the twenty-first century began (some were calling them "dot-bombs"), the future of online business seems wide open.

In addition to expanding global communications, many businesses are physically crossing boundaries. Some companies form strategic alliance relationships that allow companies to share skills and resources with foreign companies. Chrysler, a U.S. auto giant, and Daimler–Benz, a top German auto manufacturer, formed an alliance to enable Chrysler to sell cars in Europe and to improve sales of Daimler–Benz's Mercedes–Benz cars in the United States. Many companies become multinational by building facilities, including factories, in other nations. Chains like the Gap and McDonald's have opened stores on nearly every continent. Big computer companies hire most of their technical support service workers in countries where labor is cheap, such as India and Eastern Europe. The major American automakers have moved many of their production lines to Mexico.

But not everyone is happy about the "Americanization" of the world. A Frenchman who damaged a McDonald's in southern France in 2001 became a hero to the antiglobalization movement. Meetings of the World Trade Organization (WTO) are often marked by protests. Protestors at the 1999 WTO conference in Seattle injured a number of people and caused significant damage to businesses. Another hot topic in international business politics is "sweatshops," factories in foreign countries where consumer goods like clothing and tennis shoes are made much more cheaply than they could be in America. While some people protest against paying foreign workers a fraction of what American workers make, others point out that these same foreign workers are among the highest paid in their homelands. In the United States many people in the manufacturing sector and even in the service industries are upset that more and more jobs are being sent overseas. At the very least, doing business globally requires a sensitivity to these viewpoints.

As businesses increase international activities, they seek people with special skills to help them succeed in the global marketplace. They need accountants, lawyers, and personnel managers who are familiar with the laws, languages, and cultures of the countries where they do business. Corporate bankers and investment professionals must understand how economic conditions abroad affect the cost of foreign loans and the profitability of foreign investments. Another consideration with foreign loans is the likelihood of default, as many poor nations find it difficult to repay loans. Many third-world countries, which otherwise represent promising new markets, are deep in debt. Third-world debt is a rallying cry for some, who think that much of it should be forgiven if these nations are to be solvent again.

Many global businesses also hire experts to teach business customs to managers who work with foreign contacts. In Texas, beginning a meeting with a joke might put an audience at ease, but in Japan, where business is conducted in a more formal manner, coworkers and clients might be offended. In some cases human resources departments prepare employees who are sent abroad for the challenges of living and working in a different culture.

Along with new opportunities, globalization brings special challenges for the years ahead.

The main activity of the electronic office is information processing, which entails gathering, manipulating, storing, and transmitting data. All industries need to process information of some type to keep their operations running smoothly and to facilitate decision making. Information processing has three main areas: telecommunications, word processing, and data processing.

Telecommunications The word "telecommunications" means sending and receiving messages and data over distances via telephone lines, wireless communications systems, fiber-optic cables, television cable lines, or computer networks. Modern telecommunications encompasses much more than voice telephone calls, although telephone wires are used to transmit a wide variety of messages. Fax machines, for example, use simple telephone wires to transmit printed words and graphics. With electronic mail (e-mail), a computer router or modem transmits information to another computer in an office on the other side of town or in an office on the other side of the world. The most obvious advantage of telecommunications—in contrast to postal mail or overnight delivery services—is that messages often are delivered within seconds. But there are also other advantages, such as the saving of the time and effort required to prepare and print paper mail.

Teleconferencing, another form of telecommunications, enables businesses to conduct meetings among people who are at separate locations. Participants at one site can both see and hear the participants at the other sites via teleprompters.

A company can establish its own information networks within one office or between offices. By linking its computer equipment within the office building, a company establishes a local area network (LAN). Such networks enable employees to communicate more quickly than they could otherwise, which increases productivity. For example, a LAN could allow an employee working at a computer terminal in the human resources department to send the payroll records of a new employee directly to a computer in the payroll department. Through the use of modems and Internet routers, telephone and data lines, and satellites, a company can establish a remote-distance network, or wide area network (WAN). This type of information network allows a company to transmit information instantly to branch offices and plants and to other companies. For example, a chain store in one city can check instantly on the availability of merchandise at the chain's central warehouse in another city hundreds of miles away.

Companies and individuals can obtain a wide variety of information from online services and the Internet. Information available online includes stock market prices, mutual fund rates, airline schedules, hotel reservation rates, and weather reports, as well as many more specialized databases.

Word Processing Word processing means manipulating alphabetic and numeric characters for various communications purposes. Office workers have always been involved in word processing. Until the introduction of computers and word processing software, however, producing a document often required tedious and time-consuming retyping to make corrections or revisions. With word processing software, text can be added, deleted, corrected, and revised easily, without the need for retyping the entire document. Documents created on a computer can be stored, then retrieved at a later time for revising or copying.

Today, desktop publishing systems enable a single worker to write, edit, lay out, and print documents such as flyers and newsletters. Prior to the development of computer technology, producing such documents required the services of typesetters and printers.

Data Processing Data processing means gathering, calculating, organizing, sorting, and storing facts and figures. Electronic data processing gives administrators and support personnel immediate access to the information needed to make decisions. It also enables accountants and clerks to quickly and accurately perform tasks such as payroll management and budgeting. Companies use database management programs for many other purposes, such as tracking inventory, maintaining lists of customer names and addresses, sending bills, and generating mass mailings. In addition, businesses use spreadsheet programs to keep track of their financial records.

The Office Environment

Electronic technology changed not only the way work was formerly done in offices but also the environment of the office itself. In general, modern offices are quieter than those of previous eras, because computers, laser printers, and other electronic equipment make much less noise than typewriters and other outmoded office machines did. Electronic documents, such as e-mail and word processor documents, reduced the amount of paper used in offices, so modern offices are usually less cluttered than offices of the past. In addition, today most businesses recognize that a pleasant working environment increases employee productivity, so the modern office is likely to be air-conditioned, carpeted, well lighted, and comfortable. Due to the health risks of secondhand smoke, most businesses now provide a smoke-free office environment.

Telecommuting

Telecommunications technology has created a new class of worker—"telecommuters". These employees work at home using a computer and send their work to the office via the Internet or e-mail. Many companies are experimenting with policies to allow employees to work at home part or most of the time via telecommunications. This is due in part to the Clean Air Act of 1990, which mandates that large companies reduce the number of vehicle miles that their workers travel during each morning rush hour. Allowing employees to telecommute benefits companies by reducing expenses on office space, utilities, and parking. Telecommuting appeals to many workers, including those who have small children, those who value a flexible work schedule, and those who have difficulty commuting because of disabilities.

In May 2004 the U.S. Bureau of Labor Statistics reported in their *Current Population Survey* that approximately 20.7 million Americans worked part of the time at home either as telecommuters or self-employed workers. Some observers predict that people working from home will play an increasingly significant role in the transactions of American business and that the home might, in fact, become the office of the future.

THE BUSINESS WORK FORCE

Approximately one quarter of the work force in the United States is employed in what is traditionally known as business. According to the Bureau of Labor Statistics' May 2004 *Occupational Employment Statistics and Wages* survey, there were about 22.6 million administrative support workers, the largest occupational group in the country. Roughly 6.2 million people in management occupations directed these workers.

Management Roles

Managers and administrators are responsible for making decisions about how an organization should be run. Depending on the industry, an administrator's title may be manager, president, chief executive officer (CEO), superintendent, director, consultant, contractor, or one of many others. Administrators typically have general management training as well as training in the specific industry in which they are employed. Many administrators, however, can apply their management skills to a variety of industries.

In most offices administrators are organized into a hierarchy. Top managers are responsible for developing product plans and directing policies and operations. Supervisory managers directly oversee the

work of the administrative support staff. Between top managers and supervisory managers are middle managers. Large corporations, in particular, generally depend on a strict organizational hierarchy.

In recent years American managers have begun to change the nature of their organizational hierarchies. Large corporations are finding that they can respond to economic changes and develop products faster if they have fewer layers of managers. Consequently, many companies are laying off administrators to make a leaner organization. Middle management has been hardest hit by this trend.

As might be expected, downsizing—the process of creating smaller companies through job layoffs—has caused hardships. Former middle managers, most of whom are middle-aged, have had difficulty finding new positions suitable to their skills and experience. After many years of work many ex-managers also have difficulty retraining themselves for new careers. Companies, too, must face the problem of how to motivate their remaining managers. Often these employees must assume a heavier workload without the traditional incentives of clearly defined promotion or higher pay.

Innovations in office equipment such as the notebook computer allow employees to continue working while they are away from their offices. (© Michael Prince/Corbis.)

Workers who enter the workforce as administrative support personnel can often advance to more challenging and interesting positions within their companies. (Royalty-Free/Photo Disc, Inc. Reproduced by permission.)

Supporting Roles

Administrative support personnel perform the day-to-day tasks that help a business run smoothly, such as maintaining files, answering phones, paying bills, and dealing with correspondence and orders. Their job titles include secretary, receptionist, administrative assistant, word processor, clerk, and teller.

Today's offices need many of the same administrative support personnel, such as bookkeepers, clerks, and secretaries, that traditional offices needed. Many of the responsibilities of these workers have remained the same, but the ways in which they perform their jobs have changed dramatically. Although new office machines and computers eliminated the need for some jobs and reduced the time required to do others, they also created entirely new jobs—such as computer programmer—that did not exist previously. In addition, automation created new departments that offer substantial advancement opportunities. For example, almost all medium-sized and large companies have their own data processing departments. A worker who starts out as a computer operator in a data processing department may, with experience and additional training, become the manager of the department.

Because automation has significantly reduced the amount of time required to perform many tasks, office workers may have more time and freedom to take on tasks that were once reserved for lower-level managers. They may be asked to train and supervise other office workers, edit and proofread a company newsletter, or plan and arrange a business trip. In this way, automation has generally upgraded the status and image of office workers and made their work more challenging and interesting than it used to be.

Office automation is not without its drawbacks, however. Office workers in an automated office usually have less face-to-face contact with their coworkers than did their counterparts in a traditional business office. Sometimes office workers may be expected to perform one specific task, such as word processing or data entry, rather than being able to perform a variety of jobs.

TRENDS IN BUSINESS

Business, perhaps more than any other sector of society besides medicine, was transformed by the technological innovations of the late twentieth century. The development of computers and the evolution of new management theories—started in the computer hardware and software industries—brought about the growth of the "Information Society." These new technologies and management theories contributed greatly to the expansion of certain areas of business, including the service sector, the temporary help industry, computer consulting, and management consulting.

The Service Sector

The United States government and many business analysts predict that most of the employment growth in this country will occur in businesses that provide services rather than in businesses that produce goods. These businesses sell a service, rather than a manufactured product, for profit. The Bureau of Labor Statistics predicted in their 2004–14 employment projections that 18.9 million new jobs would be created through 2014. Of those jobs, more than 18.7 million were projected to be in the service sector, and none were expected in the goods-producing sector.

In the past, "service" was usually a straightforward activity, such as hair styling or auto repair. Now, however, the service sector of the economy grows more vast and complex every day. Although the service industry still includes traditional services, it has grown to encompass businesses as varied as small day care centers and huge software corporations.

Because this diversity can cause confusion, many economists propose that a third job sector—information—be added to goods and services. The information sector would include software companies, most financial services, publishers, and the many other businesses that provide, move, or manipulate information.

The Temporary Help Industry

As companies have downsized and sought to reduce their overhead costs, corporate payrolls have shrunk accordingly. However, the need to meet the challenge of increased competition and productivity has grown. Consequently, many companies rely on temporary workers.

Temporary workers have varied backgrounds and work histories. Some are displaced workers who were laid off. Others are people who enjoy the flexibility of working on an assignment basis. Many temporary workers want full-time employment, usually because better benefits (such as medical insurance, sick days, and paid vacations) accompany it. These benefits are costly to an employer, however, and have become one of the main reasons that companies hesitate to take on too many full-time employees. A temporary assignment offers the employer and the employee a chance to screen each other and may result in a full-time position.

The temporary help industry is thriving and is expected to continue to grow. Although most temporary help firms still place only clerical workers, others are discovering that they can serve highly specialized markets. The placement of science and engineering professionals in temporary jobs has become an important source of revenue for the temporary help industry.

As the demand for skilled temporary workers grows, temporary agencies are trying to make temporary work as attractive as possible. Some offer health insurance at reduced cost to the employee, making it easier for workers to remain temporary. Many agencies provide training to teach valuable new skills.

Computer Services

The growth of the computer service industry has slowed down substantially since the high-tech explosion of the late 1990s. After the burst of the "dot-com" bubble, many lower level computer jobs, such as technical support specialist and programmer, were shipped overseas, and the amount of money large companies invested in computer technology leveled off. Yet, even with these setbacks, the industry as a whole continues to thrive. Employment of computer specialists was expected to increase 31.4 percent through the year 2014, according to the Bureau of Labor Statistics. Overall, high-level computer specialists, such as security specialists, should be in greater demand than low-level computer specialists, such as computer programmers. Employment of network systems analysts and computer software engineers was predicted to increase the fastest by 2014, rising 54.6 percent and 48.4 percent, respectively.

Computer specialists working for computer systems design and related services, in particular, should have the greatest opportunities and the highest salaries. Firms in the computer systems design industry help companies to set up Web sites, networks, computer databases, and other information technology systems. These firms usually send a team of specialists out to first design and then build or implement changes to the client's computer systems. In their 2006–07 *Career Guide to Industries*, the Bureau of Labor Statistics reported that employment in computer design firms was expected to grow 39.5 percent though the year 2014.

Management Consulting

There has been tremendous growth in the number and variety of management consultants in the American economy as well. During the economic recession in the late 1980s and early 1990s, many high-level executives were released from their contracts at major consulting firms or laid off from corporations. Some of these experienced professionals formed their own small consulting firms, usually specializing in one particular area of expertise such as management analysis. According to the Bureau of Labor Statistics, management, scientific, and technical consulting services were projected to experience a 60.5 percent increase in employment growth through the year 2014.

One area where management consultants will be in high demand is in facilities management, or "outsourcing." Outsourcing refers to a company's practice of focusing on its principal activities and hiring outside specialists to perform supportive business activities such as accounting, telecommunications, and human resources.

THE WORLD OF FINANCE

Many employment opportunities exist in businesses providing financial services. The fields involved in finance include banking, investment, accounting, and insurance. Most workers in these fields hold administrative or administrative support positions. According to the Bureau of Labor Statistics' May 2004 *Occupational Employment Statistics* survey, some 5.1 million workers were employed in the business and financial operations occupations.

Banks

Years ago, bank business was conducted Monday through Friday from 9 a.m. to 3 p.m. Bank jobs were thought to be comfortable, steady, and secure. Hence, the phrase "banker's hours" referred to jobs

To remain competitive, commercial banks offer many different products and services. Customers can choose which ones will best meet their needs. *(Photograph by Kelly A. Quin. Thomson Gale. Reproduced by permission.)*

that were fairly easy and did not require too much of a person's time. This comparison is no longer valid, however. Today banking is a fiercely competitive, complex business, conducted around the clock.

The U.S. banking industry has had its share of ups and downs in recent years. At the beginning of the 1990s the banking industry was in serious trouble. Hundreds of commercial banks had gone out of business, and profits at the nation's top banks plummeted. Economic downturns and large losses on foreign loans and real estate loans were contributing factors in the banking industry's problems. Banks also felt competitive pressure from investment firms, insurance companies, pension funds, and corporations. During the 1980s federal deregulation allowed nonbank organizations to offer financial services that had previously been the exclusive domain of banks. These services included checking and savings accounts, loans, and credit cards. Further deregulation by Congress in 1999 allowed banks more inroads into the financial services industry, allowing them to sell stocks and bonds, insurance policies, and mutual funds.

Whereas nonbank companies have been assuming traditional banking functions since the 1980s, commercial banks have only been as free to move into nonbank businesses since the turn of the century. Largely as a result of this situation, the banking industry's dominance of finance has declined. Many bank customers still do not regard banks as a place to go for anything other than checking and savings accounts, CDs, and mortgages. Banks, however, are fighting to remain competitive in several ways.

Mergers To cut operation costs and offset competition, many banks have merged and laid off thousands of workers in the process. Regional banks have banded together to form super-regionals. Small community banks will not disappear altogether, however, because there will always be areas where "mega-banks" choose not to establish offices.

Additional Services In the competition for consumer dollars, banks are developing and aggressively marketing new products and offering additional services. For example, bank customers can choose from a wide array of checking accounts, annuities, certificates of deposit, credit cards, buyer protection insurance on checking accounts, telephone and online transaction services, stocks and bonds, and much more. Bank tellers are often told to sell such services to customers who have a lot of money deposited with the bank.

Top-Dollar Jobs in Computers, Business, and Office

These are high-paying jobs described in this volume. The figures represent typical salaries or earnings for experienced workers.

$100,000–$250,000	• Controller • Investment Banker
$60,000–$130,000	• Actuary • Bank Officer and Manager • Computer and Information Systems Manager • Computer Consultant • Computer Software Engineer • Credit Manager • Financial Analyst • General Manager • Human Resources Manager • Management Analyst and Consultant • Securities Broker
$35,000–$75,000	• Accountant (Management and Public) • Auditor • Brokerage Clerk • Claims Adjuster • College/University Administrator • Compensation and Benefits Analyst • Computer Database Administrator • Computer Network Technician • Computer Programmer • Computer Security Specialist • Computer Software Documentation Writer • Computer Systems Analyst • Employee Benefits Manager • Employment Counselor • Employment Interviewer • Financial Planner • Insurance Underwriter • Meeting Planner • Network Administrator • Office Manager • Office Planner • Operations Research Analyst • Outplacement Consultant • Recruiter • Statistician • Training and Development Specialist

Industry Snapshots

COMPUTER SERVICES

The computer services industry encompasses an incredibly diverse group of companies. Computer talent is in great demand as companies worldwide seek to automate their offices and factories and keep pace with rapid advances in technology. Computer specialist occupations were projected to be among the fastest growing in the economy, with employment expected to increase 31.4 percent through the year 2014, according to the Bureau of Labor Statistics.

MANAGEMENT CONSULTING

In an ever-changing marketplace, many businesses find that they need expert help to restructure their organizations, develop quality-control procedures, and manage employees. Although the management consulting industry will continue to grow throughout the twenty-first century, the rapid proliferation of consulting firms has sparked intense competition for market share. To ensure survival, firms have expanded their range of services and their areas of specialty in hopes of securing a market niche. Consulting will be one of the fastest-growing industries in coming years. According to the Bureau of Labor Statistics, management, scientific, and technical consulting services are expected to experience a 60.5 percent increase in employment growth through the year 2014. The only industry expected to grow faster was the home health care industry.

TEMPORARY HELP

Employment in agencies placing temporary workers was estimated to increase by more than 45 percent through the year 2014, with nearly 1.5 million new jobs being created, according to Bureau of Labor Statistics projections. Companies that are downsizing and streamlining their operations strive to save money in employee benefits and wages by using more temporary workers. The tremendous growth in the temporary help industry represents a major trend away from long-term job security in the United States.

FINANCE

After a period of expansion and volatility in the 1980s, investment firms have adopted a more conservative outlook. They continue to look to new markets, however, especially international ones. Investment firms have become one of the healthiest industries within the financial sector, and they are considered one of the country's faster-growing industries. A successful investment firm needs a skillful sales force, well versed in computer technology, to compete for consumers' investment dollars. Employment for financial services and investment industry was expected to grow 15.8 percent through the year 2014, according to the Bureau of Labor Statistics.

INSURANCE

To gain financial momentum in the new millennium, insurance companies are expanding overseas, finding specialized markets, and developing new products to meet the needs of a changing population. The skyrocketing cost of insurance, especially health insurance, will continue to be an important public policy issue. Employment in this field was expected to grow by 9.5 percent, or by 215,000 jobs, through the year 2014, according to the Bureau of Labor Statistics.

ACCOUNTING

Public accounting is dominated by a handful of large firms. These firms are competing against one another for clients in the United States and around the world. Accountants are becoming increasingly important in business management. In their 2004–14 projections, the Bureau of Labor Statistics forecasted that about 264,000 jobs in accounting and auditing would be added to the labor market through the year 2014, which would represent a 0.9 percent increase.

BANKING

The distinction between commercial banks and other financial institutions is blurring. Faced with competition from investment firms and insurance companies, banks are developing new products and services. Many banks have merged as a result of competition. Employment in banking was forecasted to decline by 1.8 percent, according to the Bureau of Labor Statistics.

New Technology Virtually every bank in existence uses computers and other electronic equipment to speed check-handling transactions and other services. Electronic funds transfer (EFT), an even more advanced system, may eventually eliminate the use of checks entirely. EFT automatically transfers money from one account to another, as in the case of automated teller machines (ATMs), which allow customers to do their banking twenty-four hours a day, seven days a week. EFT also allows people to au-

Alternative Work Styles in Computers, Business, and Office

TELECOMMUTING

Telecommuting allows employees to work at home on a computer connected to an office computer network. Many employees are more productive when they spend some or all of their time working at home. Telecommuting offers opportunities for the disabled or for parents of young children who need to be at home. It also allows employees to live farther from the office. Some workers who telecommute include:
- computer programmers
- computer software documentation writers
- insurance underwriters
- tax preparers
- operations research analysts

FREELANCING

Freelancing is done by workers who produce projects or provide services for one or more clients. They are not permanently employed by any one client but are paid for each assignment on an hourly basis or at a fixed rate. Freelancers frequently must spend part of their time looking for clients and assignments. Some workers doing freelance work include:
- meeting planners
- accountants
- computer consultants
- computer systems analysts
- tax preparers
- office planners
- training and development specialists

JOB SHARING

Job sharing allows two or more people to hold one full-time position. Responsibilities, salary, and benefits are all shared. A time schedule is established to fulfill job requirements and meet employee needs. Job sharers should enjoy working on a team, and they need to be flexible and well organized. Some workers involved in job sharing include:
- secretaries
- administrative assistants
- correspondence clerks
- computer and office machine repairers

FLEXTIME

Flextime allows workers to adjust work hours to suit personal needs. The total number of hours in the week remains the same. Flextime can also mean a change in workdays, such as four ten-hour days or six short days. Some workers on flextime schedules include:
- receptionists
- file clerks
- mail clerks
- claims adjusters
- employment interviewers
- data entry keyers

TEMPORARY EMPLOYMENT

Temporary workers generally receive their assignments through temporary employment agencies. They work for firms that require additional help on an occasional basis. They receive an hourly rate of pay for the time they work. Assignments differ in length and location, offering some variety. Among temporary workers are:
- secretaries
- word processors
- messenger service workers
- computer programmers

---

tomatically transfer money for regular payments (such as mortgage payments or utility bills) from their accounts to the biller's account. Many banks also offer consumers the opportunity to conduct their banking online, using personal computers and modems to deposit and transfer funds. Services such as online banking allow smaller banks, which have fewer branch offices, to compete with larger banks. In 2005, some 44 percent of Americans with a personal computer at home used it for banking online, according to a February 2005 data memo from the Pew Internet and American Life Project.

Investment Firms

The 1980s were a heady decade for investment firms. The sale of stocks, bonds, and other securities soared. Investment firms expanded greatly, hiring staff and opening branch offices in the United States and abroad. In October 1987, however, a stock market crash led many investment firms to lay off staff and adopt a more conservative and serious style. The mid-1990s saw one of the longest stock market expansions in history, fueled primarily by the growth of mutual funds. As the twenty-first century began, however, the stock market was falling, and it fell even more after September 11, 2001. By 2006 the market had made a substantial recovery, but many stocks still hadn't reached their 1990 prices, especially in the high-tech industry.

In 2001 the investment business was in crisis for another reason—declining investor confidence. Large companies like Enron and Global Crossing folded, leaving ordinary shareholders with large losses that company executives had avoided by selling off stock before the collapse. Some of the largest investment firms were indicted for fraud when they recommended failing companies' stock to investors in order to set up profitable stock offerings with the companies. At the heart of the crisis was the dual nature of such investment firms, which both recommend stocks to investors and underwrite them. This potential conflict of interest was behind many reforms.

Despite the current economic slump and crisis in confidence, the investment business is still one of the fastest-growing industries within the financial sector. Employment for financial services and investment industry was expected to grow 15.8 percent through the year 2014, according to the Bureau of Labor Statistics. Workers in this field will need to have the latest computer skills and varying degrees of knowledge regarding the emerging global market. In addition, many brokerage firms have en-

larged their sales and research departments in an attempt to remain competitive with rival firms, banks, and nonfinancial institutions. Stock and bond trading, as well as other investing, can now be done online.

Accounting Firms

According to the Bureau of Labor Statistics, there were more than 1.2 million accountants and auditors in the United States in 2004, most of whom were employed in the corporate sector. Even in bad economic times, businesses must keep financial records and pay taxes. Consequently, job prospects in accounting remain bright. In recent years there has been an increased demand for accountants, due in part to more complicated tax rules and business regulations. It was estimated in the Bureau of Labor Statistics projections that about 264,000 jobs in accounting and auditing would be added to the labor market through the year 2014.

Some accountants work as part of the administrative staff of businesses or government agencies. Others—known as public accountants—work for firms that supply accounting services to businesses. At the beginning of the twenty-first century, the field of public accounting was dominated by a handful

The business world is constantly changing. Workers must be able to adapt to new challenges and developments as companies attempt to satisfy market demands for new services and products. (© Paul Barton/Corbis.)

of huge companies. These firms offer one of the fastest-growing areas of employment.

Because computer spreadsheets now do much of the actual calculating required in accounting, to-day's accountants do more than balance daily ledgers. Accountants have become increasingly important in helping to manage businesses. They use financial information to analyze a company's needs, solve problems, and make projections. Accountants with specializations such as bankruptcy, debt restructuring, benefits consulting, corporate reorganization, and fraud investigation are especially valuable to businesses.

The corporate accounting business suffered an image crisis in 2001, when Arthur Andersen, one of the Big Five accounting firms, was indicted for fraud for its role in the Enron scandal. Instead of exposing financial trouble spots in the failing Enron's books, the Arthur Andersen staff admitted to concealing losses to curry favor with its client. As a result, Andersen went out of business. History shows that accountants and auditors must be objective if they want long-term success.

The Insurance Industry

The insurance industry is made up of three main branches: life insurance, health insurance, and property and liability insurance. In the recent past, the U.S. insurance industry endured both good and bad times. In the 1990s insurance companies were trying a number of tactics to regain a strong financial position. One tactic was to diversify products or to find a specialized niche within the insurance market. Some companies specialized in an area related to insurance, such as benefits counseling or financial and risk management. A second tactic was to develop new products. Many of these new products were aimed at senior citizens, who represent a large market. Yet another tactic was to develop an international market. Companies could do this by establishing offices or divisions overseas or by buying established insurance companies in foreign countries.

Medical Insurance Crisis One major problem that the insurance industry has had to contend with is the skyrocketing cost and the increasing complexities of insurance coverage. The problem is especially acute in the area of medical insurance. Medical insurance has become so expensive that millions of Americans cannot afford medical coverage.

Although solutions to this insurance crisis are not easy, the industry is making some attempts to control premium rates. For example, many health and life insurance companies are switching to or emphasizing managed care. Managed-care services include helping policyholders find the lowest-cost

health provider, negotiating with medical-care providers for lower costs, and checking on the necessity of certain medical procedures. Often in these systems, referred to as health maintenance organizations (HMOs), the patient has a limited choice of primary care physicians. Only a primary care physician can determine if a patient should see a specialist. Many patients complain about the lack of choice when selecting doctors under managed-care plans. Many also find that some expensive treatments are not covered under their HMO plan.

The Use of Computers Computers have greatly affected all industries, and the insurance industry is no exception. Online computer networks link branch offices of insurance companies, greatly decreasing the amount of time that used to be needed to process policies, claims, and service inquiries. The use of computers saves insurance companies both time and money and enables them to offer their clients more efficient service.

Employment Opportunities in Insurance The insurance industry is one of the largest employers in the country, and future prospects are good. Employment in this field was expected to grow by 226,000 jobs through the year 2014, according to the Bureau of Labor Statistics. Although approximately half of the insurance positions are clerical, career mobility is often swift. Those new to the field might consider specializing in areas such as international business insurance, workers' compensation, and product and pollution liability.

A LOOK INTO THE FUTURE

Throughout the early twenty-first century, jobs in computers, business, and the office will most likely be characterized by the same far-reaching trends affecting the entire economy. These trends include constantly evolving computer technology, an expanding global marketplace (aided in part by trade agreements such as NAFTA and GATT), and a shift toward an information-oriented society. These trends will require workers to seek continuing education and to improve and expand their skills. More than ever, workers who are versatile and can adapt to changing needs will be in demand.

Growth in Employment

The expanding computer and data processing services industry will offer increasing opportunities for computer specialists, although the demand for computer programmers and technical support specialists will not be as great as that for computer software engineers, computer systems analysts, database administrators, and network administrators. Computer technology has led to the near-elimination of jobs for stenographers and statistical clerks, and virtually all typing is now done on computers. Any workers in business, administration, or office occupations who do not achieve computer literacy will find their employment options severely limited.

Through the year 2014, employment in the human resources field was expected to increase by more than 18 percent, according to the Bureau of Labor Statistics. A constantly changing workplace will create a demand for people who can attract skilled workers, place them in positions best suited to their talents and the company's goals, and manage their training, benefits, and problems. Employment for management consultants, particularly in the human resources field, should also increase faster than average as more companies hire consultants to perform tasks previously assigned to middle managers. In addition, the number of receptionists and information clerks, whose work is not easily automated, was expected to rise 21.4 percent through the year 2014. These positions should occur in fast-growing industries such as business services.

The Evolving Workplace

The American workforce will most likely grow more ethnically diverse in the next century. In their 2014 projections the Bureau of Labor Statistics estimated that white workers would comprise 80.2 percent of the total workforce by 2014, a 4.6-percentage-point decrease from 1994. By 2014 the Hispanic labor force was projected to grow faster than the African-American labor force, primarily because of faster population growth. The Asian-American labor force was expected to equal more than 5 percent of the total labor force. The number of women in the workforce was expected to increase from 46.4 percent in 2004 to 46.8 percent by 2014. In addition, the baby boomer generation is aging. Compared with young workers, the pool of experienced workers should increase. It was projected that the median age of the American worker should be 41.6 years in 2014, compared with 37.7 years in 1994.

Competition for jobs in the computers, business, and office workplace will be high in the twenty-first century, and education and specialized training will increasingly become the norm. Projected rates of employment growth are faster than average for occupations requiring a college degree or other postsecondary education or training. The trend toward higher education is expected to continue. Whereas a high school diploma is required even for most entry-level jobs, a college degree is necessary for higher-level business jobs. In addition, even after a person starts working, further education, training, and retraining are essential to keeping up with and adapting to new developments in the ever-changing world of business.

These continual changes in the workplace, workers' roles, and the skills required of workers are both exciting and challenging. The workplace of the future may be far different from the one we have known. Nevertheless, opportunities in the business world abound for those ready to face new challenges.

Getting Into

Good jobs do not magically appear. Anyone who has been in the job market knows that landing the right job takes planning, preparation, perseverance, and patience. This is true whether you are looking for your first job, reentering the job market, trying to get a new job, or planning a mid-career change. This essay is designed to guide you through the process of finding a job, from helping you define your career objectives to suggesting ways to prepare yourself for interviews. Use the advice and checklists below to help identify the kind of work that fits your personality, skills, and interests. Then learn how to locate job openings that match your criteria. Finally, use these tips to help you create a resume and prepare for the interview that helps you land the job that's right for you.

PLANNING YOUR CAREER

What are your unique skills? What kind of workplace appeals to you? What do you find most rewarding in your daily life? Answering these questions can help you identify a career path that will enrich your life, financially and otherwise. Most people enjoy doing a job well. There is an inner satisfaction that comes from taking on a challenge and accomplishing something worthwhile. Whether you are just starting out in the working world or you are at the midpoint of a career, it is worth taking some time to consider whether or not you are in the right kind of work—or looking for the right kind of job. If you are unhappy or dissatisfied in your daily work and are just trying to do enough to get by, you may not be in the right job or the right field. The following ideas can help you match your skills and interests with the kind of work you will find most rewarding.

Evaluate Yourself

Before you make any career decisions, think about subjects or topics that interest you and tasks you do well. This can help you pinpoint the kind of work you would be happy doing. One way to go about this is to compile a self-inventory chart. Such a chart will be helpful as you decide which jobs you want to consider. Including details about your work history and educational background will also make the chart useful to you as you compile your resume, write cover letters, complete job application forms, and prepare for job interviews.

Begin your self-inventory chart by listing all the jobs you have ever had, including summer employment, part-time jobs, volunteer work, and any freelance or short-term assignments you have done. Include the dates of employment, the names and addresses of supervisors, and the amount of money you earned. Then compile a similar list of your hobbies and other activities, including any special experiences you have had, such as travel. Next, do the same for your educational history, listing schools attended, major courses of study, grades, special honors or awards, courses you particularly enjoyed, and extracurricular activities.

At this point, you may see a career pattern emerging: perhaps your list is already suggesting a direction for your career search. If the picture still lacks detail or focus, expand your self-inventory chart by compiling a list of standard workplace aptitudes, and rate yourself *above average*, *average*, or *below average* for each one. Some skill categories to include in your list are administrative, analytic, athletic, clerical, language, leadership, managerial, manual, mathematical, mechanical, sales, and verbal abilities. Also rate your willingness to accept responsibility and your ability to get along with people. In combination with your educational background, work history, and list of personal interests, this information should help you understand why some kinds of work appeal to you and others do not.

Evaluate Workplace Characteristics

Another tool to help you find a rewarding job is the "Work Characteristics Checklist" below. Some of these characteristics will be attractive to you. Some will not. Perhaps you will discover that having a workplace with flexible hours, for example, is more important to you than being able to work outdoors. Or maybe you will find that these are both very significant issues in your quality of life.

This checklist can be useful as a guide as you compile your own list of what is important to you in a job or workplace. Do not expect a job to meet all your requirements, however. Focusing on the job

Work Characteristics Checklist

Do you want a job in which you can

- work outdoors?
- be physically active?
- work with your hands?
- be challenged mentally?
- work with machines?
- work independently?
- work on a team?
- follow clear instructions?
- earn a lot of money?
- have a chance for rapid advancement?
- have good benefits?
- travel in your work?
- work close to home?
- work regular hours?
- have a flexible schedule?
- have a variety of tasks?
- have supervisory responsibilities?
- express your own ideas?
- be a decision maker?

characteristics that are most important to you will help you identify the type of work you would find most rewarding. It will also be helpful when it is time to decide whether or not to apply for jobs you discover during the search process.

Evaluate Career Options

Now that you've evaluated your personal skills, aptitudes, interests, and experience, and you've identified the kinds of workplace characteristics that are important to you, do you feel confident that you know what kinds of jobs you'd be good at? If not, you may wish to consult an experienced career counselor or take advantage of online resources that can help you find a good career field match.

Most high schools, vocational schools, and colleges provide vocational testing and career counseling guidance for students and alumni. Some local offices of the state employment services affiliated with the federal employment service offer free counseling. Commercial career centers also offer guidance services.

There are many tools available to test your interests and aptitudes for the purpose of career counseling. The personal profile that emerges from a skills inventory can be matched with potential career fields to show you what kinds of jobs might be good matches for your interests. These assessment tools will also show you what kind of training is necessary to qualify for jobs in these career fields. You may find programs like this online that you can try for yourself. For a more comprehensive approach, you may prefer to look into aptitude tests that are administered and interpreted by a career counselor.

Most major cities have professional career consultants and career counseling firms. You should make sure to check their reputations before pay-ing for their services. A list of counseling services in your area is available from the American Counseling Association in Alexandria, Virginia (http://www.counseling.org).

You can also search the Internet for many services that career counselors provide. Some sites have online counselors who can help you with a variety of tasks, such as obtaining information on jobs, careers, and training. They may be able to provide information on available services, including housing assistance, day care facilities, and transportation. A list of career planning resources, including Web sites, is available at the end of this volume.

EVALUATE SPECIFIC JOBS

After you have considered what you do well and what you enjoy doing, and identified some career options that provide a good match with your interests and abilities, you're ready to focus on the specific types of jobs that may be available to you. First, make a note of all the jobs in this volume that interest you. Then examine the education and training required for these jobs. Decide whether you qualify or would be able to gain the qualifications.

If possible, talk with people who have the kinds of jobs you are considering. Firsthand information can be invaluable. Also look through the appropriate trade and professional journals listed at the end of this essay and check the section at the end of the volume called "Resources" for books and Web sites that contain more detailed information about the jobs. In addition, counselors are usually helpful. For more detailed information, you can contact the trade and professional associations listed at the end of each occupational profile.

Once you have found out all you can about a particular type of job, compare the features of the job with your work characteristics checklist. See how many characteristics of the job match your work preferences. By completing these steps for all the jobs that appeal to you, you should be able to come up with a list of jobs that match your interests and abilities.

FINDING JOB OPPORTUNITIES

Once you've decided what kind of job suits you, the next step is to look for available positions. Obviously, the more openings you can find, the better your chance of landing a job. People usually apply

Job Finder's Checklist

The following list of job-hunting tips may seem obvious, but getting all the bits and pieces in order beforehand helps when you're looking for a job.

Resume Find out whether you will need a resume. If so, bring your resume up to date or prepare a new one. Assemble a supply of neatly printed copies and have an electronic version ready to e-mail to prospective employers.

References Line up your references. Ask permission of the people whose names you would like to use. Write down their addresses, phone numbers, and job titles.

Contacts Put the word out to everyone you know that you are looking for a job.

Job market Find out where the jobs are. Make a list of possible employers in your field of interest.

Research Do a little homework ahead of time—it can make a big difference in the long run. Find out as much as you can about a job, the field, and the company before you apply. A knowledgeable job applicant makes a good impression.

Organization Keep a file on your job- hunting campaign with names and dates of employers contacted, ads answered, results, and follow-up.

Appearance Make sure that the clothes you plan to wear to an interview are neat and clean. You may need to dress more formally than you would on the job, particularly if you are visiting a personnel office or meeting with a manager. Keep in mind that people will form an opinion of you based on their first impressions.

---

for many job openings before they find the right employment match.

There are many ways to find out about or apply for job openings. Some of these job-hunting techniques are explained on the pages that follow, along with information about how to follow up on job leads.

Applying in Person

For some jobs, especially part-time or entry-level jobs, you may be able to find employment by visiting the company or companies for which you would like to work. This works best when a company is expanding or jobs are plentiful for other reasons, or when a "help wanted" sign is posted at the company. Applying in person can sharpen your interviewing techniques and give you a chance to see a variety of workplaces. This direct approach is best for hourly labor or service jobs; when applying for other types of work, it is not the method to use unless you are directed to do so. Applicants for professional or supervisory jobs should always send a letter and resume to the company.

Phone and Letter Campaigns

To conduct a phone campaign, use the business listings of your telephone directory to build a list of companies for which you might like to work. Call their personnel departments and find out whether they have any openings. This technique is not useful

in all situations, and it has its drawbacks: you may not be able to make a strong impression by phone, and you will not have a written record of your contacts.

Letter writing campaigns can be very effective if the letters are well thought out and carefully prepared. Your letters should always be typed. Handwritten letters and photocopied letters convey a lack of interest or motivation.

You may be able to compile a good list of company addresses in your field of interest by reading the trade and professional publications listed at the end of this essay. Many of the periodicals publish directories or directory issues. Other sources you can use to compile lists of companies are the trade unions and professional organizations listed at the end of each job profile in this volume. The reference librarian at your local library can also help you find appropriate directories.

You can also e-mail letters to human resource departments of many companies. Be sure to follow all the same guidelines as you would for traditional letter correspondence.

Whether they are paper or electronic, your letters should be addressed to the personnel or human resources department of the organization. If possible, send the letter to a specific person. If you don't know who the correct person is, try to find the name of the personnel director through the directories in the library. You can also call on the phone and say, "I'm writing to ask about employment at your company. To whom should I address my letter?" If you can't find a name, use a standard salutation. It's a good idea to enclose a resume (described later in this essay) with the letter to give the employer a brief description of your educational and work experience.

Keep a list of all the people you write to, along with the date each letter was mailed, or keep a photocopy of each letter. Then you can follow up by writing a brief note or calling people who do not reply within about three weeks.

Job Databases Online

The World Wide Web can be an excellent resource for job hunters. The Internet currently has thousands of career-related sites where you can read about job openings or post your resume in a database for a possible match with available jobs. Some sites, such as The Monster Board (http://www.monster.com), help you build a resume and post it online as well as allow you to search through a massive database of help-wanted listings. Others employ

a search engine to find jobs that match your background, then post your resume online for employers. The Web site called CareerBuilder (http://www.careerbuilder.com) uses an interactive personal search program that lets you select job criteria such as location, title, and salary; you are then notified by e-mail when a matching position is posted in the database.

Many companies post job openings in their human resource Web pages. You can usually access these lists by visiting the Web site of a company and clicking on a link called "jobs," "careers," or "employment opportunities." If you find a job that interests you during your online search, whether it's posted at a company's own Web site or on a general listing of jobs, follow the directions given for applying for the position. Some online ads will provide the contact information you need to send your resume and cover letter directly to the employer, either by e-mail or by traditional mail, but other ads direct job hunters to apply directly through a link at the job description.

Many career-related Web sites can be found on the Internet. This hypothetical site (for illustration purposes only) allows job-seekers to search for a position by location and by job category.

Job hunters can often find job listings through the Web sites of the professional associations in their career fields. State government Web sites may also provide links to job listings—or to non-government sites that list available jobs.

Help-Wanted Ads

Many people find out about job openings by reading the "help-wanted" sections of newspapers, trade journals, and professional magazines. Employers and employment agencies often, though not always, use these classified ad sections to publicize available jobs.

Classified ads use unique terms to convey basic information. You will find some common abbreviations in the chart in this essay titled "Reading the Classifieds." You can usually decode the abbreviations by using common sense, but if something puzzles you, call the newspaper and ask for a translation. Classified ads usually list the qualifications that are required for a particular job and explain how to contact the employer.

As you find openings that interest you, answer each ad using the method requested. Record the date of your contact, and if you don't hear from the employer within two or three weeks, place another call or send a polite note asking whether the job is still open. Don't forget to include your phone number and address in your initial contact.

Some help-wanted ads are "blind ads." These ads give contact information for replying but provide no name, phone number, or address that would identify the company. Employers and employment agencies may place these ads to avoid having to reply to all of the job applicants or being contacted directly by job-seekers.

Situation-Wanted Ads

Another way to get the attention of potential employers is with a situation-wanted ad. You can place one of these in the classified section of your local newspaper or of a trade journal in your field of interest. Many personnel offices and employment agencies scan these columns when they're looking for new employees. The situation-wanted ad is usually most effective for people who have advanced education, training, or experience, or who are in fields where their unique skills are in great demand.

A situation-wanted ad should be brief, clear, and to the point. Its main purpose is to interest the employer enough so you are contacted for an interview. It should tell exactly what kind of job you

Reading the Classifieds

HELP WANTED

ADMIN. ASST.
Growing real estate mgt. co., challenging position. Excel. oppty. for conscientious person looking for a future. Must be organized, possess good administrative abilities along with bus. exp. and good skills. Phone for appt. 000-0000.

BANK TELLER—Prestigious bank seeks indivs. w/ 6 mos.–2 yrs. Teller (IRAs, Keoghs) or any bnfts. exp. Call Dave Spencer at 000-0000 or send resume to Box 123 Times.

BOOKKEEPER
For downtown insurance broker. Full charge including trial balance and payroll taxes. Insurance exp. and typ. essential. Phone 000-0000.

CORRESPONDENCE CLERK—good writing and typing skills. Knwl. office machs. Responsible, diversified position in large export firm. Excellent opportunity for self-starter. Salary open. Call Ms. Stonner 000-0000.

COMPUTER SERVICER
Progressive co. needs EDP machine servicer to repair computers. Digital and analog exp. req. Good income & bnfts. Call 000-0000.

CREDIT OFFICER
Co. needs individual with 3–5 yrs. exp. in dealing with building contractors. Must know credit and collections. Send resume to Box 247, City, State.

FILE CLERK—Good alphabetical filing. Oak Lane Court. 000-0000, ext. 7.

MAIL CLERK
Industrial Park co. seeks individual to process incoming/outgoing mail, handle general office services work. Gd. benefits. Please send resume or letter stating qualifications & desired sal. to: X7610 Gazette.

SECRETARY—Modern downtown brokerage. WordPerfect 8 and MS Excel preferred. Good sal. Contact Ms. Gibbs, 000-0000.

CLASSIFIED ABBREVIATIONS

appt.	appointment
assoc.	associate
avail. immed.	available immediately
begnr.	beginner
bkpr.	bookkeeper
bus. exp.	business experience
clk.	clerk
col.	college
DP	data processing
EDP	electronic data processing
excel. oppty.	excellent opportunity
exec.	executive
exp.	experience
fee neg.	fee negotiable (fee can be worked out with employer)
f/p., f/pd.	fee paid (agency fee paid by employer)
f/t	full time
gd. bnfts.	good benefits
K	thousand
M	thousand
machs.	machines
mfg.	manufacturing
mgr.	manager
mgt.	management
pfd.	preferred
p/t	part time
sal.	salary
sec., secy.	secretary
temp.	temporary
typ.	typist, typing
w/	with
wpm	words per minute

SITUATION WANTED

ACCOUNTANT (CPA)
4-year national CPA experience available for per diem work / audit systems review, special projects. L7559 Times.

ACTUARY
3 exams, 2 yrs life exp. for P/T & or summer employment 000-0000.

ADMIN. ASST.—HS Grad with Admin. and word processing skills seeks position in fashion industry, national magazine pfd. Hardworking, intelligent, personable, quick learner.

BKPR., CLERICAL—Recent grad. of 2-yr. bus. col. Avail. immed. employment. 000-0000

CONTROLLER—18 yrs. excel. private and CPA experience seeks position in county. Reply K46 Chronicle.

GENERAL MANAGER
With expertise in business world. Many years diversified exp. in mfg./retail/showroom areas. Excellent correspondent, articulate, well groomed. Call weekdays—000-0000

FILE CLK. AVAIL.—Knowledge typ., ofc. machs., conscientious begnr., 000-0000.

MANAGEMENT
Bright, ambitious MBA, with marketing & general management exp. seeks challenging position with progressive co. E2647 Dispatch.

MESSENGER—mature, reliable, own car. 000-0000 or F37 News.

SECRETARY—Mature, heavy exp. mutual funds, securities and banking seeks challenging position, downtown pfd. 000-0000.

WORD PROCESSOR—Excel. seeks all types of home work. Call 000-0000 mornings.

want, why you qualify, and whether you are available for full-time or part-time work. Use the same abbreviations that employers use in classified ads.

If you are already employed and do not want it known that you are looking for a new position, you can run a blind ad. A blind ad protects your privacy by listing a box number at the publication to which all replies can be sent. They are then forwarded to you. You do not need to give your name, address, or phone number in the ad.

Networking

A very important source of information about job openings is networking. This means talking with friends and acquaintances about your area of interest. If any of them have friends or relatives in the field, ask if they would be willing to speak with you. There's nothing wrong with telling anyone who will listen that you are looking for a job—family, friends, counselors, and former employers. This will multiply your sources of information many times over.

You can use the Internet to make contacts, too. You can meet people with similar interests in news groups, which are organized by topic. Then you can correspond individually via e-mail. Many fields have professional organizations that maintain Web sites. These can help you keep current on news affecting your field, including employment opportunities.

Sometimes a contact knows about a job vacancy before it is advertised. You may have an advantage, then, when you get in touch with the employer. Don't, however, use the contact's name without permission. Don't assume that a contact will go out on a limb by recommending you, either. Once you have received the inside information, rely on your own ability to get the job.

Notes on Networking

Let people know you're looking. Tell friends, acquaintances, teachers, business associates, former employers—anyone who might know of job openings in your field.

Read newspapers and professional and trade journals. Look for news of developments in your field and for names of people and companies you might contact.

Use the World Wide Web. Make contacts through news groups, or find information on Web sites for professional organizations in your field.

Join professional or trade associations. Contacts you make at meetings could provide valuable job leads. Association newsletters generally carry useful information about people and developments in the field.

Attend classes or seminars. You will meet other people in your field at job-training classes and professional development seminars.

Participate in local support groups. You can gain information about people and places to contact through support groups such as those listed by *The Riley Guide,* available online at http://www.rileyguide.com/support.html, as well as through alumni associations.

Be on the lookout. Always be prepared to make the most of any opportunity that comes along. Talk with anyone who can provide useful information about your field.

Placement Services

Most vocational schools, high schools, and colleges have a placement or career service that maintains a list of job openings and schedules visits from companies. If you are a student or recent graduate, you should check there for job leads. Many employers look first in technical or trade schools and colleges for qualified applicants for certain jobs. Recruiters often visit colleges to look for people to fill technical and scientific positions. These recruiters usually represent large companies. Visit your placement office regularly to check the job listings, and watch for scheduled visits by company recruiters.

State Employment Services

Another source of information about job openings is the local office of the state employment service. Many employers automatically list job openings at the local office. Whether you're looking for a job in private industry or with the state, these offices, which are affiliated with the federal employment service, are worth visiting, online or in person, if there are offices locally.

State employment service offices are public agencies that do not charge for their services. They can direct you to special programs run by the government in conjunction with private industry. These programs, such as the Work Incentive Program for families on welfare, are designed to meet special needs. Some, but not all, of these offices offer vocational aptitude and interest tests and can refer interested people to vocational training centers. The state employment service can be a valuable first stop in your search for work, especially if there are special circumstances in your background. For example, if you did not finish high school, if you have had any difficulties with the law, or if you are living in a difficult home environment, your state employment service office is equipped to help you.

Private Employment Agencies

State employment services, though free, are usually very busy. If you are looking for more personal service and want a qualified employment counselor to help you find a job, you might want to approach a private employment agency.

Private employment agencies will help you get a job if they think they can place you. Most of them get paid only if they're successful in finding you a job, so you need to show them that you are a good prospect. These agencies will help you prepare a resume if you need one, and they will contact employers they think might be interested in you.

Private employment agencies are in the business of bringing together people who are looking for jobs and companies that are looking for workers. For some positions, usually mid- and higher- level jobs, the employment agency's fee is paid by the employer. In such cases, the job seeker pays no fee. In other cases, you may be required to pay the fee, which is usually a percentage of your annual salary. Paying a fee can be a worthwhile investment if it leads to a rewarding career.

Some agencies may also ask for a small registration fee whether or not you get a job through them. Some agencies may demand that you pay even if you find one of the jobs they are trying to fill through your other contacts. Be sure to read and understand the fine print of any contract you're expected to sign, and ask for a copy to take home. Since the quality of these agencies varies, check to see if an agency is a certified member of a state or national association.

Some employment agencies, called staffing services, operate in a different way. They are usually paid by employers to screen and refer good candidates for job openings. They earn money when they refer a candidate who is hired by the employer. The employee pays no fee. Staffing firms, however, only spend time on candidates they think they may be able to place.

Private employment agencies are usually helping many people at one time. They may not have the time to contact you every time they find a job opening. Therefore, you may need to phone them at reasonable intervals after you have registered.

Civil Service

In your search for work, don't forget that the civil service—federal, state, and local—may have many jobs in your field. You may contact the state employment office or apply directly to the appropriate state or federal agency. The armed services also train and employ civilians in many fields. Don't neglect these avenues for finding jobs. Civil service positions usually require you to take a civil service examination. Books are available to help you prepare for these exams, and your local civil service office can also provide information.

Unions

In certain fields, unions can be useful sources of information. If you are a member of a union in your field of interest, you may be able to find out about jobs in the union periodical or through people at the union local. If you do not belong to a union, you may contact a union in the field you are interested in for information about available employment services. You will find addresses for some unions in the job profiles in this book.

Temporary Employment

A good way to get a feel for the job market—what's available and what certain jobs are like—is to work in a temporary job. There are both private and state agencies that can help place people in short-term jobs. Some jobs are seasonal, and extra workers may be needed in the summer or at another busy time.

Temporary employment can increase your job skills, your knowledge of a particular field, and your chances of hearing of permanent positions. In today's tight labor market, many companies are using the services of temporary workers in increasing numbers. In fact, temporary agencies may sign multimillion-dollar contracts to provide businesses with a range of temporary workers. In some cases, temporary workers are in such demand that they may receive benefits, bonuses, and the same hourly wages as equivalent permanent employees. Some temporary agencies are even joining with companies to create long-term career paths for their temporary workers.

MARKETING YOURSELF

An employer's first impression of you is likely to be based on the way you present yourself on print. Whether it is in an application form or on a resume, you will want to make a good impression so that employers will be interested in giving you a personal interview. A potential employer is likely to equate a neat, well-written presentation with good work habits, and a sloppy, poorly written one with bad work habits.

Writing an Effective Resume

When you write to a company to follow up a lead or to ask about job openings, you should send information about yourself. The accepted way of doing this is to send a resume with a cover letter.

The work resume is derived from the French word résumer, meaning "to summarize." A resume does just that—it briefly outlines your education, work experience, and special abilities and skills. A resume may also be called a curriculum vitae, a personal profile, or a personal data sheet. This summary acts as your introduction by mail or e-mail, as your calling card if you apply in person, and as a convenient reference for you to use when filling out an application form or when being interviewed.

A resume is a useful tool in applying for almost any job, even if you use it only to keep a record of where you have worked, for whom, and the dates of employment. A resume is required if you are being considered for professional or executive jobs. Prepare it carefully. It's well worth the effort.

DO YOU KNOW YOUR RIGHTS?

JOB DISCRIMINATION—WHAT IT IS

Federal and State Law

An employer cannot discriminate against you for any reason other than your ability to do the job. By federal law, an employer cannot discriminate against you because of your race, color, religion, sex, or national origin. The law applies to decisions about hiring, promotion, working conditions, and firing. The law specifically protects workers who are over the age of forty from discrimination on the basis of age.

The law also protects workers with disabilities. Employers must make their workplaces accessible to individuals with disabilities—for example, by making them accessible to wheelchairs or by hiring readers or interpreters for blind or deaf employees.

Federal law offers additional protection to employees who work for the federal government or for employers who contract with the federal government. State law can also provide protection, for example by prohibiting discrimination on the basis of marital status, arrest record, political affiliations, or sexual orientation.

Affirmative Action

Affirmative action programs are set up by businesses that want to make a special effort to hire women and members of minority groups. Federal employers and many businesses that have contracts with the federal government are required by law to set up affirmative action programs. Employers with a history of discriminatory practices may also be required to establish affirmative action programs.

Discrimination against Job Applicants

A job application form or interviewer may ask for information that can be used to discriminate against you illegally. The law prohibits such questions. If you are asked such questions and are turned down for the job, you may be a victim of discrimination. However, under federal law, employers must require you to prove that you are an American citizen or that you have a valid work permit.

Discrimination on the Job

Discrimination on the job is illegal. Being denied a promotion for which you are qualified or being paid less than coworkers are paid for the same job may be forms of illegal discrimination.

Sexual, racial, and religious harassment are forms of discrimination and are prohibited in the workplace. On-the-job harassment includes sexual, racial, or religious jokes or comments. Sexual harassment includes not only requests or demands for sexual favors but also verbal or physical conduct of a sexual nature.

JOB DISCRIMINATION—WHAT YOU CAN DO

Contact Federal or State Commissions

If you believe that your employer practices discrimination, you can complain to the state civil rights commission or the federal Equal Employment Opportunity Commission (EEOC). If, after investigating your complaint, the commission finds that there has been discrimination, it will take action against the employer. You may be entitled to the job or promotion you were denied or to reinstatement if you were fired. You may also receive back pay or other financial compensation.

Contact a Private Organization

There are many private organizations that can help you fight job discrimination. For example, the American Civil Liberties Union (ACLU) works to protect all people from infringement on their civil rights. The National Association for the Advancement of Colored People (NAACP), National Organization for Women (NOW), and Native American Rights

The goal of a resume is to capture the interest of potential employers so they will call you for a personal interview. Since employers are busy people, the resume should be as brief and as neat as possible. You should, however, include as much relevant information about yourself as you can. This is usually presented under at least two headings: "Education" and "Experience." The latter is sometimes called "Employment History." Some people add a third section titled "Related Skills," "Professional Qualifications," or "Related Qualifications."

If you prepare a self-inventory such as the one described earlier, it will be a useful tool in preparing a resume. Go through your inventory, and select the items that show your ability to do the job or jobs in which you are interested. Plan to highlight these items on your resume. Select only those facts that point out your relevant skills and experience.

Once you have chosen the special points to include, prepare the resume. At the top, put your name, address, and phone number. After that, de-

Fund may negotiate with your employer, sue on your behalf, or start a class action suit—a lawsuit brought on behalf of all individuals in your situation.

WHAT TO DO IF YOU LOSE YOUR JOB

Being Fired and Being Laid Off

In most cases, an employer can fire you only if there is good cause, such as your inability to do the job, violation of safety rules, dishonesty, or chronic absenteeism.

Firing an employee because of that employee's race, color, religion, sex, national origin, or age (if the employee is over forty) is illegal. Firing an employee for joining a union or for reporting an employer's violation (called whistle-blowing) is also prohibited. If you believe you have been wrongfully discharged, you should contact the EEOC or the state civil rights commission.

At times, employers may need to let a number of employees go to reduce costs. This reduction in staff is called a layoff. Laying off an employee has nothing to do with the employee's job performance. Federal law requires employers who lay off large numbers of employees to give these employees at least two months' notice of the cutback.

Unemployment Compensation

Unemployment insurance is a state-run fund that provides payments to people who lose their jobs through no fault of their own. Not everyone is entitled to unemployment compensation. Those who quit their jobs or who worked only a few months before losing their jobs may not be eligible.

The amount of money you receive depends on how much you earned at your last job. You may receive unemployment payments for only a limited period of time and only so long as you can prove that you are actively looking for a new position.

Each claim for unemployment compensation is investigated before the state makes any payments. If the state unemployment agency decides to deny you

compensation, you may ask the agency for instructions on how to appeal that decision.

OTHER PROTECTIONS FOR EMPLOYEES

Honesty and Drug Testing

Many employers ask job applicants or employees to submit to lie detector tests or drug tests. Lie detector tests are permitted in the hiring of people for high security positions, such as police officers. Some states prohibit or restrict the testing of applicants or employees for drug use. Aptitude and personality tests are generally permitted.

Other Federal Laws

The Fair Labor Standards Act prescribes certain minimum wages and rules about working hours and overtime payments. Workers' compensation laws provide payment for injuries that occur in the workplace and wages lost as a result of those injuries.

The Occupational Safety and Health Act sets minimum requirements for workplace safety. Any employee who discovers a workplace hazard should report it to the Occupational Safety and Health Administration (OSHA). The administration will investigate the claim and may require the employer to correct the problem or pay a fine.

Rights Guaranteed by Contract

Not every employee has a written contract. If you do, however, that contract may grant you additional rights, such as the right to severance pay in the event you are laid off. In addition, employees who are members of a union may have certain rights guaranteed through their union contract.

Before you sign any contract, make sure you understand every part of it. Read it thoroughly and ask the employer questions. Checking the details of a contract before signing it may prevent misunderstanding later.

CAROLINA HERNANDEZ

200 High Street West, Louisville, KY 12345
(123) 456-7890
hernandez@sach.com

OBJECTIVE: To obtain a legal assistant position with a high-technology company.

EXPERIENCE:

2003 to present   *Paralegal*, Slate, Sachs & Fielding, Louisville, KY.
Responsibilities include document production, deposition digests, and brief preparation including Shepardizing.

2000 to 2003   *Copy Editor*, High-Technology Times, Louisville, KY.
Responsibilities included copy editing and proofreading all feature articles; also edited the "Legal Adviser" column.

1998 to 2000   *Copy Editor*, The Barclay Agency, Louisville, KY.
Freelance copy editing for area businesses and legal periodicals; major clients were *State News* and *The State Law Review*.

1997 to 1998   *Editorial Assistant, The State Law Review*, Bensalem, PA.
Responsibilities included copy editing, research, and citation checking for the historical features editor.

EDUCATION:

2003   Attended weekend seminars on "Patent and Copyright Law" and "Data Processing and the Law" offered by the State Bar Association.

2002 to 2003   *Certificate in Paralegal Studies*, The Paralegal Institute of Louisville, Louisville, KY. Emphasis on corporate law. 4.0 GPA.

1994 to 1998   *Bachelor of Arts* with Distinction and Honors, Ivy College, Philadelphia, PA. English major, with history minor. Thesis on the written style of the Declaration of Independence. 3.75 GPA.

RELATED SKILLS: Familiar with various computer programs for experienced with Lexis; fluent in Spanish an

REFERENCES: References available upon request.

- State your name, address, telephone number, and email first.
- State job objective or general career goal in a few words.
- List education and work experience in reverse chronological order, with most recent item first.

- List your work experience first if it is more important than your educational background.
- Keep descriptions of your education and work experience brief.
- List special skills and qualifications if they are relevant to the job.

NATHAN HALEY

76 University Park
Dallas, TX 12345
(765) 123-4567
nathal@cic.com

EMPLOYMENT OBJECTIVE:

To obtain a position in banking or financial services.

FINANCIAL EXPERIENCE:

As an ***evening cashier,*** I closed out the register, restocked shelves, and reconciled invoices. I was also responsible for large sums of money (in cash, check, and credit slips) and store security. Nite 'n Day Minimart, Dallas, TX. Weekends. 2005 to present.

Elected ***chapter treasurer*** for the Junior Jaycees. I am responsible for all dues collection, fund-raising management, bookkeeping, and banking for my chapter. Junior Jaycees of Dallas, Dallas, TX.

While a ***business student,*** I successfully completed courses in accounting, bookkeeping, office machines, and data processing. I maintained a 4.0 GPA in all my business courses.

CUSTOMER SERVICE EXPERIENCE:

As a ***waiter and shift supervisor,*** I learned to handle customers' diverse needs simultaneously. I also learned how to supervise employees and reconcile scheduling and other conflicts. Burger Box Restaurants, Dallas, TX. Summers. 2003 to 2005.

Being a volunteer ***operator for the ACTION! Hotline*** taught me how to respond to difficult problems quickly and effectively. I was named Dallas's "Outstanding Youth of 2004" for preventing an armed robbery.

BUSINESS MACHINES:

I am proficient with computerized cash registers and adding machines. Through my course work, I have learned the fundamentals of data processing and word processing.

EDUCATION:

Graduate, Greater Dallas Vocational-Technical High School, Plano, TX. June 2006. Business curriculum.

REFERENCES:

References are available upon request.

cide which items will be most relevant to the employer you plan to contact.

State Your Objective Some employment counselors advise that you state a job objective or describe briefly the type of position for which you are applying. The job objective usually follows your name and address. Don't be too specific if you plan to use the same resume a number of times. It's better to give a general career goal. Then, in a cover letter, you can be more specific about the position in which you are interested.

Describe What You've Done Every interested employer will check your educational background and employment history carefully. It is best to present these sections in order of importance. For instance, if you've held many relevant jobs, you should list your work experience first, followed by your educational background. On the other hand, if you are just out of school with little or no work experience, it's probably best to list your educational background first and then, under employment history, to mention any part-time and summer jobs you've held or volunteer work you've done.

Under educational background, list the schools you have attended in reverse chronological order, starting with your most recent training and ending with the least recent. Employers want to know at a glance your highest qualifications. For each educational experience, include years attended, name and location of the school, and degree or certificate earned, if any. If you have advanced degrees (college and beyond), it isn't necessary to include high school and elementary school education. Don't forget to highlight any special courses you took or awards you won, if they are relevant to the kind of job you are seeking.

Chronological and Functional Resumes Information about your employment history can be presented in two ways. The most common format is the chronological resume. In a chronological resume, you summarize your work experience year by year. Begin with your current or most recent employment and then work backward. For each job, list the name and location of the company for which you worked, the years you were employed, and the position or positions you held. The order in which you present these facts will depend on what you are trying to emphasize. If you want to call attention to the type or level of job you held, for example, you should put the job title first. Regardless of the order you choose, be consistent. Summer employment or part-time work should be identified as such. If you held a job for less than a year, specify months in the dates of employment.

It is important to include a brief description of the responsibilities you had in each job. This often reveals more about your abilities than the job title. Remember, too, that you do not have to mention the names of former supervisors or how much you earned. You can discuss these points during the interview or explain them on an application form.

The functional resume, on the other hand, emphasizes what you can do rather than what you have done. It is useful for people who have large gaps in their work history or who have relevant skills that would not be properly highlighted in a chronological listing of jobs. The functional resume concentrates on qualifications—such as familiarity with particular equipment, organizational skills, or managerial experience. Specific jobs may be mentioned, but they are not the primary focus of this type of resume.

Explain Special Skills You may wish to include a third section called "Related Skills," "Professional Qualifications," or "Related Qualifications." This is useful if there are points you want to highlight that do not apply directly to educational background or work experience. Be sure these points are relevant to the kind of work you are seeking. This section is most effective if you can mention any special recognition, awards, or other evidence of excellence. It is also useful to mention if you are willing to relocate or can work unusual hours.

Have References Available Employers may also want to know whom they can contact to find out more about you. At the start of your job search, you should ask three or four people if you may use them as references. If you haven't seen these people for a while, you may want to send them a copy of your resume and let them know what kind of position you're seeking. Your references should be the kind of people your potential employer will respect, and they should be able to comment favorably on your abilities, personality, and work habits. You should indicate whether these people are personal references or former work supervisors. Avoid using any relatives. You can list the names and addresses of your references at the end of your resume or in a cover letter. Or, you can simply write, "References available upon request." Just be sure you have their names, addresses, and phone numbers ready if you are asked.

Present Yourself Concisely Tips for making your resume concise include using phrases instead of sentences and omitting unnecessary words. When appropriate, start a phrase with a verb, such as "maintained" or "coordinated." There is no need to say "I"—that is obvious and repetitive.

CAROLINA HERNANDEZ

200 High Street West, Louisville, KY 12345
(123) 456-7890
hernandez@sach.com

December 15, 2005

Mr. Thurston Moore, Director
Personnel Department
Sonic Concepts, Inc.
Louisville, KY 12345

Dear Mr. Moore:

This letter is in response to your advertisement in the *High-Technology Times* for a legal assistant. As you requested in the ad, I enclose my resume and two letters of recommendation.

As my resume indicates, I have a certificate in paralegal studies and a working knowledge of data processing and patent legislation. I am well versed in the filing procedures, court system, and law firms of the state of Kentucky. My research and communication skills have always been considered superior by my employers.

I became particularly interested in the legal issues inherent in high technology while editing the "Legal Adviser" column for the *High-Technology Times*. At the present time, I am a paralegal for Slate, Sachs & Fielding. As you may know, they are no longer handling technology clients. Given my interest in computers and law, I am looking for a position where I can continue to combine both.

I would like very much to talk with you in person about the
pany. I can arrange to be available for an interview any after
considering me for the position.

Very truly yours,

Carolina Hernandez

Carolina Hernandez

Enclosures, 3

NATHAN HALEY

76 University Park
Dallas, TX 12345
(765) 123-4567
nathal@cic.com

September 1, 2005

Ms. Laetitia Johnson, Director
Personnel Department
United Bank & Trust
Market Street
Dallas, TX 12345

Dear Ms. Johnson:

I am writing to inquire about possible openings with your bank. A friend of mine and an employee of yours, Claudia Camino, told me that you might be hiring for the Maple Street branch. My resume is enclosed.

I am a 2001 graduate of the Greater Dallas Vocational-Technical High School where I majored in business. As my resume indicates, I held both a weekend job as a cashier and a summer job as a waiter and shift supervisor while going to school. My other activities include being the treasurer for the Junior Jaycees of Dallas and volunteering with the ACTION! Hotline. Through my paid and unpaid experiences, I have acquired effective customer service skills and some knowledge of small business finance. I also have strong computer and word processing skills.

I am a longtime resident of Dallas and plan to live here permanently. I would like to make my career in banking. I am eager to learn and hope to continue my education in the evenings.

If United Bank and Trust has any job openings at this time, I would appreciate being considered for a position. I can be available for an interview at any time. I look forward to hearing from you.

Sincerely,

Nathan Haley

Nathan Haley

Enclosure

Present Yourself Well Employment counselors often recommend that resumes be no longer than one page because employers won't take the time to read a second page. If you've held many positions related to your occupation, go on to the second page, but don't include beginning or irrelevant jobs. If you have a lot of work experience, limit the education section to just the essentials.

You should also concentrate on the appearance of your resume. A traditional resume should be printed on a good grade of 8½" x 11" white paper. Consult a resume preparation guide for specific information about the best ways to format a resume that will be processed by e-mail or other electronic means. If you don't have access to a computer and printer, you can pay someone to type your resume, but it is up to you to read it carefully and ensure that it is error-free. Be sure that it is neatly typed with adequate margins. The data should be spaced and indented so that each item stands out. This enables a busy executive or personnel director to see at a glance the facts of greatest interest.

These suggestions for writing a resume are not hard-and-fast rules. Resumes may be adapted to special situations. For example, people with a variety of work experience often prepare several versions of their resumes and use the experience that's most relevant when applying for a particular job.

If this is your first resume, show it to someone else, perhaps a guidance counselor, for constructive advice. Make sure there are no spelling or punctuation mistakes anywhere on the page. No matter what, be truthful while emphasizing your assets. You can do that by showing the abilities, skills, and specific interests that qualify you for a particular job. Don't mention any weaknesses or deficiencies in your training. Do mention job-related aptitudes that showed up in previous employment or in school. Don't make things up; everything that's in your resume can, and often will, be checked.

Writing Cover Letters

Whenever you send your resume to a prospective employer, whether it's on paper or in e-mail form, you should send a cover letter with it. This is true whether you are writing to apply for a specific job or just to find out if there are any openings.

A good cover letter should be neat, brief, and well written, with no more than three or four short paragraphs. Since you may use your resume for a variety of job openings, your cover letter should be very specific. Your goal is to get the person who reads it to think that you are an ideal candidate for a particular job. If at all possible, send the letter to a specific person—either the personnel director or the person for whom you would be working. If neces-

sary, call the company and ask to whom you should address the letter.

Start your letter by explaining why you are writing. Say that you are inquiring about possible job openings at the company, that you are responding to an advertisement in a particular publication, or that someone recommended that you should write. (Use the person's name if you have received permission to do so.) Let your letter lead into your resume. Use it to call attention to your qualifications. Add information that shows why you are well suited for that specific job.

Completing the Application Form

Many employers ask job applicants to fill out an application form. This form usually duplicates much of the information on your resume, but it may ask some additional questions. Give complete answers to all questions except those that are discriminatory. If a question doesn't apply to you, put a dash next to it.

You may be given the application form when you arrive for an interview, or it may be sent to your home. When filling it out, print neatly in ink. Follow the instructions carefully. For instance, if the form asks you to put down your last name first, do so.

The most important sections of an application form are the education and work histories. As in your resume, many applications request that you write these in reverse chronological order, with the most recent experience first. Unlike your resume, however, the application form may request information about your earnings on previous jobs. It may also ask what rate of pay you are seeking on the job you are applying for.

Be prepared to answer these and other topics not addressed on your resume. Look at the sample application form, and make note of the kinds of questions that you are likely to be asked—for example, your Social Security number, the names of previous supervisors, your salary, and your reason for leaving. If necessary, carry notes on such topics with you to an interview. You have a responsibility to tell prospective employers what they need to know to make an informed decision.

Neatness Counts Think before you write on an application form so you avoid crossing things out. An employer's opinion of you may be influenced just by the general appearance of your application form. A neat, detailed form may indicate an orderly mind and the ability to think clearly, follow instructions, and organize information.

Know Your Rights Under federal and some state laws, an employer cannot demand that you answer

1 Always print neatly in blue or black ink. When completing an application at home, type it, if possible.

2 Read the application carefully *before* you start to fill it out. Follow instructions precisely. Use standard abbreviations.

3 If you aren't applying for a specific job, indicate the kind of work you're willing to do.

4 You don't have to commit to a specific rate of pay. Write "open" or "negotiable" if you are uncertain.

5 Traffic violations and so on do not belong here. Nor do offenses for which you were charged but not convicted.

6 If a question doesn't apply to you, write "NA" (for not applicable) or put a dash through the space.

7 Take notes along to remind you of school names, addresses, and dates.

8 If you're short on "real" employment, mention jobs such as babysitting, lawn mowing, or any occasional work.

9 Your references should be people who can be objective about you, such as former employers, teachers, and community leaders.

10 Under the heading "Reason for Leaving," a simple answer will do. Avoid saying "better pay"—even if it's so.

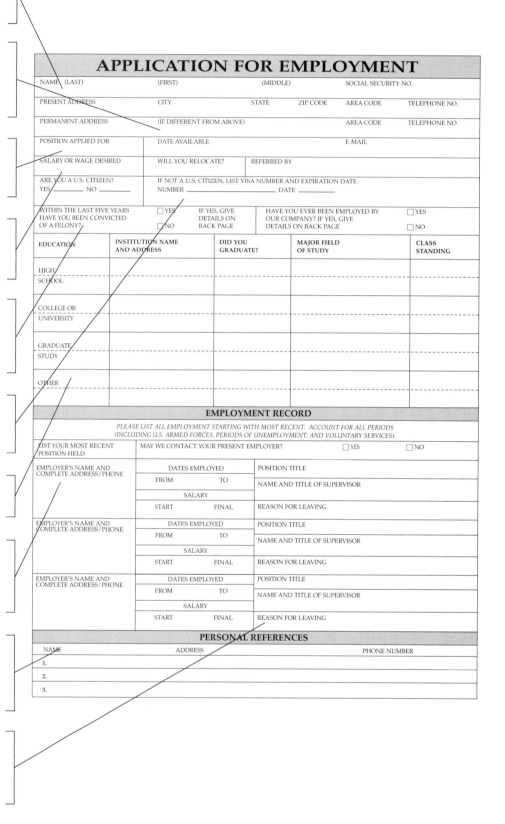

APPLICATION FOR EMPLOYMENT

NAME (LAST)   (FIRST)   (MIDDLE)   SOCIAL SECURITY NO.

PRESENT ADDRESS   CITY   STATE   ZIP CODE   AREA CODE   TELEPHONE NO.

PERMANENT ADDRESS   (IF DIFFERENT FROM ABOVE)   AREA CODE   TELEPHONE NO.

POSITION APPLIED FOR   DATE AVAILABLE   E-MAIL

SALARY OR WAGE DESIRED   WILL YOU RELOCATE?   REFERRED BY

ARE YOU A U.S. CITIZEN?   IF NOT A U.S. CITIZEN, LIST VISA NUMBER AND EXPIRATION DATE:
YES_____ NO _____   NUMBER _____ DATE _____

WITHIN THE LAST FIVE YEARS HAVE YOU BEEN CONVICTED OF A FELONY?   ☐ YES   ☐ NO   IF YES, GIVE DETAILS ON BACK PAGE   HAVE YOU EVER BEEN EMPLOYED BY OUR COMPANY? IF YES, GIVE DETAILS ON BACK PAGE   ☐ YES   ☐ NO

EDUCATION	INSTITUTION NAME AND ADDRESS	DID YOU GRADUATE?	MAJOR FIELD OF STUDY	CLASS STANDING
HIGH SCHOOL				
COLLEGE OR UNIVERSITY				
GRADUATE STUDY				
OTHER				

EMPLOYMENT RECORD

PLEASE LIST ALL EMPLOYMENT STARTING WITH MOST RECENT. ACCOUNT FOR ALL PERIODS (INCLUDING U.S. ARMED FORCES, PERIODS OF UNEMPLOYMENT, AND VOLUNTARY SERVICES).

LIST YOUR MOST RECENT POSITION HELD   MAY WE CONTACT YOUR PRESENT EMPLOYER?   ☐ YES   ☐ NO

EMPLOYER'S NAME AND COMPLETE ADDRESS/PHONE	DATES EMPLOYED	POSITION TITLE
	FROM TO	NAME AND TITLE OF SUPERVISOR
	SALARY	
	START FINAL	REASON FOR LEAVING
EMPLOYER'S NAME AND COMPLETE ADDRESS/PHONE	DATES EMPLOYED	POSITION TITLE
	FROM TO	NAME AND TITLE OF SUPERVISOR
	SALARY	
	START FINAL	REASON FOR LEAVING
EMPLOYER'S NAME AND COMPLETE ADDRESS/PHONE	DATES EMPLOYED	POSITION TITLE
	FROM TO	NAME AND TITLE OF SUPERVISOR
	SALARY	
	START FINAL	REASON FOR LEAVING

PERSONAL REFERENCES

NAME	ADDRESS	PHONE NUMBER
1.		
2.		
3.		

any questions about race, color, creed, national origin, ancestry, sex, marital status, age (with certain exceptions), number of dependents, property, car ownership (unless needed for the job), or arrest record. Refer to the information on job discrimination in this essay for more information about your rights.

PRESENTING YOURSELF IN AN INTERVIEW

If your qualifications, as presented in your resume, cover letter, and application, are a strong match for the requirements of the job, you may be invited to a job interview. On the basis of this meeting, the prospective employer will decide whether or not to hire you, and you will decide whether or not you want the job.

Prepare in Advance

Before an interview, there are a number of things you can do to prepare. Begin by giving thought to why you want the job and what you have to offer. Then review your resume and any lists you made when you were evaluating yourself so that you can keep your qualifications firmly in mind.

Learn as much as you can about the organization. Check with friends who work there, read company brochures, search the Internet, or devise other information-gathering strategies. Showing that you know something about the company and what it does will indicate your interest and demonstrate that you are a well-informed job candidate.

Try to anticipate some of the questions an interviewer may ask and think about how you would answer. For example, you may be asked: Will you work overtime when necessary? Are you ready to go to night school to improve some of your skills? Preparing answers in advance will make the process easier for you. It is also wise to prepare any questions you may have about the company or the position for which you are applying. The more information you have, the better you can evaluate both the company and the job.

Employers may want you to demonstrate specific skills for some jobs. An applicant for a job in a lumber mill or a mine, for example, might be required to demonstrate mechanical ability. Prospective technicians might be expected to demonstrate mathematical skills.

On the appointed day, dress neatly and in a style appropriate for the job you're seeking. When in doubt, it's safer to dress on the conservative side, wearing a shirt and tie rather than a turtleneck or wearing a dress or blouse and skirt rather than pants and a T-shirt. Be on time. Find out in advance exactly where the company is located and how to get there. Allow extra time in case you get lost, get caught in a traffic jam, can't find a parking spot, or encounter another type of delay.

Maintain a Balance

When your appointment begins, remember that a good interview is largely a matter of balance. Don't undersell yourself by sitting back silently, but don't oversell yourself by talking nonstop about how wonderful you are. Answer all questions directly and simply, and let the interviewer take the lead.

Instead of saying, "I'm reliable and hardworking," give the interviewer an example. Allow the interviewer to draw conclusions from your example.

It's natural to be nervous before and during a job interview. However, you need to try to relax and be yourself. You may even enjoy the conversation. Your chances of being hired and being happy if you get the job are better if the employer likes you as you are.

Avoid discussing money until the employer brings it up or until you are offered the job. Employers usually know in advance what they are willing to pay. If you are the one to begin a discussion about the salary you want, you may set an amount that's either too low or too high.

Be prepared to ask questions, but don't force them on your interviewer. Part of the purpose of the interview is for you to evaluate the company while you are being evaluated. For instance, you might want to ask about the company's training programs and its policy on promotions.

Don't stay too long. Most business people have busy schedules. It is likely that the interviewer will let you know when it's time for the interview to end.

Don't expect a definite answer at the first interview. Employers usually thank you for coming and say that you will be notified shortly. Most employers want to interview all the applicants before they make a hiring decision. If the position is offered at the time of the interview, you can ask for a little time to think about it. If the interviewer tells you that you are not suitable for the job, try to be polite. Say, "I'm sorry, but thank you for taking the time to meet with me." After all, the company may have the right job for you next week.

Follow Up after the Interview

If the job sounds interesting and you would like to be considered for it, say so as you leave. Follow up after the interview by writing a brief thank-you note to the employer. Express your continued interest in the position and thank the interviewer for taking the time to meet with you.

It's a good idea to make some notes and evaluations of the interview while it is still fresh in your mind. Write down the important facts about the job—the duties, salary, promotion prospects, and so on, which will help you make a decision should you be offered the job. Also evaluate your own performance in the interview. List the things you wish you had said and things you wish you had not said, which will help you prepare for future interviews.

Finally, don't hesitate to contact your interviewer if you haven't heard from the company after a week or two (unless you were told it would be longer). Write a brief note or make a phone call in which you ask when a decision might be reached. Making such an effort will show the employer that you are genuinely interested in the job. Your call will remind the interviewer about you and could work to your advantage.

TAKE CHARGE

Job hunting is primarily a matter of organizing a well-planned campaign. Scan the classified ads, search through online job banks, watch for trends in local industry that might be reported in the news, and check with people you know in the field. Take the initiative. Send out carefully crafted resumes and letters. Respond to ads. Finally, in an interview, state your qualifications and experience in a straightforward and confident manner.

TRADE AND PROFESSIONAL JOURNALS

The following is a list of some of the major journals in fields relating to computers, business, and office jobs. These journals can keep you up to date with what's happening in your field of interest. They can also lead you to jobs through their own specialized classified advertising sections.

Computers

Computer, 10662 Los Vacqueros Circle, P.O. Box 3014, Los Alamitos, CA 90720-1314.
http://www.computer.org
Computerworld, One Speen St., Framingham, MA 01701.
http://www.computerworld.com
Infoworld, 501 Second St., San Francisco, CA 94107.
http://www.infoworld.com

PC World, 501 Second St., San Francisco, CA 94107.
http://www.pcworld.com
SysAdmin, CMP Media LLC, 600 Community Dr., Manhasset, NY 11030.
http://www.samag.com

Data Processing

Datamation, Jupitermedia Headquarters, 23 Old Kings Hwy. South, Darien, CT 06820.
http://itmanagement.earthweb.com
Management Science, Institute for Operations Research and the Management Sciences, Northwestern University, Dept. of Industrial Engineering and Management Science, Evanston, IL 60208-3119.
http://www.informs.org

Finance

The Accounting Review, American Accounting Association, 5717 Bessie Dr., Sarasota, FL 34233.
http://aaahq.org/pubs/acctrev.htm
American Banker, 1 State St. Plaza, New York, NY 10004-1549.
http://www.americanbanker.com
Financial Executives International, 200 Campus Dr., Florham Park, NJ 07932-0674.
http://www.fei.org
Forbes, 60 Fifth Ave., New York, NY 10011.
http://www.forbes.com
Management Accounting, 10 Paragon Dr., Montvale, NJ 07645-1718.
http://www.imanet.org/
The Wall Street Journal, 200 Liberty St., New York, NY 10281.
http://www.wsj.com

Management

Associations Now, American Society of Association Executives, 1575 I St. NW, Washington, DC 20005.
http://www.asaecenter.org/
Business Week, 1221 Avenue of the Americas, 43rd Fl., New York, NY 10020.
http://www.businessweek.com
Business 2.0, Time & Life Building, Rockefeller Center, New York, NY 10020-1393.
http://money.cnn.com/magazines/business2/
Financial Management, Financial Management Association International, University of South Florida, College of Business Administration, Tampa, FL 33620-5500.
http://www.fma.org/fm.htm
Manage, National Management Association, 2210 Arbor Blvd., Dayton, OH 45439.
http://nma1.org/breaktime/index.htm

Office Work and Services

Purchasing, c/o Reed Business Information, 225 Wyman St., Waltham, MA 02451. *http://www.manufacturing.net/magazine/ purchasing*

Bank Clerk

Definition and Nature of the Work

Banks simplify people's lives, but the business of banking is anything but simple. Every transaction—from cashing a check to taking out a loan—requires careful record keeping. Behind the scenes in every bank or savings and loan association there are dozens of bank clerks, each an expert at keeping one area of the bank's business running smoothly.

New account clerks open and close accounts and answer questions for customers. Interest clerks record interest due to savings account customers, as well as the interest owed to the bank on loans and other investments. Exchange clerks, who work on international accounts, translate foreign currency values into dollars and vice versa. Loan clerks sort and record information about loans. Statement clerks are responsible for preparing the monthly balance sheets of checking account customers. Securities clerks record, file, and maintain stocks, bonds, and other investment certificates. They also keep track of dividends and interest on these certificates.

Other clerks operate the business machines on which modern banks rely. Proof operators sort checks and record the amount of each check. Bookkeeping clerks keep records of each customer's account.

In addition to these specialists, banks need general clerical help—data entry keyers, file clerks, mail handlers, and messengers—just as any other business does.

Education and Training Requirements

Bank clerks usually need a high school education with an emphasis on basic skills in typing, bookkeeping, and business math. Knowledge of computers and business machines is also helpful. Prospective bank workers may be tested on their clerical skills when they are interviewed. Most banks provide new employees with on-the-job training.

Getting the Job

Sometimes bank recruiters visit high schools to look for future employees. High school placement offices can tell students whether this is the practice at their school. If not, prospective bank workers can apply directly to local banks through their personnel departments. Bank jobs may be listed with state and private employment agencies. Candidates can also check Internet job sites and the classified ads in local newspapers as well.

Advancement Possibilities and Employment Outlook

Banks prefer to promote their employees rather than hire new workers for jobs that require experience. Clerks frequently become tellers or supervisors. Many banks encourage their employees to further their education at night.

Education and Training
High school

Salary
Median—$23,317 to $27,310 per year

Employment Outlook
Poor

According to the U.S. Bureau of Labor Statistics, employment of bank clerks was expected to decline through the year 2014, because many banks are electronically automating their systems and eliminating paperwork as well as many clerical tasks. Workers with knowledge of data processing and computers will have the best opportunities. In addition to jobs created through expansion, openings at the clerical level often occur as workers move up to positions of greater responsibility.

Working Conditions

Although banks usually provide a pleasant working atmosphere, clerks often work alone, at times performing repetitive tasks. Bank clerks generally work between thirty-five and forty hours per week, but they may be expected to take on evening and Saturday shifts depending on bank hours.

Earnings and Benefits

The salaries of bank clerks vary widely depending on the size and location of the bank and the clerk's experience. According to the Bureau of Labor Statistics, median salaries ranged from $23,317 to $27,310 per year in 2004 depending on experience and title. Generally, loan clerks are on the high end of this range, whereas general office clerks are on the lower end.

Banks typically offer their employees excellent benefits. Besides paid vacations and more than the usual number of paid holidays, employees may receive health and life insurance and participate in pension and profit-sharing plans. Some banks provide financial aid so that workers can continue their education.

Where to Go for More Information

American Bankers Association
1120 Connecticut Ave. NW
Washington, DC 20036
(800) BANKERS
http://www.aba.com

National Bankers Association
1513 P St. NW
Washington, DC 20005
(202) 588-5432
http://www.nationalbankers.org

Bank Administration Institute
1 N. Franklin St., Ste. 1000
Chicago, IL 60606
(312) 683-2464
http://www.bai.org

Bank Teller

Education and Training
High school

Salary
Median—$21,120 per year

Employment Outlook
Fair

Definition and Nature of the Work

Bank tellers receive and process money when customers make deposits. They also distribute money when customers write checks on their accounts or withdraw savings. Tellers perform many other services as well. They cash payroll checks, exchange foreign currency, receive loan payments, and issue traveler's checks. Tellers work in large city banks as well as small branch banks in suburbs, towns, and rural areas. Some tellers work for other financial institutions such as savings and loan associations.

Tellers are also responsible for recording the transactions they perform. For instance, each deposit is recorded on a deposit slip that is filled in by the customer. The teller validates, or checks, the deposit slip and stamps it by machine to show that it was checked and accepted at that date and time. Some tellers work with machines that automatically enter deposits and withdrawals into the bank's ledger or records. Tellers also validate checks before cashing them. Tellers must be able to identify the customers for whom they cash checks by asking for a personal identification number, checking for photo identification, or comparing the customer's signature to the one the bank has on file. In addition, tellers often check the computer at their station to see whether customers have enough money in their accounts to cover the personal checks they want to cash.

Tellers start the day with a certain amount of cash in their cash drawer. They are responsible for this money and for all the checks, deposits, loan payments, and other monies they receive during the day. As they work, tellers keep track of all the transactions that they perform. After banking hours the tellers settle their accounts by filling out a settlement sheet. The settlement sheet reflects the day's activities. It helps the tellers check their own work to see that their transactions have been done accurately. Tellers calculate the amounts on the deposit slips to find the total amount of money received for the day. They add up the amounts on all the checks to find the total amount of money paid out. After accounting for all of the transactions and entering them onto the settlement sheet, the teller knows how much cash should be in the cash drawer. The teller counts the cash to see whether the dollar total is the same as that on the settlement sheet. If the totals match, the teller has finished work for the day. If the totals do not match, the teller must look for the mistake. Tellers are required to settle before leaving the bank.

Bank tellers deposit checks and withdraw money for customers. Eventually they can specialize in more complex transactions such as taking real estate loan payments. (© William Taufic/Corbis.)

Some tellers perform specialized tasks. In large banks one teller may take only savings account deposits and another may cash payroll checks. Sometimes experienced tellers are given specialized jobs that are more complex. Vault tellers, for instance, keep records of the cash and checks that come in and out of the bank's vault over the course of a day. All tellers must be able to work with details. It is important for tellers to be able to perform routine tasks quickly and accurately.

Education and Training Requirements

Banks usually hire high school graduates. They prefer those who have had some clerical experience. Students can prepare in high school for a job as a teller by taking business math or courses in which they learn to use computers and other business machines. Many banks offer a few classroom training sessions to new tellers. These sessions are followed by on-the-job training, during which a trainee observes an experienced teller. The trainee gradually learns the bank's methods and record-keeping techniques as well as how to operate any machines used by the bank.

Bank tellers are responsible for large sums of money. Therefore banks bond, or insure, their tellers against possible losses of money through error or theft. The bonding company asks for references from the teller and may investigate the teller's background before selling the insurance to the bank.

Getting the Job

Many tellers are promoted to their jobs from beginning clerical jobs. However, some people start as tellers without any previous bank experience. Prospective tellers can contact banks directly or through state and private employment agencies. They can also check Internet job sites and classified ads of local newspapers for advertised openings.

Advancement Possibilities and Employment Outlook

In large banks beginners usually specialize in doing one simple type of transaction, such as taking checking account deposits. Eventually they learn to handle other transactions. Then tellers can specialize in more complex transactions, such as taking real estate loan payments. Some tellers become head tellers who supervise the work of the other tellers in their branches. They also direct the training of new tellers. Some tellers become assistant managers in a branch office of their bank. These tellers usually take college courses in banking or courses offered by the banking industry.

According to the U.S. Bureau of Labor Statistics, tellers held about 558,000 jobs in 2004. Roughly one-third of these were part-time employees. Employment of tellers was expected to grow more slowly than the average for all occupations through the year 2014 because of the increased use of automatic teller machines and automated systems that allow customers to do their banking over the Internet and the phone. However, there will be new positions for full- and part-time tellers because banking provides a relatively large number of job openings.

Working Conditions

Banks are usually pleasant places to work. Full-time tellers work between thirty-five and forty hours a week. Overtime may be required once per week or more. As banks expand their service hours, tellers may find it necessary to work shifts that include evenings and Saturdays. Tellers spend a lot of time on their feet, and their work is repetitive. Because they deal with the public, tellers must be quick, courteous, and efficient when people are waiting to be served.

Earnings and Benefits

The median yearly salary for an experienced, full-time teller was $21,120 in 2004, according to the Bureau of Labor Statistics. Some banks offer incentives whereby tellers earn extra money for inducing customers to use special financial services that the bank offers.

Banks usually offer generous benefits to their employees. Besides paid vacations and up to twelve paid holidays per year, employees may participate in pension and profit sharing plans. Employees usually receive health, life, and accident insurance. Some banks help pay tuition for employees who are continuing their education.

Where to Go for More Information

American Bankers Association
1120 Connecticut Ave. NW
Washington, DC 20036
(800) BANKERS
http://www.aba.com

National Bankers Association
1513 P St. NW
Washington, DC 20005
(202) 588-5432
http://www.nationalbankers.org

Bank Administration Institute
1 N. Franklin St., Ste. 1000
Chicago, IL 60606
(312) 683-2464
http://www.bai.org

Billing Clerk

Definition and Nature of the Work

Billing clerks calculate how much money customers owe a business and then prepare customers' bills. To calculate a statement, the billing clerk will compile documents and records, such as purchase orders, sales tickets, and hospital records. They then tally the bill and calculate if any discounts or special rates apply. In a hospital, for instance, a billing clerk would call up the insurance company to inquire about how much of the bill the insurance covers and if any insurance deductions apply. In a large accounting firm, the billing clerk would calculate the number of hours that the accountant spent on a client's finances and multiply that by the rate the accountant charges. After billing clerks come up with a total for a customer, they prepare the bill and enter the amount into the accounting records.

Many billing clerks employ computer programs that prepare the bill automatically once charges have been calculated and input the amount automatically into the company's accounting records. In such systems, billing clerks are required to closely check that the numbers on the computer match up to those on the receipts. Some billing clerks operate billing machines, which print out the bills and then stuff them into envelopes. Increasingly, billing clerks are sending off bills to customers electronically via e-mail, which the customers then pay online or automatically with a credit card or bank transfer. Depending on the office, billing clerks may be required to handle billing questions from customers.

Education and Training Requirements

Most employers require a high school education. Completion of high school business programs provides a good background for entry-level positions. Courses in mathematics, business software, and accounting are essential, especially to prepare candidates for calculating bills. Some employers prefer to hire graduates of two-year business schools or junior college programs that teach office skills. Others prefer beginners with no specialized education but a good general background. On-the-job training is provided and may last from a few days to several weeks.

Getting the Job

School placement offices may be able to help prospective workers find a position as a payroll clerk. Jobs may be listed with state and private employment agencies. Newspaper ads and Internet job sites often list openings in this area. If interested in a government job, apply to take the necessary civil service test. Candidates can also apply directly to the billing departments of large businesses.

Advancement Possibilities and Employment Outlook

Beginning billing clerks usually receive on-the-job training in the billing methods of a business and in any computer billing software used by the business. Billing clerks may receive promotions with increases in pay and eventually rise to a supervi-

Education and Training
High school

Salary
Median—$27,040 per year

Employment Outlook
Fair

Billing clerks are responsible for processing bills and payments and reconciling billing conflicts. *(Photograph by Kelly A. Quin. Thomson Gale. Reproduced by permission.)*

sory level. Clerks with a bachelor's degree may even advance to become human resource specialists or buyers in a company.

According to the U.S. Bureau of Labor Statistics, 523,000 billing clerks were employed in the United States in 2004. Roughly one third of all billing clerks were employed in the health-care industry. Employment of billing clerks was expected to grow more slowly than the average for all occupations through the year 2014. Automated billing systems and software are allowing fewer workers to send out more bills faster. In many companies, billing clerks are being phased out. Their duties are being taken over by accounting and bookkeeping clerks. The greatest number of new jobs for billing clerks will be in the health-care industry due to the complexity of health-care billing.

Working Conditions

Billing clerks work in large offices with enough business to require a billing clerk. Much of the work is performed while seated at a desk. Clerks usually work at routine tasks that may be repetitive. They usually work thirty-five to forty hours a week. Many belong to labor unions that are active in the industry in which they work.

Where to Go for More Information

Office and Professional Employees
International Union
265 W. 14th St., 6th Fl.
New York, NY 10011
(800) 346-7348
http://www.opeiu.org

Earnings and Benefits

Billing clerks' earnings depend largely on the type and size of the organization in which the clerk is employed. In 2004 full-time billing clerks earned a median annual salary of $27,040 per year, according to the Bureau of Labor Statistics. Experienced clerks may earn more. Benefits usually include paid vacations, paid holidays, medical and life insurance coverage, and some type of retirement plan.

Bookkeeper

Education and Training
High school

Salary
Median—$28,570 per year

Employment Outlook
Fair

Definition and Nature of the Work

Bookkeepers keep financial records that track a company's expenditures, profit and loss, cash flow, and other financial activities. Bookkeepers usually work for the accounting departments of their companies. Bookkeepers employ database and spreadsheet computer programs to do their record keeping.

Most small firms have one general bookkeeper, also called a full-charge bookkeeper. General bookkeepers verify and enter into ledgers the details of their firm's financial transactions. They then summarize these details in a general ledger. Periodically, a general bookkeeper balances the books. When the books are balanced, it is possible to tell at a glance how much cash has been spent and how much received, what the company owes and what is owed to the company, and whether the company has made a profit or suffered a loss. In addition to keeping records, general bookkeepers may prepare payrolls, tax reports, and customers' monthly invoice statements.

Large firms break down the bookkeeping responsibilities into specialized areas. Each area is handled by one or more bookkeeping clerks, also called accounting clerks, who are supervised by a head bookkeeper. Accounts receivable clerks are responsible for the ledger that records the firm's sales of goods and services, whereas accounts payable clerks are responsible for the ledger that records the firm's purchases of goods and services. Auditing clerks check records posted by other workers to make certain they are correct.

The widespread use of computers and bookkeeping programs has dramatically cut down on the amount of time required for bookkeepers to perform their bookkeeping duties. As such, many offices now require bookkeepers to take on additional responsibilities, such as payroll, customer service, or billing.

Education and Training Requirements

A high school education, with emphasis on business math, bookkeeping, and accounting, is needed to get a job as a bookkeeper. Some employers prefer to hire junior college or business school graduates for the position of full-charge bookkeeper. Good performance in business subjects such as business software, typing, accounting, bookkeeping, and business mathematics is an asset. The ability to use a computer is essential, and knowledge of basic spreadsheet and database programs is helpful.

Many employers prefer to train bookkeepers themselves. An aptitude for mathematics and the ability to concentrate on detail are basic requirements. Once on the job, a bookkeeper with some business education beyond high school will have a better chance for advancement.

Bookkeepers at small companies have many responsibilities and tasks, including determining whether their company has made a profit or suffered a loss. (© Terry Wild Studio. Reproduced by permission.)

Bookkeepers with two years of bookkeeping experience can obtain a Certified Bookkeeper designation, which is awarded by the American Institute of Professional Bookkeepers. The certification ensures employers that bookkeepers can carry out all standard bookkeeping duties. In order to obtain the certification, a bookkeeper must pass three exams and adhere to a code of ethics. Many colleges offer preparatory courses for these exams.

Getting the Job

School placement offices may be able to help a student find a position as a bookkeeper. Other jobs may be listed with state and private employment agencies, on Internet job sites, and in newspaper classified ads. If interested in a government job, apply to take the necessary civil service test.

Because almost every business has at least one bookkeeper, prospective workers might try applying to any firm that interests them. Even if there are no job openings at the time of applying, candidates may be considered for future openings.

Advancement Possibilities and Employment Outlook

Bookkeeping clerks usually begin by recording routine transactions. Then they advance to supervisory work. Talent, training, and experience all help determine a bookkeeping clerk's chances for promotion. Bookkeepers who take courses in college accounting may go on to become accountants. General book-keepers may advance if they assume other responsibilities.

According to the U.S. Bureau of Labor Statistics, bookkeepers, accounting clerks, and auditing clerks held two million jobs in 2004. Employment of bookkeepers was expected to grow more slowly than average for all occupations through the year 2014. Though the demand for accounting services will continue to grow, the increased use of computers and bookkeeping and accounting software in the office has eliminated much of the need for bookkeepers. However, the turnover rate among bookkeepers is high, so there should be jobs available.

Working Conditions

Most bookkeepers work a standard forty hours per week. They mostly work in pleasant offices. The pace of the work is steady and often repetitive, particularly for bookkeeping clerks. Some overtime may be expected during periodic book balancing and at the end of the fiscal year. Some of these workers belong to labor unions that are active in their industry.

Earnings and Benefits

Bookkeeping salaries vary by region and industry. The median annual salary for bookkeeping, accounting, and auditing clerks was $28,570 in 2004, according to the Bureau of Labor Statistics.

The benefits that bookkeepers receive depend entirely on the industry in which they work. Generally, however, a bookkeeper can expect paid vacations, holidays, and health insurance.

Brokerage Clerk

Education and Training
High school

Salary
Median—$35,235 per year

Employment Outlook
Fair

Definition and Nature of the Work

Brokerage clerks work for securities or brokerage firms. They are responsible for preparing and maintaining the records of financial transactions involving stocks, bonds, and other types of investments.

Purchase-and-sale clerks match orders to buy with orders to sell and balance and verify stock trades. Dividend clerks pay stock or cash dividends to a firm's clients. Transfer clerks make sure that stock certificates comply with banking regulations. They also handle customer requests for security registration changes. Receive-and-deliver clerks handle the receipt and delivery of securities among firms. Margin clerks are responsible for monitoring customers' margin accounts (cash advance/credit accounts customers set up with the brokerage firm) and ensuring customers make their payments.

Brokerage clerks use the most current computer equipment and software. Many use custom-designed software programs to process transactions.

Education and Training Requirements

A high school diploma or its equivalent is usually required for a brokerage clerk position. Computer knowledge—especially of word processing and spreadsheet programs—is very important. When hired, new brokerage clerks usually receive on-the-job training that sometimes involves formal classroom study.

Because brokerage clerk jobs are usually entry-level positions, some college graduates with degrees in business or finance apply for them as a means of beginning a career in the financial field. Many brokerage firms have a set course of promotion for these graduates that advances them from brokerage clerk jobs into managerial positions.

The National Association of Securities Dealers (NASD) offers a Series 7 brokerage license that qualifies a clerk to take on more responsibilities in a brokerage firm. The designation gives the clerk the ability to pass along securities recommendations from a broker and to answer more clients' questions. In general, the designation makes a clerk more valuable to a brokerage firm. A clerk must be employed by a registered firm for four months before taking the Series 7 exam for the license.

Brokerage clerks should be organized and detail oriented, and they should have good interpersonal skills. Because they handle finances and confidential material, they must also be honest and trustworthy.

Getting the Job

The local state employment agency, Internet job sites, and the help wanted section of the newspaper are good places to look for job openings. Sometimes contacting a financial institution's personnel department directly can lead to a job opportunity. Large firms often send representatives to schools and colleges to recruit qualified people.

Advancement Possibilities and Employment Outlook

Brokerage clerks frequently advance by assuming more duties in the same position with higher pay. Some are promoted to low-level, then senior, supervisory positions. With additional experience and education, a clerk may become a qualified broker.

According to the U.S. Bureau of Labor Statistics, brokerage clerks held seventy-five thousand jobs in 2004. Nine out of ten worked for securities and commodities firms, banks, and other financial institutions. Employment of brokerage clerks was expected to grow more slowly than average for all occupations through the year 2014, due primarily to automation and changes in business practices and to the small size of the occupation.

Working Conditions

Brokerage clerks usually work forty hours per week in a pleasant office environment. Overtime may be required during periods of heavy stock and bond market activity. The work can be repetitive and sometimes tedious. Often there are joint tasks that require working closely with others.

Earnings and Benefits

Salaries for brokerage clerks vary depending on geographic location, type and size of the institution, level of education and training, and complexity of the clerk's duties. The median annual salary for brokerage clerks in 2004 was $35,235, according to the Bureau of Labor Statistics. Brokerage clerks generally receive a benefits package that includes life and health insurance, retirement plans, and paid vacation time.

Business Machine Operator

Education and Training
High school

Salary
Varies—see profile

Employment Outlook
Poor

Definition and Nature of the Work

Business machine operators run equipment such as duplicators and copiers that perform routine office tasks. An office that regularly produces a large volume of printed material may have its own copying department. Copying machine operators make copies of reports, charts, drawings, letters, and circulars. They may operate photocopy machines or small printing presses. They may have to enlarge or reduce the copy. They may have to collate pages of lengthy documents by hand, although some copiers collate automatically. The operators must renew the supply of paper and toner or ink in the machines. They must be able to fix minor breakdowns. In the case of major breakdowns, they must arrange for professional repair service. In some offices the operators must keep a log of each job. In others the information is recorded automatically.

Offices that send out mass mailings employ a number of mail preparing machine operators. These workers use various machines that collate, fold, and insert material into envelopes. They use other machines to seal, address, and bundle the envelopes by zip code. The operators sometimes maintain the mailing lists by making corrections, deletions, and additions. They make new address labels using computer software and printing equipment. Large offices of all kinds usually employ mail handling machine operators. They use machines that weigh, meter-stamp, and bag letters and packages.

Office machines now do many of the more complicated tasks previously done by office clerks. The machines are faster and more accurate. The result is that many clerks now use computers and business machines. However, these workers are not usually called business machine operators. They do other work besides operating a special machine. Their titles usually refer to the departments in which they work (for example, accounting assistant). Some large offices and government departments have workers with such titles as billing machine operator. These operators are not expected to do other work.

Education and Training Requirements

Employers generally prefer to hire high school graduates. High school business courses and good typing skills can help prospective workers get a job. An aptitude for mathematics is useful for jobs in which math-related machines are used. Basic computer skills may also be required, because many photocopiers, printing presses, and mail machines are hooked up to computer networks and controlled through computer terminals.

Business machine operators must be willing to learn how to operate, maintain, and repair increasingly complex machinery. (© Earl Dotter. Reproduced by permission.)

Business machines are becoming more complex, and many employers now prefer applicants with general training in machine operation and business practice. Courses are available at vocational/technical institutes and community colleges.

Most employers give on-the-job training even to experienced machine operators, because every manufacturer's machines work differently. The training period can range from a few days to a few weeks. In the case of very complex equipment, the trainee may work under an experienced operator for several months. Sometimes training is provided by the machine manufacturer, particularly when a machine is new to the office.

Getting the Job

School placement offices may be able to help a student find a position as a business machine operator. Jobs are also listed with state and private employment agencies, in the classified ads of local newspapers, and on the Internet. If candidates are interested in a government job, they should apply to take the necessary civil service test.

If there is a firm that an individual would particularly like to work for, he or she should contact its personnel office for an interview. Even if there are no job openings at the time of application, applicants may be considered for future openings.

Advancement Possibilities and Employment Outlook

Business machine operators can advance by mastering more complex machines. Some experienced operators train new employees or assume other supervisory positions. According to the 2002–12 employment predictions by the U.S. Bureau of Labor Statistics, the employment of business machine operators was expected to decline during this decade. Many new machines will be introduced. However, some will do the work of two or more existing machines, thus eliminating jobs.

Working Conditions

Offices are generally pleasant places to work. Because of the noise generated by some business machines, operators are sometimes isolated from other employees. They may have to spend a great deal of time on their feet, and the work tends to be repetitive. Operators usually work between thirty-five and forty hours per week. Some workers belong to labor organizations that are active in the industry in which they work.

Earnings and Benefits

Wages vary depending on experience, level of responsibility, and the size, type, and location of the company. In wage data released in the 2003 *Occupational Employment Statistics* survey, the Bureau of Labor Statistics reported that mail machine operators earned an annual median salary of $21,920 per year. Duplicating machine operators made a median salary of $22,940 per year. The benefits business machine operators receive depend entirely on the industry in which the operators work. Generally, however, they can expect paid vacations, holidays, and health insurance.

Where to Go for More Information

Office and Professional Employees
International Union
265 W. 14th St., 6th Fl.
New York, NY 10011
(800) 346-7348
http://www.opeiu.org

Correspondence Clerk

Education and Training
High school

Salary
Median—$29,340 per year

Employment Outlook
Poor

Definition and Nature of the Work

Offices that receive large quantities of mail and e-mail depend on correspondence clerks, or correspondents. These clerks answer letters and e-mail that do not require the personal attention of an executive. Some replies are routine, allowing the correspondent to send a form letter or e-mail. For replies that must be researched, the correspondent gathers information from a number of sources and then interprets company policy carefully before drafting the response. A correspondent's job is one of great responsibility, and it requires excellent judgment. Correspondence clerks work for publishing and media companies, retail operations, mail order companies, and government agencies.

On a typical day a correspondence clerk first goes through the mail and e-mail, arranging it so that the most important letters and e-mails will be answered first. After putting together the necessary facts, the correspondent either types or dictates replies. The remainder of the day is spent answering less pressing correspondence. Companies frequently expect their correspondents to meet quotas—that is, to produce a certain number of replies each day. By the end of the day all letters and e-mail dictated by the correspondent are typed and proofread. The correspondent attaches the necessary enclosures and puts the letters in the mail.

Some correspondence clerks specialize in a particular aspect of their company's business. For example, credit correspondents are skilled at writing letters urging customers to pay bills. Other correspondents answer product queries regarding, for example, what a product does or how much it costs. Still others deal only with customer complaints.

Correspondents may have an area of skill that permits them to deal more effectively with certain types of requests. Technical correspondents, for example, can explain the workings of tools or machinery in the language of the industry.

Education and Training Requirements

Many employers hire high school graduates as correspondents. Some companies, however, prefer applicants with a degree from a two-year college. Writing skills and a solid knowledge of grammar and spelling are essential. Typing, computer, and business courses are important for some jobs. Regardless of prior training, beginning correspondents usually receive several months of supervision while learning company policy, office routine, and, in some offices, how to use dictating machines or voice recognition software.

A correspondence clerk gathers information about company policy before she replies to a customer's query. *(Photograph by Kelly A. Quin. Thomson Gale. Reproduced by permission.)*

Getting the Job

School placement offices may be able to help a graduating student find a position as a correspondence clerk. The classified ads of local newspapers list job openings, as do state or private employment agencies. Candidates can also apply directly to companies that employ correspondence clerks. When contacting prospective employers, individuals should be sure to do so by letter. It is a perfect opportunity to impress them with writing skills.

Advancement Possibilities and Employment Outlook

Many correspondence clerks are promoted to their jobs from secretarial positions. A talented correspondent who demonstrates an ability to handle difficult problems may advance to senior correspondent and then to a training or supervisory position.

As of 2004 some twenty-three thousand Americans were employed as correspondence clerks, according to the U.S. Bureau of Labor Statistics' 2004–14 projections. Employment of correspondence clerks was expected to decline through the year 2014.

Working Conditions

Some companies provide private offices or partitioned rooms for their correspondents. Many others expect correspondence clerks to work in large, open rooms. The noise and distraction of this setting demands that clerks have the ability to concentrate.

The normal work week for correspondence clerks ranges from thirty-five to forty hours. Some firms, such as mail order houses, have seasonal peaks when correspondents may be expected to work overtime. Some workers belong to labor unions that are active in the industry in which they work.

Wages vary depending on experience, level of responsibility, and location of the work. The Bureau of Labor Statistics reported in their November 2004 *Occupational Employment Statistics* survey that correspondence clerks earned a median salary of $29,340 per year. The benefits that correspondence clerks receive depend largely on the size of the business and the particular industry in which they work. Generally, however, a correspondent can expect paid holidays, vacations, and health insurance.

Where to Go for More Information

Office and Professional Employees
International Union
265 W. 14th St., 6th Fl.
New York, NY 10011
(800) 346-7348
http://www.opeiu.org

Credit Authorizer, Checker, and Clerk

Education and Training
High school

Salary
Median—$29,058 per year

Employment Outlook
Poor

Definition and Nature of the Work

Credit has existed in one form or another for years. In the days of the general store, for example, it made good business sense for the storekeeper to extend credit privileges to customers who would pay in the future. This encouraged purchases by making it more convenient for would-be buyers who did not have the necessary cash on hand. Extending credit still makes good business sense, but deciding which customers are worthy of credit is not as intuitive as it once was. Modern businesses must depend on credit departments or outside credit agencies to help determine who should receive credit and who should not. Credit clerks, credit checkers, and credit authorizers are employed by departments and agencies to get to know customers and evaluate their creditworthiness.

When applying for a credit card, for example, a customer presents his or her personal information to a customer service agent or credit clerk. In some cases, a credit checker is contacted to confirm the information on the application by faxing or calling the applicant's employer and references. A credit checker then may evaluate the information and decides whether credit should be extended. The credit clerk or customer service agent then informs the customer of the decision.

Most credit purchases by existing customers are approved automatically. Sometimes, however, problems arise when accounts are past due or overextended or the amount being charged is unusually large. In these cases the transaction will not go through, and a credit authorizer must be contacted by the credit card holder or a salesperson. These authorizers evaluate the customers' credit records and payment histories and decide whether to approve new charges.

Some businesses that extend credit do not have their own credit investigation staffs. These firms use outside agencies called credit bureaus to do the credit checking. Firms that subscribe to a credit bureau get up-to-the-minute information on an applicant's credit standing by phone or by computer. Credit bureaus keep files on credit customers. Bureaus employ credit analysts and credit checkers who check information on credit applications.

Education and Training Requirements

Most companies prefer to hire high school graduates. English, speech, and business courses are useful. Some college or business courses may be required depending on the area of specialization. Those who have skills in computers and data processing advance more quickly. Typing skills are necessary for some jobs. New workers receive several weeks of on-the-job training.

Getting the Job

Interested individuals can ask their school placement office about jobs in the credit field. They can check Internet job sites and classified ads of newspapers for job openings. They can also apply directly to credit bureaus and large retail companies that have credit departments. Even if there are no openings at that time, applicants may be considered for future openings. Prospective workers can register with private employment agencies that have job listings in the credit field.

Advancement Possibilities and Employment Outlook

In 2004 more than sixty-seven thousand people were employed as credit authorizers, checkers, and clerks in the United States, according to the U.S. Bureau of Labor Statistics. Employment of credit checkers was expected to decline through the year 2014.

The job outlook is affected by changes in the economy. When credit or loans are restricted, job openings become limited. Department stores have also been discontinuing their store credit cards, further decreasing the need for checkers. Automated credit checking systems are also making it possible for customer service representatives to handle the jobs once done by credit checkers. However, openings will still occur to replace credit workers who leave their jobs. An experienced credit checker can advance to a supervisory position.

A credit authorizer, checker, or clerk examines pages of credit histories to help determine the customers' needs. (© Earl Dotter. Reproduced by permission.)

Working Conditions

Most credit authorizers, checkers, and clerks work thirty-five to forty hours per week in pleasant offices. Those who work for retail stores may be expected to work some evenings and on Saturdays. Some credit authorizers, checkers, and clerks deal with confidential information and should be discreet. Authorizers, checkers, and clerks who deal with the public must be courteous and tactful.

Earnings and Benefits

Earnings vary depending on experience, education, and the size and location of the employer. In 2004 the median salary for credit authorizers, checkers, and clerks was $29,058 per year, according to the Bureau of Labor Statistics. Benefits generally include paid vacations, holidays, and health insurance. Checkers in department stores may receive discounts on merchandise.

Where to Go for More Information

ACA International (formerly American Collectors Association)
PO Box 390106
Minneapolis, MN 55439
(952) 926-6547
http://www.acainternational.org

Consumer Data Industry Association
1090 Vermont Ave. NW, Ste. 200
Washington, DC 20005-4905
(202) 371-0910
http://www.cdiaonline.org

Credit Research Foundation
8840 Columbia 100 Pkwy.
Columbia, MD 21045
(410) 740-5499
http://www.crfonline.org

Credit Collector

Education and Training
High school

Salary
Median—$27,456 per year

Employment Outlook
Very good

Definition and Nature of the Work

Credit collectors, also known as bill and account collectors, try to convince debtors—people who owe money—to pay their overdue bills. They work from bad debt files given to them by creditors who have not been able to get the debtors to pay through normal billing procedures. Credit collectors may first try to contact debtors by telephone to talk to them about their reasons for nonpayment. They may have to trace debtors who have moved by checking for forwarding addresses with the post office, searching telephone directories, and interviewing former neighbors. If customers have stopped payment because they are dissatisfied with the merchandise or services they purchased, credit collectors usually refer them to the original seller or a customer service department. If the debtors' complaints are not valid, collectors then try to convince the debtors verbally that their bill is fair and should be paid. Collectors visit debtors in person when telephone conversations are unsuccessful.

If nonpayment is due to financial difficulties, credit collectors may work out a new payment schedule with debtors. At times they suggest to creditors that the case should be handled by an attorney. Credit collectors may also perform other tasks such as supervising repossession of merchandise that was not paid for. Although most credit collectors work for collection agencies, some are employed by retail stores, real estate firms, credit unions, insurance companies, banks, and loan companies.

Education and Training Requirements

Credit collectors are trained on the job by working under the supervision of experienced workers. Most employers require applicants to be high school graduates. A person can prepare for the field while in high school by taking courses in psychology, business mathematics, speech, and foreign languages. On-the-job training consists of learning collection procedures, budgeting, and telephone and in-person interviewing techniques.

Getting the Job

Direct application to firms that employ credit collectors is one way to get a job. Jobs in the field are also advertised in the classified sections of newspapers and on Internet job sites. State and private employment agencies may offer job leads.

When creditors cannot get debtors to pay their bills, they hire credit collectors to handle the process. *(Photograph by Kelly A. Quin. Thomson Gale. Reproduced by permission.)*

Advancement Possibilities and Employment Outlook

Advancement in the field is limited. Outstanding workers may be promoted to the position of collection manager or credit collection supervisor. Some workers become bank loan officers. Opportunities for advancement to a managerial position increase when workers take courses in credit and finance at professional associations and colleges.

In 2004 bill and account collectors held 456,000 jobs, and roughly one fifth of these collectors worked for collection agencies, according to the U.S. Bureau of Labor Statistics. Employment was expected to grow faster than the average for all occupations through the year 2014. Companies on the whole have become more aggressive about collecting overdue debts. A greater number of companies are also lending money to customers and issuing credit cards. As such, debt levels and delinquent payments should continue to rise. Finally, the high turnover rate in the debt collection industry will result in job openings each year.

Working Conditions

Credit collectors generally work thirty-five to forty hours per week. Since debtors are usually unavailable during the day, the workweek may include night and weekend hours. Seasonal overtime work often occurs. Credit collectors work out of offices that are usually pleasant and well lighted, but they may spend most of their working hours in the field searching for forwarding addresses and visiting debtors. Since debtors are generally less than willing to talk to credit collectors, successful workers must be persuasive talkers who remain calm through difficult situations. They must be able to deal with people who are under stress. Employers look for workers with clear, pleasant speaking voices, because credit collectors often spend many hours talking on the telephone. Some companies provide field workers with a car or repay them for the use of their own vehicle.

Earnings and Benefits

In 2004 credit collectors earned a median salary of $27,456 per year. Credit collectors with the highest 10 percent of salaries in their profession earned over $41,808 per year, according to the Bureau of Labor Statistics. Income varies greatly because many workers receive, in addition to a base salary, commissions or bonds based on the amount of debts they collect. Benefits generally include paid vacations and health insurance.

Where to Go for More Information

ACA International (formerly American Collectors Association)
PO Box 390106
Minneapolis, MN 55439
(952) 926-6547
http://www.acainternational.org

Consumer Data Industry Association
1090 Vermont Ave. NW, Ste. 200
Washington, DC 20005-4905
(202) 371-0910
http://www.cdiaonline.org

Customer Service Representative

Definition and Nature of the Work

Customer service representatives are employed by all types of companies to field questions and concerns from customers. They typically work at the front desk of a local office branch or at a cubicle in a corporation's call center. They may communicate with customers over the phone, by e-mail, fax, or regular mail correspondence.

Companies hire customer service representatives to be the first point of contact for customers who have problems or questions about a product or service. Customer service representatives are usually provided with the means to answer the most basic questions. At a phone service company, for instance, a customer service representative is typically stationed in front of a computer that allows him or her to see a customer's account. When a customer calls, the representative is able to answer basic questions about the customer's balance, update the customer's information, or sign the customer up for new services. If a customer calls with a more complicated question, perhaps involving erroneous charges, the representative will route the customer's call to a specialist who can help them.

Education and Training
High school

Salary
Median—$27,020 per year

Employment Outlook
Very good

Customer service representatives respond to customer inquiries and problems by providing information or directing requests to others who can supply the necessary information or service. (© Martha Tabor/Working Images Photographs. Reproduced by permission.)

Those customer service representatives who work in phone banks are typically monitored by supervisors to ensure that the representatives are helpful and answer questions quickly. Those representatives who work in branch offices and stores may be required to perform other duties, such as make photocopies or keep the office or store clean. Customer service representatives can be found in just about any business, including electronics manufacturers, clothing stores, hospitals, and even produce suppliers. Wherever they work, customer service agents are required to be polite and maintain their poise even when confronted with an irate customer.

Education and Training Requirements

Many companies prefer applicants who are high school graduates. Applicants should have basic computer skills and be able to type. Companies will usually train customer service representatives on how to deal with customer questions and how to use the computer and phone systems. Training typically lasts several weeks. In some instances, such as with an electronics store, the customer service representative has an advantage in landing the job if they know something about the products being sold.

Intelligence, a pleasant personality, and a neat appearance can be more important for the job than a formal education. A customer service agent must be patient and enjoy working with people.

Getting the Job

A student's high school placement office may be able to help him or her find a position as a customer service representative. Jobs may be listed with state and private employment agencies, on Internet job sites, and in the classified ads of local newspapers. If prospective workers are interested in a government job, they should apply to take the necessary civil service test.

Advancement Possibilities and Employment Outlook

Customer service representatives can go on to become supervisors of customer service. In a branch office or store, they can often go on to become a store manager. With a college degree they may even rise to a job in product development or human resources.

According to the U.S. Bureau of Labor Statistics, 2.1 million people were employed as customer service representatives in the United States in 2004. One quarter of all customer service representatives were employed in the finance and insurance industries. Employment of customer service agents was expected to grow faster than the average for all occupations through the year 2014. Because of the expansion of the professional and information service industries in the United States, many new jobs will be created. The high turnover rate of customer service representatives will also ensure ample job opportunities. Because people like to voice their concerns and questions to other people, office automation will not likely have too negative of an impact on the field.

Working Conditions

Customer service representatives usually stand or sit behind a counter in stores or office branches, and conditions can vary depending on the store. Customer service representatives who work in phone banks usually sit in clean, well-lit office spaces at a desk or a cubicle. Phone banks that receive a high volume of calls can be noisy. Because customer service representatives typically spend all day at a computer, they are susceptible to eye strain, back problems, and injuries such as carpel tunnel syndrome.

Earnings and Benefits

The size and location of the customer service representative's employer affects earnings. Customer service representatives earned a median salary of $27,020 per year in 2004, according to the Bureau of Labor Statistics. Those who worked for an insurance carrier earned a median salary of $29,790 per year, and those who worked for a business support service earned a median salary of $21,390 per year. Most customer service representatives receive benefits that include paid vacations and holidays as well as health insurance.

Where to Go for More Information

Office and Professional Employees
    International Union
265 W. 14th St., 6th Fl.
New York, NY 10011
(800) 346-7348
http://www.opeiu.org

Data Entry Keyer

Definition and Nature of the Work

A large and ever increasing amount of information is stored on computers. Banks store information on every check written against their customers' accounts. State governments record information on drivers' licenses and motor vehicle registrations. Insurance companies keep records of their clients' policies and claims.

Data entry keyers, also called data entry operators and key entry operators, enter lists of items, numbers, or other data into computers, where it is stored or used for research purposes. They often help to transfer information from checks, licenses, or other paper documents into a computer. Data entry keyers normally use data or number keypads to feed information directly into a com-

Education and Training
High school

Salary
Median—$23,250 per year

Employment Outlook
Poor

puter. Others work with nonkeyboard data entry devices such as scanners, which scan documents into a computer. Computer software then automatically recognizes the characters on the document. After the document is scanned, the data entry keyer fills in any data the computer software did not recognize.

Data entry keyers must be fast and accurate. In some organizations data entry keyers are divided into two levels. Those in the first level work under close supervision. The material they work with is standardized, and they do not have to use their judgment to select or code the data. Any questions can be referred to a supervisor. Those in the higher level are more experienced. They may select and code the data that they enter. They may have to consult several documents to find what they need. They may also have to select the correct procedure for dealing with each piece of information.

Data entry keyers may also be required to operate other equipment, such as printers or tape readers. However, most of the work data entry keyers do is repetitive.

Education and Training Requirements

Most employers require applicants to be high school graduates and to be able to enter data accurately at a given speed. A person can learn to operate data entry equipment in high school or in a private business school. Individuals may have to take a test when applying for a job. Some organizations transfer workers from other departments (such as bookkeeping) and give them on-the-job training in data entry.

Getting the Job

A student's school placement office may be able to help him or her to get a job as a data entry keyer. Prospective workers should check the classified ads of local newspapers. They can also apply directly to organizations that employ data entry keyers. The biggest employers are companies that provide computer and data processing services. Banks, wholesalers, and state governments are among other large employers.

Advancement Possibilities and Employment Outlook

Data entry keyers can advance from lower- to higher-level jobs. Some may advance to supervisory positions. However, opportunities are limited and usually are available only after several years on the job. With further training, a few data entry keyers may advance to jobs such as administrative assistant.

According to the U.S. Bureau of Labor Statistics, 330,000 people held data entry keyer jobs in 2004. Employment of data entry keyers was expected to decline through the year 2014. Technological advances are making it possible to enter a great deal of information into computers automatically. The devices that read bar codes on items purchased at supermarkets are examples of this type of innovation. Others are scanners, or machines that can read printed letters and figures. Also, many professionals now work from personal computers, enabling them to do their own data entry as they perform their regular jobs.

Working Conditions

A data entry keyer usually works in an office with many others doing the same work. These offices may be noisy because of the various types of equipment they contain. Keyers can be subject to eyestrain from long hours looking at video display terminals. They may also suffer from back strain from sitting at a computer for most of the day and can develop repetitive motion injuries such as carpal tunnel syndrome.

Earnings and Benefits

The median annual salary of a full-time data entry keyer in 2004 was $23,250, according to the Bureau of Labor Statistics. Experienced keyers and those who work for the federal government can earn more. Benefits generally include paid vacations and health insurance.

Where to Go for More Information

International Association of Administrative
  Professionals
10502 NW Ambassador Dr.
PO Box 20404
Kansas City, MO 64195
(816) 891-6600
http://www.iaap-hq.com

Office and Professional Employees
  International Union
265 W. 14th St., 6th Fl.
New York, NY 10011
(800) 346-7348
http://www.opeiu.org

File Clerk

Definition and Nature of the Work

Education and Training
High school

Salary
Median—$21,029 per year

Employment Outlook
Poor

File clerks are the guardians of a company's important documents. They are responsible for creating and maintaining an efficient and accessible filing system. Clerks gather material from the company's departments, sort it, and arrange it. While some offices still use a paper file and folder system, many have installed computerized filing and retrieval systems that employ electronic storage media, such as hard drives, floppy drives, and CD-ROMs. Still other companies maintain microfilm or index card files such as those found in libraries. When a company worker needs information from the paper files or computer media, a clerk locates the appropriate materials and delivers them to the desk of the company worker.

File clerks must arrange incoming records numerically, alphabetically, or by subject matter. Some file clerks are responsible for more than one set of files. They then must store the information in either a paper filing system, on microfilm, or on an electronic storage media device. Many use scanners to convert forms, receipts, and reports into electronic format.

Company records must be kept up to date. File clerks regularly clean out files, throwing away old material and making certain that all material has been filed correctly. File clerks must keep track of all the materials in the files and ensure that nothing is lost. Although file clerks are employed by many different companies, more than nine tenths of all file clerks work in service-providing industries, including government. Roughly one fourth of all file clerks worked in the health-care industry in 2004, according to the U.S. Bureau of Labor Statistics.

Education and Training Requirements

Most companies prefer to hire file clerks who have finished high school. Courses in business, computers, typing, and English are helpful. File clerks should have a talent for organization and enjoy detail work.

Training is usually given on the job. In small offices training may entail nothing more than a quick explanation of the filing system. Clerks who operate mecha-

File clerks must organize, sort, and file documents so that they are easy to locate when other employees make requests. *(Photograph by Kelly A. Quin. Thomson Gale. Reproduced by permission.)*

nized or microfilm files or specialized computer databases may require training.

Getting the Job

A student's school placement office should be able to help him or her find a position as a file clerk. Jobs may be listed with state and private employment agencies. Internet job sites and newspaper classified ads often list openings for file clerks. If candidates are interested in a government job, they should apply to take the necessary civil service test. A person can also apply directly to companies that employ large crews of file clerks. If there is a firm a person would like to work for, he or she should contact its personnel office for an interview. Even if there are no job openings at that time, applicants may be considered for future openings.

Advancement Possibilities and Employment Outlook

In most cases file clerks must learn another skill, such as typing, if they want to advance. Experienced file clerks may eventually supervise the work of others.

The 2006–07 *Occupational Outlook Handbook* reported that about 255,000 people worked as file clerks in 2004. Employment of file clerks was expected to decline through the year 2014 due to an increase in office automation. Powerful, centralized computer storage devices and networks allow any individual in an organization to easily access files, thus eliminating the need for file clerks. However, demand for file clerks is expected to be strong in the health sector. Openings will also become available as file clerks leave their jobs and replacements are needed.

Working Conditions

File clerks generally work from thirty-five to forty hours per week in pleasant offices. They spend much of their time on their feet. They may do much bending, stretching, and reaching in the course of a working day. Filing may become repetitious.

Where to Go for More Information

Office and Professional Employees
    International Union
265 W. 14th St., 6th Fl.
New York, NY 10011
(800) 346-7348
http://www.opeiu.org

Earnings and Benefits

Salaries vary depending on the size and location of the office. Full-time file clerks earned a median annual salary in 2004 of $21,029, according to the Bureau of Labor Statistics. Clerks with experience can earn more. The benefits that clerks receive depend on the industry in which they work. In general, benefits include paid holidays, vacations, and health insurance. Some of these workers belong to labor unions that are active in the industry in which they work.

Human Resources Assistant

Definition and Nature of the Work

Human resources assistants assist human resources managers or administrators. They provide clerical and technical support in such areas as recruiting, hiring, compensation, and benefits. These assistants gather information on employees' training, skills, wages, promotions, and general work history. They record this information by hand or on a word processor. Then they use the data to update personnel files. Human resources assistants maintain these files and search them for information requested by current and prospective employers and even credit agencies. They also prepare employee reports for managers in the organization.

Those human resource assistants with more training and experience may perform some of a human resource manager's work. They may interview prospective employees, determine benefits, and process dismissals. Human resource assistants often administer and score any required aptitude and personality tests. They may also be responsible for preparing and filing reports of on-the-job accidents and injuries.

Human resource assistant positions may be found in any organization that employs more than a few people. Jobs can be found in business and manufacturing firms, schools of all levels, government agencies, and nonprofit organizations.

Education and Training Requirements

Employers prefer to hire people who have completed high school. Courses in general mathematics, office practices, bookkeeping, basic computer software office applications, and data processing are helpful. Human resources assistants should enjoy detailed work. Training is usually given on the job.

Getting the Job

A student's school placement office may be able to help him or her find a position as a human resource assistant. Job openings are also listed with state and private employment agencies and in newspaper ads and on job Internet sites. If individuals are interested in a government job, they should apply to take the necessary civil service test. They can also apply directly to companies. Those with a large number of employees are most likely to employ human resource assistants. If there is a firm a person would like to work for, he or she should contact the human resource office for an interview. Even if there are no jobs available immediately, a person's application may be kept on file for future openings.

Advancement Possibilities and Employment Outlook

With additional training, education, or experience, human resource assistants can advance to other positions in human resource departments. They may become personnel schedulers and human resource specialists. Some may move into supervisory positions. Human resource assistants may choose to move into other clerical positions, such as credit clerk or charge account clerk.

> ### Education and Training
> High school
>
> ### Salary
> Median—$31,750 per year
>
> ### Employment Outlook
> Good

Human resources assistants should enjoy recording numerical data and reading forms. Experienced human resources assistants may have contact with other employees. (Photograph by Kelly A. Quin. Thomson Gale. Reproduced by permission.)

According to the U.S. Bureau of Labor Statistics, about 172,000 people worked as human resource assistants in 2004. Employment was expected to grow as fast as the average for all occupations through the year 2014. The growth of computer use and electronic data transactions will eliminate some human resource jobs, but many openings will be created as personnel clerks leave or advance to other positions. In addition, economic downturns do not always have a negative impact on human resources departments. Companies need human resource assistants to handle the paperwork when employees are laid off.

Working Conditions

Human resource assistants generally work from thirty-five to forty hours per week in pleasant offices. Most of the work is performed while sitting at a desk. These assistants do a great deal of typing and recording of numerical data. Much of their time is spent reading detailed forms. More experienced human resource assistants may have a lot of contact with other employees and should enjoy talking to people.

Where to Go for More Information

American Payroll Association
30 E. 33rd St., 5th Fl.
New York, NY 10016-5386
(212) 686-2030
http://www.americanpayroll.org

Office and Professional Employees
   International Union
265 W. 14th St., 6th Fl.
New York, NY 10011
(800) 346-7348
http://www.opeiu.org

Earnings and Benefits

Salaries vary depending on the size and location of the office. Human resource assistants earned a median salary of $31,750 per year in 2004, according to the Bureau of Labor Statistics. Human resource assistants with the most experience and those working for large firms earn the highest salaries. Salaries also vary with the amount of responsibility of the position. The benefits that human resource assistants receive depend on the industry in which they work. Benefits include paid holidays, vacations, and health insurance.

Interviewer

Education and Training
High school

Salary
Median—$23,670 to $33,114 per year

Employment Outlook
Fair

Definition and Nature of the Work

Interviewers assist people with such tasks as opening bank accounts and filling out medical documents, charge account applications, consumer surveys, and other forms. Interviewers may work for financial institutions (such as banks or credit unions), health-care facilities, market research companies, or the government.

Job responsibilities include gathering and verifying information, creating files, and performing processing tasks. The type of employer determines the specific duties of interviewers. Admitting interviewers work in hospitals, clinics, or doctors' offices. They gather information for patients' admissions, fill out discharge records, and process payments. Interviewers working in outpatient areas may also schedule appointments, provide general information, and escort patients. Market research interviewers usually work for market research firms conducting surveys on various topics. They interview people using a prepared list of questions and forward the results to their employer. Eligibility interviewers work for the government and assess the eligibility of individuals who would like to take part in government assistance programs such as welfare and public housing. They gather financial and personal information on the applicants and determine if they qualify for government aid.

Education and Training Requirements

Most employers expect interviewers to have a high school diploma, although there are no formal educational requirements. Courses in word processing and a familiarity with computers are valuable. Interviewers must have good communication skills and a strong command of the English language. They must also be detail oriented. Some experience with telemarketing or other telephone-oriented work is an advantage. Employers generally provide on-the-job training.

Getting the Job

Interested individuals can consult the classified ads in local newspapers or Internet job sites for job openings. They can also apply in person to the personnel offices of financial, medical, or research companies.

Interviewers must have strong communication skills in order to obtain accurate information about people. *(Photograph by Kelly A. Quin. Thomson Gale. Reproduced by permission.)*

Advancement Possibilities and Employment Outlook

Successful interviewers can become supervisors. Advancement to other positions within the financial, medical, or marketing fields is possible with additional training and education.

According to the U.S. Bureau of Labor Statistics, 515,000 interviewers were employed in the United States in 2004. Employment of interviewers was expected to grow more slowly than average for all occupations through the year 2014. Employment growth for interviewers should vary by industry, but it was expected to be fastest in the health-care industry and social assistance sectors. The slowest growth rates were anticipated in the financial sector. Many new jobs for interviewers should become available with personnel services, since more companies are contracting out for clerking services instead of maintaining a full-time staff.

Working Conditions

Full-time interviewers usually work a forty-hour week in offices or at designated workstations. Much of the work is routine. Interviewers may sit for long periods, often in front of a computer screen from which they access information while dealing with customers on the phone. They communicate with individuals in person, by telephone, or by mail. Angry or upset customers can make the job stressful at times. Many interviewers work part time.

Earnings and Benefits

In 2004 the average annual salary for interviewers varied depending on the industry. Eligibility interviewers for the government earned the most, with a median annual salary of $33,114, according to the Bureau of Labor Statistics. The median salary for interviewers who did not work in the financial industry or for government eligibility programs was $23,670 per year. Interviewers receive standard benefits packages, which generally include health insurance, paid vacations, and a retirement plan.

Where to Go for More Information

American Federation of State, County, and
    Municipal Employees, AFL–CIO
1625 L St. NW
Washington, DC 20036-5687
(202) 429-1000
http://www.afscme.org

Service Employees International Union
1313 L St. NW
Washington, DC 20005
(202) 898-3200
http://www.seiu.org

Mail Clerk

Definition and Nature of the Work

Mail clerks sort and deliver mail that comes to business offices. They prepare mail to be turned over to the post office or to a private shipping company. Mail clerks work for government agencies, insurance companies, advertising agencies, schools, mail order firms, and almost every business that receives or sends a great deal of mail.

Part of the mail clerks' job is to distribute mail to the different departments of the company. Mail clerks usually put sorted piles of letters, packages, and other mail into a large rolling bin that resembles a shopping cart. Then they follow a systemized route to deliver the mail to all parts of the building. They may collect outgoing mail from the departments at the same time. Mail clerks also carry memorandums and messages from one department to another. When companies have offices in more than one building, the mail clerks deliver mail from building to building.

Mail clerks also may be required to send out packages. Clerks wrap the packages according to standards set by the U.S. Postal Service and private shipping companies such as Federal Express. Mail clerks weigh packages and letters and put the correct postage on them. In some companies they operate computerized printing and mailing systems, which print out the shipping labels and postage for a package.

Mail clerks must know their company's policy for mailing letters and packages. If they use the wrong postal rate to send a letter, mail clerks could cost the company money and lost business. They may also have to decide for themselves the most efficient way to send mail. Therefore, they must know postal and shipping rates and regulations.

In addition to sorting and delivering mail from the post office, a mail clerk may sort and deliver material going from one department to another. (Photograph by Kelly A. Quin. Thomson Gale. Reproduced by permission.)

Education and Training Requirements

Most employers prefer to hire high school graduates. However, a high school education is not required for the job of mail clerk. Clerks are trained on the job to follow the company's mail handling procedures. Mail clerks usually begin by doing simple mail handling tasks, such as sorting letters or delivering mail. They should become familiar with the layout of the office building and with the names of the departments. They also should learn about postal rates and regulations. They must be comfortable with computers, because most mail rooms now use computerized mailing systems.

Getting the Job

High school placement offices may be able to help graduating students find jobs as mail clerks. Some companies hire students for summer or part-time jobs. These jobs often lead to full-time jobs after graduation. Check the classified ads of local newspapers or Internet job sites for openings. Some private employment agencies specialize in placing clerical workers. Interested individuals can also apply directly to organizations that employ mail clerks. If a person is interested in a government job, he or she can apply to take the necessary civil service test.

Advancement Possibilities and Employment Outlook

Advancement for mail clerks usually depends on their ability, education, and training. Some clerks become supervisors of mail rooms. Others go into other types of clerical work.

According to the employment predictions by the U.S. Bureau of Labor Statistics, employment of mail clerks was expected to decline through the year 2014. Electronic mail (e-mail) will cause a decrease in the number of workers needed, and the use of mail-handling machinery and computerized mail systems has eliminated some mail room jobs. But people are still needed to deliver mail. Mail clerk jobs will continue to provide good short-term employment opportunities.

Working Conditions

Mail clerks work in many different settings. Some clerks who work in small offices do much of their work by hand. Others work in large mail rooms with noisy machines. Many mail handling tasks are repetitive. Clerks who distribute mail spend a lot of time on their feet. However, they get to meet many of their coworkers. Many mail clerks belong to labor unions that are active in the industry in which they work.

Earnings and Benefits

Salaries and benefits vary widely depending on the location of the job and the kind of mail handling tasks that are being performed. In their November 2004 *Occupational Employment Statistics* survey, the Bureau of Labor Statistics reported that mail clerks earned a median salary of $23,650 per year. Supervisors of mail rooms can earn more. Benefits often include paid vacations and holidays, health insurance, and retirement plans.

Where to Go for More Information

Office and Professional Employees
 International Union
265 W. 14th St., 6th Fl.
New York, NY 10011
(800) 346-7348
http://www.opeiu.org

Mail Service Worker

Definition and Nature of the Work

Many nongovernmental agencies provide express delivery service of mail and packages in the United States and abroad. These shipping companies will guarantee overnight or express delivery, or customers are refunded their money. They also offer some additional mail-related services. Many employees are needed to keep these operations running smoothly and efficiently. Entry-level positions in these companies are customer service agents, drivers/couriers, and handlers.

Customer service agents work either in a shipper's branch location or at a telephone bank at a regional office. Customers typically call the agents or stop by a branch office in person to inquire about delivery rates, pick-up times, and other details. The agents need to be able to supply customers with price and delivery information for letters and packages being sent all over the world. Additionally, customer service agents can be asked to locate a package at any step along the

Education and Training
High school

Salary
Varies—see profile

Employment Outlook
Fair

This mail service worker uses a hand-held computer to help track deliveries. (AP Images.)

delivery route. The agents do this by using a computer terminal linked by the Internet to the main office. The locations of packages are updated via computer by employees all along the route. The agents may also order supplies and do general office duties at branch stations.

Unless a customer brings a package into a branch office, a driver's/courier's truck must come and pick up the package. Some couriers carry handheld computers so that they can pick up a customer's package or letter within an hour or two of the call to the service agent. Couriers check each package that they pick up to make sure it meets the company's weight and mailing requirements. At the end of their shift couriers drive all the packages they picked up to a specified airport where handlers load the mail onto a plane. The plane flies to the shipper's central airport hub and sorting complex. At the central complex other handlers take the packages off the plane, sort the packages by destination, and load the packages onto waiting planes, which then carry the packages to airports near the delivery destinations. When the packages arrive at these destination airports, local couriers pick them up and deliver them to branch stations. They are then sorted once more, loaded onto the couriers' vans, and delivered to their destinations.

Employees in all three positions must be able to lift a package weighing a specified amount and to maneuver heavier packages using appropriate equipment. Handlers must also know how to use power and hand tools. Because they work so closely with the public, customer service agents and drivers/couriers must enjoy working with people and have good communication skills.

Education and Training Requirements

Most companies require a high school diploma. Because of the computer tracking system, an introductory course in computer use might prove helpful. Drivers/couriers need a valid driver's license and a good driving record. In mail and package services that are unionized, all workers must join the union.

Getting the Job

Applicants can get information about applying for jobs at their local branch agencies. Companies often place ads through the state employment agencies, the classified section of newspapers, or on the Internet.

Advancement Possibilities and Employment Outlook

Some companies promote their employees to supervisory positions almost exclusively from within. The greater use of electronic mail (e-mail) is expected to cause a moderate decrease in all mail handling. However, an increase in package handling is also expected.

Working Conditions

These jobs require lifting and moving heavy packages. Agents and couriers deal constantly with the public. All three entry-level jobs require overtime work, but employees are usually paid for their time. Some employees must work variable shifts, including weekends and holidays.

Earnings and Benefits

Wages vary widely by company, geographic location, and job description. Full-time customer service representatives in all industries made a median wage of $27,020 per year in 2004, according to the U.S. Bureau of Labor Statistics. Couriers who drove delivery trucks earned a median salary of $37,315 per year in 2004, and handlers made $20,300 per year. Many employees start part time with express mail companies; their salaries and benefits are figured on a part-time basis, and are therefore lower.

Where to Go for More Information

Office and Professional Employees
    International Union
265 W. 14th St., 6th Fl.
New York, NY 10011
(800) 346-7348
http://www.opeiu.org

Parcel Shippers Association
1211 Connecticut Ave. NW, Ste. 610
Washington, DC 20036
(202) 296-3690
http://www.parcelshippers.org

Messenger Service Worker

Definition and Nature of the Work

The efficiency of every business depends in part on the flow of letters, paperwork, and packages. This flow may be between departments in the same company and building or between businesses in different locations. It is the job of a messenger service worker to make pickups and deliveries of some of this material. Most of the letters and packages messengers transport need immediate attention.

Messengers or couriers who make deliveries between businesses may travel by foot, public transportation, bicycle, motorcycle, or truck. They must be familiar with the geographic area, know the fastest routes, and be able to maneuver through heavy urban congestion. Most messengers transport items only within a defined delivery area, such as a city's financial district.

With the increased use of facsimile machines and computer networks to transfer documents, many messenger services now specialize in transporting items that cannot be sent electronically. For instance, some may transfer medical specimens from hospitals to medical laboratories. Others transport emergency spare parts for aircraft and other equipment.

Law firms, brokerage houses, banks, and some other businesses deal with large numbers of original documents such as stock certificates. Often these documents need to be transported from one place to another. Some large businesses hire messenger services to run not only these messenger operations but also their mail rooms. If a business does not employ its own outside messengers, it may use an independent messenger service.

Education and Training
None

Salary
Median—$20,190 per year

Employment Outlook
Poor

Education and Training Requirements

Some employers prefer to hire high school graduates. More important than having formal education, however, is being responsible, independent, and very punctual. Good references are also necessary, because most companies bond, or insure, their messengers.

Training for new messengers is brief, informal, and done on the job. New outside messengers are given assistance in planning their routes. Couriers may be expected to know their area well when they join a messenger service.

Getting the Job

A high school placement office may be able to help an interested individual find a job as a messenger. Internet job sites and local newspapers in large metropolitan areas often carry job listings for messengers. Candidates can also apply directly to companies that usually employ messengers. Even if there are no openings at the time of applying, a person's application may be kept on file until positions become available. If a person is interested in a government job, he or she should apply to take the necessary civil service test.

Advancement Possibilities and Employment Outlook

Some companies hire messengers who have more qualifications than the job demands with the intention of promoting them to positions of greater responsibility. Banks, for example, often promote messengers to bank clerk jobs after an introductory period. Other firms expect messengers to remain in that job for the course of their employment.

Couriers and messengers held 147,000 jobs in 2004, according to the U.S. Bureau of Labor Statistics. Employment of messengers was expected to decline through the year 2014. The spread of electronic document delivery technologies such as e-mail and fax will continue to erode at the courier industry. Employment is also very dependent on the economy. When workers are laid off, messengers are often the first to go. Full-time jobs with commercial messenger services may offer greater security. Still, messenger work is plentiful, easy to obtain, and provides a good source of short-term employment and income.

Working Conditions

Messengers employed full time usually work between thirty-five and forty hours per week. Those employed by banks and newspapers sometimes work in shifts. Messengers employed by independent services often work very irregular hours and operate more like self-employed independent contractors. Many messengers work flexible part-time hours and provide their own transportation. Their hours fit their schedules and the work available.

Inside messengers and those who deliver on foot are on their feet all day. They are also under pressure to complete several deliveries at once. Couriers using cars and vans or bicycles are constantly on the move. They have the stress of dealing with heavy traffic while trying to make their deliveries as fast as possible. All messengers must be very efficient and reliable. They must be able to plan their routes quickly and remember many detailed instructions.

Earnings and Benefits

Earnings vary widely depending on the location of the job. Messengers working full time in 2004 could expect a median wage of $20,190 annually, according to the U.S. Bureau of Labor Statistics. The highest-paid 10 percent of messengers earned more than $30,510 annually.

Couriers working for messenger services are usually paid by the errand. Those who use their own cars are paid a mileage allowance for each mile they drive. Many of these couriers work part time, so their earnings depend on how many hours they work and how many errands they complete.

Where to Go for More Information

Office and Professional Employees
   International Union
265 W. 14th St., 6th Fl.
New York, NY 10011
(800) 346-7348
http://www.opeiu.org

Office Clerk

Definition and Nature of the Work

Office clerks do many jobs that are basic to office work. Clerks make up payrolls and bills. They enter data on a computer, scan documents, sort mail, answer e-mail, and file papers and reports. Clerks work in government offices, insurance companies, and hospitals. They work for department stores, manufacturers, and other businesses. In small offices general office clerks perform a variety of tasks according to a schedule. For instance, clerks might prepare payroll checks every Thursday and stock the supply closet every Friday. Some clerks move from job to job as the need arises. These clerks are called floaters. For instance, a clerk might enter invoices into a database one day and help secretaries type letters the next day.

In large companies the work of office clerks is usually more specialized. One clerk might be in charge of copying letters, manuscripts, or other materials on photocopying machines. Another clerk might spend each day working in the bookkeeping department. Office clerks are often supervised by secretaries or office managers. Many clerks operate office machines such as fax machines, photocopiers, and computers. Some organizations have specialized clerical jobs that are not found elsewhere. For instance, hospitals employ clerks to enter information into a computer as patients are admitted to the hospital.

Education and Training Requirements

Most employers prefer people who have a high school education. High school courses in business software and business math are helpful. Any knowledge a student can gain about computers and business machines is also useful. Some high schools have work–study programs in which students can work in clerical jobs while still in school. Sometimes students can get summer jobs in which they can learn to do various clerical jobs.

Getting the Job

A person's school placement office may be able to help him or her find openings. Interested individuals can apply to companies directly or answer the classified ads in their local newspaper or on Internet job sites. Candidates who want to work for the government should arrange to take the necessary civil service examination. State and private employment agencies list clerical openings.

Advancement Possibilities and Employment Outlook

A person may start as a general office clerk and advance to a specialized job such as bookkeeping clerk. Some clerks become word processors by increasing their typing speed and accuracy. Some clerks who are proficient at word processing go

Although some clerical jobs have been eliminated due to increased use of computer and business machines, the general outlook is still good for office clerks. *(Royalty-Free/Photo Disc, Inc. Reproduced by permission.)*

back to school to take shorthand in order to become secretaries. Clerks sometimes seek further training and become bookkeepers.

Roughly 3.1 million general office clerks were employed in the United States in 2004, according to the U.S. Bureau of Labor Statistics. The average growth for all occupations was expected to outpace the growth of general office clerk employment through the year 2014. The increased use of computers and other technology will lead to further office automation and result in the elimination of some clerical jobs. Clerks who remain in their jobs will likely be required to take on more duties around an office. Some positions, however, will become available as clerical workers move up to more specialized jobs. Other new jobs will be created throughout the country as new businesses form that require the service of a general office clerk.

Working Conditions

Clerks work in many different settings, from offices in big cities to those in suburban or rural office parks. Offices can be hectic and noisy or quiet and well organized. Clerks usually perform routine tasks that may be repetitive. They usually work a standard forty hours per week. Many clerks belong to labor unions that are active in the industry in which they work.

Where to Go for More Information

Office and Professional Employees
    International Union
265 W. 14th St., 6th Fl.
New York, NY 10011
(800) 346-7348
http://www.opeiu.org

Earnings and Benefits

Wages vary depending on the level of responsibility and the size and location of the employer. In 2004 general office clerks earned a median salary of $22,770 per year, according to the Bureau of Labor Statistics. Some clerks earn more by working overtime. Many clerks receive paid vacations, paid holidays, health insurance, and pension plans.

Payroll Clerk

Education and Training
High school

Salary
Median—$30,350 per year

Employment Outlook
Good

Definition and Nature of the Work

Payroll clerks compute and record the earnings owed to each company employee on a computer and ensure employees are paid on time. This recording is known as posting. The information for the calculations is often taken from paper worksheets and work tickets. In offices where automated timekeeping systems are in place, the payroll numbers are already in the computer system, and the payroll clerks are required to check the electronic data for errors.

Payroll clerks are also responsible for calculating deductions, such as income tax withholding, Social Security payments, insurance, and union dues. These clerks may also prepare and distribute pay envelopes to employees and set up automatic electronic transfers between the company and an employee's bank. In addition to these duties, payroll clerks may keep records of benefit deductions, sick leave and vacation pay, 401(k) contributions, and other nontaxable wages.

In large organizations payroll responsibilities may be broken down into specialized areas. For instance, in some businesses bonus and commission systems may be in operation. In these organizations some payroll clerks may be known as bonus clerks and commission clerks.

Education and Training Requirements

Most employers require a high school education. Completion of a high school business program provides a good background for entry-level positions. Courses in mathematics, business software, and accounting are essential, especially when calculating bonuses and commissions. Some employers prefer to hire graduates of two-year business schools or junior college programs that include office skills. Others prefer beginners with no specialized education but a good general background. On-the-job training is provided and may last from a few days to several weeks.

Payroll clerks need a strong background in mathematics and accounting to calculate employees' earnings and deductions. (Photograph by Kelly A. Quin. Thomson Gale. Reproduced by permission.)

Some organizations offer classes and certification programs for those who would like to become payroll clerks. The American Payroll Association, for instance, offers the Fundamental Payroll Certification for job seekers who wish to demonstrate a basic understanding of payroll operations.

Getting the Job

A student's school placement office may be able to help him or her find a position as a payroll clerk. Jobs may be listed with state and private employment agencies. Newspaper ads and Internet job sites often list openings in this profession. If candidates are interested in a government job, they should apply to take the necessary civil service test. A person can also apply directly to the personnel departments of companies that employ payroll clerks.

Advancement Possibilities and Employment Outlook

Beginning payroll clerks usually perform routine clerical duties. As they gain experience and skill, they will be assigned more difficult tasks. Some employers have different levels of clerical positions with progressively more responsibility. Clerks may receive promotions to these higher levels with increases in pay.

According to the U.S. Bureau of Labor Statistics, 214,000 payroll clerks were employed in the United States in 2004. Employment of payroll clerks was expected to grow about as fast as average through the year 2014. Although many of the duties traditionally associated with payroll are becoming automated, the job itself is becoming more multifaceted. Many companies are offering a wide array of benefits and retirement plans, and they need payroll clerks to sort through and keep track of these plans. In the future more companies will also likely contract out to firms that specialize in payroll operations. As such, a greater number of payroll jobs will be found in the bookkeeping and payroll service industry.

Working Conditions

Payroll clerks work in many different settings. Some work in small, quiet offices; others in large, hectic ones. Much of the work is performed while seated at a desk. Clerks usually work at routine tasks that may be repetitive. They usually work thirty-five to forty hours per week. Many belong to labor unions that are active in the industry in which they work.

Earnings and Benefits

A payroll clerk's earnings depend on the clerk's particular duties, skill, and experience. Earnings also depend on the type and size of the organization in which the clerk is employed. In 2004 full-time payroll clerks earned a median annual salary of $30,350 per year, according to the Bureau of Labor Statistics. Experienced clerks may earn more. Benefits usually include paid vacations, paid holidays, medical and life insurance coverage, and some type of retirement plan.

Receptionist

Education and Training
High school

Salary
Median—$21,840 per year

Employment Outlook
Very good

Definition and Nature of the Work

Most people form an impression of a company the instant they walk through the front door. If visitors are greeted by an alert and pleasant receptionist and are then efficiently directed to their destination, they will have the feeling that the company is well run. On the other hand, if the receptionist is indifferent or rude, visitors may get the idea that the company is not properly managed.

In addition to greeting visitors, receptionists frequently answer phones, compose documents and letters, and perform other clerical tasks around the office. In many firms the receptionist keeps a log of each day's visitors, noting arrival and departure times. Other duties may include taking down client's personal information, sorting mail, maintaining a log of employee attendance, proofreading outgoing letters, reports, and e-mails, and keeping the reception area neat.

All kinds of businesses employ receptionists, from beauty shops to factories to doctors' offices. In these and many other businesses, the pleasant demeanor of an efficient receptionist is an asset.

Education and Training Requirements

Many companies prefer applicants who are high school graduates. However, intelligence, a pleasant personality, and a neat appearance can be more important for the job than a formal education. Good word processing and computer skills are also a plus. A receptionist must be patient and enjoy working with people. Receptionists are sometimes trained on the job.

Getting the Job

A high school placement office may be able to help a student find a position as a receptionist. Jobs may be listed with state and private employment agencies, on Internet job sites, and in the classified ads of local newspapers. If candidates are interested in a government job, they should apply to take the necessary civil service test.

Advancement Possibilities and Employment Outlook

Receptionists are in an excellent position to get to know all the aspects of their company's business. Furthermore, it is unlikely that a receptionist who handles the job well will go unnoticed by management. Receptionists often become secretaries or take on other positions of responsibility.

According to the U.S. Bureau of Labor Statistics, more than 1.1 million people were employed as receptionists in the United States in 2004. Roughly 90 percent of all receptionists worked in the service-providing industry. One third of all receptionists were employed by the health-care and social assistance industries. Employment of receptionists was expected to grow faster than the average for all occupations through the year 2014. Because of the expansion of business and professional services, many new jobs will be created. The high turnover rate of receptionists will also ensure ample job opportunities. Because reception jobs require many interpersonal skills, office automation will not likely have too negative of an impact on the field. Employment prospects will be best for those with word processing and other office skills.

Working Conditions

Receptionists are usually seated in the most attractive area of the company. Even in a factory, a receptionist's office is clean and quiet. While receptionists have limited contact with fellow employees, dealings with the public are frequent. As representatives of their company, receptionists should get along well with people.

Earnings and Benefits

The receptionist's experience and the size and location of the employer affect earnings. Receptionists earned a median salary of $21,840 per year in 2004, according to the Bureau of Labor Statistics. Those with more experience and skills earned more. Receptionists working for the federal government earned from \$22,937 to \$27,818 per year. Most receptionists receive benefits that included paid vacations and holidays as well as health insurance. Some employers provide educational assistance for their receptionists.

Statistical Assistant

Education and Training
High school

Salary
Median—\$31,390 per year

Employment Outlook
Fair

Definition and Nature of the Work

Statistical assistants establish and check numerical facts in many different areas of business, government, and industry. Statistical assistants compile and record data and make computations. Statistical assistants work for insurance companies, banks, and stock brokerages. They also work for research firms, manufacturers, wholesalers, and retailers, as well as for the government at all levels.

Businesses of all kinds employ statistical assistants in shipping, receiving, billing, data processing, and research departments. Some statistical assistants count products or raw materials and make note of the number on hand. Others post, or record, numerical entries on shipment records, tally sheets, and handheld computers. They may also work in research fields doing routine computations with figures supplied by research workers. For instance, a statistical assistant might figure out the average income of a group of consumers being studied by market researchers. Assistants often compute freight rates for airlines, railroads, and trucking companies. Many statistical assistants do scheduling work.

In certain industries people who compile statistics have specific job titles. Insurance companies employ many actuarial assistants to help actuaries figure out the risk involved in insuring people's lives, cars, and homes. Actuarial assistants compile facts about things such as traffic accidents. They might figure out which areas of a city have the most accidents by counting up the accidents at different locations and comparing the totals. Many such computations provide the actuary with the facts needed to determine insurance rates.

Statistical assistants are employed by government agencies, such as the Food and Drug Administration and the Department of Agriculture, to compile statistics for government research and publications. Crew schedulers are statistical assistants who assign airline pilots to specific flights and then keep track of the miles each pilot flies.

Many statistical assistants use electronic calculators and hand-held computers. They keep track of and manipulate data with the help of computer spreadsheets and databases. No matter what their field, statistical assistants must work accurately and take responsibility for the facts they pass along.

Education and Training Requirements

An individual must have a high school education to be hired as a statistical assistant. Employers look for people who have taken high school courses in business math, bookkeeping, and business applications software. A person will receive on-the-job training in procedures used by the company after he or she is hired. The length of time needed to learn how to be a statistical assistant varies depending on the chosen field. Most employers train inexperienced assistants to use calculators, hand-held computers, and computer programs such as spreadsheets.

Statistical assistants often use advanced statistical software to compile and analyze data. (© Martha Tabor/Working Images Photographs. Reproduced by permission.)

Getting the Job

A high school placement office may be able to help a graduating student find a job as a statistical assistant. Candidates can also apply directly to insurance companies and manufacturers as well as to other firms that employ statistical assistants. If individuals are interested in a government job, they should apply to take the necessary civil service test. Check Internet job sites and classified ads of local newspapers for possible openings.

Advancement Possibilities and Employment Outlook

Statistical assistants usually begin as general assistants who do routine counting or data collecting. After they learn their employer's methods, they are given more difficult assignments. A few become chief assistants or supervisors. Other assistants seek additional training and go into computer programming or other data processing jobs.

According to the 2004–14 employment predictions by the U.S. Bureau of Labor Statistics, nineteen thousand people held statistical assistant jobs in 2004. Employment of statistical assistants was expected to grow more slowly than average through the year 2014. Although the amount of statistical data is expected to increase substantially, many routine tasks now performed by statistical assistants will be handled by computers. This increases productivity and reduces the need for these workers. There will, however, continue to be openings due to replacement needs.

Working Conditions

Most statistical assistants work from thirty-five to forty hours per week in a variety of settings. Some assistants work on shipping platforms, while others work in offices, railroad yards, and computer centers. Statistical assistants often perform repetitive tasks. They may be under pressure to work quickly yet accurately in their calculations. Many statistical assistants belong to labor unions that are active in the industry in which they work.

Earnings and Benefits

In their November 2004 *Occupational Employment Statistics* survey, the Bureau of Labor Statistics reported that statistical assistants earned a median salary of $31,390 per year. Benefits vary depending on the company and the kind of work performed. Generally, assistants can expect to receive health and life insurance plus retirement benefits as well as paid vacations and holidays.

Telephone Operator

Education and Training
High school

Salary
Median—$28,392 per year

Employment Outlook
Poor

Definition and Nature of the Work

Although the majority of telephone calls are dialed directly, some calls require the assistance of a telephone operator. An operator may be needed to place a collect call, supply a telephone number in a distant city, or find out the cost of a call.

Two types of telephone operators provide these services. The operators who work for the telephone companies are probably the most familiar to the average phone user. However, many large businesses and organizations receive so many calls that they require operators to run their private branch exchange (PBX) switchboards. These workers are called PBX operators.

Telephone company operators may function as central office operators or as directory assistance operators. Operators who help customers with person-to-person and collect calls are called central office operators. They obtain the information needed to complete the call and record the details for billing. Many of the tasks previously performed manually are now totally computerized, leaving the central office operator free to answer a larger volume of calls more quickly. Operators who look up local or long-distance telephone numbers are called directory assistance operators. Directory assistance operators answer customer inquiries for telephone numbers by using computerized alphabetical or geographical directories. Since the 1990s many of the responsibilities of the directory assistance operators have been automated. A computerized recording provides the customer with the number requested.

Additional types of operators include overseas, mobile, and marine operators who place calls abroad and to and from ships and cars.

Education and Training Requirements

A high school diploma or its equivalent is the usual minimum requirement for telephone operators. High school courses in speech, office practices, and business math provide a helpful background for persons interested in this occupation. Patience, courtesy, and good spelling skills are also needed.

New operators are taught how to use the phone equipment, keep records of calls, and simulate the customer assistance procedure by placing practice calls. After operators have learned how to handle the most complex calls, they begin to work on their own. They also receive instruction on customer service procedures.

Getting the Job

Part-time work for operators is often available and may lead to a full-time job later. Many telephone operators who start out as young part-timers working for a company after school and on weekends end up landing full-time positions with the same company after graduating from high school. Generally their part-time work experience is counted toward benefits such as vacations, holiday pay, and seniority.

Individuals interested in this type of work should consult with state or private employment agencies, apply to private companies, and answer classified ads in local newspapers. Business firms, answering services, schools, hospitals, and public offices all need operators to run their switchboards.

Advancement Possibilities and Employment Outlook

After gaining one to two years of experience, a telephone company operator may be promoted to junior service assistant or service observer, assisting the supervisor by monitoring customer service telephone conversations. Some operators advance to other clerical jobs or to telephone craft jobs such as equipment installers and repairers.

Employment of telephone operators is expected to decline through the year 2014. Technological advances in areas such as directory assistance, long distance, and PBX systems will reduce the need for operators. Also, many jobs in this field are being outsourced to foreign countries. As with most occupations in the early twenty-first century, the majority of job openings for telephone operators will result from the need to replace experienced employees who retire or transfer to other positions. Employment prospects for switchboard operator/receptionists seemed the most promising as of 2006. PBX systems with direct inside dialing leave operators free to concentrate on other clerical tasks. This flexibility appeals to employers and will stimulate a demand for these workers. The increasing demand for voice recognition systems will also affect future employment levels.

Working Conditions

Operators who work for telephone companies, hospitals, hotels, and other locations where telephone service is needed on a twenty-four-hour basis work shifts, holidays, and weekends. Some operators work split shifts—that is, they are on duty during the peak calling periods in the late morning and early evening and have time off in between. The scheduled hours of PBX operators are usually the same as for other clerical positions in the business.

Operators usually work in pleasant, air-conditioned surroundings. The job of a telephone operator requires little physical exertion; however, during peak calling periods the work may become hectic and stressful. Job performance is monitored closely by management, so operators must be able to maintain their composure under pressure.

Earnings and Benefits

According to the U.S. Bureau of Labor Statistics, telephone operators earn a median hourly salary of $13.65, which for full-time workers translates to $28,392 per year. Other types of communication equipment operators typically earn a median salary of $15.23 per hour. Unionized telephone company operators usually receive extra pay for overtime. Benefits include paid vacations, holidays, and sick leave.

Where to Go for More Information

Communications Workers of America
501 3rd St. NW
Washington, DC 20001-2797
(202) 434-1100
http://www.cwa-union.org/

Information Technology and
    Telecommunications Association
PO Box 278076
Sacramento, CA 95827-8076
(415) 777-4647
http://www.tca.org/

International Brotherhood of Electrical
    Workers
900 7th St. NW
Washington, DC 20001
(202) 833-7000
http://www.ibew.com/

Telephone Service Representative

Definition and Nature of the Work

Telephone service representatives work for telephone companies. They deal directly with the public, handling requests for new telephone services and answering questions about bills or payments. Customers typically contact them through a toll-free telephone number.

During the course of their conversations with customers, telephone service representatives try to sell the latest services available. They may arrange to have new service installed for customers who have moved. They tell customers about monthly charges and installation fees. When customers decide what kinds of services they want, the service representative records this information and gives it to the telephone installers. In addition, the information is fed into a computer system that handles billing and directory listings.

Service representatives also check mistakes in billing. When necessary, they adjust the charges and issue credits to customers. They are trained to check customer accounts quickly and keep them in proper order.

Business telephone service is more complicated than residential service. The service representative who deals with businesses is generally called a sales representative. These representatives must be familiar with the wide range of services available and know the rates for these services. When a customer's needs for services and equipment are very complex, the representative will call in a specialist to design a system for that business. That specialist is known as an account executive.

Service and sales representatives usually take many calls per hour from different people and businesses. They must have all the information they need at their fingertips and convey it clearly and quickly. Most of the information is computerized, so representatives spend the bulk of their working hours in front of a computer. Telephone service representatives must be courteous and patient at all times, regardless of the pressures of their job.

A telephone service representative receives on-the-job training to learn how to sell telephone services to customers. (© Jose Luis Pelaez, Inc. Corbis.)

Education and Training Requirements

Telephone service representatives need at least a high school diploma or its equivalent. High school courses such as English, typing, speech, and business are helpful. Some employers may also require an associate's degree from a community college plus two years of sales experience. Candidates will probably have to pass a sales aptitude test to get the job.

Most telephone companies train new employees both in the classroom and on the job. New service representatives learn about company policy and the kinds of services offered. They learn how to apply rates, taxes, and tariffs. They also study customer relations and sales techniques. Sales representatives generally receive additional training in business services and equipment.

Getting the Job

Most telephone companies use tests as one way of finding out if candidates are well suited for the job of service representative. Interested individuals should apply directly to their local telephone company. School placement offices also may have some useful job information.

Advancement Possibilities and Employment Outlook

The opportunity to advance in telephone companies is good. Service representatives, for example, can become service analysts, group supervisors, or business office supervisors.

The proliferation of telecommunication services and companies has provided a steady demand for knowledgeable, courteous service representatives. Despite outsourcing of some jobs to foreign countries, employment projections from the U.S. Bureau of Labor Statistics suggest a faster than average growth in this field through the year 2012.

Working Conditions

Telephone service representatives usually work in large, well-lighted offices. The offices are crowded places, and representatives work closely with their coworkers and supervisors. Some sit at desks; others stand most of the day. The pressure and standards are high.

Service representatives work forty hours per week. They sometimes work evenings and weekends. When service representatives work overtime, they are usually paid time and a half. Many telephone service representatives belong to unions.

Earnings and Benefits

Wages for service representatives vary according to regional pay scales. According to the Bureau of Labor Statistics, the median salary for a service representative is $27,020 per year.

Many service representatives belong to a union. The union contract covers benefits, wage progression, and internal placement. Service representatives receive pension plans, sick leave, and paid vacations and holidays.

Where to Go for More Information

Communications Workers of America
501 3rd St. NW
Washington, DC 20001-2797
(202) 434-1100
http://www.cwa-union.org

International Brotherhood of Electrical
    Workers
900 7th St. NW
Washington, DC 20001
(202) 833-7000
http://www.ibew.com

United States Telecom Association
607 14th St. NW, Ste. 400
Washington, DC 20005
(202) 326-7300
http://www.usta.org

Word Processor

Education and Training
High School

Salary
Median—$28,030 per year

Employment Outlook
Poor

Definition and Nature of the Work

Word processors set up and prepare reports, letters, mailing labels, and other materials on a computer using a keyboard and word processing software. The word processor uses word processing commands to format the material and instruct the machine to correct spelling or grammar errors, number pages automatically, adjust the margins or line length, or perform a host of other functions. After inspecting the completed document, the word processor can print out and arrange copies of the document for presentation or for filing. Word processors also often perform other clerical duties around an office such as copying documents and answering telephones.

Word processing has become an everyday part of office technology in private industry and government. In addition to the job of word processor, this new technology has given rise to a number of related positions. Word processing trainers train terminal operators and instruct users in machine capabilities and formatting options. Proofreader/format designers, in addition to proofreading hard copy, set standards for the word processor's automated grammar and spelling correction and formatting processes. Word processing managers and supervisors coordinate and oversee other word processors and may be involved in the evaluation, design, and implementation of future word processing systems.

Education and Training Requirements

To become a word processor, a person generally needs a high school education. Employers look for applicants with all-around clerical skills, including a good command of the English language, fast and accurate typing, experience with basic word processing programs, and some secretarial experience. The actual technology of word processing—the use of computers and the software—is often acquired on the job or through employer-sponsored training programs. Many two-year colleges and business schools certify word processors who have completed a program in business and word processing. Some temporary placement services offer preliminary word processing training to clerical workers.

Word processing has become an everyday part of office technology in private industry and government. *(Photograph by Kelly A. Quin. Thomson Gale. Reproduced by permission.)*

Getting the Job

A high school or business school placement office may be able to help a student find a job as a word processor. Interested individuals can check Internet job banks and classified ads of local newspapers for job openings. State and private employment agencies may be able to lead a person to openings in word processing. For a government job, arrange to take the necessary civil service examination.

Advancement Possibilities and Employment Outlook

Word processors who work quickly and accurately can advance to positions as supervisors or to specialized clerical or administrative assistant jobs within their companies after gaining additional training in programming applications.

According to the U.S. Bureau of Labor Statistics, 194,000 people held word processing jobs in 2004.

Employment of word processors was expected to decline through the year 2014. In more and more companies professionals and other office personnel are doing their own word processing. Some experienced word processors will be needed because the occupation is a large one.

Working Conditions

Some word processors work independently at separate terminals. Others are clustered in a clerical pool. Word processors generally must sit at their machines for hours at a time. Their work can be tedious and can cause backaches, eyestrain, and repetitive motion injuries such as carpal tunnel syndrome.

Word processors usually work forty hours per week, although rotating or swing shifts and flexible time (for example, four ten-hour days a week) are options at some companies. Overtime may be expected during peak periods.

Earnings and Benefits

The median salary in 2004 for word processors and typists was $28,030 per year, according to the Bureau of Labor Statistics. The highest-paid 10 percent earned more than $43,190 per year. Most word processors receive benefits such as health insurance and paid vacations.

Where to Go for More Information

International Association of Administrative
  Professionals
10502 NW Ambassador Dr.
PO Box 20404
Kansas City, MO 64195-0404
(816) 891-6600
http://www.iaap-hq.com

Office and Professional Employees
  International Union
265 W. 14th St., 6th Fl.
New York, NY 10011
(800) 346-7348
http://www.opeiu.org

Administrative Assistant

Definition and Nature of the Work

Administrative assistants work for managers and executives. Some organizations do not distinguish between executive secretaries and administrative assistants. In organizations that distinguish between the two, administrative assistants tend to spend more time on long-range assignments. The secretaries have to do more detailed, day-to-day tasks and are more closely supervised by their employers.

Administrative assistants often help their employers prepare reports. They attend meetings with their employers, collect and research documents, and may do much of the writing themselves. They may produce computer graphics such as illustrations. Administrative assistants often edit and enter reports and in-house publications into the computer. Some administrative assistants conduct Internet research and collect facts and figures to be included in budgets.

In some organizations, such as universities, administrative assistants may work on planning. They look at different ways of organizing certain office tasks and recommend changes. In research companies each project director may have an administrative assistant. The assistants take responsibility for all routine administrative chores. They keep track of funds spent and produce monthly budget reports. They keep track of vacation schedules. They may deal with the accounting department regarding errors in paychecks and withholding taxes. They may be responsible for seeing that a project has enough office space and equipment. Administrative assistants may arrange for the maintenance and repair of equipment and even negotiate prices with office supply vendors.

Administrative assistants must be highly organized and able to work independently. They nearly always need strong secretarial skills. They frequently need computer skills to deal with budgets, word processing, and desktop publishing. Good writing and analytical skills are a requirement. Administrative assistants often must talk to clients or discuss problems with other staff members. They must work easily with other people.

Education and Training Requirements

Administrative assistants need a high school diploma, basic typing skills, and computer skills. In companies where high-level secretaries may be called administrative assistants, advanced secretarial skills and experience are essential. In companies where administrative assistants have distinct duties, a basic knowledge of accounting and business administration is often helpful. Employers also often require competency in spreadsheets, database management, and other software applications. Some organizations require a bachelor's degree for these positions.

Getting the Job

A school placement office may be able to find a job for a graduating student as an administrative assistant. Interested individuals can contact companies directly, Internet job sites, or the classified ads in local newspapers for openings. Try to find out exactly what duties the employer requires for a position before

The duties of administrative assistants vary according to the company for which they work. Some may work on budgets and schedules, while others may edit and help produce in-house publications. *(Photograph by Kelly A. Quin. Thomson Gale. Reproduced by permission.)*

applying; duties may vary from business to business. If candidates are interested in a government job, they should arrange to take the necessary civil service test. State and private employment agencies may be able to lead prospective workers to administrative assistant openings.

Advancement Possibilities and Employment Outlook

Administrative assistants may advance to managerial positions. However, additional training is often required. They may also move into such areas as sales.

According to the U.S. Bureau of Labor Statistics, 1,547,000 administrative assistants and executive secretaries held jobs in 2004. Employment of administrative assistants was expected to grow more slowly than the average for all occupations through the year 2014. Continued office automation in the form of computer programs, voice messaging systems, and scanners will allow fewer administrative assistants to accomplish more in less time.

Working Conditions

Administrative assistants work in many kinds of offices. They usually work in a room close to their executives or managers. They often share office space with secretarial or other staff. Assistants to top administrators may have their own offices. Most administrative assistants work thirty-five to forty hours per week. The need to work additional hours depends on the type of organization. The job of an administrative assistant in a major industry tends to be more high pressure than that of an assistant in a university. Some employers allow administrative assistants to work flexible schedules.

Earnings and Benefits

Earnings depend on the type, size, and location of the organization. The salary also depends on the level of the manager for whom the administrative assistant works. The median salary for administrative assistants and executive secretaries was $34,970 per year in 2004, according to the Bureau of Labor Statistics. The highest-paid 10 percent made more than $53,460 per year. Full-time employees usually receive paid holidays and vacations, health and life insurance, and fringe benefits.

Where to Go for More Information

International Association of Administrative
  Professionals
10502 NW Ambassador Dr.
PO Box 20404
Kansas City, MO 64195-0404
(816) 891-6600
http://www.iaap-hq.com

Office and Professional Employees
  International Union
265 W. 14th St., 6th Fl.
New York, NY 10011
(800) 346-7348
http://www.opeiu.org

Claims Adjuster

Education and Training
High school; license

Salary
Median—$44,080 per year

Employment Outlook
Good

Definition and Nature of the Work

Claims adjusters ascertain how much money people are entitled to receive on their insurance claims. Most claims adjusters work for property-liability insurance companies. Property-liability insurance covers such losses as fires, thefts, and accidents. People who buy this insurance protect themselves and their property against these events. The claims adjuster goes to the scene of the accident or fire to see that the claim is valid and that it is settled as quickly as possible. This work requires a thorough knowledge of insurance policies and practices.

As soon as a loss is reported, an adjuster investigates the claim by talking to witnesses and studying police reports before determining the amount that should be paid to the policyholder. Part of the adjuster's job is to determine whether the amount of the claim has been inflated and whether fraud has been committed. The claims adjuster may prepare written reports of the findings.

Sometimes the amount of a claim is discussed or negotiated with the policyholder. This is especially true when the loss is extensive. The claims adjuster must work out a settlement that is fair to both the policyholder and the insurance company.

Whereas most claims adjusters work for insurance companies, some are employed by large policyholders, such as banks, and others work for independent adjusting firms. Some handle several types of insurance, whereas others specialize in one kind, such as automobile coverage. Although a few have desk jobs, most adjusters conduct investigations in the field.

Education and Training Requirements

Many claims adjusters have college training, although it is not always a requirement for the job. A high school diploma is necessary, however. A course in business law may be helpful, because adjusters must understand the legal language of insurance and be able to explain it to their customers. Some claims adjusters learn the business through on-the-job training and evening courses sponsored by their companies. Others take part in work–study programs offered by schools of insurance. Insurance companies also like to employ adjusters with some experience in the products the company insures. A person with a college degree and a background in automobile repair, for instance, would have an advantage over someone with just a college degree when applying for a job as an auto damage insurance appraiser.

Most states require claims adjusters to be licensed. Although licensing regulations vary widely from state to state, typical requirements include proof of state residency, a written examination covering the fundamentals of adjusting, successful completion of an approved insurance course, and proof of good character. Some states also require that examiners enroll in continuing education courses each year to maintain their license. Beginning adjusters almost always work on small claims under the supervision of more experienced workers.

Getting the Job

Most claims adjusters, particularly those without college training, are promoted to their positions from beginning clerical jobs. In some companies, however, it is possible to start as a junior adjuster even with no previous insurance experience. In this case a training period is usually provided for new employees.

Interested individuals can contact insurance companies directly for jobs. State and local insurance associations may offer suggestions about the best places to apply and the correct people to see when applying for a position. Jobs are sometimes listed in the classified ads of local newspapers or on the Internet.

Advancement Possibilities and Employment Outlook

Talented and experienced claims adjusters may work toward the job of chief adjuster or claims department supervisor. Workers who take advanced law courses may become home office legal managers.

Employment for claims adjusters was expected to grow as fast as the average for all occupations through the year 2014, according to the U.S. Bureau of Labor Statistics. Many openings will occur as experienced workers retire or leave their jobs for other reasons. Although computers have taken over some of the routine tasks that were done by examiners in the past, the demand for skilled claims adjusters will keep pace with the rest of the economy. Growth in the proportion of the population over age twenty-five, together with the expansion of the economy, will lead to a steadily increasing volume of insurance claims.

Working Conditions

Claims adjusters spend much time away from the office conducting investigations. Adjusters often work during the evening. Their workweek is generally forty hours, but adjusters must arrange their own schedules.

Some claims adjusters are on twenty-four-hour call. However, on-call duty nearly always rotates among several adjusters. Claims adjusters have contact with many different kinds of people.

Earnings and Benefits

Earnings vary depending on experience, location of the work, and level of responsibility. The median salary of an inside claims adjuster was $44,080 per year, according to salary.com.

Usually claims adjusters either are given company cars or are reimbursed for the use of their own cars. Company benefits are usually good. Adjusters can expect to receive paid vacations and holidays and health and pension plans. Job-related educational expenses are often paid by the employer.

Claims Examiner

Claims examiners work for insurance companies, reviewing medical bills and accident reports to determine whether the policyholder's claims are covered under their insurance policies. (© Terry Wild Studio. Reproduced by permission.)

Definition and Nature of the Work

Claims examiners review claims made against insurance companies. Examiners, who are sometimes called reviewers, are employed by life and health insurance companies. Claims examiners are responsible for approving or rejecting claims or arranging settlements.

Unlike claims adjusters, who do much of their work at the scene of the loss or accident, claims examiners have desk jobs. They do much of their work by telephone and by mail. When policyholders file claims, examiners check both the insurance policies and the claims to make sure that all the information is correct and to determine whether the claims are covered under the policies. (A policy is a contractual agreement between an insured person or business and an insurance company.) Examiners also talk with policyholders, insurance agents, and other companies. Examiners may review medical bills or accident reports, or they may consult specialists. For example, an examiner might ask a doctor whether a claimed injury could have resulted from the type of accident that is being investigated.

When a claim has been carefully reviewed, the settlement is calculated and the claims examiner authorizes payment of the specified amount. Most claims examiners deal with cases in which the loss value is comparatively low. Large or unusual claims and possible false claims are referred to a senior examiner.

Claims examiners must keep careful records detailing the outcome of each step in the settlement process. They are often responsible for preparing summary reports. Some must testify in court, especially in cases where claims are being contested.

Education and Training Requirements

Two years of college is usually the minimum requirement for employment as a junior claims examiner. Courses in law, business, math, and economics are helpful. Junior examiners are trained on the job by experienced workers.

Many companies prefer to hire applicants who have a bachelor's degree. Insurance companies also like to employ examiners with some expertise in those areas that the company focuses on. For instance, a person with some medical training would have an advantage when applying for a job as a health insurance examiner. Many life and health claims examiners take company-sponsored courses to improve their skills. They may also take part in work–study programs offered by schools of insurance.

Getting the Job

Interested individuals can contact insurance companies directly for jobs. State and local insurance associations may offer suggestions about the best places to apply and the appropriate people to see when applying. Openings for claims examiners are often advertised in newspapers and on the Internet.

Advancement Possibilities and Employment Outlook

Claims examiners may become senior claims representatives, supervisors, underwriters, or administrators. Those with college training have the best chance for advancement.

According to the U.S. Bureau of Labor Statistics, claims examiner employment was expected to grow as fast as the average for all occupations through the year 2014. Many openings will occur as experienced workers retire or leave their jobs for other reasons. Although computers have taken over some of the routine tasks that were done by examiners in the past, the demand for skilled claims examiners will keep pace with the rest of the economy. Jobs in the health-care insurance industry should increase the most. As the American population ages, the number of health insurance claims and life insurance policies are expected to balloon.

Working Conditions

Claims examiners normally work from thirty-five to forty hours per week in pleasant offices. Their work involves thorough investigation of insurance claims. When quarterly or yearly statements are prepared, examiners may work overtime.

Earnings and Benefits

Salaries vary depending on experience, location of the work, and the type of insurance involved. The median annual salary for claims examiners was $33,669 in 2006, according to salary.com.

The benefits offered by insurance companies are usually good. Examiners generally receive health and life insurance in addition to paid vacations and holidays. Many companies reimburse examiners for job-related educational expenses.

Where to Go for More Information

American Council of Life Insurance
1001 Constitution Ave. NW
Washington, DC 20001-2133
(202) 624-2000
http://www.acli.com

American Institute for Chartered Property
 Casualty Underwriters and the Insurance
 Institute of America
720 Providence Rd.
PO Box 3016
Malvern, PA 19355
(800) 644-2101
http://www.aicpcu.org

Insurance Information Institute
110 William St.
New York, NY 10038
(212) 346-5500
http://www.iii.org

International Claim Association
1 Thomas Circle NW, 10th Fl.
Washington, DC 20005
(202) 452-0143
http://www.claim.org

Property Casualty Insurers Association of
 North America
2600 S. River Rd.
Des Plaines, IL 60018
(847) 297-7800
http://www.pciaa.net

Computer and Office Machine Repairer

Definition and Nature of the Work

Computer and office machine repairers install, maintain, and repair the hardware components of computer systems, copiers, faxes, and other office equipment. Hardware components are the physical components of a computer or office machine, such as the microprocessor, memory boards, monitors, and paper feeders. Software consists of computer programs and applications. Most office machines contain many of the same hardware components as computers. Copying machines, for instance, house microprocessors, memory chips, and small LCD display screens, which allow them to perform a wide array of functions.

If a problem with a computer or office machine occurs, repairers talk to the computer operators. They find out if the system is experiencing problems and look for the causes. They may run special diagnostic programs through the computer or office machine to check for hardware problems. These programs often discover where the problem lies. Repairers may also use testing devices, such as voltmeters, ohmmeters, and oscilloscopes. Computers and office machines have very complicated circuitry. Repairers may have difficulty in locating the cause of the problem. If the problem is software related, the repairer may have to contact a computer technical support specialist.

Making repairs to a computer or office machines' circuitry and subsystems usually takes very little time. Faulty circuit boards are simply taken out and replaced. The repairer uses ordinary tools such as small pliers, wire strippers, and soldering equipment. Printers and copiers may require mechanical repairs, lubrication, and toner. When a major breakdown develops, repairers must work long hours to repair it. A company can suffer heavy losses if its computer systems stop working.

Computers have very complicated circuitry. Computer and office machine repairers have mechanical skills and specialize in diagnosing and solving problems with computer systems and other office machines. (© Chuck Savage/Corbis.)

Repairers sometimes install office machines and computers and hook up any peripherals or network devices to computers with network cables. Peripheral devices include printers and disk drives, and network devices include hubs or wireless routers. Setting up a computer system typically involves running cables between offices through walls and ceilings. For more complicated computer networks, repairers may be closely supervised by a network technician. After setting up, computer and office machine repairers then test the system to make sure that it works properly, and they put together a maintenance schedule.

Repairers often specialize in working on one type of machine or one model of computer. For example, at a large installation one repairer may specialize in maintaining and repairing high-speed printers. Repairers keep written records of all maintenance work and repairs. They also order new parts and keep a list of those parts that are immediately available. In addition, computer and office machine repairers sometimes modify the uses of a machine by adding parts. Sometimes they expand systems by installing new auxiliary machines.

Many repairers are employed by the manufacturers who make the equipment. Some repairers work for companies that provide maintenance services. In both cases the repairers work in the customers' offices. Government agencies and insurance and utility companies often employ their own repairers.

Computer and office machine repairers must like solving problems and be mechanically skillful. Good vision with no color blindness is necessary because the wires in a computer are color coded. Repairers must be interested in electronics and keep up with the latest technical manuals. They must also be skilled in talking to operators and answering their questions. Repairers must be able to work without supervision.

Education and Training Requirements

A high school education and some training in electronics are required to become a computer repairer. High school students should take mathematics and electronics courses. Most employers prefer applicants who have completed one to two years of electronics training at a technical school or college or while in the armed services. Courses in science are also helpful. Many computer manufacturing companies offer training programs for repairers. Trainees study for a number of months both in the classroom and in the field. Practical experience as well as courses in computer science and circuitry theory form the basis of the training program. Once training is completed, repairers spend a year working under the supervision of an experienced worker. Repairers must keep up with new developments in data processing.

Getting the Job

A school placement office can usually put a graduating student in touch with manufacturers and other businesses that employ computer repairers. Interested individuals can apply directly to companies that make or repair data processing equipment. They should also check the classified sections of newspapers for job openings.

Advancement Possibilities and Employment Outlook

Experienced repairers can become troubleshooters. They remain at the main office and help the repairers in the field to solve difficult problems. They may also develop maintenance procedures and instruct trainees. Repairers can be promoted to supervisors or service managers. They may transfer to other work, such as sales and production.

According to the U.S. Bureau of Labor Statistics, computer and office machine repairer employment was expected to grow more slowly than the average for all occupations through the year 2014. Most computer and office equipment, such as faxes and printers, have become so inexpensive that replacing a broken machine is often more cost effective than repairing it. In addition, computer support technicians are taking over many of the responsibilities once held by computer and office machine repairers.

Working Conditions

The normal workweek for computer and office machine repairers is forty hours. However, working long hours of overtime on emergency repairs is common. Some employers rotate their repairers between day and night shifts. Repairers who work for manufacturers may have to travel to their clients. Repairers on emergency repairs may have to work under stress and deal with anxious customers. Their jobs may also require a lot of lifting and bending.

Earnings and Benefits

According to the Bureau of Labor Statistics, the median annual salary for a computer, automated teller, and office machine repairer in 2004 was $35,152. Repairers working for equipment manufacturers made a median wage of $38,500 per year, and those working for electronics and appliance stores made a median wage of $29,203 per year. Benefits include paid vacations and holidays as well as health insurance and retirement plans.

Where to Go for More Information

Computer Technology Industry
   Association
1815 S. Meyers Rd., Ste. 300
Oakbrook Terrace, IL 60181
(630) 678-8300
http://www.comptia.org

ETA International
5 Depot St.
Greencastle, IN 46135
(800) 288-3824
http://www.eta-i.org

International Society of Certified
   Electronics Technicians
3608 Pershing Ave.
Fort Worth, TX 76107
(800) 946-0201
http://www.iscet.org

Office and Professional Employees
   International Union
265 W. 14th St., 6th Fl.
New York, NY 10011
(800) 346-7348
http://www.opeiu.org

Computer Operator

Education and Training
High school plus training

Salary
Median—$31,070 per year

Employment Outlook
Poor

Definition and Nature of the Work

Computer operators manage the operation of computer hardware systems. They are often required to work with most types of computers, including minicomputers, mainframes, and networks of personal computers. Computer operators must maintain the computer hardware as well as solve any problems that occur. A computer operator's duties vary depending on the computer system.

Computer operators are essential to the day-to-day operations of older mainframes and minicomputers. These computer systems consist of a network of smaller computer terminals (monitors and keyboards) hooked up to a central core that contains all the system's software and memory. Most of the older mainframes and minicomputers have a central control panel. While the computer is running, a computer operator watches closely for error lights on the console that may go on to indicate that the computer is not operating properly. If a light goes on or the computer stops, the operator must locate the problem and solve it. Operators maintain log books and operating records for the equipment and record all malfunctions and errors. If the computer system's files and programs are on discs or tapes, the operator has to see to it that the computer has been loaded with these storage media. Experienced operators may help computer programmers or systems analysts test programs.

For a personal computer network, the computer operator may assist a network administrator in ensuring all network connections are in place and that the network and the servers are running smoothly. They may also assist users in connecting computer peripherals, such as printers or lab equipment, or help new employees set up a computer.

Computer operators work for many businesses and industries, including banks, insurance companies, and manufacturers. They are also employed by government agencies, educational institutions, and companies that provide computer services.

The trend toward networking and the use of sophisticated software have enabled computers to perform tasks previously done by operators. With the advancement of technology and the move away from mainframe computers and toward personal computing networks, the jobs of computer operators are shifting from equipment maintenance to network support, user support, and database maintenance.

A computer operator holds hard drives while standing in the server room. (© Helen King/Corbis.)

Education and Training Requirements

In the past a high school diploma, previous experience with an operating system, and familiarity with the latest technologies were the minimum requirements for employment. However, employers increasingly require operators to have some formal computer-related training, perhaps through a community college or technical school. Employers then train workers until they are familiar with specific equipment and routines.

Getting the Job

A student's school placement office may list jobs for computer operators. Interested individuals should check state and private employment agencies for job leads. Internet job sites or classified ads in a local newspaper are a good source of openings. For a government job, candidates should arrange to take the necessary civil service test.

Advancement Possibilities and Employment Outlook

Computer operators can advance to supervisory positions. With experience and further education, some operators become computer programmers and network administrators.

According to the Bureau of Labor Statistics, computer operators held roughly 149,000 jobs in 2004. Employment of computer operators was expected to decline through the year 2014. Technology improvements over the past twenty years have given rise to user-friendly software that automatically controls and monitors the operations of even the largest computer networks. Computer operators are simply not needed. When a problem does arise in these complicated systems, the assistance of highly trained programmers, systems analysts, or network administrators is required.

Working Conditions

Computer operators generally work between thirty-five and forty hours per week. Many companies schedule computer operation twenty-four hours a day, so operators may work in shifts. Because they may work without supervision during their shift, operators must be able to work independently. Some computer operators belong to labor unions.

Earnings and Benefits

Earnings vary depending on the size and location of the company. The median annual salary for a computer operator was $31,070 per year in 2004, according to the Bureau of Labor Statistics. Benefits depend on the industry in which the operator works. Generally, operators receive paid vacations and holidays and health insurance.

Employment Interviewer

Education and Training
High school plus training

Salary
Median—$40,970 per year

Employment Outlook
Very good

Definition and Nature of the Work

Employment interviewers are matchmakers; they help job seekers find suitable job openings and employers find qualified staff. They may work for private employment agencies or for state government employment services.

Employers often ask private agencies to search for workers to fill specific jobs. Job seekers come to agencies on their own or in response to classified ads that agencies place to advertise specific jobs. At the agencies job seekers are asked to fill out application forms with information about education, job experience, and references. The applicants also list the kinds of jobs they want. The applications are kept on file on paper or in a computer database. Also on file are job openings submitted by employers. Employment interviewers interview the applicants to explore their interests and abilities. The interviewers then attempt to match the applicants with jobs that are on file. If suitable jobs are not already on file, the interviewers may contact nearby companies in an effort to find jobs for their clients. Interviewers then send clients for interviews with employers who are hiring workers. The interviewer may give the prospective employee advice on how to handle him- or herself during an interview or on how to arrange

Employment interviewers spend most of their time interviewing applicants and talking with employers on the telephone. (© Martha Tabor/ Working Images Photographs. Reproduced by permission.)

a resume. Interviewers often check applicants' references, because they don't want to recommend unqualified applicants to employers.

Some private agencies place only certain kinds of workers, such as engineers, teachers, or clerical workers. Some of the fastest-growing agencies are those that provide temporary workers for employers. In these agencies employment interviewers have a large number of people on file who can be called to fill in for absent staff or on a temporary basis.

All private agencies are paid a fee each time they match a worker with a job. The fee may be paid by the employer, the applicant, or both.

In state government employment offices, a similar matching process takes place. However, much of the searching is done with the help of computerized job banks. In these offices employment interviewers talk with applicants, review their application forms, and may help them identify the type of work for which they are most suited. Employment counselors recommend training and educational programs to people who need to develop new skills to get jobs.

Education and Training Requirements

Most public and private employment agencies prefer to hire college graduates. Agencies look for people who have a degree in psychology, guidance, vocational counseling, or business administration. However, high school graduates with some college training or work experience in fields such as personnel may be hired. Many private agencies also require college graduates to have previous work experience in related fields. Private agencies that specialize in certain kinds of work such as engineering or teaching sometimes prefer to hire college graduates with backgrounds in those fields. Typing skills and computer skills may be necessary. Private agencies generally offer several months of on-the-job training to newcomers. In some states employees of private agencies must pass a licensing exam to become fully qualified workers.

Getting the Job

Jobs with private agencies can be found by applying directly to the agencies or by checking job banks on the Internet and classified ads in local newspapers. Civil service examinations are required for jobs in government employment services. Apply to take the necessary test for federal, state, and local government jobs.

Advancement Possibilities and Employment Outlook

Privately employed interviewers who are good at their work and place many applicants may advance to management-level jobs. In large agencies they may become department heads or office managers. Some go on to open their own employment agencies. An interviewer can become a certified personnel consultant by passing an examination given by the National Association of Personnel Services. Certification carries with it the association's approval of the interviewer's business practices and gives the interviewer professional status.

Employment interviewers who work for government agencies undergo initial training during which they learn interviewing skills. After gaining some experience, they can take additional training programs to prepare them for more responsible jobs. Some interviewers go back to school to earn college or graduate degrees required for jobs in counseling and supervision.

According to the 2002–12 employment projections by the U.S. Bureau of Labor Statistics, 175,000 Americans held jobs as employment interviewers in 2002. Growth in employment in this field between 2002 and 2012 was expected to be faster than the average for all occupations.

Working Conditions

Private agencies range in size from those with branches in several cities and many employees to those with as few as three or four employees. Employment interviewers must enjoy working with people. They spend most of their time interviewing applicants or talking with employers on the telephone. Because they earn commissions, privately employed interviewers are under pressure to place as many job seekers as possible. Interviewers in temporary employment agencies are also under pressure to supply employers with temporary staff at short notice. Employment interviewers generally work thirty-five to forty hours per week. Some interviewers in private agencies work longer hours to accommodate working people with evening or Saturday appointments.

Where to Go for More Information

National Association of Personnel Services
PO Box 2128
The Village at Banner Elk, Ste. 108
Banner Elk, NC 28604
(828) 898-4929
http://www.napsweb.org

National Employment Counseling Association
5999 Stevenson Ave.
Alexandria, VA 22304
(800) 347-6647
http://www.employmentcounseling.org

Earnings and Benefits

Starting salaries for employment interviewers in state government agencies vary. In their 2003 *Occupational Employment Statistics* survey, the Bureau of Labor Statistics reported that the median salary for employment interviewers was $40,970 per year in 2003.

Interviewers in private agencies generally earn commissions based on a percentage of the annual salaries of the positions they fill. Commissions can provide opportunities for higher earnings. Employment interviewers working in temporary employment agencies may receive a salary alone or a small salary plus commissions. Salaries vary geographically and are higher in large cities. Benefits may include paid holidays, insurance, and vacations. Some workers may be eligible for pension plans.

Meeting Planner

Definition and Nature of the Work

Meeting planners are professional decision makers who manage all facets of meeting preparation and presentation. Depending on their employer, meeting planners may be known as association executives, corporate meeting planners, or independent meeting planners. An association executive plans meetings for a small business association or organization. A corporate meeting planner is employed by a large company or business. An independent meeting planner works on a freelance basis for businesses that do not have meeting planners on staff.

All meeting planners have similar responsibilities, which include establishing meeting objectives, selecting and inspecting the meeting site, scheduling the meeting, budgeting expenses, lining up speakers, and negotiating with suppliers of materials, food, and entertainment. In addition, meeting planners may make travel arrangements and provide audiovisual and technical equipment when needed.

Education and Training Requirements

Although a college degree is not always required for a meeting planner, many large corporations and associations prefer to hire college graduates. Courses in business management, economics, hotel and hospitality management, and communications are recommended. Meeting planners should have good interpersonal skills to communicate well with attendees, good quantitative skills to formulate and follow budgets, and good organizational skills. Meeting planners with three years' experience and a good track record may choose to earn the Certified Meeting Professional (CMP) designation, which is given on the basis of experience and an examination. This certification, awarded by the Convention Industry Council, may help with career advancement.

Getting the Job

Most entry-level positions will be as a member of the administrative or planning staff at a large corporation or business association. A good way to locate job openings is through the college placement office or on the Internet. Interested candidates can also check the newspaper classified ads for clerical or administrative positions or contact a company's personnel office directly.

Advancement Possibilities and Employment Outlook

Planning staff members can become head meeting planners at large corporations or business associations. After gaining experience and further education, they can establish their own consulting firms.

According to the U.S. Bureau of Labor Statistics, meeting planners held forty-three thousand jobs in 2004. Employment of professional meeting planners was expected to grow faster than the average for all occupations through the year 2014. The increase was expected to be due in part to a rise in the number of conferences in the health-care and high-technology industries. The continued globalization of big business will also likely fuel the need for more conferences. As businesses spread out around the world, more and more meetings will be needed to bring employees together for important face time

Meeting planners try to make the most cost-effective arrangements for their clients. They often travel to inspect potential meeting sites. (Photograph by Kelly A. Quin. Thomson Gale. Reproduced by permission.)

Education and Training
Varies—see profile

Salary
Median—$39,620 per year

Employment Outlook
Very good

with one another. Freelance meeting planners will be especially in demand as smaller companies opt to hire outside consultants on an as-needed basis.

Working Conditions

Meeting planners work in pleasant offices. They often travel to inspect meeting sites to evaluate all aspects of the site. They must be good negotiators in order to make the most cost-effective arrangements for their employers. On the whole, meeting planners' schedules can be erratic. They can work eighteen-hour days in the weeks leading up to a big meeting. Afterward, however, their workload may drop drastically. Planners also need to be adaptable and creative. They must work well under pressure and be able to deal with unexpected problems.

Earnings and Benefits

Salaries for meeting planners depend on the size of the company and the amount of responsibility the planner has. Freelance planners who have a good reputation, many years of experience, and an established clientele earn the most money. The median annual salary for all meeting planners was $39,620 in 2004, according to the Bureau of Labor Statistics.

Full-time meeting planners generally receive benefits that include paid vacations and holidays, medical insurance, and a pension plan. Freelance planners must provide their own benefits.

Secretary

Education and Training
Varies—see profile

Salary
Varies—see profile

Employment Outlook
Fair

Definition and Nature of the Work

Secretaries perform several office tasks within one job. They do word processing and data entry. They may take shorthand. Secretaries also file papers, answer telephones, schedule appointments, and handle mail for their employers. Secretaries are employed by business, professional, government, and nonprofit organizations.

The exact nature of the work varies widely from job to job. Secretaries in small firms may spend most of their time dealing with the mail and answering the phone. In a very small organization, one secretary may be responsible for all office functions.

In the past, every middle manager in a large corporation would have a secretary working for him or her. Office automation has eliminated many secretarial jobs. Managers now use e-mail to send and receive correspondences, and they get their phone messages through voice mail. There is less paper to file because so much information is stored on computers.

In most modern, automated offices, one secretary provides services for several managers. Those who work for only one or two managers are usually given additional responsibilities. They may be given tasks that formerly were done by administrators. The tasks vary with the type of office and the special skills of the secretary. A secretary to a human resources director might administer and score tests or check applicants' references. A secretary to an advertising manager might check copy for printing errors and layout. In some offices experienced secretaries are given the same responsibilities as administrative assistants.

Large organizations may have five or more levels of secretaries. Those at the top level are usually called executive secretaries. Those at the middle level may be called senior secretaries or administrative secretaries, but the titles vary from one organization to another. Secretary is sometimes an entry-level title. Inexperienced secretaries may start out by working in a group. Middle- or senior-level secretaries often teach newcomers how to use the company's computer equipment and programs. If the equipment changes, they may help to retrain other office workers.

A secretary's duties can range from answering phones to supervising personnel and managing office operations. *(Photograph by Kelly A. Quin. Thomson Gale. Reproduced by permission.)*

In any office, experienced secretaries may be given a great deal of responsibility. They may order supplies, schedule meetings, handle petty cash, and make travel arrangements. Some secretaries perform supervisory duties or act as office managers.

Many secretaries specialize in one type of office work. For instance, legal secretaries are familiar with the terms and procedures used by lawyers. Medical secretaries work in doctors' offices, hospitals, and other places where a knowledge of medical terms is essential. Bilingual secretaries work for the government and for other organizations that maintain contact and exchange letters with offices abroad.

Education and Training Requirements

Secretaries generally must have a high school education. Many employers prefer to hire graduates of administrative support schools. Business executives may prefer applicants with a liberal arts degree and secretarial training. Typing or word processing skills of at least sixty-five words per minute are often required for jobs in big cities. Shorthand skills are no longer needed for many secretarial jobs. A basic knowledge of computers is increasingly required. Employers usually provide training for their particular equipment and programs. Communication skills are also valuable on the job.

Getting the Job

A high school or business school placement office may help a graduating student to find a secretarial job. Interested individuals can contact companies directly or check the classified ads in their local newspapers. They can also check for jobs on the Internet. If candidates are interested in a government job, they should arrange to take the necessary civil service exam. State and private employment agencies may find suitable openings for prospective secretaries.

Another approach is to register with an agency supplying temporary secretaries to local companies. A person could gain experience that might lead to a permanent job.

Advancement Possibilities and Employment Outlook

A secretary in a small firm may advance to office manager or transfer to a more responsible job in a larger organization. In large firms good secretaries may be given more administrative responsibility. They may become administrative assistants. Some take college courses in administration and progress to entry-level management positions. Secretaries who work in government may train to qualify for higher civil service jobs.

According to the U.S. Bureau of Labor Statistics, 2.6 million secretaries were employed in the United States in 2004. The number of secretaries employed was expected to increase more slowly than the average for all occupations through the year 2014. Employment opportunities for legal and medical secretaries were expected to be much better than those for general secretaries. Many general secretary jobs will be lost as offices continue to update their technology and more and more secretarial duties become automated.

Working Conditions

Secretaries work in many types of offices. An executive secretary may work in a roomy office in a large office building. Entry-level secretaries may work in a large room as part of a group. Medical secretaries may work in busy doctors' offices. Most secretaries meet and work with a variety of people. All secretaries are subject to pressures at least some of the time. Most secretaries work thirty-five to forty hours per week. Some offices permit secretaries to work flexible schedules.

Earnings and Benefits

Secretaries' salaries vary a great deal. Skills, experience, and the type and location of the job affect earnings. In their November 2004 *Occupational Employment Statistics* survey, the Bureau of Labor Statistics reported that the median yearly salary for general secretaries was $27,520. Medical secretaries made $28,250, and legal secretaries brought in $38,870. Full-time employees usually receive paid holidays and vacations, health and life insurance, and fringe benefits.

Where to Go for More Information

International Association of Administrative
    Professionals
10502 NW Ambassador Dr.
PO Box 20404
Kansas City, MO 64195
(816) 891-6600
http://www.iaap-hq.org

Office and Professional Employees
    International Union
265 W. 14th St., 6th Fl.
New York, NY 10011
(800) 346-7348
http://www.opeiu.org

Software Quality Assurance Technician and Analyst

Education and Training
Varies—see profile

Salary
Varies—see profile

Employment Outlook
Good

Definition and Nature of the Work

Software quality assurance technicians and software quality assurance analysts conduct tests on computer software programs to make sure the programs perform properly and are fairly easy to use. The testing may be done on both new programs and updated or modified versions of existing programs.

A software quality assurance technician deliberately tries to do things that will crash the program—that is, make it stop functioning—to determine weaknesses in the computer code. Game testing often involves entering commands or making moves very quickly or very slowly. The testing of word processing programs or other kinds of computer applications may involve typing characters as rapidly as possible to see if the program can process the commands properly. The software quality assurance technician may also use the mouse to click on inappropriate places on the screen to see how the program responds.

A software quality assurance technician keeps a detailed log of all the keystrokes and/or commands entered during testing and how the computer responds to them. He or she also notes any error messages or codes displayed by the computer. All problems are noted, along with the series of commands that produced the problem. The technician then writes up a detailed report of the test and passes it along to the programmers, who use this information to correct errors in the computer code. Sometimes the technician meets directly with the computer programmers to discuss the test results. In other cases the technician's report is submitted to a quality assurance supervisor or manager who works with the programmers. Because the job involves performing the same types of tasks for hours at a time, the technician should also have a fairly high tolerance for repetition and a low boredom threshold.

Many software developers hire software quality assurance analysts to develop programs that automatically test software in development. A software quality assurance analyst will analyze the software that requires testing. They will then develop a testing program from scratch or modify an existing testing program. The testing program looks for defects in the code that makes up the software being tested. The analyst must keep detailed records of the defects the testing program finds, analyze these defects, and recommend ways to fix the problems. In addition, the quality assurance analyst will test if the software being developed interferes with other software typically found on a computer. They may also be responsible for defining the operating standards that the software must meet in order to be released to the public.

Sometimes software developers will use software quality assurance analysts early in the testing process to weed out the major bugs in a piece of software. They will then use technicians to experiment with the program some more and flush out any additional bugs in the software just before release.

Education and Training Requirements

A person can obtain a temporary or part-time position as a software quality assurance technician with little or no advanced education. Many companies hire high school or college students who are familiar with computers to do this type of work on a short-term basis. Those seeking a full-time position in this field should have a background in computer technology such as software programming or network administration, although a four-year degree is rarely required. Some companies even prefer to hire people who have only a modest amount of computer experience, because most of the users of the product will not be computer experts. In this way, the technician will approach the task from a perspective similar to that of the typical user.

Software quality assurance analysts must have at least a four-year degree in computer science, mathematics, or information systems and knowledge of the major programming languages. National certification courses are offered for most major computer languages, including C + +, Java, and XML. Private companies will also offer certification on their newer programming languages and software. Quality assurance analysts must also be aware of the standard methodologies used in quality assurance testing.

Getting the Job

Many computer companies have a permanent software quality assurance department that hires qualified technicians and analysts, but some independent technicians and analysts work for companies on a contract or consulting basis. Positions in this field may be advertised in trade magazines or on Internet job banks. Information about such jobs is also passed on by word of mouth, so having contacts within the computer industry is helpful. Some firms provide quality assurance testing to software companies, but they tend to be located in areas with a large amount of high-tech industry.

Advancement Possibilities and Employment Outlook

A software quality assurance analyst with experience and college training may go on to a position as a quality assurance manager or supervisor. This type of position involves more administrative work and less hands-on testing. Another managerial path is supervisory sales or marketing, a position in which an individual can use knowledge of the strengths and weaknesses of a company's product to work with customers or potential customers.

Working Conditions

Software quality assurance technicians and analysts usually work in an office or laboratory environment, whether they are self-employed or employed by a software firm. The job often requires sitting in front of a computer screen and working with the same program for hours at a time. If a project is under a tight deadline, the software quality assurance technician or analyst may work long or irregular hours to meet the software developer's schedule.

Where to Go for More Information

Association for Computing Machinery
1515 Broadway
New York, NY 10036
(212) 626-0500
http://www.acm.org

IEEE Computer Society
1730 Massachusetts Ave. NW
Washington, DC 20036
(202) 371-0101
http://www.computer.org

Institute for Certification of Computing
  Professionals
2350 Devon Ave., Ste. 115
Des Plaines, IL 60018
(847) 2899-4227
http://www.iccp.org

Earnings and Benefits

Software quality assurance technicians' pay varies widely. Video game developers often do not even pay people to test games in the late development stages. Many gamers are eager to test a game simply for the privilege of being the first to play it. Software quality assurance analysts typically make the same salary as systems analysts. According to salary.com, software quality assurance analysts made a median annual wage of $59,306 in 2006. Self-employed technicians and analysts are usually paid an hourly fee, which varies with the experience of the analyst and the nature and difficulty of the testing performed.

Tax Preparer

Education and Training
High school plus training

Salary
Median—$32,000 per year

Employment Outlook
Good

Definition and Nature of the Work

Tax preparers work for independent or franchised tax preparation services and sometimes for lawyers or accountants involved in tax work. They use their knowledge of federal, state, and local tax codes and publications to prepare tax returns and make sure that their clients do not pay unnecessary taxes. Tax preparers usually specialize in preparing tax returns for individuals rather than for businesses or corporations.

Tax laws are subject to frequent change and vary from one area to another. For example, some states have community property laws that affect the taxes owed by married couples who file joint returns. Tax preparers must be aware of all the provisions and annual changes in the tax laws to advise their clients competently.

Tax preparers use their knowledge of federal, state, and local tax codes and duplications to prepare tax returns and make sure that their clients do not pay unnecessary taxes. (Tim Boyle/Getty Images News/Getty Images.)

Tax preparers work intensively from January to April, which is considered the tax season. Evening and weekend work is required during this period to complete the workload. Because work tapers off after April 15, the annual deadline for submission of tax returns, few workers are employed full time as tax preparers for the entire year. Many work at other occupations during the remaining months or moonlight as tax preparers during tax season.

If the Internal Revenue Service (IRS) or the courts have reason to question the legitimacy of an individual's tax return, the tax preparer may testify about the preparation of the tax return. Tax preparers who have taken a special examination given by the IRS may represent their firm's clients before the IRS during a tax audit.

Tax preparation involves considerable research and attention to detail, so an ability to read quickly and thoroughly is essential. In addition, tax preparers must have an aptitude for working with figures and mathematical formulas. Because tax preparation firms use computers to complete clients' tax returns, familiarity with computer technology is also helpful.

Education and Training Requirements

Applicants must have a high school diploma as well as a thorough knowledge of tax laws and proficiency in math and computer applications. Many tax preparers have college training. Courses in accounting and business math provide useful preparation. Because tax laws are revised every year, preparers must continue their professional education. The National Association of Tax Practitioners offers continuing education classes yearly.

Getting the Job

The best way to get a job as a tax preparer is to apply directly to tax preparation services. Classified ads in local newspapers and ads on the Internet may also offer job leads.

Advancement Possibilities and Employment Outlook

Tax preparers can advance by taking the IRS-sponsored Special Enrollment Examination. Passing this exam enables tax preparers to represent their clients formally before the IRS during tax investigations or audits. Some experienced tax preparers open their own tax preparation services.

According to the U.S. Bureau of Labor Statistics, eighty-six thousand tax preparers were employed in the United States in 2004. Employment of tax preparers was expected to grow about as fast as the average for all occupations through the year 2014. These workers will be in demand as individuals continue to seek outside help in preparing their tax returns.

Working Conditions

Tax preparers usually work in the office of their firm. They may travel to meet with their clients or to visit libraries or government offices. Beginners usually work under the close supervision of an experienced tax preparer. After gaining experience, they work independently.

Tax preparers must be able to work rapidly, accurately, and under pressure, because they must often meet tight deadlines. They should enjoy working with the public, because an important aspect of their work involves face-to-face consultations with clients.

Earnings and Benefits

Tax preparers can work on a commission basis. Their commission is usually a percentage of the fee charged to the client and depends on the preparer's experience and the complexity of the tax return. In their November 2004 *Occupational Employment Statistics* survey, the Bureau of Labor Statistics reported that the median annual salary for tax preparers in 2004 was $32,000. Because tax preparers generally are hired for only part of the year, few tax preparation firms offer benefits to their workers.

Where to Go for More Information

National Association of Tax Professionals
720 Association Dr.
PO Box 8002
Appleton, WI 54912-8002
(800) 558-3402
http://www.natptax.com

Union Business Agent

Education and Training
Varies—see profile

Salary
Varies—see profile

Employment Outlook
Fair

Definition and Nature of the Work

Union business agents represent the interests of the members of their labor union. They are elected by the members and paid by the union to speak on its behalf to both management and the public. Business agents work at the level of the union local. The term "union local" refers to a branch of the union membership. The actual duties of a business agent vary with each union local and depend on its size and needs. In a small local, which may be made up of the workers of one factory or company, the business agent heads the union office. The business agent not only handles negotiations and grievances but also sets up the office. The agent hires staff, keeps records, and collects membership dues. The locals of very large unions sometimes represent all the workers in a wide geographic area. In large locals the business agents work in large offices with other union officers, such as the local president or secretary.

Business agents participate in contract negotiations. Negotiations are held with management to work out a labor contract that is acceptable to both workers and management. The contract terms include specified wage scales, hours, and working conditions. When a contract is signed, it is in force for a stated length of time. Union business agents work to protect their members' rights guaranteed under the contract.

One of the union business agent's main tasks is to handle grievances as head of the local's grievance committee. Grievances are complaints that workers have against management. Workers make their complaints about salaries, benefits, safety standards, and working conditions to a member of the grievance committee who works in their department. The committee member meets with the workers' supervisor to settle the problem. When matters cannot be settled at this level, the business agent is called into the grievance procedure. Business agents are familiar with the terms of the contract. They are in a good position to bargain with managers for fair grievance settlements for workers.

In addition to these duties, union business agents handle general union business, such as writing reports and correspondence. They also encourage new people to join the union. They collect membership dues from those who already belong to the union. Many agents set up union meetings. They are re-

Union business agents protect the rights of union members. They often handle workers' grievances or complaints against management. (© Earl Dotter. Reproduced by permission.)

sponsible for planning meetings and finding meeting places. Some business agents arrange for outside speakers to come to the meetings. Agents often give time to individual union members who have questions about union matters or personal finances.

Besides representing the union to members and management, union business agents are active in the community. Some agents lobby for new labor laws or support political candidates who pledge to support labor causes.

Education and Training Requirements

There are no formal educational requirements for this job. The main requirement is union membership support, which is necessary because agents are elected to their jobs by union members. Most union officials have spent many years in their unions as unpaid committee workers and leaders.

Most union business agents have a high school education, and many have some college training. Some unions offer training programs in labor relations and union leadership. Officials may also take college courses in labor relations.

Getting the Job

Union business agents must run for election and win a majority of the votes. Active members of the union and current officials can advise workers about how to campaign for the post. However, membership support is the only way to get the job.

Advancement Possibilities and Employment Outlook

Advancement depends on performance and popularity. Business agents can be elected to positions as president, vice president, or secretary of the union local. A few successful leaders go on to become officers of the national union after many years of service.

Although membership in labor unions continues to grow, this growth is slow relative to growth in the work force as a whole. Workers trained in labor relations will have the best job opportunities.

Working Conditions

Working hours for a business agent vary from day to day, but they are generally long. Agents sometimes work around the clock during drawn-out negotiations. They also work under considerable pressure at times and usually have a busy schedule. They spend much of their time speaking to people. The job calls for leadership and dedication.

Earnings and Benefits

Salaries vary with the union. Union business agents usually receive a salary that is figured as an increase over the salary of the highest-paid journeyman in the union. Benefits include paid vacations, health insurance, and pension plans.

Where to Go for More Information

American Federation of Labor–Congress
   of Industrial Organizations
815 16th St. NW
Washington, DC 20006
(202) 637-5000
http://www.aflcio.org

Accountant, Management

Definition and Nature of the Work

Businesses have money coming in—income—and money going out—expenditures. Records must be kept of all this money. Companies must keep accurate records of their costs and their profits and losses to satisfy legal requirements and appease shareholders. Accurate financial records also help business people to see whether they are using their money efficiently. Management accountants, often referred to as corporate accountants or private accountants, preside over the financial record keeping of a business. They keep records of and analyze all the company's financial data such as revenue, income, taxes owed, and the amount of cash a company has. They prepare financial statements such as balance sheets, cash-flow statements, and income statements. They also present additional reports to senior managers so that they can make important decisions. In addition, management accountants supervise record-keeping departments, such as bookkeeping and data processing.

Management accountants often specialize in one area of accounting. Tax accountants keep track of how much tax a company owes local, state, and federal governments. They also look into all the ways a company can save money on its taxes through deductions and tax shelters. At the beginning of each year they compile all their tax data from the previous year and prepare and file returns. Cost accountants determine the exact cost of producing a product. Once the costs are known, accountants can suggest a selling price for the product that will recover costs and provide a profit. Cost accountants also try to identify ways to control production costs to keep them as low as possible. Budget accountants plan budgets for their firms and agencies. They plan expenditures so that money is used efficiently. They work with cost accountants to keep expenditures low. They analyze the budget on a regular basis to ensure that the company is on track financially and make budget recommendations if the company is not.

Education and Training Requirements

A person must have a degree in accounting to become a management accountant. Interested individuals should begin to prepare in high school by taking math courses. In college they should follow an organized program of courses to build a well-rounded knowledge of accounting. Many employers prefer to hire people with a master's degree in accounting, but some firms hire people with an undergraduate accounting degree directly out of college. However, a master's program gives a person a chance to develop a special area of interest, such as cost or tax accounting.

> **Education and Training**
> College

> **Salary**
> Median—$50,770 per year

> **Employment Outlook**
> Very good

Management accountants develop and maintain financial systems for business, industry, and government agencies. They must be able to give their employers accurate financial information. (Photograph by Kelly A. Quin. Thomson Gale. Reproduced by permission.)

While certification is an advantage for management accountants, it is not always a necessity. The most widely accepted is the Certified Public Accountant (CPA) designation. The CPA designation is awarded to accountants who pass an examination given by the state board of accountancy. All states use the four-part Uniform CPA Examination issued by the American Institute of Certified Public Accountants (AICPA). The exam lasts for two days and typically has a pass rate of only 25 percent. Before candidates can take the exam, most states require that they have 150 hours of college-level coursework, which is the equivalent of a master's degree and an undergraduate degree.

Getting the Job

A college or graduate school placement office can help a student find a job in management accounting. Many employers send representatives to college campuses to recruit accountants. Interested individuals can also contact business and industrial firms directly. If individuals are interested in government work, they should arrange to take the necessary civil service examination. Candidates can check the classified ads of their local newspapers and Internet job banks for openings in all areas of accounting. Employment agencies that specialize in placing professional workers may offer job leads.

Advancement Possibilities and Employment Outlook

Management accountants have many opportunities to advance because their work is essential to the operation of any business or agency. Management accountants can start in junior positions assisting experienced accountants. Then they can advance to more responsible jobs in cost accounting, tax accounting, or systems accounting. Some accountants become supervisors of large bookkeeping departments. Others become the chief auditors or chief budget accountants of a company. A few go on to become treasurers or controllers.

According to the U.S. Bureau of Labor Statistics, employment of accountants was expected to increase faster than the average for all professions through the year 2014. As the economy and businesses continue to grow more complex, more accountants will be needed to keep track of company finances and tax regulations. In addition, the continued globalization of big businesses will create a demand for accountants who understand international accounting rules. After the accounting scandals at large corporations at the turn of the twenty-first century, there is increasing pressure on businesses and government agencies to improve their accounting procedures, which should also lead to more opportunities for accountants.

Working Conditions

Accountants have frequent contact with people on various levels of their organizations. They usually work thirty-five to forty hours per week. However, they may have to work extra hours during the months before taxes or annual reports are due. Accountants who work for the government may have to travel often.

Earnings and Benefits

Accountants and auditors in general earned a median yearly salary of $50,770 in 2004, according to the Bureau of Labor Statistics. Earnings vary somewhat between accounting specialties. Salary.com estimated that mid-level cost accountants made $50,966 per year in 2006, and mid-level tax accountants made

$53,964 per year. Entry-level accountants made much less. A 2005 salary survey conducted by staffing services firm Robert Half International revealed that accountants and auditors with one year of experience earned between $28,250 and $45,000 per year. Accountants usually receive paid holidays and vacations, health and life insurance, and pension plans.

Accountant, Public

Definition and Nature of the Work

Accountants are experts at preparing and analyzing financial reports. These reports include balance sheets, income and loss statements, and tax returns. Public accountants work for firms that offer their services to the public on a fee basis. Accounting firms may be retained by individuals who need help with their tax returns or by large corporations that need help setting up accounting systems. Some public accounting firms are small partnerships. Others are large companies with offices in many cities. Some public accountants are self-employed.

Businesses and individuals have money coming in—income—and money going out—expenditures. Records must be kept of all this money. Some individuals have relatively simple accounting problems, but businesses have a more complicated set of accounts. Companies must keep accurate records of their costs and their profits and losses to satisfy legal requirements. Accurate financial records also help business people to see whether they are using their money efficiently.

Public accountants divide their time among their clients. They travel to the customer's office or store to audit (check the accuracy of) the company's record keeping. Public accountants prepare reports, such as quarterly earnings statements. They also see that records are kept for tax purposes and that a firm's tax returns are filled out properly. Companies that do not employ their own accountants retain public accountants to keep their accounts. Even large firms that have their own accountants hire public accountants on a consulting basis to handle special problems. Public accountants can give companies independent, unbiased advice concerning their finances. Public accountants are also hired to

| **Education and Training** |
| College |

| **Salary** |
| Median—$50,770 per year |

| **Employment Outlook** |
| Very good |

prepare annual reports that are presented to the stockholders of corporations. These reports show the state of a company's finances to the people who own stock in the company.

Public accountants must be familiar with the tax laws concerning their clients' professions or businesses. They must be able to communicate well with their clients. Sometimes public accountants discuss the records they prepare with government auditors or Internal Revenue Service officials.

Education and Training Requirements

A person should have a degree in accounting if he or she wants to become a public accountant. Interested individuals should begin to prepare in high school by taking math courses. In college they should follow an organized program of courses to build a well-rounded knowledge of accounting. Many public accounting firms prefer to hire people with a master's degree in accounting, but some firms hire people with an undergraduate accounting degree directly out of college. However, a master's program gives a person a chance to develop a special area of interest, such as cost or tax accounting.

Public accounting firms usually require their accountants to become certified by passing an examination given by the board of accountancy in each state. All states use the four-part Uniform CPA Examination issued by the American Institute of Certified Public Accountants (AICPA). The exam lasts for two days and typically has a pass rate of only 25 percent. Before candidates can take the exam, most states require that they have 150 hours of college-level coursework, which is the equivalent of a master's degree and an undergraduate degree. Many firms hire new graduates as junior public accountants to assist certified public accountants (CPAs). Junior accountants learn on the job. They also spend a good deal of time studying on their own or through coursework to prepare for the CPA test. Even after certification, accountants must continue to study and take courses to keep up to date on new tax laws or accounting techniques, such as computerized record keeping.

Getting the Job

A college placement office can help a student find a job in a public accounting firm. Many large firms send recruiters to college campuses to look for qualified graduates. Candidates can also apply directly to public accounting firms in their area. Private employment agencies that specialize in placing professional workers may offer job leads. Interested individuals should also check the classified ads of their local newspaper and job banks on the Internet.

Advancement Possibilities and Employment Outlook

Accountants can advance rapidly after they have passed their CPA exam. As they become more experienced, they are given greater responsibility and become senior accountants. Some accountants become supervisors or partners in their firms. Other accountants open their own public accounting firms.

According to the Bureau of Labor Statistics, employment of public accountants was expected to increase at a rate faster than the average for all professions through the year 2014. As the economy and businesses continue to grow more complex, more accountants will be needed to keep track of company finances and tax regulations. In addition, the continued globalization of big businesses will create a demand for accountants that understand international accounting rules. After the accounting scandals at large corporations at the turn of the twenty-first century, there has been increasing pressure on businesses and government agencies to improve their accounting procedures, which should also lead to more opportunities for accountants. CPAs and accountants familiar with computer applications in accounting and internal auditing will have the best opportunities.

Working Conditions

Public accountants usually work thirty-five to forty hours per week. During the tax season, which lasts from January 2 to April 15, when taxes are due, many public accountants work long hours preparing tax returns for individuals and companies. The job involves much contact with customers and considerable travel from one customer's office to the next. Accountants must be patient and accurate, because their job involves details and numbers.

Earnings and Benefits

Accountants and auditors in general earned a median annual salary of $50,770 in 2004, according to the Bureau of Labor Statistics. A 2006 salary survey conducted by staffing accounting services firm Robert Half International revealed that the yearly salaries of public accountants with one to three years' experience averaged between $35,500 and $47,000 in a small accounting firm and between $42,750 and $60,000 in a large firm. Starting salaries for partners in public accounting firms came in around $175,000 per year. Accountants generally receive benefits, including paid vacations, health and life insurance, and pension plans.

Where to Go for More Information

American Institute of Certified Public Accountants
1211 Avenue of the Americas
New York, NY 10036
(212) 596-6200
http://www.aicpa.org

National Association of State Boards Accountancy
150 4th Ave., Ste. 700
Nashville, TN 37219
(615) 880-4200
http://www.nasba.org

National Society of Accountants
1010 N. Fairfax St.
Alexandria, VA 22314
(800) 966-6679
http://www.nsacct.org

Actuary

Definition and Nature of the Work

What are the chances that a twenty-one-year-old will live to age sixty-five? How much do people lose every year because of fires, floods, or robbery? Actuaries work with numbers and facts to answer such questions.

By checking facts, working with statistics programs, and constructing probability charts, actuaries are able to tell insurance companies how much to charge a policyholder for a particular type of coverage. The fee, or premium, must be sufficient so that the company will be able to pay the customer in case of loss and still make a profit.

More than 60 percent of all actuaries work for private insurance companies. Many work for life insurance companies. The rest work for property-liability companies and are sometimes called casualty actuaries. Some actuaries work for state or federal government agencies. In the federal government actuaries handle particular insurance programs, such as Social Security or life insurance for veterans and members of the armed services. Actuaries who work for state agencies are concerned with unemployment insurance, workers' compensation, or state retirement or pension plans. State-employed actuaries regulate the rates that are charged by private insurance companies. Actuaries also work for consulting firms and rating bureaus. Rating bureaus are associations that supply actuarial data to member companies. Consulting actuaries set up and evaluate pension and welfare plans for private companies, unions, and government agencies.

Education and Training
College

Salary
Median—$76,340 per year

Employment Outlook
Very good

Education and Training Requirements

To become an actuary, a person needs a bachelor's degree with a strong background in mathematics and statistics. Courses in insurance law and accounting can also help. Some colleges offer undergraduate and graduate programs in actuarial science. Before becoming a fully qualified actuary, an individual must pass a series of examinations over a period of five to ten years. Students can begin by taking the first two examinations while they are still in college. Then they have a better chance of securing a beginning job as an actuary when they graduate.

Professional organizations give the examinations that a person must take to become an actuary. The number of examinations required varies from one insurance field to another. Generally, the first few examinations test mathematical skills that are learned in college. Because the various actuarial societies recognize each other's examinations, individuals can apply the examinations administered by one to the requirements of another if they decide to switch to another field of actuarial work. However, some of the tests are specific to various branches of the profession.

Getting the Job

Candidates can apply directly to insurance companies and rating bureaus where they think they would like to work. Many entry-level actuary jobs can also be found in actuarial consulting firms. Interested individuals can also find out about jobs by searching Internet job banks, from classified ads in their local newspapers, or by asking a job placement counselor at their college. If candidates are interested in a government job, they should arrange to take the necessary civil service examination.

Advancement Possibilities and Employment Outlook

Actuaries' advancement depends on how well they do their job and how quickly they pass their exams. Early promotion is most likely for those who have passed two examinations while still in college. Actuarial trainees do fairly routine work at first. Once hired, actuaries are encouraged to finish their examinations to attain first an associate level designation and then a fellowship designation. Some fully qualified actuaries who have passed all the exams may rise to top managerial jobs, such as vice president of an insurance company. Others may become associates in consulting firms.

According to the U.S. Bureau of Labor Statistics, eighteen thousand actuaries held jobs in 2004. Employment of actuaries was expected to increase faster than the average for all occupations through the year 2014. The main reason for the favorable outlook is that the insurance industry is projected to grow substantially. In addition, the regulation and spiraling costs of managed health care will provide new work for actuaries. Actuarial consulting firms will also likely be hiring more actuaries as companies increasingly hire consulting firms to analyze their risks.

Working Conditions

Actuaries generally work between thirty-five and forty hours per week in pleasant offices. Longer hours are not unusual in this profession. Trainees are closely supervised; however, this supervision decreases quickly as they pass exams. Fully qualified actuaries are highly ranked executives and consultants with a great deal of responsibility. Actuaries working as consultants have to travel to clients' offices. Others are frequently required to travel to meetings and conventions.

Earnings and Benefits

The median annual salary for actuaries was $76,340 in 2004, according to the Bureau of Labor Statistics. Top actuarial executives receive salaries in excess of $107,650 per year. Benefits usually include paid holidays, ample vacations, health insurance, and pension plans.

Where to Go for More Information

American Academy of Actuaries
1100 17th St. NW, 7th Fl.
Washington, DC 20036
(202) 223-8196
http://www.actuary.org

American Society of Pension Professionals
  and Actuaries
4245 N. Fairfax Dr., Ste. 750
Arlington, VA 22203
(703) 516-9300
http://www.aspa.org

Casualty Actuarial Society
4350 N. Fairfax Dr., Ste. 250
Arlington, VA 22203
(703) 276-3108
http://www.casact.org

Society of Actuaries
475 N. Martingale Rd., Ste. 600
Schaumburg, IL 60173
(847) 706-3500
http://www.soa.org

Auditor

Definition and Nature of the Work

An auditor is a type of accountant. The main job of the auditor is verification of a company's financial records. Auditors study various sources to find out whether a company's records present its true financial situation. They check the company's bookkeeping and accounting methods by analyzing its books and records. They compare the company's books with the records of the banks, brokers, creditors, and others who deal with the company. They check the books of the departments within the company as well. These objective analyses and reports often help management cut costs, save on taxes, and increase profits.

There are two types of auditors—external and internal. External or independent auditors work for public accounting firms or are self-employed. Businesses, industries, and government agencies contract with auditors to verify and certify their financial statements. Well-run companies usually have their books audited once a year. An independent audit gives shareholders and creditors an outside, expert opinion of a company's financial condition.

The work of internal auditors is similar to that of external auditors, but internal auditors work for and receive a salary from one company. These auditors examine and evaluate the financial system of their firm to ensure that it is being run efficiently and economically. They examine all financial records, including ac-

Education and Training
College

Salary
Median—$50,770 per year

Employment Outlook
Very good

counting books, payroll records, and equipment and inventory records. They submit reports to management on how well accounting policies are working and where changes should be made.

Education and Training Requirements

To become an auditor, a person must have at least a bachelor's degree with a major in accounting. Courses in economics, communications, computers, and the humanities are also helpful. Many external auditors receive advanced degrees, such as a master's degree in business administration (MBA) or a law degree.

Many public accounting firms require their external auditors to pass their state's certification examination and earn a Certified Public Accountant (CPA) designation. All states use the four-part Uniform CPA Examination issued by the American Institute of Certified Public Accountants (AICPA). The exam lasts for two days and typically has a pass rate of only 25 percent. Before candidates can take the exam, most states require that they have 150 hours of college-level coursework, which is the equivalent of a master's degree and an undergraduate degree.

Getting the Job

The best way to get started in this field is in a public accounting firm. After individuals have gained some experience in general accounting, they can begin to specialize in auditing. Candidates can find out about job openings from accounting firms, Internet job banks, and from classified ads in newspapers. State and private employment offices may also offer job leads.

Advancement Possibilities and Employment Outlook

The more training and experience an auditor has, the greater the opportunities for advancement. Experienced auditors often go into business for themselves. According to the U.S. Bureau of Labor Statistics, employment of auditors was expected to increase at a rate faster than the average for all professions through the year 2014. After the accounting scandals at large corporations at the turn of the twenty-first century, there had been increasing pressure on businesses and government agencies to improve their accounting procedures, which should also lead to more jobs for auditors.

Working Conditions

Auditors travel often and do much of their work in the offices of their clients and in banks and other financial organizations. They often come into contact with people. They usually work between thirty-five and forty hours during a five-day week. However, they may be expected to work overtime without additional pay.

Earnings and Benefits

Accountants and auditors in general earned a median annual salary of $50,770 in 2004, according to the Bureau of Labor Statistics. Salary.com estimated that mid-level internal auditors made a median annual salary of $54,445 in 2006. Entry-level auditors made much less. A 2005 salary survey conducted by staffing services firm Robert Half International revealed that accountants and auditors with one year of experience earned between $28,250 and $45,000 per year. Auditors usually receive paid holidays and vacations, health and life insurance, and pension plans. Some employers also offer profit-sharing plans. Self-employed auditors arrange for their own benefits.

Where to Go for More Information

American Institute of Certified Public
  Accountants
1211 Avenue of the Americas
New York, NY 10036
(212) 596-6200
http://www.aicpa.org

Institute of Internal Auditors
247 Maitland Ave.
Altamonte Springs, FL 32701
(407) 937-1100
http://www.theiia.org

Institute of Management Accountants
10 Paragon Dr.
Montvale, NJ 07645
(201) 573-9000
http://www.imanet.org

Bank Officer and Manager

Definition and Nature of the Work

Bank officers and managers manage banks. They work at various levels of the banking industry. Within the industry there are many different kinds of banks offering full service or specialized types of checking, savings, loan, and trust fund services. Banks vary in size, from the small local bank with just one branch to the super-regional banks. These larger banks are made up of a parent bank with many branches. The top officers and managers of the parent bank include the chief executive officer, president, vice presidents, assistant vice presidents, controller, and treasurer. These people supervise the activities of all the branch banks. In addition, each officer works with a number of assistants and trainees.

Each bank department and service is administered by a bank officer or financial manager. The number and type of officers and managers found in each branch depend on the services offered. In a small community bank, one bank manager may be responsible for many different departments.

Loan officers are responsible for a bank's primary concern, which is to make money by charging interest on loans. Because the amount of money available for loans is limited, personal and commercial loan officers evaluate credit reports on the individual or corporation to determine which applicants will be able to pay back their loans with interest. Credit department managers prepare these credit reports. Real estate loan officers investigate whether the house a customer wants a loan to buy is worth the selling price. These officers also want proof that the buyer will receive a clear title to the house. Loan officers usually work with a single type of loan, such as mortgages, so they can gain enough experience in their field to make correct loan decisions for their bank.

Trust officers supervise the investment of trust monies. From estates, foundations, or businesses, banks receive the power to hold and invest trust money (called a trust fund) through legal documents such as wills or deeds of trust. Trust department officers may oversee personal and corporate trusts. These officers consult with investment specialists employed by the bank and then decide the best investment for each customer's account. Trust officers are responsible for seeing that the beneficiaries (people named to receive income from the trust fund investments) receive income checks on time and that all provisions of the trust are followed.

Operations managers generally work in a bank's corporate offices and are responsible for all the information and data processing services the bank requires. These include jobs such as check processing, record keeping, and bookkeeping that are carried out using computers and other automated machinery. Operations managers also coordinate the flow of work from one bank department or branch to another.

There are many other kinds of bank managers. Among these are the bank investment managers, who are responsible for investing bank funds. Financial managers prepare and interpret financial reports for the president, the vice presidents, and the officers who supervise the departments of accounting, records, and public relations. Each branch of a parent bank is also run by a branch manager, who supervises all the operations of the branch.

Education and Training Requirements

A person must have a college education to become a bank officer or management trainee. Interested individuals should take a college preparatory program in high school with a special emphasis on mathematics. A college program in

Bank officers manage banks on various levels, or they administer financial services that the banks offer. (© Keith Dannemiller/Corbis.)

business administration, accounting, or finance will give a person a good background for bank work. Some banks prefer to hire people with graduate training in business administration or economics. Most banks have management training programs in which trainees work for a short time in a few different bank jobs. They learn the banking business and then specialize in one aspect of bank work. Some banks hold seminars or send trainees to outside classes sponsored by the American Institute of Banking, a division of the American Bankers Association. Many banks finance the education of promising people who go to school while they work for the bank.

Getting the Job

A college placement office can help a student find a job as a management trainee in a bank. Some private employment agencies also place bank personnel. Banks often advertise for trainees in newspaper classified ads and on the Internet. Many banks send personnel workers to recruit on college campuses. Candidates can also find out about openings by writing to the personnel officers of the banks in which they are interested. If applying for a banking job while in school, students can take advantage of work–study programs.

Advancement Possibilities and Employment Outlook

Many bank management trainees advance to become bank officers and managers. The competition is intense for top-level executive jobs such as treasurer or head of operations. Although only a small number of officers reach senior-level positions, many more jobs are available in middle management. Some trainees start as assistant branch managers and eventually go on to manage their own branches. Trust department trainees may assist trust officers and go on to manage several trust accounts. Many bank employees seek further education to prepare themselves for high-level jobs. For example, loan officers study real estate or business accounting. There are many advancement possibilities in banking, especially for those who continue to learn about finance.

According to the U.S. Bureau of Labor Statistics, 432,000 bank managers and officers held jobs in 2004. Employment in most all banking professions was expected to decline through the year 2014. Consolidation among banks will continue to eliminate management positions. Advances in telecommunications, the computerization of customer records, and automated credit checking systems are expected to decrease the need for loan officers as well. Nevertheless, openings for bank officers and managers will occur as experienced officers and managers retire or leave their jobs for other reasons.

Working Conditions

Working conditions vary depending on the location of the bank and the type of work performed. However, a bank's business depends on customers' impressions, so banks are usually pleasant places to work. Bank officers, such as loan and trust officers, spend their days seeing customers, doing paperwork, and attending meetings. Assistant managers of branch banks must be available to handle employees' and customers' questions while the banks are open for business. Many officers and managers do paperwork after banking hours. Most bank officers and managers work thirty-five to forty hours per week, although they must frequently bring work home with them. Also, most bank officers participate in civic functions and attend trade association meetings. This may require some overtime work. Some branch managers work irregular hours when banks are open nights or Saturdays. Bank officers and managers are under pressure to do their work accurately and efficiently and to take full responsibility for the departments or branches they manage.

Earnings and Benefits

Bank salaries vary widely from job to job. According to salary.com, the median yearly salary for an entry-level loan officer was $34,516 in 2006. Officers with experience who specialized in one type of loan or service made much more. Commercial loan officers, for instance, made a median annual salary of $53,989 in 2006, and trust officers brought in $62,292 per year. Salary.com reported that the median annual salary for bank managers was $94,037. The size of a bank significantly affects bank officers' and manager's salaries. Benefits include paid holidays and vacations, health and life insurance, and pension and profit sharing plans.

College/University Administrator

Definition and Nature of the Work

College/university administrators maintain, develop, coordinate, and oversee the various programs in public and private colleges and universities. There are many different types of administrators. They may be responsible for a variety of tasks ranging from financial aid to student activities.

The president directs the entire campus operation and oversees all other administrators. The provost handles all aspects of the academic program, including curriculum, library, research, and faculty matters. Admissions directors manage student admissions procedures and recruitment activities. They plan and pro-

Education and Training
Advanced degree

Salary
Varies—see profile

Employment Outlook
Good

duce application and admissions materials, review student applications, maintain student files, and develop the recruiting program.

Financial aid directors manage the loan programs, scholarships, and grant-in-aid programs, which provide financial assistance to students. Registrars direct class scheduling and student registration, oversee collection of tuition and fees, maintain student transcripts, and supervise commencement. The dean of students, or student affairs administrator, is responsible for overseeing extracurricular activities, student housing, and counseling services. Many colleges and universities have additional administrative positions such as director of public relations, director of alumni affairs, and chief planning officer or development officer.

Education and Training Requirements

To become a college or university administrator, a person must at minimum have a master's degree in a field such as student counseling, finance, or higher education administration. The larger and more prestigious academic institutions often require that top administrators have a Ph.D. Knowledge of computer science and data processing is helpful. Strong organizational and managerial skills as well as efficiency and decisiveness are essential characteristics for college administrators.

Getting the Job

Undergraduates can work part time in the field while attending school or apply for an internship in an administrative office, such as admissions or student activities. This experience gives them an advantage when applying for an administrative position after graduation. In most colleges only a bachelor's degree is needed for an entry-level position, such as an admissions counselor or a recruiting officer.

Advancement Possibilities and Employment Outlook

Advancement from entry-level positions depends on the size and organization of the administrative office. In smaller offices an assistant can become director after completing a graduate degree. In larger offices an administrator can advance by specializing in one area, such as foreign student admissions or minority admissions. Administrators can also advance by starting out at a lesser-known college or junior college and then moving to a larger college or university.

According to the U.S. Bureau of Labor Statistics, postsecondary education administrators held 132,000 jobs in 2004. Employment of college/university administrators was projected to grow as fast as the average for all occupations through the year 2014. Growth will likely be seen in schools that offer continuing education for adults who want to earn a degree or receive training for work. However, job availability will depend on the enrollment and financial status of individual colleges and universities.

Working Conditions

College campuses provide a pleasant setting in which to work. Administrative offices are usually large and comfortable. Unlike many who work in academics, many administrators work a twelve-month schedule and may work long hours during certain periods, such as the beginning of each semester or quarter. Some administrators, such as admissions director and dean of students, may also work some evenings and weekends. Administrators often travel to professional conferences or to other colleges. College/university administrators must have leadership skills, patience and tact in dealing with staff and students, and the ability to handle diverse personalities and unexpected situations.

Earnings and Benefits

Salaries for administrators vary widely between public and private institutions and between two- and four-year schools. Earnings also vary between administrative positions. According to the College and University Professional Association for Human Resources—as noted by the Bureau of Labor Statistics—registrars earned a median annual salary of $61,953 in 2004. Financial aid directors brought in a median annual salary of $63,130 in 2004, dean of students made $75,245, and chief development officers made $114,400. Benefits usually include paid holidays and vacations, health insurance, and retirement plans and contributions.

Where to Go for More Information

American Association of Collegiate
    Registrars and Admissions Officers
1 Dupont Circle NW, Ste. 520
Washington, DC 20036
(202) 293-9161
http://www.aacrao.org

American Association of University
    Administrators
National Office
Roberts Hall 407
Rhode Island College
Providence, RI 02908-1991
(401) 456-2808
http://www.aaua.org

College and University Professional
    Association for Human Resources
2607 Kingston Pike, Ste. 250
Knoxville, TN 37919
(865) 637-7673
http://www.cupa.org

Compensation and Benefits Analyst

Definition and Nature of the Work

To attract and keep competent employees, employers must pay salaries and provide benefits that are competitive and equitable. Compensation and benefits analysts evaluate existing and proposed jobs and classify them according to their levels of responsibility and importance to the employer. They research what comparable jobs pay and what benefits are given elsewhere and develop appropriate salary and benefit structures.

Compensation and benefits analysts work for federal, state, and local governments; school systems and universities; and medium and large businesses. Their role is particularly important in civil service systems, where they must develop compensation structures for entire government bodies, and in large firms, where they must develop salary structures and benefit plans that remain consistent throughout the entire corporation. Compensation and benefits analysts usually work in personnel departments.

A compensation and benefits analyst's job is sensitive and exacting. Compensation and benefits analysts must be familiar with laws and regulations concerning affirmative action, fair labor standards, and veterans' preference. They must know how salaries and benefits in other firms compare with the salaries and benefits of their firm or agency. They must be sure that the salaries and benefits within their firm provide incentives for hard work and long-term commitment.

Compensation and benefits analysis has become even more crucial with expanded interpretations of equal pay laws. The new concept of "comparable worth," which aims to establish the comparability (for salary purposes) of job

Education and Training
College

Salary
Median—$47,490 per year

Employment Outlook
Very good

types and job titles across industries and employers, has made compensation and benefits analysis increasingly sophisticated. Compensation and benefits analysts must have strong analytical and verbal skills as well as an understanding of how organizations function.

Education and Training Requirements

A bachelor's degree is almost always required for entry into the field of compensation and benefits analysis, although some employers may be willing to substitute professional experience for education. Employers increasingly look for additional formal education—a master's or a doctoral degree—for senior positions in compensation work. For entry-level positions there is no specific major required. However, course work in business or public or personnel administration provides good preparation for the field.

Getting the Job

Civil service systems and large companies in private industry most often hire compensation specialists. Classified advertisements in newspapers, on the Internet, and in professional journals are good sources of job leads for private sector jobs. Jobs with government agencies usually require passing a civil service exam; interested individuals should contact a federal or local branch of the Civil Service Commission for information about the exams and job openings.

Advancement Possibilities and Employment Outlook

From the entry-level position of compensation and benefits analyst, it is possible to advance to the job of compensation manager—with responsibilities for the functioning of an office or division—or to that of personnel director of an agency or firm. Many compensation analysts take an exam on the practice and theory of compensation, administered by the WorldatWork Society of Certified Professionals. Passing the exam earns the practitioner a Certified Compensation Professional (CCP) designation, which can be useful for professional advancement. Compensation analysts can also gain accreditation in the general field of personnel.

According to the U.S. Bureau of Labor Statistics, compensation and benefits analysts held ninety-nine thousand jobs in the United States in 2004. Employment of compensation and benefits analysts was expected to grow faster than the average for all occupations through the year 2014. The increasing complexity of laws and regulations covering personnel and pay practices has resulted in the expansion of in-house personnel staff with expertise in compensation, especially in large companies. Unlike other personnel positions that may be eliminated during recessionary periods, compensation analysts are considered particularly important at such times so that salaries can be adjusted and jobs can be reclassified.

Working Conditions

Compensation and benefits analysts generally work with large numbers of employees. They work a thirty-five- or forty-hour week. Occasional overtime may be required.

Earnings and Benefits

Earnings vary depending on education and experience and on the size and location of the employing company. The median annual salary for compensation and benefits analysts in 2004 was $47,490, according to the Bureau of Labor Statistics. Benefits generally include paid holidays and vacations, health and life insurance, and pension plans.

Computer and Information Systems Manager

Definition and Nature of the Work

Computer and information systems managers direct and manage various computer-related activities of a company. They construct business plans, oversee Internet and computer operations, assign projects to staff members, and direct the flow of work. Computer and information systems managers work in manufacturing, industry, government, and educational institutions. They generally are in charge of facilities that have many programmers, systems analysts, and peripheral equipment operations. They report to the top management of their organizations.

Computer and information systems managers must have general management ability as well as specific knowledge of the firm's computer systems. They must have a thorough working knowledge of programming and systems analysis. Computer and information systems managers must be able to communicate with all department heads in the company that require computer and network systems. They must be able to translate the requirements of each department into a workable computer operation. Then they must be able to instruct the information technology staff to carry out these procedures.

Computer and information managers must ensure that their departments have the necessary machines and personnel to process information as it is needed. They develop budgets for their departments and plan for new equipment purchases. Managers must keep up with new developments in computers.

Education and Training Requirements

A bachelor's degree and many years of experience are generally the minimum requirements to become a computer and information systems manager. Knowledge of programming or systems analysis is also essential. In small computer installations, people without degrees who have experience as programmers can move up to become computer and information systems managers. Some college graduates gain their experience by working as a manager's assistant. College courses in mathematics, programming, and business help students prepare for jobs in data processing. A master's in business administration (MBA) may also be necessary, especially for those who want to be a manager at a large company. Many companies have training programs for their computer personnel. The federal government also sometimes offers training to people hired in lower level computer jobs.

Getting the Job

Computer and information systems managers usually are chosen from the ranks of programmers and systems analysts or are brought in from outside the company. A college placement office can help students find a job in an information technology company that has an executive training program. If interested individuals have suitable experience, they should check newspaper classified ads and Internet sites for managerial jobs. Employment agencies that specialize in placing professional workers may offer job leads. In addition, candidates can contact computer manufacturers and organizations with large computer centers. Insurance companies, utilities, and universities and colleges often have sizable installations. If a person is interested in a government job, he or she should apply to take the necessary civil service examination.

Education and Training
College plus training

Salary
Median—$92,570 per year

Employment Outlook
Very good

Advancement Possibilities and Employment Outlook

Information technology is becoming more and more important in business. For this reason, computer and information systems managers are often promoted to the top management of their organizations. For example, managers can advance to the position of vice president of information systems. Computer and information systems managers also may be given management jobs outside the field of data processing. Computer and information systems management prepares them well for the planning and organization needed by successful managers.

According to the U.S. Bureau of Labor Statistics, 280,000 computer and information systems managers were employed in 2004. Employment of computer and information systems managers was predicted to grow faster than the average for all occupations through the year 2014. The use of computers in business and government will continue to increase. Qualified people will be needed to run the growing number of computers, computer networks, and Internet operations. However, there will be stiff competition for computer and information systems management jobs. Those with advanced education or experience in specific types of computer applications will have the best chance of employment. The employment outlook is very good for skilled people who keep up with new developments in this ever-changing field.

Working Conditions

Computer and information systems managers usually work in offices close to computer rooms. Much of their work is done independently. They are often the main link between computer personnel and the rest of their organization. They work under some pressure to deliver information technology solutions that suit their firms' needs. Computer and information technology managers work forty hours per week and can expect to work extra hours to meet project deadlines.

Earnings and Benefits

The Bureau of Labor Statistics reported that the median yearly wage for computer and information systems managers in 2004 was $92,570. According to the "Computerworld Salary Survey 2005" (*Computerworld*, October 24, 2005), the median yearly wages for mid-level computer and information systems managers varied depending on the type of work. Network managers, for instance, made a median annual wage of $68,822 in 2005, whereas applications development managers made $100,841. In a very large company a manager who supervises many staff members may earn considerably more. Benefits usually include paid vacations and holidays, health and life insurance, and pension plans.

Computer Consultant

Definition and Nature of the Work

The widespread use of computers in businesses of all sizes has created a need for computer consultants. Companies that are large enough to computerize their operations but too small to need a computer specialist on staff usually hire computer consultants on a contract or retainer basis.

Most computer consultants work independently, although some are employed by consulting firms. Their duties vary according to the needs of their client companies. A computer consultant might spend only a few hours helping a dentist select and learn to operate a small office system. For a larger company, the consultant might spend several months establishing a complicated database, creating a network of small and large computers, writing user manuals, designing a Web site, or conducting computer training classes. Consultants also may recommend and design security features for a computer system. Computer consultants can be software programmers, hardware system installers, networking specialists, database specialists, systems analysts, or a combination of the above.

Education and Training Requirements

Most computer consultants are college graduates. They may have degrees in computer science or data processing. Experts recommend that aspiring consultants gain experience as staff computer specialists before working independently.

Getting the Job

Interested individuals can apply directly to computer consulting firms. If someone wants to work independently, he or she can advertise in computer magazines or send a resume directly to firms that potentially require the services of a computer consultant.

Advancement Possibilities and Employment Outlook

According to the 2004–14 employment projections by the U.S. Bureau of Labor Statistics, the employment of computer and other technical consultants was expected to grow much faster than the average for all occupations through the year 2014. Both the use of computers and the need for sound computer advice are expected to grow. However, computer consultants face competition from computer manufacturers and salespeople as well as from other consultants. Moreover, many computer stores are starting to offer free consulting services to attract buyers. Consultants who remain alert to trends in computer use and are flexible enough to adjust their services accordingly will have the best chances for success.

Working Conditions

Consultants may have to work long hours, because clients usually need their systems installed or upgraded quickly. Assignments may last from several days to several months. Self-employed consultants

Self-employed computer consultants enjoy independence and diversity in their jobs, but they may not have a steady flow of work. (© Royalty-Free/Corbis.)

Education and Training
College

Salary
Median—$85,904 per year

Employment Outlook
Excellent

enjoy independence and diversity in their jobs, but they may not have a steady flow of work.

Computer consultants must have good communication skills so that they can identify their clients' needs quickly and explain their recommendations clearly.

Earnings and Benefits

Computer consultants' earnings vary greatly depending on experience, the complexity of their task, and specialty. According to the "Computerworld Salary Survey 2005" (*Computerworld*, October 24, 2005), the median hourly rate for consultants was $61 in 2005. The median annual base pay rate for consultants working at a consulting firm was $85,904.

Computer Database Administrator

Education and Training
College

Salary
Median—$60,650 per year

Employment Outlook
Excellent

Definition and Nature of the Work

Computer database administrators design, write, and take care of computer database systems so that the right person can get the right information at the right time. A database is simply a collection of computer files full of information that a company may wish to track. This information may include customer addresses, inventory, and payroll figures. A database administrator might set up and organize a database or reorganize an existing database. To organize a database, an administrator writes precise instructions for the computer. These instructions, called a computer program, tell the computer how to collect and sort data and how to give data to the people who need them. Database administrators also write programs to perform queries to extract useful information and to produce reports as necessary. The database administrator also watches over the system to ensure that users do not tamper with the information or the structure of the database. In cases where the database system contains private information about a business or its customers, the database administrator makes sure that only people with authorization are allowed access to confidential information. They may also design programs to protect the database from computer hackers or to weed out problems in the database.

The database administrator makes current and accurate information available to all branches and personnel at all times. Computer database administrators can use the database to help management make informed decisions. For instance, they can create computer models from the database system that will predict the results of a product design change, a move to a new location, or a change to the billing process. Centralized control by a computer database administrator avoids the problem of missing or duplicate information and simplifies the updating of files.

Education and Training Requirements

Employers hiring database administrators look for candidates with formal training in computer science. Educational requirements usually include at least a bachelor's degree in computer science, systems science, telecommunications, or a related field of study. High school students interested in pursuing this type of work should study mathematics, computer science, and physics.

Candidates for jobs in this field may also need specific training certification in various networking specialties. For example, Microsoft Corporation has established a training program in which candidates can earn a Microsoft Certified Database Administrator (MCDBA) certificate after passing a series of tests that cover all aspects of planning, setting up, maintaining, and using a Microsoft SQL Server.

Getting the Job

Newspapers and Internet job sites carry advertisements every day for computer database administrators. Many employment agencies specialize in placing applicants in computer-related positions.

Advancement Possibilities and Employment Outlook

According to the Bureau of Labor Statistics, 104,000 database administrators were employed in the United States in 2004. Employment of computer database administrators was expected to grow much faster than the average for all occupations through the year 2014. Computer database administrators may be promoted to higher-level jobs in large companies with data processing departments. If they demonstrate skills in managing people as well as database systems, they can move into executive-level jobs in these areas and manage groups of other database administrators. Because of the importance of tracking information accurately in companies, they can eventually become the chief information officer in their company. With rapid increase in networking—linking computers together—more job openings will become available for computer database administrators.

Working Conditions

Computer database administrators can work in any business that uses computer systems. For example, they may work in large industries with enormous database systems or in small offices where the database may contain only the company's payroll and customer address list.

Computer database administrators work a forty-hour week. However, they may have to work substantial amounts of overtime, which may or may not be paid. Database administrators may work on weekends to perform routine maintenance and create system backups. They also have to be present whenever there is a problem with the database.

Earnings and Benefits

The salary range of a computer database administrator can vary widely, depending on the size of the database system. The Bureau of Labor Statistics reported that the median yearly wage for database administrators in 2004 was $60,650. According to the "Computerworld Salary Survey 2005" (*Computerworld*, October 24, 2005), the median yearly salary for a database administrator was $81,152 in 2005. Those in management jobs earn more.

Most companies offer attractive benefit plans, including medical insurance, vacations, savings or profit sharing plans, and pension plans.

Where to Go for More Information

Association for Computing Machinery
1515 Broadway
New York, NY 10036
(212) 626-0500
http://www.acm.org

Computing Technology Industry Association
1815 South Meyers Rd., Ste. 300
Oakbrook Terrace, IL 60181
(630) 678-8300
http://www.comptia.org

IEEE Computer Society
1730 Massachusetts Ave. NW
Washington, DC 20036
(202) 371-0101
http://www.computer.org

Institute for Certification of Computing Professionals
2350 Devon Ave., Ste. 115
Des Plaines, IL 60018
(847) 299-4227
http://www.iccp.org

Computer Network Technician

Education and Training
College

Salary
Median—$60,600 per year

Employment Outlook
Excellent

Definition and Nature of the Work

Computer network technicians build and maintain computer networks used by business, education, government, and health-care institutions. Networks linking desktop computers allow users to send electronic mail (e-mail) and to share data, computer applications, and Internet connections. As more institutions establish computer networks, the demand for skilled computer network technicians will grow.

Computer network technicians, which are also known as computer network engineers or network specialists, must know current standards and terminology used for local area networks (LANs) and larger wide area networks (WANs). They often help plan their employers' computer networks and then implement the planned networks. Most commonly, network technicians administer existing computer networks and troubleshoot problems as they arise.

Planning a computer network entails analyzing costs and needs of a company and then selecting the appropriate media (e.g., twisted-pair copper wire, coaxial cable, fiber-optic cable, wireless) for a given situation. Computer network technicians may also recommend appropriate network addressing systems, appropriate layouts for various network configurations, and appropriate connection devices.

Implementing a computer network entails designing and following administrative plans to meet specific needs such as account management and security. Much of the work involved in implementing a network consists of installing, configuring, and resolving conflicts among different hardware used in the network, such as network adapters.

Administering and troubleshooting a network entails identifying and resolving network performance problems. Technicians identify problems common to

Computer network technicians plan or design, implement, and troubleshoot computer networks for businesses and other institutions. (Photograph by Kelly A. Quin. Thomson Gale. Reproduced by permission.)

components of the network, such as cards, cables, and other related hardware. They also establish disaster recovery plans for various situations if the network were to malfunction.

In addition to knowing relevant computer and networking terminology, protocols, and hardware, computer network technicians must have mastered necessary software, including different operating systems such as Novell NetWare, Unix, and Windows. They must also understand basic network architecture models such as peer-to-peer and client-server.

Computer network technicians need self-discipline and the ability to balance a variety of tasks. A technician must be able to spend long hours at a keyboard debugging a program and be dexterous and patient enough to weave a complex web of wires.

Because network technicians often provide technical support to network users, they must be able to help nontechnical people understand and use complex equipment and software. In addition to technical expertise, employers often require network technicians to excel in verbal and written communication and to have good interpersonal skills.

Education and Training

Employers hiring computer network technicians look for candidates with formal training in computer science. Educational requirements usually include at least a bachelor's degree in computer science, electrical engineering, telecommunications, or a related field of study. High school students interested in pursuing this type of work should study mathematics, computer science, and physics.

Candidates for jobs in this field may also need specific training certification in various networking specialties. For example, Novell Software has established a training program in which candidates earn certification as a Certified NetWare Engineer (CNE) after passing a series of seven tests that cover all aspects of planning, installing, maintaining, and communicating between networks using the Novell NetWare operating system. A consortium of computer technology companies including Hewlett–Packard and Cisco Systems offers an examination and certification program, awarding successful candidates the title Certified Network Expert (CNX). Other manufacturers and industry groups offer certification programs for specific network specialties.

Getting the Job

Computer network technicians are employed by businesses or institutions that operate a computer network or by consulting firms hired by an institution to plan, implement, and/or maintain a network. Candidates can find listings for these jobs on a variety of Internet sites, in trade publications, and in newspaper classified ads. Colleges and trade schools preparing students for CNX or another type of certification may also provide job placement services for successful students.

Advancement Possibilities and Employment Outlook

According to the U.S. Bureau of Labor Statistics, 231,000 network technicians were employed in 2004. Employment of qualified computer network specialists was expected to grow much faster than the average for all occupations through the year 2014. The number of computer network users will likely increase, and the underlying technology will evolve. Skilled technicians who keep their skills current will be valuable employees to the businesses, institutions, or consulting firms who hire them.

In a typical career path, a computer network technician could start out as a basic troubleshooter or equipment servicer. The technician would gain more responsibility as the existing network grows. Adding CNE and/or other certifications would qualify the technician for a position as a network manager.

Technicians with a knack for communicating with nontechnical associates may advance to careers as network trainers. To teach the rapidly evolving technologies, network trainers must continually update their knowledge.

Working Conditions

Computer network technicians usually work in clean, well-lighted office buildings. The nature of their work may require them to spend time working in a variety of locations, solving problems with individual computers or other parts of the network such as servers or connecting cables.

The growing importance of computer networks to business, education, and health-care institutions demands that technicians often work long hours, including weekends and holidays, troubleshooting and/or setting up needed extensions to their employers' networks. Technicians can face fatigue and stress-related illness. They also may encounter eye and back strain along with other physical problems associated with prolonged computer use.

Earnings and Benefits

Computer network technicians' salaries vary widely based on experience, certification, and place of employment. The Bureau of Labor Statistics reported that the median annual wage for network technicians in 2004 was $60,600. According to the "Computerworld Salary Survey 2005" (*Computerworld*, October 24, 2005), the median yearly wage for a network engineer was $70,365 in 2005. Those in management jobs earn more. Because qualified technicians are in such demand, employers offer competitive benefits packages as well as incentive bonuses.

Computer Programmer

Education and Training
College

Salary
Median—$62,890 per year

Employment Outlook
Fair

Definition and Nature of the Work

Computer programmers write the step-by-step instructions that direct computers to process information. These instructions, or programs, tell the computer what to do in a series of logical steps. Programmers work on a wide range of projects. The kind of work a programmer does depends on the employer. Programmers work in manufacturing, industry, engineering, government offices, hospitals, and educational institutions.

Programmers receive detailed job descriptions that identify the goal of the program. Programmers then may prepare systems flow charts that show diagrammatically how information will flow through the computer and its peripheral, or related, equipment. If much creativity and expertise are demanded at this step, systems analysts or computer software engineers may prepare the systems flow charts. In most medium to large computer installations, programmers receive their instructions from systems analysts or computer software engineers.

When the preliminary stages are completed, programmers write the actual program using special computer languages. Different computer languages are used for different applications. For instance, HTML and XML are useful when creating Web applications, and COBOL is useful for business applications. Since most programs are long and complex, they must be tested to see whether they run as expected. This step is called debugging. If the test run is not satisfactory, the programmers examine the program for errors in logic and data and make corrections or report the problem to a software engineer. It may take a few days to write a simple program, while more than a year may be required to develop a sophisticated one.

Most programmers are involved in applications programming. They work on specific tasks that have a direct application, such as designing accounting procedures. Applications programmers usually specialize in either writing programs just for one professional field, such as science or business. Applications programmers meet with clients and designers to understand the scope of the project before they begin to write the code. They work alone or in teams depending on the budget, deadline, and the size of the project.

Systems programmers write programs to maintain and control systems software that may run systems such as a large office's computer network. They would, for instance, write a program that enables a new printer to work with an old computer. They generally work for computer manufacturers or for companies that have large computer installations. Some are involved in developing new computer languages. Computer software engineers, who are very experienced programmers, design and implement complex programs from scratch. They are familiar with computer hardware design, memory, and the inner workings of computers.

Education and Training Requirements

Educational requirements usually include at least a bachelor's degree in computer science, mathematics, or information systems, as well as knowledge of the major programming languages. In addition, employers often require that new hires know how to work with database systems such as Oracle and Sybase. National certification courses are offered for most major computer languages, including C++, Java, and XML. Private companies will also offer certification on their newer programming languages and software. Certification on a language increases a programmer's job prospects, because it proves to an employer that a programmer knows that language.

Sometimes employers will hire inexperienced college graduates who show promise and send them to special computer training schools to update their skills at the company's expense. Larger firms may have their own formal training programs. It usually takes a year or more before new programmers are capable of working without supervision. Programmers usually continue their training for the rest of their careers as new programming languages and technologies continually arrive on the marketplace.

High school students interested in pursuing this type of work should study mathematics, computer science, and physics. They should also take computer programming courses in school or learn computer languages in their spare time.

Getting the Job

Many job openings for computer programmers are listed on the Internet and in the classified sections of newspapers. College placement bureaus and employment agencies can also help a person enter the field. Another way to get a job as a computer programmer is through direct application. If candidates want to work for the government, they should apply to take the necessary civil service exam.

Advancement Possibilities and Employment Outlook

Experienced programmers can advance to various supervisory positions that concentrate on either administrative or operational areas. Those interested in the analytical aspects of programming can become systems analysts. Additional education and training may be required for this position.

According to the U.S. Bureau of Labor Statistics, 455,000 people were employed as computer programmers in the United States in 2004. Employment of computer programmers, however, was expected to grow more slowly than average for all occupations through the year 2014. Sophisticated computer software now exists that automatically writes basic code and software routines. This software allows analysts and computer engineers to design and write programs without help from computer programmers. Many low and mid-level computer-programming jobs have also been outsourced to India, China, and Eastern Europe where wages are lower. Jobs for programmers in the United States should be available in data-processing service firms and computer consulting businesses.

Working Conditions

Computer programmers work in especially clean, comfortable surroundings. Most programmers work a forty-hour week that at times includes evenings and weekends. Often programmers work long hours to meet deadlines. They are expected to work both independently and as part of a team. Programmers who work for a consulting company may have to travel to a client's location to work. Because they spend all day at a computer, programmers are susceptible to eye strain, back problems, and injuries such as carpel tunnel syndrome.

Earnings and Benefits

Computer programmers generally earn salaries much higher than those earned by nonsupervisory workers in other fields. The Bureau of Labor Statistics reported that the median annual wage for computer programmers in 2004 was $62,890. According to the "Computerworld Salary Survey 2005" (*Computerworld*, October 24, 2005), the median yearly wage for a computer programmer/analyst was $67,685 in 2005. Benefits vary according to individual employer, but most programmers receive paid vacations, sick leave, and insurance plans. Some companies offer profit sharing and pension plans.

Where to Go for More Information

Association for Computing Machinery
1515 Broadway
New York, NY 10036
(212) 626-0500
http://www.acm.org

IEEE Computer Society
1730 Massachusetts Ave. NW
Washington, DC 20036
(202) 371-0101
http://www.computer.org

Institute for Certification of Computing
  Professionals
2350 Devon Ave., Ste. 115
Des Plaines, IL 60018
(847) 2899-4227
http://www.iccp.org

Computer Security Specialist

Definition and Nature of the Work

As computer networks grow and more sensitive data is stored on computer files, the need for trained, skilled computer security specialists will also grow. Computer security specialists help businesses, educational institutions, and government organizations to control access to their computer networks and protect important data stored there. This is accomplished through a variety of means.

Computer security specialists, who are also known as information security specialists, design and implement network control mechanisms that serve to control users' access to a computer network through such processes as firewalls. Computer security specialists also implement application access controls, such as password authentication, that keep unauthorized users from accessing a particular computer or network or program. Computer security specialists take steps to deny hackers access to a system and set up programs that detect hackers who do intrude onto a system. Computer security specialists also may be responsible for controlling site-specific physical access to computers.

Computer security specialists work with employees at all levels of an organization. Managers communicate the organization's needs to computer security specialists. Management and security specialists then work together to balance the organization's security needs with the security system's ease of use. Computer security specialists also communicate procedures and passwords to users of the systems. This entails keeping up-to-date lists of users and passwords as well as helping workers who have forgotten passwords or accidentally violated security procedures. Computer security specialists monitor who is using a computer network. They also send reports of use to various members of the organization for verification. Finally, computer security specialists are responsible for keeping accurate and up-to-date backup files of all important data shared on a computer network.

Education and Training Requirements

People interested in work as computer security specialists need some training beyond high school. A bachelor's degree in computer science is highly recommended. Computer security specialists must be familiar with a variety of networking technologies, such as TCP/IP, Windows NT, and Unix. They must have a thorough understanding of computer programming, and they should be trained in risk management. Computer security specialists must also be able to communicate technical information clearly and concisely.

The International Information Systems Security Certification Consortium, a nonprofit corporation, awards a Certified Information Systems Security Professional (CISSP) accreditation to individuals who pass an exam on computer security procedures. Such accreditations improve a potential employee's prospects greatly.

Getting the Job

Trained computer security specialists are hired by corporations and institutions needing their services and by independent consulting firms. Jobs are posted on the Internet by groups such as the

Computer security specialists help control access to computer systems. They design and implement mechanisms and programs that deny access to hackers and other unauthorized users. (Photograph by Kelly A. Quin. Thomson Gale. Reproduced by permission.)

Computer Security Institute (CSI) and the Information Systems Auditing and Control Association (ISACA). Positions also are advertised in trade publications.

Advancement Possibilities and Employment Outlook

According to the U.S. Bureau of Labor Statistics, employment of computer security specialists was expected to grow faster than the average for all occupations through the year 2014. Although most organizations using computer networks have security needs, the number of individuals trained to meet those needs, in each case, is relatively small. Reliable, highly skilled, and well-trained individuals will be in great demand to meet those needs.

Working Conditions

Computer security specialists work in pleasant, well-maintained offices and they usually work a forty-hour week or more. They may work unpredictable hours and be on constant call to handle emergencies. Because of the high level of responsibility, the job can be very stressful. Computer security specialists face the same risks as other computer workers, including eyestrain, carpal tunnel syndrome, and backache.

Where to Go for More Information

Computing Technology Industry
   Association
1815 S. Meyers Rd., Ste. 300
Oakbrook Terrace, IL 60181
(630) 678-8300
http://www.comptia.com

IEEE Computer Society
1730 Massachusetts Ave. NW
Washington, DC 20036
(202) 371-0101
http://www.computer.org

Earnings and Benefits

The Bureau of Labor Statistics regards computer security specialists as a type of network and computer systems administrator. In their 2006–07 *Occupational Outlook Handbook*, the Bureau reported that the median annual wage for all network and computer systems administrators in 2004 was $58,190. According to the "Computerworld Salary Survey 2005" (*Computerworld*, October 24, 2005), the median yearly wage for an information security specialist in 2005 was $81,035.

Because they are in such demand, computer security specialists can expect attractive benefits packages from corporations and consulting firms, although the nature of the work makes it difficult for computer specialists to take advantage of vacations and time off.

Computer Software Documentation Writer

Education and Training
College

Salary
Median—$53,490 per year

Employment Outlook
Very good

Definition and Nature of the Work

A computer software documentation writer is the most common type of technical writer. Computer software documentation writers research and write the instructional guides, online and desktop help guides, reference manuals, and job aids for computer software. Software is a term for the computer programs that run on a computer. The documentation ranges from descriptions of complicated systems software installations to an on-screen help guide for a word-processing program. Software documentation writers try to make sure that the documentation is clear enough to help the beginner and detailed enough to be useful for advanced users. The increasing trend toward more types of new and sophisticated software necessitates writers who can produce manuals and help guides in very short time frames.

To prepare documents, software documentation writers work closely with software developers. The writers compose the manuals in a logical format on word processors. They often are required to find graphics, pictures, or illustrations to go along with the documentation. Writers are usually responsible for posting documentation on the Web or directly into a computer program as well. As such, they may need to know basic programming languages. In some small offices they may prepare a print publication by using a desktop publishing software package or electronic typesetting.

Large organizations may have several levels of software documentation writers. Those at the top are the senior writers. In addition to writing documents, senior writers may manage the activities of several other writers. Copy editors check the text for grammar, correct spelling, information accuracy, and punctuation. Copy editors also make sure that the usage of computer terms is correct. Depending on their technical knowledge, copy editors may check the technical content of the document. Production editors oversee the preparation of the camera-ready copy for the printer. They work with writers, artists, customers, and sometimes the printer and electronic typesetters to design the document. In smaller companies, the software documentation writer may perform all these tasks.

Computer software documentation writers make sure that instructional guides and reference manuals for computer hardware and software are clear enough to help beginning users and detailed enough for advanced users. *(© Martha Tabor/Working Images Photographs. Reproduced by permission.)*

Education and Training Requirements

Most software documentation/technical writers have at least a bachelor's degree in technical writing, communications, journalism, or English. Some companies now require technical writers to have a technical degree and experience in programs and programming languages, such as RoboHelp or XML, that are typically used by software documentation writers. Extra courses in book design, page layout, and readability requirements are extremely helpful. Many companies send their writers to seminars and courses for this training.

Software documentation writers must have a good technical understanding of the system with which they are working. They need excellent communication skills to gather useful information from the developer and to present the information clearly to the user. In addition, writers must have a knowledge of book design, page layout, readability requirements, and graphics.

Getting the Job

Companies employ writers either directly or on a consulting basis. Consultants work for an agency that signs a contract with the firm that needs the writer. This contract specifies the amount of money that the writer will make and the length of the assignment. For example, a writer may be employed only until the documentation is delivered to the customer. However, the writer is still employed by the agency, which usually finds the writer a new assignment quickly. Prospective writers can check the classified sections of their local newspaper for job openings.

Advancement Possibilities and Employment Outlook

The next step up from a software documentation level is usually a supervisory position. Writers can also go to other departments in a company to use their communication and organizational skills. According to the U.S. Bureau of Labor

Statistics, fifty thousand technical writers were employed in the United States in 2004. Due to expected increase in computer applications, employment of software documentation writers was expected to increase faster than the average for all occupations through the year 2014.

Working Conditions

Most software documentation writers work in a pleasant atmosphere in an office with high technology equipment. The hours are normally advertised as nine to five. When there are deadlines, writers can expect to be asked to work overtime. Because software documentation writer positions are usually management positions that are exempt from the requirements of the Fair Labor Standards Act, company policy will determine if this overtime is paid or unpaid.

Where to Go for More Information

Institute for the Certification of Computer Professionals
2350 E. Devon Avenue, Ste. 115
Des Plaines, IL 60018-4610
(847) 299-4227
http://www.iccp.org

Society for Technical Communications
901 N. Stuart St., Ste. 904
Arlington, VA 22203
(703) 522-4114
http://www.stc.org

Earnings and Benefits

Technical writers made an average annual salary of $53,490 in 2004, the Bureau of Labor Statistics reported. According to the Society for Technical Communicators, entry-level technical writers made a median annual wage of $42,500 in 2004. Writers who are directly employed by a corporation full time will receive vacations and benefits. Consultants are paid at a daily or hourly rate, which can be substantial. However, consultants normally must supply their own benefits, which can be very expensive. In addition, if an agency finds the writer a job, the agency can collect a flat fee or a percentage of the salary from either the writer or the business that hires the writer.

Computer Software Engineer

Education and Training
College

Salary
Median—$80,519 per year

Employment Outlook
Excellent

Definition and Nature of the Work

Computer software engineers develop and maintain computer software programs, which are coded instructions that tell the computer what to do in logical steps. Software engineers work on a wide range of projects. They work in manufacturing, industry, engineering, government offices, and educational institutions. Sometimes they work on improving computer systems already in use. When asked to develop a program, a software engineer would first analyze the task and apply techniques of computer science, engineering, and mathematical analysis to come up with the best solution. The software engineer would then prepare systems flow charts that show diagrammatically how information would flow through the computer and its peripheral equipment to get the job done. Finally, they would create an outline of the actual program. In a large organization, such as a computer software company, computer engineers would instruct computer programmers to write the actual code that makes up the program and intercede only when the programmers have a problem. Once the program has been developed, the software engineer may test it for problems and examine it for errors in logic or data. Some programs require days to write, while others may require a year or so.

Software engineers generally fall into two camps—computer applications software engineers and computer systems software engineers. Computer applications software engineers develop applications programs that have a specific task, such as controlling a robot arm in a factory. They use different programming languages for different tasks. C and C++ are useful for programs used by scientists, whereas Java is useful for Web applications. Applications software engineers meet with clients and designers to understand the scope of the project before they begin to design a program. They work alone or in teams, depending on the budget, deadline, and the size of the project.

Computer systems software engineers develop the software necessary to run computer systems. They design the software around a client's present and future needs. In a large company they may coordinate each of a department's needs. A systems software engineer may, for instance, design a program that links the inventory systems to the accounting department so that changes in inventory are automatically updated in the accounting records. These engineers typically work for computer design firms or manufacturers that configure, implement, and install computer systems for other companies. Systems software engineers will work with a team of engineering, marketing, manufacturing, and design people to set up a system for the client company.

Education and Training Requirements

Most employers require that computer software engineers have a college education in computer science or software engineering. For more demanding jobs, a graduate degree is preferred. Knowledge of the major computer languages is a must. National certification courses are offered for most major computer languages, including C++, Java, and XML.

Sometimes employers will hire inexperienced college graduates who show promise and train them further at the company's expense. It usually takes a year or more before new programmers are capable of working without supervision. Programmers usually continue their training for the rest of their careers as new programming languages and technologies continually arrive on the marketplace.

High school students interested in pursuing this type of work should study mathematics, computer science, and physics. They should also take computer-programming courses in school or learn computer languages in their spare time. When in college, students should try to gain experience by getting an internship with software engineers.

Those interested in becoming a computer software engineer must be analytical and detail oriented. They must be good at solving logic problems. Because they often supervise programmers and work with team members, software engineers should be able to communicate effectively.

Getting the Job

A good way to find a job as a computer software engineer is to contact the larger computer manufacturers and consulting firms. The federal government has computer systems in operation all over the country. If candidates are interested in a government job, they should apply to take the necessary civil service examination. College placement offices can help graduating students in contacting employers. Classified ads in newspapers and trade journals and Internet job banks are other sources of jobs.

Advancement Possibilities and Employment Outlook

Entry-level software engineers will likely spend their time testing and verifying programs in development. With experience, they will be asked to design and develop software on their own. Those who show management abilities may become department supervisors and managers. Some experienced software engineers start their own computer firms.

According to the U.S. Bureau of Labor Statistics, eight hundred thousand people worked as software engineers in 2004. Employment was expected to grow much faster than the average through the year 2014. New openings will occur as businesses continue to streamline and incorporate new technologies into their computer systems. Software engineers who can develop Internet applications will be in especially strong demand as the Web continues to expand into all aspects of American life. The rapid growth of computer centers that sell computer services to other businesses will also provide jobs.

Working Conditions

Computer software engineers work in clean, comfortable surroundings. Most work a forty-hour week that at times includes evenings and weekends. Often they work long hours to meet deadlines. They are expected to work both independently and as part of a team. They meet with many people to define problems, discuss solutions, and explain new programs. Software engineers who work for a consulting or computer design company may have to travel to a client's location to work. Because they spend all day at a computer, they are susceptible to eye strain, back problems, and injuries such as carpel tunnel syndrome.

Earnings and Benefits

The Bureau of Labor Statistics reported that the median annual wage in 2004 for computer applications software engineers was $74,980, and for computer systems software engineers, it was $79,740. According to the "Computerworld Salary Survey 2005" (*Computerworld*, October 24, 2005), the median yearly wage for computer software engineers in 2005 was $80,519. Benefits generally include paid holidays and vacations, sick leave, and health insurance.

Where to Go for More Information

Association for Computing Machinery
1515 Broadway
New York, NY 10036
(212) 626-0500
http://www.acm.org

IEEE Computer Society
1730 Massachusetts Ave. NW
Washington, DC 20036
(202) 371-0101
http://www.computer.org

Institute for Certification of Computing
    Professionals
2350 Devon Ave., Ste. 115
Des Plaines, IL 60018
(847) 2899-4227
http://www.iccp.org

Society for Information Management
401 N. Michigan Ave.
Chicago, IL 60611
(312) 527-6734
http://www.simnet.org

Computer Support Specialist

Definition and Nature of the Work

Computer support specialists help people with computer problems. Some computer support specialists called help-desk technicians field phone calls or e-mails or make house calls for people who are having difficulty with a particular piece of computer hardware or software. Most of these people who need help have no technical expertise. The support specialist asks the user to describe the problem as well as the commands that were entered or steps taken that led up to the problem. The support specialist may then repeat those steps on his or her own computer to try to duplicate the problem. If the problem was caused by user error, the specialist explains how the problem occurred and how to fix it. If the problem is due to a fault with the software or hardware, the specialist tries to determine the cause of the problem. This may require consulting with supervisors or computer programmers. Once the cause of the problem has been determined, the specialist walks the user through the steps required to fix it.

Other computer support specialists known as technical support specialists provide support to people in the information processing department of a company. In addition to troubleshooting problems, they may be responsible for the operation of the company's computer systems. They may assign work to employees in the department and determine the priorities of various tasks. They may look over computer programs to make sure they are installed properly and are compatible with existing programs. They may look over projects to make sure they are completed properly and meet the company's goals. They may also evaluate computer systems to see if they need to be expanded or upgraded. Technical support specialists may also modify software produced by other computer firms to meet the needs of the company.

Still other support specialists specialize in setting up computer systems that are delivered to customers. This includes installing the operating system (the program that tells the computer how to run software programs loaded onto it) and any software the client will need. The support specialist may also train personnel at the client's office to use the computer system and answer questions about getting started with the system. A support specialist may be assigned to user support for a particular client, taking all calls from that client to resolve problems that arise.

All computer support positions require strong analytical thinking and problem-solving abilities. Support specialists must write technical reports about the problems they encounter. Computer programmers use these reports to modify existing products or to help avoid similar problems when designing new products. Support specialists must deal with both inexperienced users and computer-savvy programmers or software designers. They must be able to reduce technical information to simple language.

Education and Training Requirements

Most employers require that computer support specialists have at least some college education. College programs in math and sciences, particularly computer sciences, are valuable, as are courses that develop communication skills. There are no courses specifically devoted to technical support because the technology changes too quickly and individual products require different knowledge bases. Most firms that make computer software or hardware train employees to provide support for each of their products.

High school students interested in pursuing this type of work should study mathematics, computer science, and physics. They should also take computer programming courses in school or study computers and computer languages in their spare time.

Getting the Job

Almost all computer hardware or software companies maintain their own in-house technical support staff. Often this is a basic entry-level position within the company. Large companies that use computers extensively may also have an in-house support group. Support positions are often advertised in local newspapers as well as with career placement offices at local schools. Someone working for a company that has an in-house support staff might speak to the personnel department about the possibility of transferring to such a position. The company may pay for the cost of training or provide its own training program.

Advancement Possibilities and Employment Outlook

According to the U.S. Bureau of Labor Statistics, some 518,000 computer support specialists were employed in the United States in 2004. Employment of computer support specialists was expected to increase faster than the average for all occupations through the year 2014. Although many help-desk technician jobs are being outsourced overseas to countries such as India and Eastern Europe, developments in new technology and the need for in-house technical support staffs will create many new jobs in the United States. Technical support specialists may go on to supervisory positions in which they oversee the work of a support staff and handle more complicated problems. With additional training or education, a support specialist may pursue a career as a quality assurance engineer who tests computer programs for problems, or designs software to perform such tests. Other career paths that require additional training include software engineer and systems analyst.

Working Conditions

Support specialists usually work a standard forty-hour week in an office environment. They may have to work evenings or weekends to provide timely support to users. Technical support specialists who work with a particular client may have to travel to the client's place of business. This may mean working overtime or irregular hours. The job often involves working with frustrated users who do not understand the technology. This requires patience and the ability to work under stress.

Earnings and Benefits

The Bureau of Labor Statistics reported that the median annual wage for computer support specialists in 2004 was $40,430. The "Computerworld Salary Survey 2005" (*Computerworld*, October 24, 2005) gave a higher figure, reporting that the median yearly wage for a computer support specialist was $47,464 in 2005. Because most support jobs are with established companies, benefits include paid vacations, medical benefits, and retirement packages.

Computer Systems Analyst

Definition and Nature of the Work

Computer systems analysts analyze business or scientific tasks and plan and develop the hardware systems and software that allow a computer to complete these tasks. These analysts, sometimes called systems analysts, may also work on improving computer systems already in use. They are employed by a wide variety of organizations, including businesses, universities, hospitals, and government agencies. Consulting firms that contract to develop new computer systems also employ systems analysts.

A typical type of problem for a computer systems analyst would be to develop software for a new computerized inventory system used by a large retail store. The analyst first discusses the current system with managers to establish what the new system should do. The analyst then breaks the system down into steps and collects information about what has to happen at each of these stages. The systems analyst uses cost accounting, mathematical modeling, and sampling techniques to plan a new system that will best keep track of the store's stock. The analyst then describes the new system to management and makes any necessary changes. After the system has been accepted, the analyst then prepares specifications, process diagrams, and system flow charts. These charts and diagrams are instructions that tell computer programmers how to program the computer to operate the system. The analyst then explains the system to the people who will be using it and decides on any computer hardware and additional software that is required to run the system. If a complex program is needed for the system, the analyst may enlist the help of a computer software engineer to design and write the program.

For systems already in operation, analysts work to develop more efficient or faster procedures. They also modify systems when changes are made in the task the computer has to complete. Computer systems analysts can develop systems to handle billing and payrolls, predict future sales, or build rockets. Because systems problems are so diverse, many analysts specialize in either business, engineering, or scientific applications. All analysts must keep up to date with current data processing methods, programming languages, and machines.

Education and Training Requirements

Most employers require that computer systems analysts have a college education. Many prefer an undergraduate degree in computer science or related subjects. A background in accounting and business management or even a master's in business administration (MBA) is helpful for those interested in business applications. Scientific organizations may require courses in physical science, mathematics, or engineering. Work in very specialized fields, such as scientific research, requires a graduate degree or training in the field. A knowledge of one or more computer languages is very valuable. Many

Computer systems analysts will be in great demand due to advances in telecommunications technology and scientific research. (© Chris Jones/Corbis.)

colleges, vocational schools, and computer companies offer training in computer science, computer programming, and data processing.

Many systems analysts have transferred into this field from other occupations, especially computer programming. Increasingly companies are looking to hire programmer–analysts, who can both come up with solutions to computer problems and write software. Programmers usually continue their training for the rest of their careers as new programming languages and technologies continually arrive on the market.

High school students interested in pursuing this type of work should study mathematics, computer science, and physics. They should also take computer programming courses in school or study computers and computer languages in their spare time.

Getting the Job

A good way to find a job in systems analysis is to contact the larger computer manufacturers. The federal government has computer systems in operation in many states. Those who are interested in a government job should apply to take the necessary civil service examination. College placement offices can help graduating students to contact employers. Classified ads in newspapers and trade journals and Internet job banks are other sources of jobs.

Advancement Possibilities and Employment Outlook

A junior systems analyst may advance to senior and then to lead systems analyst positions. Those who show management abilities may become department supervisors and managers. Some experienced analysts start their own computer firms.

According to the U.S. Bureau of Labor Statistics, 487,000 people worked as computer systems analysts in 2004. Employment was expected to grow much faster than the average through the year 2014. New openings will occur because of the development of new applications for computers and sophisticated technologies. The rapid growth of computer centers that sell computer services to other businesses will also provide jobs. Advances in telecommunications technology and scientific research mean that systems analysts with specialized science backgrounds will be in great demand.

Working Conditions

Computer systems analysts often spend time working independently. They spend some time in the office and some time observing the systems with which they work. They meet with many people to define problems, discuss solutions, and explain new systems. Systems analysts usually work forty hours per week with occasional evening or weekend work to meet project deadlines.

Earnings and Benefits

The Bureau of Labor Statistics reported that the median yearly wage for computer systems analysts in 2004 was $66,480. According to the "Computerworld Salary Survey 2005" (*Computerworld*, October 24, 2005), the median yearly wage for a systems analyst/programmer in 2005 was $67,685. Benefits generally include paid holidays and vacations, sick leave, and health insurance.

Where to Go for More Information

Association for Computing Machinery
1515 Broadway
New York, NY 10036
(212) 626-0500
http://www.acm.org

IEEE Computer Society
1730 Massachusetts Ave. NW
Washington, DC 20036
(202) 371-0101
http://www.computer.org

Institute for Certification of Computing
   Professionals
2350 Devon Ave., Ste. 115
Des Plaines, IL 60018
(847) 2899-4227
http://www.iccp.org

Society for Information Management
401 N. Michigan Ave.
Chicago, IL 60611
(312) 527-6734
http://www.simnet.org

Controller

Definition and Nature of the Work

Controllers are in charge of coordinating, planning, and reporting on the financial activities of a large organization. Controllers work for banks, corporations, and government agencies. They set financial policies. Often they are in charge of the accounting, bookkeeping, and auditing departments and sometimes choose the accounting method a company employs. They supervise record keeping and set up controls to ensure efficiency and honesty. All financial reports made within a company go to the controller. The controller reports directly to the president or board of directors of a company or organization. The controller also supervises the financial reports that are sent out of the company. These include annual reports to stockholders, tax returns, and reports to government agencies.

Controllers explain financial policies to people who work in their organizations. They are often responsible for assets and investments. For example, they are in charge of planning purchases of new equipment. Sometimes they borrow money from banks to be used by their companies to build new factories or offices. Controllers also plan budgets. They set limits on the amount of money to be spent by their firms each year. For example, a controller working for a city government may plan the sanitation department's budget for a one-year period. The controller allocates $1 million as the budget for the year. Using this amount, the controller decides how much is to be spent on new trash trucks, salaries, dump operations, and other operating expenses.

Education and Training Requirements

Controllers must have extensive knowledge of accounting and finance as well as working knowledge of the industry they serve. Training in accounting and finance is essential. Cost and budget accounting are important courses for those interested in becoming controllers. Courses in statistics and management are helpful, because they offer exposure to various aspects of business methods. The increased use of computers in accounting and record keeping makes knowledge of data processing important to a controller. People with a master's degree in accounting or a master's in business administration (MBA) have the best chance to be hired for executive training programs that lead to top-level jobs such as that of controller.

The Institute of Management Accountants offers the Certified Public Accountant (CPA) and the Certified Management Accountant (CMA) designations for financial managers specializing in accounting. Both designations would improve an employee's chances of becoming a controller.

Getting the Job

Only the most experienced workers become controllers. Some advance to the position by being promoted from the ranks of accountants and auditors in their company, whereas others are brought in from the outside to head the company's accounting departments.

A graduating student's college placement office can help him or her find an accounting job. The placement office can also provide information on companies and organizations that have executive training programs. A person can start as a trainee and advance to more responsible positions. Junior auditors can advance to senior auditors and then to controllers of branch stores. State and pri-

Education and Training
College

Salary
Median—$167,898 per year

Employment Outlook
Good

vate employment offices and newspaper classified ads may offer job leads. For government jobs, interested individuals should apply to take the necessary civil service exam.

Advancement depends on a good knowledge of accounting, an ability to pay attention to details, an ability to think creatively, and a talent for management. Those who want to become executives must keep up with new accounting and data processing techniques. Many consultants take seminars and courses offered by professional associations.

Advancement Possibilities and Employment Outlook

Controllers are already at the top of their field. They may decide to move to organizations that offer higher salaries or more prestige. Controllers are sometimes picked to become a company's chief financial officer (CFO) or chief executive officer (CEO).

According to the U.S. Bureau of Labor Statistics, employment of financial managers at all levels was expected grow about as fast as the average for all occupations through the year 2014. The need for financial managers typically grows at the rate of the overall economy. Many entry-level financial managers advance to jobs such as cost accountant, chief cost accountant, budget director, or senior internal auditor. Only a few go on to become treasurers, controllers, or financial vice presidents. However, all of these positions are well-paid, challenging jobs.

Working Conditions

Controllers and the accountants who work with them spend most of their time in the office. Controllers usually work in large corporate headquarters, banks, or government buildings in urban areas. They are often required to attend meetings with other managers to explain financial policies. They usually work more than forty hours a week without additional pay. They must also spend some time keeping up with the field by attending seminars and professional meetings.

Earnings and Benefits

According to salary.com, controllers made a median annual salary of $167,898 in 2006. Controllers usually receive good benefits, including paid vacations of up to four weeks, health insurance, and pension and profit sharing plans.

Where to Go for More Information

Association for Financial Professionals
7315 Wisconsin Ave., Ste. 600 W
Bethesda, MD 20814
(301) 907-2862
http://www.afponline.org

Financial Executives International
200 Campus Dr.
Florham Park, NJ 07932-0674
(973) 765-1000
http://www.fei.org

Institute of Management Accountants
10 Paragon Dr.
Montvale, NJ 07645-1718
(800) 638-4427
http://www.imanet.org

Credit Manager

Definition and Nature of the Work

When a credit card company or other business loans money or issues a credit card to a customer, they must ensure to some degree that the customer will be able to repay the loan/credit with interest some time in the future. Most businesses check that the customer has ample income and pays bills in full and on time. The person who makes the final decision to extend or deny credit is the credit manager.

Consumer credit managers direct the credit operations of retail stores and credit bureaus. The size of the operation determines each manager's duties. In small offices, such as those found in car dealerships, credit managers help customers fill out credit applications. They then check the references listed on the form and decide whether or not credit should be granted. Managers also handle customer complaints and look into late payments. In large credit offices, such as those found in financial institutions that issue credit cards, credit checkers perform all of these jobs except that of making the final credit decision. Managers are also responsible for hiring and supervising credit checkers and other workers in their departments. They may help to determine the minimum qualifications for who can receive credit.

Commercial credit managers make decisions that affect the credit and credit standing of a business firm. Managers do in-depth research regarding the credit record of businesses before coming to their decisions, because commercial credit applications generally involve thousands or hundreds of thousands of dollars. Managers review the credit application thoroughly and speak with company officials. Managers also contact credit information agencies, sometimes called credit bureaus, that have reports on the firm. In addition, managers may talk to bank officers who handle the firm's accounts.

Education and Training Requirements

Although not all credit managers have a college degree, employers prefer applicants with college training. Business school experience is helpful, as are college courses in accounting, finance, economics, and business administration. Requirements vary with individual companies. One firm may choose to promote a good worker who does not have a college degree, whereas another company may look for applicants who have college training in a specific field. Management trainees in retail stores or credit unions usually must have prior work experience in the credit field.

New credit managers are trained on the job. They learn the company's credit policies and how to search out credit information. In addition to on-the-job training, courses are available. There are college and home-study courses and follow-up training programs designed to keep managers up to date on new developments in credit processing procedures. Credit managers with the appropriate levels of training and experience may qualify for professional certification.

Credit managers decide whether consumers or businesses will have the ability to repay debts and interest. (© Martha Tabor/ Working Images Photographs. Reproduced by permission.)

Getting the Job

Prospective credit managers can apply directly to credit institutions for which they would like to work. Retailers, manufacturers, and sales offices also employ credit workers. A college placement office may be able to help a graduating student find a job. Both state and private employment agencies list jobs in the credit field. Newspaper classified ads and Internet job sites may also offer job leads.

Advancement Possibilities and Employment Outlook

Consumer credit managers can advance to positions of increased supervisory responsibility in their department or company. Professional certification may help in advancement. Highly qualified commercial credit managers sometimes advance to positions in general management in their firms.

According to the Bureau of Labor Statistics, employment of credit managers was projected to increase about as fast as the average for all occupations through the year 2014. The need for managers will generally grow as fast as the population and the economy grow. Advances in telecommunications, the computerization of customer records, and automated credit checking systems may negatively impact the need for credit managers. Nevertheless, openings will occur to replace experienced credit managers who retire or leave their jobs for other reasons.

Working Conditions

Consumer credit managers spend their working time in the office. Commercial credit managers who service commercial accounts may visit business offices or plants to interview current and prospective clients. Credit managers must have good judgment and consideration. Because the financial responsibilities are significant, they often work under pressure. Credit managers normally work forty hours per week. Commercial credit managers usually work longer and less regular hours than consumer credit managers.

Where to Go for More Information

American Financial Services Association
919 18th St. NW
Washington, DC 20006
(202) 296-5544
http://www.afsaef.org

Credit Professionals International
525B N. Laclede Station Rd.
St. Louis, MO 63119
(314) 961-0031
http://www.creditprofessionals.org

Earnings and Benefits

Earnings depend on experience and education and on the size of the employing firm. Salary.com estimated that the median annual salary of credit managers was $72,329 in 2006.

Credit managers can expect paid vacations and holidays. They also receive health and life insurance and retirement benefits. In addition, some companies offer their employees profit sharing plans, cash bonuses, and the opportunity to purchase stock in the firm.

Employee Benefits Manager

Definition and Nature of the Work

Employee benefits managers, sometimes referred to as employee benefits specialists or professional benefits administrators, are responsible for developing and administering employee benefits programs, such as pension plans, 401(k) retirement plans, medical and life insurance, and education benefits. Their duties include researching, designing, and evaluating the benefits options offered to employees by a business or government agency. They may also offer financial counseling for employees who are near retirement.

The complexity and scope of employee benefits has been growing in recent years. In addition to conventional health insurance and pension coverage, many employers now offer benefits in the form of dental and optical insurance, disability and accidental death insurance, homeowners' insurance, stock options, and thrift savings plans. Because of its substantial financial value, employers increasingly use their employee benefits package to recruit capable workers.

Some employers sponsor or subsidize services that provide their employees with child care, counseling, or recreation and physical fitness programs. Education benefits for employees and for their children may also be provided.

Employer-sponsored benefits sometimes encourage employees to make longer-term job commitments, because employees must wait a period of time before they can collect certain portions of their benefits package. This is particularly true in the case of thrift savings plans and retirement pensions.

Employee benefits managers must be familiar with laws and regulations governing employee benefits. In addition, they must be aware of employer tax incentives associated with certain benefits.

Employee benefits managers are employed by government agencies, by medium and large corporations, and by consulting firms that specialize in employee benefits management. Rather than maintain an in-house benefits management staff, some employers, especially smaller ones, hire independent consulting firms to design or revise their employee benefits package. They may choose firms that have expertise in the benefit needs of local government agencies, nonprofit companies, small private universities, or whatever their particular organization might require.

Education and Training Requirements

Although some employee benefits managers are high school graduates who have learned their duties through on-the-job training, most managers have a bachelor's degree. Specialized programs that offer certification in employee benefits are available at the master's level in some colleges and universities. College courses in business law and administration, economics, finance, and accounting

Education and Training
College

Salary
Median—$66,530 per year

Employment Outlook
Very good

Employee benefits managers conduct research and analyze data to design benefits packages for employees. (© Terry Wild Studio. Reproduced by permission.)

offer useful preparation for this field. Training in the use of computers is also helpful. Several states have licensing requirements for people holding this job.

Getting the Job

Employers in private industry often advertise job openings on the Internet and in newspapers and professional journals. They also recruit through employment agencies and sometimes at colleges and universities. Your school's placement office may be able to help you with job leads. If you are interested in government work, arrange to take the necessary civil service examination. You can contact your local civil service representative for information about government job openings and exam requirements.

Advancement Possibilities and Employment Outlook

College graduates with advanced degrees will have the best chances for advancement. Some employee benefits managers can advance through self-employment as benefits consultants.

According to the Bureau of Labor Statistics, employment of employee benefits managers was expected to grow faster than the average for all occupations through the year 2014. Because of the increasing complexity of laws and regulations governing employee benefits, specialists in this area will be in high demand.

Working Conditions

Employee benefits managers generally work a standard thirty-five- to forty-hour week. They may work alone or as members of a team of personnel workers. Employee benefits managers must be skilled at conducting research, analyzing complex data, working with numbers, and maintaining comprehensive records.

Earnings and Benefits

The median annual salary for employee benefits managers in 2004 was $66,530, according to the Bureau of Labor Statistics. Employee benefits managers usually receive paid vacations and holidays, health and life insurance, and pension plans.

Employment Counselor

Definition and Nature of the Work

Employment counselors work with individuals, and sometimes with groups, to assist them in making wise career decisions. To help their clients find the right type of job, counselors collect and assess information about education, previous employment experience, skills, interests, and personal information.

Counselors may also administer a variety of tests to get further information about their clients. These may include aptitude and skills tests and personality assessments. These tests are also helpful in giving clients a better understanding of their vocational interests.

After assessing all of this information, employment counselors identify possible career options. They also discuss with their clients specific jobs within these areas, the type of work that is performed, and entry requirements.

Clients then use this information to conduct a job search on their own, or they seek the services of a job placement agency. Some employment counselors may also provide job placement assistance. They will search files of job orders from employers and try to match these with their clients' qualifications. They may also contact prospective employers to find out whether suitable job openings exist.

The number of jobs for employment counselors in private industry is growing. These counselors have detailed knowledge of their company and the requirements for the different jobs within it. They may meet with employees from time to time to discuss performance and offer suggestions for improvement when necessary. When employees wish to change jobs, the counselor may work with them to find a suitable position within the company.

Employment counselors must have excellent interpersonal skills. They must have a thorough understanding of the world of work and up-to-date information about trends that affect the employment outlook.

Education and Training Requirements

Entry requirements for employment counselors vary greatly depending on the type of position and each state's licensing. The minimum requirement is a bachelor's degree in psychology, vocational guidance, or counseling. Related degrees may also be acceptable if the counselor has experience in interviewing, job placement, or personnel work. Some state agencies and many private agencies require that their employment counselors have master's degrees. In many states a master's degree is required to receive a license to practice privately. A newly hired employment counselor is often given a period of on-the-job training.

Getting the Job

The placement office of a student's college is the best source of information about job openings. Individuals may also apply directly to private agencies that hire employment counselors. Those interested in federal and state agencies should register to take the necessary civil service examinations. Professional associations, Internet job banks, and publications may also be useful sources of information.

Advancement Possibilities and Employment Outlook

Employment counselors in federal and state agencies may advance to supervisory and administrative positions. Those in private practice can work to build

Education and Training
College

Salary
Median—$45,570 per year

Employment Outlook
Very good

their practices. In private business, counselors may move into other personnel and management positions.

According to the Bureau of Labor Statistics, 248,000 employment, school, and educational counselors held jobs in 2004. Employment of employment counselors was expected to grow faster than the average for all occupations through the year 2014. Many job openings will result from the need to replace counselors who advance to other positions or transfer to other fields. Employment for counselors in private industry is also expected to grow due to the fact that people are switching jobs and careers more frequently.

Working Conditions

Employment counselors usually work a forty-hour week. In some agencies evening work is required to suit clients' schedules. Self-employed counselors often offer evening appointments and fit their schedules to the number of clients they have. Because privacy is an important part of the counseling process, counselors have their own offices. These are usually pleasant, well-lighted places to work, away from noise and other distractions.

Earnings and Benefits

The earnings of employment counselors vary greatly. Salaries of those working for state agencies vary considerably from state to state. The median salary for employment, school, and educational counselors was $45,570 per year in 2004, according to the Bureau of Labor Statistics. Counselors usually receive paid holidays and vacations, health insurance, and retirement benefits.

Where to Go for More Information

National Association of Personnel Services
PO Box 2128
The Village at Banner Elk, Ste. 108
Banner Elk, NC 28604
(828) 898-4929
http://www.recruitinglife.com

National Career Development Association
305 N. Beech Circle
Broken Arrow, OK 74012
(866) FOR-NCDA
http://www.ncda.org

National Employment Counseling Association
5999 Stevenson Ave.
Alexandria, VA 22304
(800) 347-6647
http://www.employmentcounseling.org

Executive Search Recruiter

Education and Training
College

Salary
Median—$70,192 per year

Employment Outlook
Very good

Definition and Nature of the Work

When companies want to fill a senior management position, they often use the services of an executive search firm. The job of the executive search recruiters who work for these firms is to fill high-level positions with the most suitable people available.

A company will provide an executive search recruiter with a complete description of the job and the skills needed to fill an executive vacancy. A recruiter who is not familiar with a particular company may visit its offices to learn more about it. The recruiter may spend many hours with the client discussing the job and offering advice on the company's employment needs.

The recruiter then begins a search for suitable candidates. This is done by checking the computer files of the executive search firm for resumes of people who are already known to the firm or recruiter. The people who most closely match the client's requirements are then contacted about the position.

If recruiters are unable to find qualified candidates from these files, they may try to identify and investigate people working in similar positions in other companies. The recruiter approaches these people and tries to interest them in moving to the client company. For this reason, executive recruiters are sometimes called "headhunters."

The first contact with potential candidates is usually made over the telephone. If the candidates show interest in the position, the recruiter arranges an interview. After the recruiter has interviewed several candidates, he or she gives the client written reports on them. The client company may then interview the selected candidates directly.

If a candidate is selected and accepts the position, the search is complete. If the client is not satisfied or the candidate is not interested in the position, the recruiter must begin the search again. Although executive recruiters can sometimes fill positions quickly, it often takes months to conclude a successful search.

An executive search recruiter spends a lot of time on the telephone talking to clients about high-level jobs they need to fill and contacting prospective employees. *(Photograph by Kelly A. Quin. Thomson Gale. Reproduced by permission.)*

Executive search firms are paid for each position that they fill. The client pays part of the fee as a retainer. Once a retainer has been accepted, the search firm is obligated to fill the position. The rest of the fee may be paid to the search firm when the job has been filled or as the search progresses.

Education and Training Requirements

A college degree and a familiarity with the business world is usually required to get a job at a recruiting agency. Personal qualities are more important than formal education. Recruiters come from varied backgrounds. Many recruiters have experience in some business specialty or in general management. Some have experience in sales and marketing.

Recruiters must be very good at dealing with people. They must be comfortable spending a lot of time talking on the telephone. Recruiters often speak to people they do not know and who may not want to talk with them. They have to get their point across quickly and persuasively. They may have to approach many candidates before a position is filled, so recruiters must have a lot of patience. Discretion is a very important personal quality, as recruiters often deal with confidential information about clients and candidates.

Getting the Job

Because many recruiters have experience in other areas before joining executive search firms, entry-level positions are not easy to find. The best way to find a job in this area is to approach executive search firms directly. Classified ads in newspapers and trade journals and Internet job banks are sometimes other sources of jobs.

Advancement Possibilities and Employment Outlook

In an executive recruiting firm, advancement comes in the form of earnings rather than position. As recruiters gain experience, they may be assigned to searches for more senior executives. These positions command higher salaries, and recruiters receive larger fees. They may also gain recognition by bringing new business into the firm. Some recruiters advance to supervisory positions or become partners in a firm. Some experienced recruiters start their own executive search firms.

According to the Bureau of Labor Statistics, employment of employment placement professionals of all kinds was expected to grow faster than the average for all occupations through the year 2014. Mergers and growth in financial service companies are creating positions for top executives and managers. Financial companies are turning to executive search recruiters to fill these positions.

Working Conditions

The success of executive search firms depends on the impression they make on their clients and prospective candidates. They often fill positions that command very high salaries. Executive recruiters work in pleasant surroundings. They have big, modern offices. In large firms the recruiters have secretaries and assistants to help them with their work.

A large percentage of a recruiter's time is spent talking with people. Much of this time is spent on the telephone with client companies and candidates. Travel time may be necessary to visit clients' offices and learn about their operations. Recruiters also spend much time interviewing candidates. They often need to travel to conduct interviews and follow-up meetings.

Earnings and Benefits

Where to Go for More Information

Association of Executive Search
  Consultants
12 E. 41st St.
New York, NY 10017
(212) 398-9556
http://www.aesc.org

Executive search recruiters are usually paid according to the number of positions that they fill. The recruiting firm usually receives a percentage of the annual salary and benefits package paid to the selected candidate. The recruiter will receive part of this sum.

Earnings vary widely according to the salary and the number of placements made. According to salary.com, the median annual salary for an executive recruiter in 2006 was $70,192. Benefits often include paid vacations and holidays, health and life insurance, and a retirement plan.

Financial Analyst

Education and Training
College

Salary
Median—$61,910 per year

Employment Outlook
Good

Definition and Nature of the Work

Financial analysts, also called securities or investment analysts, examine financial information in order to make sound suggestions to businesses on how to invest money. Financial analysts often use statistical software and spreadsheets to analyze the facts they gather. Financial analysts then make reports to their employers on the results of their research. They work in banks, corporations, stock brokerages, insurance companies, and government agencies. Some analysts study worldwide and national money matters. Others advise corporations on ways to invest their pension funds. Many financial analysts specialize in determining the value of securities, such as stocks and bonds.

Financial analysts who work for stock brokerages pass their research findings on to the securities brokers. Analysts help brokers and their customers look for good investments and determine when a stock or bond should be bought or sold.

Many analysts specialize in researching and evaluating the securities of companies in one industry. These analysts look at all the factors in the industry that influence the price of the companies' stocks. They study new products, market prices, and other industry-wide trends. Analysts study a company's financial status to see how much the company is earning compared with others in the industry. Some analysts visit the companies they are researching to interview the management and to determine how efficiently the companies are being operated. Analysts compare the companies' financial reports with those of previous years. Then they try to predict what will happen to the companies' earnings in the future. Sometimes they work with statisticians to get the most information from the facts they collect. Although there is no way to be sure of future earnings or stock prices, analysts increase the chances of making profitable decisions by getting the most accurate information available.

Financial analysts research and gather current financial information to analyze the status of companies and their securities. (© Gary D. Landsman/ Corbis.)

Education and Training Requirements

A person must have a college education to become a financial analyst. Employers look for people with a degree in business administration. Undergraduate courses in finance, business, economics, statistics, accounting, mathematics, and law prove helpful. Increasingly, applicants for financial analyst positions have earned a master's degree in business administration (MBA). Analysts must understand corporate accounting to analyze financial statements. Banks, corporations, and brokerage houses generally offer some form of in-house training for beginning financial analysts.

The Chartered Financial Analyst (CFA) Institute offers a CFA designation for people who have a bachelor's degree and three years of work experience in the financial industry. To acquire a CFA, a candidate must pass a series of three examinations that cover subjects such as accounting economics, securities analysis, and portfolio management. Although the CFA designation is not required to become a financial analyst, it is helpful for advancement, especially for someone working for an investment firm, a brokerage, or other financial institution.

Getting the Job

A college placement office can help a graduating student find a job in financial analysis. Large corporations, banks, and brokerages often send representatives to colleges to speak to graduating seniors about the job openings they have available. Interested individuals should check Internet job sites as well as the classified ads of local newspapers. The *Wall Street Journal* is a national business newspaper that publishes classified ads for financial analysts. Firms from all parts of the country place these ads. For government jobs, candidates should apply to take the necessary civil service examination.

Advancement Possibilities and Employment Outlook

Financial analysts may start as junior analysts and work their way up to positions as senior financial analysts in banks or brokerage firms. Some financial analysts become consultants. Analysts may also advance to positions such as the head of a securities analysis department. Advancement opportunities are good for analysts who prove themselves by offering sound advice consistently.

According to the U.S. Bureau of Labor Statistics, 197,000 people in the United States held jobs as financial analysts in 2004. Employment of analysts was expected to grow as fast as the average for all occupations through the year 2014. Financial analysts are always needed to help people make wise financial decisions. However, the number of jobs in securities analysis depends to some extent on the health of the economy. When times are good, many investors buy securities. Therefore, more analysts are needed. In times of recession, the competition for jobs increases.

Working Conditions

Financial analysts do much of their work independently. They spend most of their time in the office. Occasionally they visit companies or attend conferences with other financial experts. Financial analysts work under great pressure to be correct in their statements about the economy or specific investments. Analysts who are too often wrong are not promoted. Financial analysts generally work forty hours per week. Often they are required to work overtime.

Earnings and Benefits

The median annual salary for a financial analyst was $61,910 in 2004, according to the Bureau of Labor Statistics. Experienced analysts earned $113,490 or more per year. Some senior analysts employed by large firms earn more.

Most financial analysts receive health and life insurance, paid vacations, and pension plans. Many banks and insurance companies offer profit sharing plans to their employees.

Financial Planner

Education and Training
Varies—see profile

Salary
Median—$62,700 per year

Employment Outlook
Very good

Definition and Nature of the Work

Financial planners help individuals and groups plan the use of their savings, income, and investments. Some are self-employed consultants who offer workshops that teach people how to analyze their own financial situations. Other financial planners operate financial planning businesses or are employed by insurance companies and financial institutions—savings and loan companies, investment services companies, and banks—to sell their company's financial products. Such products might include family budgeting schemes, mutual funds, individual retirement accounts (IRAs), insurance, real estate, or tax-sheltered investment plans.

Financial planners help individuals examine their immediate and long-term financial situations. The job of the financial planner is to help each investor decide what kinds of investments are best. They advise people on what types of investments to put their money in as well as the timing of major expenditures, such as buying a house or starting retirement.

In order to be effective, financial planners must be familiar with legal restrictions and laws concerning retirement plans, tax shelters, insurance, and trusts. They must be skilled at working with numbers and budgets and be able to understand complicated financial and legal documents. In addition, they should be articulate, persuasive, and have sales ability to build a clientele. Financial planners are also sometimes called personal financial analysts, personal financial advisers, or financial consultants.

Education and Training Requirements

The majority of workers in this occupation are college graduates. In fact, a growing number of colleges offer programs specifically for financial planners. Although few employers require such specialized academic training, it is helpful to take courses in marketing, accounting, business law, economics, and financial and estate planning. In preparing to become a financial planner, a person must have good math skills and the ability to work with budgets and accounting systems.

The Certified Financial Planner (CFP) Board of Standards offers a CFP credential for people who have some experience in financial planning. To acquire a CFP, a candidate must pass an examination that covers subjects such as financial planning processes, insurance and risk management, and taxes and retirement planning. Although the CFP designation is not needed to become a financial planner, it is helpful for advancement, especially for someone working for a big investment firm.

Financial planners must be skilled at working with numbers and budgets and be able to understand complicated financial and legal documents. (© Bill Varie/Corbis.)

Many financial planners obtain additional training in insurance, stocks and securities, taxes, or banking, depending on their special field. Those interested in working with securities often seek certification from the National Association of Security Dealers. Some states have bonding and licensing requirements for people who work in stocks, bonds, and securities. Individuals should contact their state government for specific requirements that may apply to financial planners.

Getting the Job

The best way to get a job as a financial planner is to apply directly to the company or financial institution for which you would like to work. Newspaper classified ads and ads on the Internet may also offer job leads. Private employment agencies that specialize in placing workers in the field of finance may also list openings.

Advancement Possibilities and Employment Outlook

Financial planners can advance by expanding the areas of their expertise and thus increasing the range of financial services or products they handle. In some companies advancement to positions of greater responsibility depends on the financial planner's ability to generate high commissions. Some planners open their own financial planning businesses. Financial planners also might advance by becoming licensed as securities brokers.

According to the U.S. Bureau of Labor Statistics, personal financial planners held 158,000 jobs in 2004. Employment of financial planners was expected to grow at a faster rate than that of all occupations through the year 2014. The increasing number of investment alternatives and continuing changes in tax laws should lead to high demand for people employed in financial planning. As the baby boomers reach retirement age, more and more will be turning to financial planners to secure their financial future. The turnover rate is high, however, owing to the competitive nature of work in this field. Many beginning financial planners fail to establish a sufficiently large clientele and leave the field.

Working Conditions

Financial planners work in offices and in the field, either alone or in teams. They may hold financial planning workshops with local community groups or at adult evening schools. Some financial planners meet their clients at their homes or businesses.

Financial planners sometimes work more than forty hours per week, especially in the beginning when they are trying to establish a clientele. Some financial planners work evenings and weekends to meet with clients.

Earnings and Benefits

Earnings of financial planners vary widely depending on their experience and the services they perform. Financial planners who are self-employed may charge a flat fee based on a percentage of the value of their client's investment. Fees are also sometimes negotiated on an hourly rate. Many financial planners who sell financial products are paid primarily on a commission basis. Some receive supplementary salaries that vary depending on the employing company. The median annual salary for financial planners was $62,700 in 2004, according to the Bureau of Labor Statistics. Experienced financial planners earned $108,280 or more per year. Some financial institutions and insurance companies offer benefits that include paid holidays and vacations, health and life insurance, and pension plans.

General Manager

Education and Training
College

Salary
Median—$77,420 per year

Employment Outlook
Good

Definition and Nature of the Work

A general manager directs and coordinates the operations of a small business or a department in a company. Medium-sized and large companies are divided into production, sales, promotion, purchasing, and other departments, and a general manager is typically in charge of each of these divisions. In a small company the general manager may be responsible for all operations. General managers usually report to the chief operating officer or to a vice president. They may report to the chief executive officer.

Each company has its own corporate ladder. Some companies give the title of general manager to those in charge of separate operating units. A department store chain might call the person in charge of each store a general manager. Sometimes the person in charge of a subsidiary company has that title. At some big, high-tech companies more than one general manager may be assigned to the same division. Despite these differences, the functions of all general managers are essentially the same.

General managers take direction from their top executives. They must first understand the executives' overall plan for the company. Then they set specific goals for their own departments to fit in with the plan. The general manager of production, for instance, might have to increase certain product lines and phase out others. General managers must describe their goals clearly to their support staff. The supervisory managers see that the goals are met.

General managers direct other people to achieve their goals. Therefore, general managers must be able to delegate responsibility. They must be skilled in hiring good middle managers and giving clear, consistent directives. They must organize their divisions so that the employees know exactly what role each has to play.

General managers must understand the work of their departments thoroughly. They are constantly required to make difficult decisions about departmental activities. To make correct decisions, they must be able to read and analyze a great deal of information in a short time. If there is no reliable information, the manager must have sound judgment to make a decision. General managers must write clear reports for their senior executives. They must have strong leadership qualities and be able to get excellent performance from their support staff.

Education and Training Requirements

Education requirements vary depending on the kind of business. For example, general managers in technical or research firms often have degrees in science or engineering. In most cases candidates need a college education to be hired for executive training programs. Occasionally people without college degrees work their way up to management positions, including that of general manager. However, most employers prefer to hire applicants who have at least a bachelor's degree in business administration. Courses in management, accounting, finance, and industrial relations will prove helpful. Some large companies prefer to take management trainees with a college degree in liberal arts and a master's degree in business administration (MBA).

Many companies have executive training programs. In many training programs candidates are assigned to various jobs for a few months or a year to give them experience in many departments. By far the most important qualification for becoming a general manager is proven success in lower managerial positions.

Getting the Job

Most general management positions are filled by promoting experienced lower-level managers. Sometimes the positions are filled from outside the firm. Those who move up from within a firm usually reach top-level management positions by advancing through executive training programs. A college placement office can put graduating students in touch with organizations that have executive training programs. Interested individuals can check the newspaper classified ads and Internet job banks for jobs in management, industrial engineering, or production and quality control. Candidates can also contact large manufacturing firms, utilities, and other businesses directly. Private employment agencies geared for professional and managerial workers may also be helpful. Executive search recruiters, or "headhunters," also find jobs for people in management. Large organizations hire professional recruiters to fill the top positions.

Advancement Possibilities and Employment Outlook

General managers are often promoted to top executive positions. They may also become general managers in larger companies. According to the U.S. Bureau of Labor Statistics, general managers held 1,807,000 jobs in 2004. Employment of general managers was expected to grow as fast as the average for all occupations through the year 2014. However, competition is strong for top management positions, because many managers are promoted from within the company.

Working Conditions

General managers usually work in comfortable offices close to the departments they direct. Many general managers travel frequently. In national companies they have to travel to the head office or to confer with the managers of other divisions or plants. Nearly all general managers meet with their counterparts in other companies. Some travel or live abroad. They may be transferred from one position to another on short notice.

General managers in large companies often work under intense pressure. They may work much more than forty-hour weeks and be required to socialize for work. General managers in small companies may face less pressure.

Earnings and Benefits

Salaries for general managers vary greatly. Earnings depend on the type, size, and location of the firm and on length of service. The estimated median annual salary of a general manager was $77,420 in 2004, according to the Bureau of Labor Statistics. Those with salaries in the top 25 percent received more than $118,310 per year. Most receive additional income in the form of bonuses, stock options, and health and life insurance. Some drive company cars and receive other benefits, such as club memberships and expense accounts.

Where to Go for More Information

American Management Association
1601 Broadway, 6th Fl.
New York, NY 10019
(800) 262-9699
http://www.amanet.org

National Management Association
2210 Arbor Blvd.
Dayton, OH 45439
(937) 294-0421
http://www.nma1.org

Human Resources Manager

Education and Training	College
Salary	Median—$81,810 per year
Employment Outlook	Very good

Definition and Nature of the Work

Human resources managers manage the needs of a company's employees. They develop and manage employment programs, salary compensation and job evaluations, benefits, promotions, equal opportunity initiatives, and education and training programs. In large companies one human resources manager may be in charge of each of these areas. However, in small or medium companies the human resources manager may manage the human resources operation of the entire business.

Human resources managers must be highly qualified and experienced. There are many state and federal regulations in place to protect employees, and the manager must know and follow these regulations. If a company's hiring or promotion policies do not follow these regulations, the government may penalize it.

Human resources managers focus on people and their needs. For example, a human resources manager's responsibilities in the benefits area may extend from

Human resources managers focus on people and their needs. To be effective they should be knowledgeable about all areas of human resources as well as every aspect of the company. (© G. Baden/zefa/Corbis.)

researching and planning programs to processing individual benefit claims, depending on the size of the department. In addition to managing human resources programs, human resources managers usually supervise other employees.

In industries that are unionized, human resources managers deal with relations between labor and upper management. They read union contracts to help upper management comply with the terms of the contracts. They examine workers' grievances and try to help settle disagreements between labor and management.

Human resources managers' tasks can be extremely interesting and varied. They develop plans for finding applicants to fill job openings. Then they interview and, where necessary, test these applicants. These managers use their knowledge of job evaluation to fit the employees into the proper jobs. They use their knowledge of salary compensation to calculate employees' salaries and to make sure that the company's entire salary program is competitive with that of other companies. Human resources managers may also develop programs that increase employees' skills, strengthen their managerial ability, or provide career counseling.

Education and Training Requirements

Human resources managers must have excellent skills in management techniques, budgeting, counseling, business planning, and organization and systems design. They should have a knowledge of all the human resources areas, including benefits, salary compensation, employment, equal opportunity, payroll, and career planning.

Most human resources managers are college graduates. Many hold a master's degree. Because many different skills are needed, many educational backgrounds are acceptable to employers. Particularly valuable majors include those in human resources, business administration, political science, and psychology.

Getting the Job

Although employment agencies may list job openings, large companies usually fill human resources management jobs from within the company. To do the job properly, human resources managers must know every aspect of the company. This knowledge comes from experience. Classified sections of newspapers or career sites on the Internet may carry ads for these positions.

Advancement Possibilities and Employment Outlook

In large companies human resources managers may rise to managerial or executive status. Those who work for smaller companies may have to move to other companies to advance to a higher level.

According to the U.S. Bureau of Labor Statistics, human resources managers held 157,000 jobs in 2004. Employment of human resources managers was expected to grow faster than the average for all occupations through the year 2014. More and more companies are viewing human resources departments as being crucial to the well-being of the organization and will continue to expand their human resources departments to take care of the needs of the growing workforce. Increasingly complex benefit packages and labor laws also will create a demand for more human resources managers.

Working Conditions

Human resources managers usually work in a pleasant office setting. They spend a great deal of time interviewing people, talking on the phone, and in meetings. They must work well with people. To recruit new employees or take part in conferences and seminars, they may be required to travel. Human resources managers generally work more than a forty-hour week.

Earnings and Benefits

The median yearly salary for human resources managers was $81,810 in 2004, according to the Bureau of Labor Statistics. The highest-paid 10 percent earned more than $118,800 per year. Salaries vary depending on the size, type, and location of the business. Benefits usually include paid holidays and vacations, health insurance, and pension plans. Some human resources managers participate in company-sponsored stock option or profit sharing plans.

Where to Go for More Information

International Personnel Management
  Association for Human Resources
1617 Duke St.
Alexandria, VA 22314
(703) 549-7100
http://www.ipma-hr.org

Society for Human Resource Management
1800 Duke St.
Alexandria, VA 22314
(703) 548-3440
http://www.shrm.org

Insurance Underwriter

Education and Training
College

Salary
Median—$48,550 per year

Employment Outlook
Fair

Definition and Nature of the Work

Insurance underwriters evaluate applications for insurance policies. They assess the degree of risk to the insurance company of the person or property listed on the application. An insurance "risk" is the probability that the applicant will have to collect under the terms of the policy. By deciding which risks to insure, insurance underwriters (often called just underwriters) affect the financial well-being of the insurance company. If underwriters appraise risks either too conservatively or too liberally, insurance companies may lose money.

Insurance underwriters generally specialize in one of three principal types of insurance: life, property and liability, or health. They handle policy applications both from individuals and from businesses.

Insurance underwriters need accurate information to decide whether a policy is an acceptable risk. For example, to review an application for automobile insurance, the underwriter takes into account the applicant's previous loss record as well as age, medical reports, credit rating, driving record, and other information that may be helpful in evaluating the risk. Insurance underwriters may compare applications with similar policies and consult actuarial studies to determine their company's record of losses.

After compiling the necessary information, the underwriter evaluates the insurance application in relation to the company's underwriting standards. The underwriter may use complex computer programs that rate applications and make recommendations. The underwriter may decide to issue the policy as requested, to modify the policy, or to reject it. The underwriter outlines the terms of the acceptable policy and determines the rates or premiums.

Education and Training Requirements

Most insurance companies prefer to hire college graduates. However, some high school graduates who begin as underwriting clerks may advance to positions as underwriters. Courses in mathematics, statistics, business, and insurance are helpful. Beginners usually start as trainees or junior underwriters. Most insurance companies offer training programs, which are considered essential to an insurance underwriter's education and career.

The American Institute for Charted Property Casualty Underwriters offers a certification for insurance underwriters. The certification, known as the Chartered Property and Casualty Underwriter (CPCU) designation, can only be earned by insurance underwriters who have been in the industry for three years. To earn the designation, candidates must pass ten exams and abide by a professional code of ethics.

Getting the Job

A college placement office may be able to help a graduating student find a job as an insurance underwriter. Interested individuals should check Internet job sites and the classified ads of local newspapers and insurance journals. Candidates can also apply to various employment agencies. A person may increase his or her chances of getting a job offer after graduation by working part time or during the summer for an insurance company.

Advancement Possibilities and Employment Outlook

Advancement possibilities depend on the size of the company. After completing the training period, the underwriter may advance to various levels within the department. An experienced underwriter may become chief underwriter or underwriting manager of the department. Some insurance underwriters are promoted to administrative positions.

According to the U.S. Bureau of Labor Statistics, insurance underwriters held 101,000 jobs in 2004. Employment of insurance underwriters was expected to grow more slowly than average through the year 2014. More and more insurance companies are using computer programs that automatically make recommendations on insurance applications and cut down on the number of underwriters needed. Many openings, however, will occur to replace experienced underwriters who retire or leave their jobs for other reasons.

Working Conditions

Most insurance underwriters work a forty-hour week. Although underwriters work primarily in their offices, they may accompany salespeople on appointments with prospective customers. Insurance underwriters must be able to make prompt decisions and communicate their ideas to others. They must be skilled at analysis and at gathering information, and they should enjoy working with details.

Earnings and Benefits

The salaries of insurance underwriters vary depending on the location, size, and type of insurance company. Insurance underwriters earned a median annual salary of $48,550 in 2004, according to the Bureau of Labor Statistics. Those with the top 10 percent of salaries earned more than $86,110. Most insurance companies offer their employees health and life insurance, paid holidays and vacations, and pension plans.

Internet Entrepreneur

Education and Training
Varies—see profile

Salary
Varies—see profile

Employment Outlook
Varies—see profile

Definition and Nature of the Work

The Internet—a worldwide network of computer networks—offers businesses and individuals a relatively inexpensive way to communicate with a global audience. The development of the Internet over the past forty years has opened an entirely new medium for communication and commerce. Creative individuals with something to say or something to sell and technical interests and abilities can use the Internet to reach vast numbers of people.

Internet entrepreneurs are individuals who are familiar with the culture and technology of the Internet and are able to apply their knowledge to sell products or services via the Internet. In general, these entrepreneurs exploit the World Wide Web (the Web)—the portion of the Internet where users post "pages" of text, images, audio, and video using the HTML programming language. On a basic level the Web provides individual entrepreneurs and business organizations with an inexpensive means to offer documents and software to a worldwide audience.

Commercial Web sites fall into two basic types: pay sites and free sites. Pay sites offer subscribers proprietary information for a fee. The information can range from financial analysis to software applications to sports statistics. Free sites attract users with interesting content, then make money through advertising or sales generated through the site. For example, "search engines" such as Yahoo and Google help users find Web pages for free while exposing the users to advertisements. Other free sites are essentially online catalogs selling products and offering feature articles and reviews. Home electronics, computer equipment, books, music, video games, and travel arrangements are among the most popular items sold over the Internet.

Many Web sites are owned and maintained by huge corporations. Nearly all *Fortune* 500 companies have Web sites. On the other hand, there are also thousands of smaller businesses represented on-line—many owned and operated by individuals. Regardless of whether they work for a large corporation or a tiny business, Internet entrepreneurs must combine marketing skills with an aptitude for using new and evolving technology.

Education and Training Requirements

The Internet has fostered a culture where highly educated and well-trained business people compete side-by-side with self-taught amateurs. In general, individuals hoping to find employment as Internet experts for large corporations need a college degree and training in business management, marketing, and/or economics. They also need to understand basic HTML and Java programming capabilities as well as the fundamental architecture of the Internet.

On the other hand, individuals interested in starting a business on the Internet need only the training and education necessary to realize their own ambitions. Knowledge of the HTML programming language and an understanding of Web architecture are basic prerequisites. Internet entrepreneurs must also come up with good ideas. Often the best way to do this is to look for valuable services that the Internet could provide but does not. Internet entrepreneurs should strive to understand the core business that they hope to break into, whether it is electronics retailing, floral arrangements, or movie memorabilia. They should conduct market research and put together a solid financial plan before launching their business.

Internet entrepreneurs combine creativity and marketing skills to sell goods and services on the World Wide Web. (© Terry Wild Studio. Reproduced by permission.)

Getting the Job

Internet entrepreneurs need access to the Internet. Most Internet service providers (ISPs) offer use of their computer servers linked to the Internet for a fee. Those entrepreneurs more experienced in computers can set up their own server on the Internet.

Like any other form of entrepreneurship, Internet entrepreneurship requires personal initiative and drive. Individuals interested in an Internet career should discover as much as possible about the growth and evolution of the Internet. They should consider setting up a personal Web page to gain hands-on experience of the Web.

Advancement Possibilities and Employment Outlook

The Internet has shown spectacular growth over the past few years and will almost certainly continue to grow. On the other hand, the failure rate of Internet businesses is high, because the medium evolves in ways that are impossible to predict.

Employment in Web-related business is volatile. Many large companies have invested heavily in developing Internet sites. Then, as those sites fail to produce revenue, companies alter their plans and "downsize" or abandon the sites, often laying off employees in the process.

Like other new industries, the Internet offers high-risk opportunities. Individuals with the right idea and the skills necessary to capitalize on it can earn a fortune. At the same time, far more Internet-based businesses will fail rather than succeed.

Working Conditions

Internet entrepreneurs working for large companies generally work in clean, well-lighted, modern offices. Small-time entrepreneurs often work out of their homes. Entrepreneurs of all types are dedicated individuals willing to work extremely long hours to make their dreams a reality. Stress and anxiety are part of the entrepreneur's daily experience.

Earnings and Benefits

Earnings on the Internet vary wildly. In established businesses looking to create or grow an Internet presence, executives responsible for managing Internet operations will earn salaries comparable to their non-Internet counterparts. According to salary.com, top division information technology executives earned a median annual salary of $150,647. Workers responsible for day-to-day work on Internet sites earned substantially less—a typical Web designer, for instance, earned a median annual salary of $60,188, according to the same survey.

The earnings of self-employed entrepreneurs depend upon the relative success of their businesses. Some lose money year after year, while others go on to become billionaires. Personal earnings, of course, come out of sales after product and marketing costs have been subtracted. Successful online businesses generate much larger sales. Unfortunately, most Internet businesses are not huge successes.

Individuals working for large companies usually receive benefits packages consisting of health and unemployment insurance and paid holidays. Self-employed entrepreneurs usually pay for their own insurance.

Where to Go for More Information

Internet Society
1775 Wiehle Ave., Ste. 102
Reston, VA 20190-5108
(703) 326-9880
http://www.isoc.org

US Internet Industry Association
1800 Diagonal Rd.
Alexandria, VA 22314
(703) 647-7440
http://www.usiia.org

US Internet Service Provider Association
1330 Connecticut Ave. NW
Washington, DC 20036
(202) 862-3816
http://www.usispa.org

Investment Banker

Definition and Nature of the Work

Investment bankers arrange and negotiate large financial transactions. They are employed by investment banking firms to act as advisers to client companies and to initiate moneymaking ventures for their own firms. Investment bankers are also employed by large commercial banks.

An investment banker's work is diverse, dictated by the financial needs of clients. If a company plans to merge with or acquire another company or sell a subsidiary, an investment banker usually negotiates the agreement. When a corporation is facing financial difficulty, such as a large budget deficit or failing operations, an investment banker is called in to study the situation and find a remedy. When a client company issues new stock, the investment banking firm might underwrite, or take financial liability for, the stock, while the investment banker finds buyers for the shares. Investment bankers may also manage the investments of their client companies.

Education and Training Requirements

A master's degree in business administration (MBA) from a top school is generally required. Some firms hire liberal arts graduates and train them to become analysts, but these trainees usually pursue a graduate degree in business if they plan to remain in the field. A few investment bankers transfer from other related fields, such as finance, law, or banking.

Getting the Job

Most investment bankers are recruited directly from colleges and business schools, and some are offered trial jobs in the summer while they are still in school. Recruiters look for well-rounded candidates who participate in extracurricular activities while maintaining excellent academic records.

Education and Training
Advanced degree plus training

Salary
Starting—$45,000 to $85,000 per year

Employment Outlook
Good

An investment banker's work is dictated by the different financial needs of clients. (© Jose Luis Pelaez, Inc./Corbis.)

Advancement Possibilities and Employment Outlook

A successful investment banker may be promoted to vice president or managing director. A large investment banking firm might have forty to eighty managing directors, or partners.

The number of job opportunities for those interested in investment banking typically grows with the economy. Investment banking firms, however, are few in number, and the competition among applicants for jobs with these firms is intense. A firm might hire less than twenty-five employees from a field of more than one thousand applicants.

Working Conditions

Because investment banking involves huge financial risks and large-scale crises, an investment banker's work is often stressful and demanding. Those employed in the field report average workdays of fourteen to seventeen hours, frequent and often unexpected travel, interrupted weekends, and all-night work sessions. Because of the ups and downs of financial markets, job security is low. However, most investment bankers find the work exciting and creative.

Where to Go for More Information

American Bankers Association
1120 Connecticut Ave. NW
Washington, DC 20036
(800) BANKERS
http://www.aba.com

National Association of Securities Dealers
1 Liberty Plaza
New York, NY 10006
(212) 858-4000
http://www.nasd.com

Earnings and Benefits

Annual salaries for investment bankers are well above $100,000 after the first few years. Entry-level salaries, however, started at $45,000 per year for someone with a bachelor's degree and at $85,000 per year for someone with an MBA in 2005, according to WetFeet.com. In addition, entry-level investment bankers often received large, year-end bonuses of $10,000 or more. Benefits usually include paid holidays and vacations as well as medical insurance.

Management Analyst and Consultant

Education and Training
Advanced degree plus experience

Salary
Median—$63,450 per year

Employment Outlook
Good

Definition and Nature of the Work

Management analysts, sometimes referred to as management consultants, provide corporations and government agencies with the expertise needed to solve management problems quickly. These problems may result from rapid expansion, business relocation, technical innovations, or competition from other corporations. For example, when one corporation takes over another, management may decide to reorganize the entire corporate structure. Outside management consultants would analyze the new organization, recommend changes to its structure, and help the corporation implement the changes. Such changes may include eliminating nonessential jobs and machinery or streamlining an inventory system.

Management consulting firms compete for contracts for their services, which usually entails preparing detailed proposals for specific consulting projects. After a consulting firm lands a project, the firm's employees analyze the problem or problems in the client's business and devise solutions. They present the solutions to their clients in written reports and oral presentations. Then the consultants may help their clients implement the proposed solutions.

Consultants typically work long hours on tight deadlines. Therefore, they must be able to manage job-related stress. The work requires creativity, self-discipline, and the ability to set and meet goals. In addition to being experts in their particular fields, successful consultants are excellent at making oral presentations and have good personnel management skills.

There are two common types of consulting operations in the United States: small consulting businesses, which usually offer expertise in a specific area, and large consulting firms, which offer a wide variety of consulting services. About 29 percent of management consultants are self-employed, according to the U.S. Bureau of Labor Statistics. Although there are many small consulting firms, most consultants are employed by large firms. Consultants offer corporations and government expertise in a variety of fields. Some consultants focus on a specific industry, such as health care or high tech. Other consultants specialize by business function, such as marketing and finance.

Education and Training

To work in the field of management analysis and consulting, individuals need a college degree. Private industry usually looks for consultants with a master's degree in business administration (MBA) or a related discipline. Candidates straight out of college with a bachelor's degree may find work as management analysts or research associates reporting to consultants with more education and experience.

Management analysts and consultants are creative, self-disciplined people who provide corporations and government agencies with the expertise needed to solve management problems. *(© Terry Wild Studio. Reproduced by permission.)*

Students interested in consulting careers should study business administration in general while gaining more detailed knowledge in a specific area of expertise. Suggested areas of study include computer and information sciences, engineering, marketing and distribution, and communications.

With the increasing globalization of the world economy, successful consultants also need to have a basic understanding of world cultures, including the ability to communicate in one or more foreign language.

In order to give themselves a competitive advantage, consultants can earn the Certified Management Consultant designation. The designation is given by the Institute of Management Consultants (IMC) USA to those who pass an exam and an interview covering the IMC USA's Code of Ethics.

Getting the Job

There are two common paths a person can take to become a consultant: a person can obtain a bachelor's degree in business administration or an MBA and then find a job at a major consulting firm; or a person can gain expertise in a specialty while working for a company and then seek employment with a large consulting firm or become an independent consultant.

Regardless of their career paths, successful consultants are able to sell themselves and their expertise. They keep a network of past and potential clients and often advertise their services in newspapers, magazines, and trade or professional periodicals.

Advancement Possibilities and Employment Outlook

Management consultants working for large firms typically follow a clearly defined corporate path to advancement. In most firms new consultants are referred to as associates or researchers. As they gain experience, consultants may be named senior associates and be given more responsibility and less supervision. After a number of years on the job, successful consultants may be named engagement managers, then senior engagement managers, with responsibility for supervising one or more projects. Ultimately, consultants at large firms hope to be named principals or partners in the firm.

Consultants with entrepreneurial ambitions often choose to start their own operations. Self-employed consultants must be able to acquire and keep enough clients to earn a profit.

The demand for management consultants is expected to grow as corporations and government rely more and more on independent experts to help identify and solve problems. According to the Bureau of Labor Statistics, 605,000 Americans were employed as management analysts in 2004. Employment in this field was expected to grow faster than the average for all occupations through the year 2014. Competition for the jobs will be keen. Companies will continue to need consultants to help them globalize their business operations and to keep pace with new technologies and management practices. Companies will also look to consulting firms to cut costs. Unlike full-time employees, consultants are not given benefits by the company that hires them and can be easily let go if they are not needed anymore.

Working Conditions

Management consultants typically work in comfortable, pleasant offices. The job often requires travel, and many consultants make extended stays away from home to analyze a client's problems and implement solutions.

Consulting work can make extreme demands on one's time, with long workweeks and tight deadlines. Self-employed consultants often work out of home offices and set their own work schedules, although the success of their business depends on their ability to satisfy their clients' demands.

Earnings and Benefits

Salaries in this industry vary greatly according to employees' education, experience, and their roles in a consulting project. The Bureau of Labor Statistics reports that the median annual salary for a management analyst in 2004 was $63,450. Another source, the Association of Management Consulting Firms, reports that entry-level research associates earned a median annual salary of $52,482; management consultants earned a median yearly wage of $89,116, whereas junior partners and partners in a firm earned between $191,664 and $317,339 per year.

Where to Go for More Information

Academy of Management
PO Box 3020
Briarcliff Manor, NY 10510-8020
(914) 923-2607
http://www.aom.pace.edu

Association of Internal Management
   Consultants
824 Caribbean Ct.
Marco Island, FL 34145
(239) 642-0580
http://www.aimc.org

Association of Management Consulting
   Firms
380 Lexington Ave., Ste. 1700
New York, NY 10168
(212) 551-7887
http://www.amcf.org

Institute of Management Consultants
   (IMC) USA
2025 M St. NW, Ste. 800
Washington, DC 20036
(202) 367-1134
http://www.imcusa.org

Network Administrator

Definition and Nature of the Work

A network administrator oversees computer networks to ensure that they function smoothly. A network consists of a grouping of computers that communicate with each other or a central computer known as a server, on which computer files, programs, and other information are stored. A network may be as small as two or three computers or as large as the Internet, the world's largest computer network.

Whereas a network technician or engineer designs and sets up the infrastructure for a computer network, a network administrator usually configures and manages an existing network. He or she may be responsible for customizing the network to an individual company's needs by connecting the necessary hardware and software to the network. Once the network is configured, the administrator adds computer programs, such as e-mail, that the company's employees use on a daily basis. A network administrator's work usually depends on the size of the network for which he or she is responsible. The smaller the network, the more duties a network administrator handles. For large networks, several individuals may perform different tasks related to the network. The administrator then monitors the performance of the network and troubleshoots any problems such as slow performance or network crashes. A crash occurs when users cannot access the network or use all of its features properly. The administrator must also work with individual users who are having network problems that are not experienced by other users.

Some network problems may result in the loss or corruption of data stored on the server. For this reason, the administrator must develop, install, and maintain emergency systems to back up the main network server. Administrators keep records of all users' problems and errors as well as the steps taken to solve the problems. This information is used to help solve future problems.

Administrators also control user access to the network. This includes setting up passwords for individual users and determining which files, programs, or features each person is allowed to use. The administrator must also create a firewall—a set of security measures designed to make sure that no one can gain unauthorized access to the system. In larger firms this task may fall to a network security specialist. Network security also involves monitoring the network to see who is using it and how. A security specialist is responsible for changing passwords periodically and updating security measures and procedures.

Education and Training Requirements

A network administrator should have a strong background in math, sciences, and computer science, as well as experience working with computers. Although a college degree in computer sci-

A network administrator installs the necessary hardware and software to set up a computer network, and customizes it to meet the needs of the company using it. *(Photograph by Kelly A. Quin. Thomson Gale. Reproduced by permission.)*

ence, systems science, math, or engineering is not required to become a network administrator, advancement is difficult without one. Administrators should be familiar with a variety of network operating systems, including Microsoft, Novell, and Unix. Because computer technology changes rapidly, administrators must constantly upgrade their knowledge base.

Several companies that produce network software also offer training and certification in network administration. For instance, network software maker Novell offers a Certified Novell Administrator (CAN) certification for administrators who pass their training courses. A company that hires a network administrator from outside will almost certainly require such certification or proof of experience in administering a network successfully.

Network administration requires good organizational and logical thinking skills, both to set up and administer a network and to diagnose and solve problems. Administrators must be able to work under pressure and meet tight deadlines when required. Because they may have to work with users who have little or no technical knowledge, they must be able to communicate complex and unfamiliar ideas easily.

Getting the Job

Network administrator jobs are often advertised in newspapers, computer industry magazines, or Internet job banks. Some firms may offer to pay for the training of interested employees, because those individuals are already familiar with the company's needs.

Advancement Possibilities and Employment Outlook

Network administrators may advance into network engineering, in which they design networks from the ground up based on a company's needs and priorities. They may also branch out into other areas of computing such as programming, systems analysis (determining how well computer systems are operating and designing ways to improve their performance), and software engineering. Computer networks are becoming a standard part of most medium-to-large firms, and even of many smaller ones.

According to the U.S. Bureau of Labor Statistics, 278,000 network administrators were employed in the United States in 2004. Employment of network administrators was expected to grow much faster than average for all occupations through the year 2014. As the use of networks expands and the technology continues to change, the demand for qualified administrators will increase.

Working Conditions

Network administrators, like other computer professionals, work in an office environment. Most put in forty hours or more of work per week. Much of the job is performed alone, but the administrator must also work with users who are not comfortable with the system or who are experiencing difficulties. Configuring a network can require long hours of work over a short period of time. Maintaining the network can alternate between routine tasks such as installing and updating programs and the more interesting but hectic work of troubleshooting and fixing network problems. If a network crashes, the administrator must work as quickly as possible, regardless of the hour, to solve the problem and restore the network to operation. For a large network, the task of updating and maintenance can require late hours and work on an irregular schedule.

Earnings and Benefits

The Bureau of Labor Statistics reported that the median yearly wage for network administrators in 2004 was $58,190. According to the "Computerworld Salary Survey 2005" (*Computerworld*, October 24, 2005), the median yearly wage for a network administrator was $52,712 in 2005. Those in management jobs earn more. Because most network administrators are salaried employees, they are also entitled to health insurance, retirement, and other benefits offered to the company's employees.

Where to Go for More Information

Association for Computing Machinery
1515 Broadway
New York, NY 10036
(212) 626-0500
http://www.acm.org

IEEE Computer Society
1730 Massachusetts Ave. NW
Washington, DC 20036
(202) 371-0101
http://www.computer.org

Systems Administrator Guild
2560 9th St., Ste. 215
Berkeley, CA 94710
(510) 548-5738
http://www.sage.org

Office Manager

Definition and Nature of the Work

Office managers supervise administrative support workers, such as office clerks and secretaries, and coordinate administrative support activities. They work in all types of business and government offices. Office managers may head the entire office in a small firm or administrative support operations in a department of a large company. In either case the manager is responsible for directing workers and seeing that their jobs are done efficiently.

Office managers often decide what administrative support duties are needed in their department or company. Office managers decide what qualifications are necessary to perform the job. For instance, an office manager in an accounting firm may decide that an applicant requires a bachelor's degree to fill the job of accounting clerk. In many offices the manager helps to hire administrative support staff and is in control of promotions. Office managers devise training programs for new workers. Some are also responsible for determining salaries and working conditions. Managers make sure that job duties are not unnecessarily duplicated in the office. Managers often redefine duties in order to achieve maximum efficiency. They may devise a new job or eliminate an existing job. For instance, if a receptionist has too much filing to do, another person may be hired to file. Then the receptionist is free to answer telephones and greet visitors.

Office managers decide how much time it should take to do each job. Much of a manager's time is spent planning and developing work schedules. If new equipment would make a process more efficient, the manager orders the necessary machinery. For example, a faster copying machine might be ordered to reduce the time it takes employees to make copies.

Office managers are responsible for reporting to higher management and acting as liaisons between administrative support and the senior management. They report on the progress made by their departments in meeting company goals. The office manager takes direction from senior management and translates

Education and Training
College

Salary
Median—$41,030 per year

Employment Outlook
Fair

Office managers work with employees at many different job levels to instruct them and see that their jobs are done efficiently. *(Royalty-Free/Photo Disc, Inc. Reproduced by permission.)*

these directions into working practice. They must be able to communicate clearly. In addition, managers should be decisive, observant, and innovative. The position requires analytical ability as well as tact.

Education and Training Requirements

Most positions in office management require a college degree in business, although workers with only a high school diploma sometimes work their way up to managerial positions. College course work in accounting, administrative and personnel management, and data processing are especially useful. There are a number of home-study courses available for people who cannot attend college.

Office managers are often trained on the job. Many companies and government offices have management trainee programs. Sometimes trainees start by working for a short time in each of the company's departments to find out how the company functions. They work under the supervision of an experienced manager. Some companies send employees to courses and seminars at business schools or colleges to learn management techniques.

Getting the Job

A college or business school placement office can help graduating students find a position as a management trainee. State employment service and private employment agencies also list jobs in management. Interested individuals can write to various companies to inquire about jobs, and they can ask to leave an application on file if there are no immediate openings. In addition, the classified sections of newspapers list both beginning and top management openings. Candidates should also look in job sites on the Internet.

Advancement Possibilities and Employment Outlook

Office managers usually start as assistants and progress to jobs of greater responsibility as supervisors of large numbers of employees. A few office managers advance to top management positions in their firm. Some go into business for themselves. Their training makes them qualified to run many kinds of businesses. They can also become management consultants to various companies.

According to the U.S. Bureau of Labor Statistics, office and administrative support supervisors and managers held 1.5 million jobs in 2004. Employment of office managers was expected to grow more slowly than the average for all occupations through the year 2014. New technologies have eliminated many administrative support jobs as well as the need for someone to manage people in these jobs. Growth in the size and complexity of organizations in both the public and the private sectors, however, will require increasingly sophisticated management techniques, and the demand for skilled administrative specialists will continue to be strong.

Working Conditions

Office managers usually work forty hours per week, although they often spend additional time working on projects or attending meetings. Most of a manager's time is spent in the office. Office managers are under pressure from top management to make the administrative support operations of their departments run smoothly. They are also under pressure from their employees who may require the manager's time and assistance. Managers must get along well with all of these people.

Earnings and Benefits

Office managers earned a median yearly salary of $41,030 in 2004, according to the Bureau of Labor Statistics. Salaries vary with the size of the office in which a manager works, with large corporations usually paying the highest salaries. Benefits often include paid vacations, holidays, and health insurance. Some companies offer pension and profit sharing plans to their managers.

Where to Go for More Information

American Management Association
1601 Broadway
New York, NY 10019
(212) 586-8100
http://www.amanet.org

International Association of Administrative
  Professionals
10502 NW Ambassador Dr.
PO Box 20404
Kansas City, MO 64195-0404
(816) 891-6600
http://www.main.org/psi/

National Management Association
2210 Arbor Blvd.
Dayton, OH 45439
(937) 294-0421
http://www.nma1.org

Office Planner

Definition and Nature of the Work

Office planners, also known as office designers or facilities engineers, design the layout of office spaces. They create new offices or redesign existing facilities, taking into account factors such as the site's functions, staff interactions, traffic flow, and the machinery that is used. Office planners provide advice in the form of a master plan of office space, often presented as a drawing or blueprint. They use computers to create these plans.

Managers have become increasingly aware of the effect the office environment has on productivity and employee incentive. As new technologies such as computerized information services and cable communications are introduced into business settings, the organization of a comfortable, efficient office space has become more difficult. The office planner has emerged as the specialist who integrates all elements of the office's environment and functions into a coherent design.

Office planners must incorporate a variety of elements into their work. They must know principles of architecture and interior design as well as mainte-

Education and Training
College

Salary
Median—$40,670 per year

Employment Outlook
Good

An office planner is a specialist who can integrate the elements of the office's environment and functions into a coherent design. *(Photograph by Kelly A. Quin. Thomson Gale. Reproduced by permission.)*

nance and operations. In addition, they must be aware of evolving product designs, energy management, and building and safety codes. Planners also must have a good sense of personal and functional interactions in offices so they can design office spaces that are comfortable and productive.

Office planners work for several types of employers. Those employed as in-house experts usually work for large companies, such as banks, insurance companies, and manufacturers. Those employed by architectural firms or office systems design firms work as part of a team of experts who provide clients with services on a contract basis. Vendors and distributors of office equipment, furniture, and related supplies also sometimes hire office planners to help them sell packages of office equipment. Self-employed office planners often work on a freelance basis for other firms or as independent consultants.

Education and Training Requirements

To become an office planner, a person must have at least a bachelor's degree. College-level training is required by most employers, including architectural or design firms and major office equipment producers. A number of colleges and universities offer undergraduate and graduate programs in interior design or facilities planning and management. Other useful majors are environmental design, architecture, and engineering. Most employers also look for a strong business background. Programs generally require from two to four years of full-time study. Some employers provide on-the-job training lasting from one to three years.

The Institute of Business Designers and the American Society of Interior Designers grant certification to office planners based on their experience and successful completion of the National Council for Interior Design Qualification Examination. The exam, which requires the test taker to solve a design problem and to produce a blueprint, covers knowledge of space allotment, furniture selection and arrangement, and lighting and electrical technology. Applicants must have a combined six years of design experience either from a school or a design firm to be eligible to take the exam. Two of the six years must be in post-secondary education.

Getting the Job

A school placement office may be able to help a graduating student find a job in office planning. A person can also apply directly to architecture and design firms, office equipment manufacturers, and other companies that employ office planners. In some cases employers advertise job openings in newspapers, on the Internet, or in trade journals. Professional associations also offer student members a job referral service.

Advancement Possibilities and Employment Outlook

Office planners working in architectural or design firms can advance to senior positions by demonstrating superior talent and cooperative achievements with their coworkers in the firm. In-house office planners can advance to supervisory staff positions within their company. Planners working for equipment vendors sometimes move into managerial positions in charge of a division or several regional outlets. Some office planners advance by entering private practice as independent consultants.

Office planning is a subset of interior design. According to the U.S. Bureau of Labor Statistics, employment of interior designers was expected to grow as fast as the average through the year 2014. An increasing recognition of the effect of the office environment on productivity will likely lead to steady demand for the services of office planners.

Working Conditions

Office planners spend most of their time in offices drafting sketches and blueprints, but they also must travel to the sites where they will create or redesign office spaces. Many office planners work a standard forty-hour week, although sometimes they must work overtime to meet tight deadlines. The work schedules of consultants and freelance office planners are generally less regular than those of in-house office planners.

Earnings and Benefits

Salaries of office planners vary depending on their education and experience and on the type, size, and location of the employer. According to the Bureau of Labor Statistics, the median annual salary of interior designers/office planners was $40,670 in 2004. Interior designers/office planners with the top 10 percent of salaries made $71,220. Office planners who work for equipment distributors or vendors often work on commission or for a base wage plus a commission or bonus. Benefits vary with the employer but may include paid holidays and vacations, health insurance, and pension plans.

Operations Research Analyst

Education and Training
College

Salary
Median—$60,190 per year

Employment Outlook
Fair

Definition and Nature of the Work

Operations research analysts are problem solvers. They try to find more efficient and effective ways to run operations such as factories, telephone networks, traffic systems, and other concerns. For example, analysts might determine how to time traffic lights to produce fewer traffic jams. Operations research analysts use mathematics, engineering, scientific methods, and computer programming to solve such problems. Analysts have been employed in manufacturing industries, government, and the military for many years. An increasing number of analysts work in industries such as telecommunications, insurance, and banking. Some work for universities, research organizations, and consulting firms.

Operations research analysts look at each problem as a unique one. For instance, an analyst might be asked to develop a new traffic pattern for a large cafeteria to make the best use of space and personnel. There may be many similar cafeterias, but no other cafeteria has exactly the same location, layout, and equipment. The analyst asks questions and collects information about the cafeteria. How many people eat there on an average day? Where will they enter? Where are the trays picked up and returned? How long do most people stay? Then the analyst makes mathematical models to figure out the many possible ways to serve customers. Using a computer, the analyst finds the best ways to arrange the tables so that as many people as possible can eat comfortably at the same time. The analyst may then help the cafeteria manager decide how many employees are needed to handle the customers efficiently. Although this example is simple, it illustrates how operations research analysts help management to use space, personnel, and equipment more efficiently.

Many large organizations need the services of operations research analysts because inefficient operating methods can result in significant financial losses. Big businesses have many managers, each making operational decisions. Operations research analysts can help to coordinate the decision-making process. Operations research analysts also work in advertising and inventory control. Some analysts develop routes and schedules for buses, trains, and planes. Regardless of the field in which they work, operations research analysts must be able to think logically. They must be able to analyze many parts of a complex problem at the same time.

Education and Training Requirements

A person needs a master's degree in operations research or in a closely related field to become an operations research analyst. In high school a student should study mathematics and prepare to enter a college program in mathematics, engineering, or economics. Whatever a student's major is, a good background in applied mathematics is essential. A thorough knowledge of computers and experience with a variety of data processing systems is also necessary.

Many employers require a Ph.D. in operations research or management science. Many universities offer complete graduate programs in operations research. If candidates plan to work in a particular field, they might want to combine a mathematics degree with a graduate degree in that field.

Employers usually give on-the-job training to all newly employed analysts (even those with advanced degrees or previous work experience). Newcomers learn about the organization before they attempt to solve some of its problems. Some employers help their operations research analysts obtain advanced degrees.

Getting the Job

Most operations research analysts get jobs with large organizations. Interested individuals should check for ads on the Internet and in the classified section of local newspapers. College placement services can also help graduating students contact employers. Teaching jobs with the universities that offer operations research programs are sometimes available. The federal government employs operations research analysts. If a person is interested in a government job, he or she should apply to take the necessary civil service test. Candidates can also contact research organizations and consulting firms that work in operations research.

Advancement Possibilities and Employment Outlook

Operations research analysts can advance steadily to assignments that are more complex and broader in scope. There are many opportunities for people who are willing to keep up with the field and adapt their knowledge to specific industries. Analysts may start as a junior member of an operations research team and work up to a leadership position. Some analysts start their own consulting firms. Operations research analysts can also become corporate executives, because their work provides them with excellent planning and management skills.

According to the U.S. Bureau of Labor Statistics, fifty-eight thousand operations research analysts were employed in the United States in 2004. Employment of operations research analysts was expected to grow more slowly than average for all occupations through the year 2014. Jobs for operations research analysts should exist in all industries. Other jobs can be found in public agencies responsible for the management of water resources, garbage disposal, and recycling facilities, for example.

Working Conditions

Operations research analysts usually work at their desks or in computer rooms. They often work in teams. However, much of their work consists of independent calculations or computer work. They spend some time consulting with their clients or managers. Analysts generally work forty hours per week, except when they must put in extra hours to meet deadlines. They also spend time keeping up with the constant changes in the field.

Earnings and Benefits

Earnings of operations research analysts vary depending on experience, education, and geographic location. Operations research analysts earned a median salary of $60,190 per year in 2004, according to the Bureau of Labor Statistics. Benefits generally include paid holidays and vacations, health and life insurance, and pension plans.

Where to Go for More Information

American Society for Information Science and Technology
1320 Fenwick Ln., Ste. 510
Silver Spring, MD 20910
(301) 495-0900
http://www.asis.org

Institute for Operations Research and the Management Sciences
7240 Parkway Dr., Ste. 310
Hanover, MD 21076
(800) 4INFORMS
http://www.informs.org

Organizational Developer

Definition and Nature of the Work

Organization development is usually considered to be a specialized branch of management consulting. Organizational developers help corporate clients plan and implement programs to increase their organization's efficiency. They also help clients institute policies that enable their organizations to evolve continually to meet new business challenges. As more businesses opt to change their organizational structures, and as the use of management consultants in general grows more widespread, the demand for organizational developers will also grow.

A corporation hires an organizational developer when it suffers from inefficiency or needs help identifying personnel needs. Like other management consultants, organizational developers spend time analyzing a business's structure. They then formulate a report identifying ways to improve the corporation's performance through reorganization or through the redefinition of specific employees' roles. In general, organizational developers focus on improving goal setting, communication, and cross-departmental cooperation, as well as clarifying roles within the corporation. The ultimate goal usually is to improve professional relationships within the organization: between managers and staff, within teams, and across department lines. Organizational developers often recommend, design, and implement corporate education programs intended to help managers and employees develop productive professional relationships.

Organizational developers often work for independent consulting firms. Many large corporations hire organizational developer specialists as permanent employees who, most often, work within the human resources department.

Organizational developers analyze the operations of businesses and design programs to help them run more efficiently. (© Terry Wild Studio. Reproduced by permission.)

Education and Training Requirements

Organizational developers need specialized training, and they almost always have at least a bachelor's degree. Many organizational developers have advanced degrees in business administration and/or psychology.

Recommended courses of study include business, finance, economics, and psychology. People interested in becoming organizational developers should study current management and leadership theory, along with principles of business organization. Organizational developers also need training in scientific survey methodology.

Getting the Job

Candidates for jobs in organizational development should apply directly to consulting firms or corporations looking to fill positions. Organizational development jobs with corporations often are advertised within a human resources department. In addition to education and training pertinent to organizational development, successful candidates must demonstrate the ability to work as part of a team. They must also have an inquisitive mind and persistence.

Advancement Possibilities and Employment Outlook

In their first years of employment, organizational developers usually work long hours on relatively low-level tasks, such as data entry or interview transcriptions.

With three to seven years of experience, organizational developers' responsibilities expand to include direct client contact, employee and manager interviews, project analysis, the writing of reports, and, eventually, project management. Most organizational developers with ten or more years of experience hold managerial positions within the organization for which they work. Organizational developers not interested in management jobs can often use their experience to find employment as another type of management consultant, such as an efficiency expert or continuing education specialist.

According to the U.S. Bureau of Labor Statistics, employment in the management consulting field is expected to grow much faster than the average for all occupations through 2014. Competition for the jobs will be keen.

Working Conditions

Organizational developers work in clean, well-lighted offices. In entry-level positions they often work long hours at dull, repetitive tasks. Organizational developers who have direct client contact must be tactful and able to elicit honest information from employees. The nature of organizational development consulting requires that organizational developers work well as team members. They must be able to study a specific aspect of an organization, then put their observations into one "big picture," reconciling different interpretations of the organization's problems and agreeing on possible solutions.

Organizational developers on average work more than forty hours per week, especially when preparing reports with a tight deadline. Organizational developers working for consulting firms often must travel or temporarily relocate to service clients.

Earnings and Benefits

Salaries for organizational developers vary according to education and experience. Salary.com estimated the average annual salary for an organizational development specialist was $61,769 in 2006. The median annual salary for management consultants in 2004 was $72,488, according to the U.S. Bureau of Labor Statistics. Organizational developers can earn considerably more with advanced education degrees.

Where to Go for More Information

Academy of Management
PO Box 3020
Briarcliff Manor, NY 10510-8020
(914) 923-2607
http://www.aom.pace.edu

Association of Internal Management
   Consultants
824 Caribbean Ct.
Marco Island, FL 34145
(239) 642-0580
http://www.aimc.org

Association of Management Consulting
   Firms
380 Lexington Ave., Ste. 1700
New York, NY 10168
(212) 551-7887
http://www.amcf.org

National Association of Professional
   Organizers
4700 W. Lake Ave.
Glenview, IL 60025
(847) 375-4746
http://www.napo.net

Outplacement Consultant

Education and Training
College

Salary
Median—$52,800 per year

Employment Outlook
Excellent

Definition and Nature of the Work

World competition and increased technology have taken their toll on middle managers. Companies now find that they have to operate with fewer managerial personnel. In the past when these managers lost their jobs, they received only financial compensation. More recently companies have been using the services of outplacement consultants who work for outplacement consulting firms. These are specially trained people who can provide many different types of assistance to the terminated employee.

An outplacement consultant is a type of human resources consultant/specialist. Outplacement consultants assist employees in obtaining new positions more quickly. Although these consultants do not actually locate new jobs, they help employees to develop the skills and attitude necessary for a successful job search.

In the initial stages of assistance, outplacement consultants counsel employees about the psychological effects of job loss and how best to prepare for looking for a new job. They may also test employees to assess personality and skills. Following this evaluation, the consultants spend time coaching employees in job-hunting skills, interviewing, resume writing, and how to market their experience and skills.

Until recently these services were available only to selected senior employees. Today many companies realize the advantages of offering outplacement services to other terminated employees. Many unions also include this benefit in their contract negotiations.

Consultants usually offer group seminars to nonmanagerial staff in company offices. They also set up workshops where employees can discuss their situation and the problems associated with losing their jobs. These meetings are followed by other workshops designed to develop job-hunting skills and to offer advice on how to begin looking for new positions.

The terminating company pays a fee to the outplacement firms for these services. Many firms also provide private one-on-one counseling and workshops for individuals who find themselves unemployed. A few large corporations employ their own outplacement specialists. They are often personnel managers with additional training in this field.

Education and Training Requirements

There is no specific training needed to become an outplacement consultant. People working in this field come from a variety of backgrounds. Many have had personnel experience in a number of industries. Some have become consultants after having lost their jobs.

Employers usually require that outplacement consultants have a college education. Courses in personnel administration, personnel management, business, psychology, and sociology provide a good background. Many outplacement consultants have master's degrees in counseling or behavioral sciences, and some have doctoral degrees.

Getting the Job

A college placement office may be a good source for locating outplacement consultant positions. Interested individuals can also check the classified ads in local newspapers and professional magazines and job sites on the Internet.

Advancement Possibilities and Employment Outlook

Outplacement specialists may advance to managerial positions within outplacement firms depending on their skills, experience, and performance. Some experienced consultants begin their own outplacement firms.

According to the U.S. Bureau of Labor Statistics, employment of human resources consultants of all types was predicted to grow much faster than the average for all occupations through the year 2014. The number of outplacement firms is expected to increase as outplacement services become an accepted part of employee benefits packages. Openings for qualified people will increase as outplacement firms begin to offer services such as management personnel assessment and preretirement counseling.

Working Conditions

Outplacement consultants generally work from their own offices. They may conduct interviews and counsel clients in pleasant rooms or hold workshop and discussion groups in large conference rooms. They also work in resource rooms where reference books and materials are kept for clients' use.

When a large corporation plans to terminate many employees, the consultants usually travel to the company offices. Here outplacement consultants use specially provided space to conduct their counseling and training. They may also have to travel to different companies to discuss the services they offer.

Earnings and Benefits

The median annual salary for a human resources consultant in 2004 was $52,800, according to the Bureau of Labor Statistics. Earnings for outplacement consultants likely depend on the size of the firm for which the consultant works and the number and type of contracts received by the firm.

Where to Go for More Information

Association of Career Firms International
204 E St. NE
Washington, DC 20002
(202) 547-6344
http://www.aocfi.org

Recruiter

Definition and Nature of the Work

Recruiters seek out, interview, and test applicants to locate qualified employees for job openings. Recruiters—also called personnel recruiters or employment, recruitment, and placement specialists—often travel to universities and colleges to interview promising students for employment. They may also select applicants from resumes that job seekers send to the company.

Whether they travel to school sites or do their recruiting in a company's human resources departments, recruiters evaluate applicants on their technical skills, education, work history, personality, salary requirements, and managerial abilities. To inform candidates of company benefits and job opportunities, they often give promotional presentations. Recruiters also test prospective employees during follow-up interviews, analyze the results, and maintain files on applicants. They may also check applicants' references.

An important part of the recruiter's job is to understand and implement the government's guidelines on discrimination. Recruiters must also know their

Education and Training
College

Salary
Median—$41,190 per year

Employment Outlook
Very good

company's needs, programs, benefits, management structure, and advancement policies.

Some recruiters work exclusively for private consultants or employment agencies, which assist companies in finding qualified employees. Other recruiters are employed by large corporations.

Education and Training Requirements

A college education is usually required in this field. Majors in human resources management, business, psychology, sociology, or economics are accepted. Some employers prefer liberal arts graduates. Courses in management, marketing, industrial relations, organizational behavior, and public relations provide excellent preparation for this field. A master's degree in business administration (MBA) may be helpful in some cases.

Getting the Job

A graduating student's college placement office may be a good source for locating recruiting positions. Interested individuals should consult the classified ads in local newspapers and job sites on the Internet. Some companies use employment agencies and human resources management magazines to locate recruiters.

Advancement Possibilities and Employment Outlook

Recruiters can advance to higher levels in human resources or other managerial departments in a company, depending on their skills, experience, and performance. Advanced jobs in the human resources field include training specialist, human resources director, and manager.

According to the U.S. Bureau of Labor Statistics, recruitment, employment, and placement specialists held 182,000 jobs in 2004. Employment of recruiters was expected to grow faster than the average for all occupations through the year 2014. In times of recession when jobs are scarce, the opportunities in recruiting may diminish. Because recruiting is often a one-step assignment on a career ladder, there will always be a need to replace recruiters who advance to higher positions. The job market will be competitive due to the abundant supply of college graduates and experienced workers with suitable qualifications.

Working Conditions

College recruiters travel extensively from city to city during the height of the recruiting season, which can be both exciting and grueling. Also, recruiters frequently may be required to work on weekends and in the evenings. They should know how to use audiovisual equipment and other office equipment, including computers.

Recruiters must have excellent communications skills and an interest in people. They must be able to quickly judge a person's suitability for a job. This part of the job creates pressure.

Earnings and Benefits

According to the Bureau of Labor Statistics, recruitment, employment, and placement specialists earned a median salary of $41,190 per year in 2004. Benefits include paid vacations and holidays and health insurance.

Where to Go for More Information

International Public Management
    Association for Human Resources
1617 Duke St.
Alexandria, VA 22314
(703) 549-7100
http://www.ipma-hr.org/

Society for Human Resource Management
1800 Duke St.
Alexandria, VA 22314
(703) 548-3440
http://www.shrm.org

Resume Writer

Definition and Nature of the Work

Resume writers prepare resumes, or summaries of the qualifications of an applicant who is searching for a job. Resume writers are aware that potential employers may only look briefly at a resume. Therefore, they prepare an applicant's resume so that it makes a favorable impression quickly. Resume writers make sure that the resume presents the applicant's qualifications, job history, and experience in a clear and readable format. Resume writers research the best design to catch a potential employer's attention. They can set up the applicant's work experience on paper in a variety of ways. They can suggest different methods for printing resumes. Resume writers also know the correct words to use when listing the applicant's qualifications, skills, education, and job history.

Many resume writers specialize in writing resumes for one type of applicant. For example, some writers prepare resumes only for executives or only for applicants to a specific industry. These writers may use specific wording in the applicant's resume ensuring that it appeals to potential employers from that industry.

Resume writers may be employed by companies that provide this service, or they may work on a freelance basis out of their homes. Many resume writers use word processing or desktop publishing software programs to prepare the resumes. The writer can use these programs to produce a high-quality, professional-looking document that is very readable.

Education and Training Requirements

Most resume writers have a college degree, although there are no specific educational requirements for this job. Resume writers should have typing skills, proofreading skills, and a basic knowledge of computers. They should be able to communicate with a customer to decide what information about him or her would be most valuable on the resume. They should write well and be able to produce error-free resumes. Many resume writers have previous experience in personnel departments, where they learned to evaluate effective resumes. This can contribute to their ability to write resumes that will attract a potential employer's attention.

Getting the Job

Resume services place help-wanted ads in newspapers and on the Internet. Writers can also call resume writing services to inquire about job openings.

Advancement Possibilities and Employment Outlook

Because most resume writers are self-employed, advancement consists mainly of acquiring more clients. Resume writers may use their desktop publishing or word processing skills in areas other than resume writing to supplement their earnings. They may also move into the job of executive search recruiter or employment counselor.

Because many people are proficient computer users and many word processing programs and books on how to write resumes are available, jobs for resume writers may decrease in the future. However, the large number of job applicants will ensure that this service is needed for highly competitive fields.

Education and Training
College

Salary
Varies—see profile

Employment Outlook
Fair

Working Conditions

Resume writers may work in their own homes or for resume writing services. They work at computers. Work hours vary. Self-employed writers may work part time or full time depending on the flow of work. Resume writers employed by companies are likely to work in an office environment, but they may do some of their work at home.

Earnings and Benefits

Writers who work for a service may get a small salary plus a commission for each resume that they prepare. Yearly salaries for resume writers can vary widely due to the types of clients the writer has and the number of clients the writer has. Most resume services charge around $150 for a basic resume. Generally, someone who writes resumes for college students will make much less than someone who writes resumes for executives.

Due to the uneven nature of resume writing, no official survey on median salary exists for resume writers. Resume writers are essentially a cross between a writer and an employment interviewer. The U.S. Bureau of Labor Statistics reported that the median salary for employment interviewers was $40,970 per year in 2003. Full-time, salaried writers made a median yearly wage of $44,350 in 2004.

Where to Go for More Information

Association of Career Professionals
    International
204 E St. NE
Washington, DC 20002
(202) 547-6377
http://www.iacmp.org

Securities Broker

Education and Training
College plus training

Salary
Median—$69,200 per year

Employment Outlook
Good

Definition and Nature of the Work

The securities broker is an essential link between a consumer and the world's financial markets. Securities brokers, also called securities, commodities, and financial services sales agents, advise customers who want to make financial investments. Securities brokers arrange for the purchase or sale of stocks, bonds, and other securities on their customers' behalf. Through the maze of investment opportunities that are available, brokers steer customers to those that best suit their needs.

The two most common types of securities are stocks and bonds. Private businesses offer the public part ownership of the business by issuing stocks. People who buy shares of stock are sometimes promised a percentage of the profits, known as dividends, in return for the use of their money. As the value of the company increases, the value of the individual's stock increases. Bonds represent loans made to companies and government agencies. In return for buying bonds, buyers receive a prescribed rate of interest and sometimes a yearly or monthly cash payment. Bonds may be sold in much the same way that stocks are sold.

Investment needs vary with individual customers. A conservative investor whose life savings amount to a small sum may be in the market for a long-term investment that will provide a regular income. The broker may advise this customer to invest in government or corporate bonds or a mutual fund. On the other hand, the broker may direct a wealthy customer to buy stock in a company that is financially uncertain but has great potential.

Brokers may specialize in one type of security, such as mutual funds or government bonds. Some specialize in commodities, a type of security that represents future ownership of such commodities as potatoes, wheat, or coffee. Although many brokers service work with both individuals and corporations, some specialize in only one type of account.

Brokers generally work for discount or full-service brokerage firms that have offices. Brokers place, buy, and sell orders with the home office and report to their customers on the outcome of transactions either in person or on the Internet. Success in their business rests on their knowledge of the field and ability to predict future developments in trading. Investors can also choose to invest with an Internet brokerage, in which customers make investments without the help of a securities broker.

Education and Training Requirements

To become a broker, a person must have a college education. Employers may prefer to hire those who major in economics, finance, or business administration. Most large brokerages have a trainee program, which includes classroom instruction and on-the-job training. Courses include accounting, corporate finance, bonds, financial statements, mutual funds, sales techniques, public speaking, and many other related subjects. A student can also get this training at accredited schools. At the end of the training, individuals must pass a qualifying examination, known as the General Securities Registered Representative Examination, to be licensed or registered representatives of the stock exchange to which they belong. The examination is administered by the National Association of Securities Dealers (NASD), and to take it candidates must be employed in a brokerage firm for four months. Depending on the state, a broker may have to take additional tests and meet additional requirements.

Getting the Job

The best way for interested individuals to find a job in the securities business is to apply directly to a company for which they would like to work. Speaking to people who work in the various aspects of the business may help candidates to decide what kind of sales work they would like to do. Private employment agencies that specialize in placing workers in the field of finance may list openings for beginners. Newspaper classified ads and Internet job sites may also offer job leads.

Advancement Possibilities and Employment Outlook

Advancement for brokers usually takes the form of an increase in the number and size of the accounts they handle. Beginning brokers generally work with the accounts of individual investors. With experience they may be made responsible for very large accounts, such as those of corporations. Some experienced brokers advance to the position of branch office manager. Managers supervise the work of other brokers while handling orders for their own customers. A few brokers become partners in their firms.

According to the U.S. Bureau of Labor Statistics, 281,000 securities, commodities, and financial services sales agents held jobs in 2004. Employment was expected to grow as fast as the average for all occupations through the year 2014. A high rate of turnover in the field also contributes to a number of openings, because many workers who fail to establish a clientele leave the field each year. The securities business depends on the health of the economy as a whole. Therefore, the job market shrinks when money is tight. Although self-service Internet securities firms take business away from brokers, brokers are benefiting from the increase in retirement-aged individuals looking to invest their money.

Where to Go for More Information

National Association of Securities Dealers
1 Liberty Plaza
New York, NY 10006
(212) 858-4000
http://www.nasd.com

New York Stock Exchange
11 Wall St.
New York, NY 10005
(212) 656-3000
http://www.nyse.com

Security Traders Association
420 Lexington Ave., Ste. 2334
New York, NY 10170
(212) 867-7002
http://www.securitytraders.org

Working Conditions

Securities brokers work in offices or cubicles that are clean and well lighted. Fluctuations in market activity may produce an atmosphere of tension within the brokerage.

Although established brokers usually work forty hours per week, beginners who are trying to get customers may work much longer hours. Securities brokers often work weekends and evenings to meet with customers.

Earnings and Benefits

Trainees generally are paid on a salary basis until they meet licensing and registration requirements. Experienced brokers work on a commission or salary-plus-commission basis. According to the Bureau of Labor Statistics, securities, commodities, and financial service sales agents earned a median yearly salary of $69,200 in 2004. The top 25 percent earned more than $131,290 per year. Benefits include pension plans and health insurance. Salaried employees may receive paid holidays and vacations.

Software Trainer

Definition and Nature of the Work

A software trainer is a type of training specialist who teaches individuals how to use computer applications or programs such as spreadsheets, desktop publishing programs, or computer network systems software. The nature of the job requires knowledge of computer software programs and strong communication skills.

The types of programs trainers must know depends on the setting in which they are teaching. Those who work for a corporation must be familiar with the software the company uses in its day-to-day operations. This may include widely used software such as Microsoft Word or Lotus spreadsheets as well as programs developed by the company to perform functions specific to that business. Trainers who work as consultants or at a school or career counseling center will need to know a broad range of programs that may be used by many different businesses. Because the Internet is being used for business as well as research, a software trainer needs to be knowledgeable about the uses of various browsers such as Netscape or Internet Explorer that allow individuals to access and navigate the World Wide Web.

Software trainers must be able to explain the technical complexities of software effectively. The trainer's audience may include people with a wide range of computer skills and educational levels. The audience may also vary in size from just a few people in a private setting to an entire roomful of people in a professional seminar. Trainers must be able to structure their presentations to fit the circumstances. Like any good teacher, the trainer must also be able to measure how well the students are absorbing the material and to adjust the presentation accordingly.

An important part of good teaching is preparation, which requires strong organizational skills. Good preparation allows a trainer to present the material quickly and efficiently. However, trainers must also be able to change course and adapt to the needs of the students. Trainers must anticipate which areas may be more difficult for students and the types of questions students are likely to ask. A trainer must also be able to address the needs of individual students without slowing down the entire class.

Education and Training Requirements

The education required of a software trainer depends on the setting in which the work is done. Schools or career centers usually require a four-year degree in a computer-related field and possibly a teaching certificate as well. Corporate trainers and consultants may only need experience using the software being taught. Many software trainers are self-taught and rely on the knowledge they have gained working with various programs. Of course, the more software programs a person knows, the better his or her chances of landing a job as a software trainer.

Education and Training
College

Salary
Median—$44,570 per year

Employment Outlook
Very good

A software trainer teaches individuals how to use computer programs. The trainer must present materials efficiently and at an appropriate level for those being trained. (Royalty-Free/Photo Disc, Inc. Reproduced by permission.)

Getting the Job

If already working for a company that uses computers in its business, a person may be able to create his or her own position as an in-house software trainer for company personnel. If individuals have extensive experience using software programs and working with others, they can market their services as consultants to businesses or as instructors for individuals. Computer stores sometimes have openings for instructors to teach their customers how to use the software they purchase. Schools and computer camps are also good places to look for jobs as software trainers. Interested individuals can check Internet job sites and classified ads of newspapers for job openings as well.

Advancement Possibilities and Employment Outlook

Experienced trainers who work in a corporate environment may move on to become the director of training, supervising other trainers. An individual who works as a consultant may expand that business to develop specialized workshops or seminars.

According to the U.S. Bureau of Labor Statistics, training and development specialists—the job title befitting software trainers—held 216,000 jobs in 2004. Employment of software trainers and other training and development specialists was expected to grow faster than average for all occupations through 2014. Because computers and the Internet are a key part of both business and education, the prospects for employment as a software trainer should continue to grow. Companies will continue to hire more software trainers to keep their aging workforces up-to-date on increasingly complex software. More jobs will also become available as existing software trainers leave their jobs or get promoted.

Working Conditions

Software trainers employed by corporations or schools work in modern offices or classrooms. They work standard business or school hours. Consultants may work at a space in the client's office or in a seminar or conference room at a hotel or other meeting facility. They may also work in an individual client's home. Those who run seminars often schedule them on weekends or evenings when people are not at work or school.

Earnings and Benefits

The median annual salary for training and development specialists, according to the Bureau of Labor Statistics, was $44,570 in 2004. Specialists with the top 10 percent of salaries made more than $74,650 per year. Benefits for salaried software trainers generally include health and life insurance, paid holidays and vacations, and pension plans.

Statistician

Definition and Nature of the Work

Statisticians collect and analyze mathematical data to solve problems and make predictions on future outcomes. They apply their knowledge to many different fields, including manufacturing, government, science, engineering, and public health. Using statistical techniques, statisticians can make forecasts on population growth, economic conditions, or the outcome of elections. Some statisticians work to develop the theories on which statistical techniques are based.

When statisticians are assigned a project, they first plan ways to collect the information they need. They draw on their knowledge of probability and sampling. For example, to predict the outcome of an election, statisticians might design a survey of a sample group of people who represent all the voters. Sampling substitutes the impossible task of asking every person how he or she plans to vote. Statisticians carefully develop questionnaires that yield clear answers and useful information. They supervise the workers who carry out the survey and tabulate the data. When all the information is collected, statisticians study and interpret it. They may then make recommendations to their superiors or clients.

Statisticians work on the research and marketing problems of many industries. The insurance industry employs statisticians, as do state and federal governments. The primary purpose of market research and public opinion research companies is to collect and interpret statistics. Statisticians in industry often work on quality control and product development issues. In a computer company, for instance, statisticians might design experiments that determine the failure rate of keyboards or the error rate of software. Universities employ statisticians both to teach and to do research.

Statisticians may have other titles according to their specialty. For example, those who conduct economic research may be called econometricians. Those

Education and Training
College

Salary
Median—$58,620 per year

Employment Outlook
Fair

Statisticians use computers to analyze data and predict population growth, economic conditions, or the outcome of elections. (© Martha Tabor/ Working Images Photographs. Reproduced by permission.)

who work to improve the basic mathematical theories behind statistical work are often called mathematical statisticians. Statisticians who collect and analyze data in the biological sciences are sometimes known as biostatisticians.

Education and Training Requirements

The minimum education required in this field is a bachelor's degree in mathematics or statistics. Depending on the particular job, a statistician may need a major in some other subject, such as economics or biology, with a minor in statistics. Courses in computers and business administration are often helpful. A statistician with only a bachelor's degree does very routine work. A graduate degree or sometimes multiple graduate degrees are required for the more advanced jobs. A doctoral degree is generally required for those who teach in colleges and universities.

Statisticians must have an aptitude for figures and be interested in working with numbers. The ability to organize figures and to think logically is also necessary.

Getting the Job

A college placement office may be able to help a graduating student find a job as a statistician. Interested individuals should check the classified ads of local newspapers and Internet job banks for openings. State and private employment agencies may offer job leads. Those who are interested in a government job should apply to take the necessary civil service examination. A person can also apply directly to firms that employ statisticians.

Advancement Possibilities and Employment Outlook

Statisticians with exceptional ability can rise to top management jobs. Those who have advanced degrees and expand their area of expertise have the best chances for advancement.

According to the U.S. Bureau of Labor Statistics, nineteen thousand people in the United States were employed as statisticians in 2004. Employment of statisticians was expected to grow more slowly than the average for all occupations through 2014. The demand for these workers was expected to grow more slowly than average in both the public and private sectors. However, openings will occur as experienced statisticians retire or leave their jobs for other reasons.

Working Conditions

Statisticians usually work in comfortable and pleasant offices. At times statisticians are under considerable pressure to meet deadlines. They are generally required to work forty hours per week, but statisticians sometimes work extra hours without pay.

Earnings and Benefits

Earnings vary with education, experience, and the size of the employing firm. The median annual salary for a statistician was $58,620 in 2004, according to the Bureau of Labor Statistics. Those with the top 10 percent of salaries made more than $100,500 per year. Statisticians employed by the federal government earned a median salary of $81,262 per year. Benefits usually include paid holidays and vacations, health insurance, and retirement contributions.

Training and Development Specialist

Definition and Nature of the Work

Training and development specialists help businesses, institutions, and government agencies to develop, carry out, and evaluate training programs for their employees. These specialists, also known just as trainers, may prepare newly recruited employees for their jobs. They often assist employees with job transitions in the event of a corporate merger or acquisition. They also may instruct employees in new technology, in a new management and reporting system, or in safety and health precautions. Trainers must analyze organizations, discover where training would be most useful, and design new programs to fit the need. They frequently use training methods that include audiovisual aids, classroom instruction, role-playing, or equipment such as computers. When the training sessions are complete, trainers evaluate the effectiveness of the training to ensure that the desired results are being achieved.

Also known as human resource development specialists or employee development specialists, these specialized human resources workers are employed by federal, state, and local government, by school systems, and by firms in private industry. Some trainers are self-employed as freelance specialists. Many more work for private consulting firms that specialize in areas such as management, marketing, or interpersonal behavior.

Training and development specialists should have strong interpersonal and verbal skills, imagination, and a good sense of humor. In addition, trainers must have a good understanding of how organizations function, together with special competence in the particular area in which they train.

Education and Training Requirements

Most training and development specialists have at least a bachelor's degree, frequently in computer science, psychology, English, or management science. Many trainers also have a master's degree in a training-related field. A doctoral

A training and development specialist uses classroom discussion and equipment to teach employees how to use new software. *(Photograph by Kelly A. Quin. Thomson Gale. Reproduced by permission.)*

degree is becoming increasingly common among personnel workers who specialize in the development of new training programs.

Two- and four-year programs or specialized courses related to training exist at many colleges and universities nationwide. Course work in communication skills such as public speaking and audiovisual techniques and in management science are especially helpful. Many people enter the field after previous experience as teachers, broadcasters, or in other professions that involve public speaking.

Getting the Job

A college placement office may be able to help a graduating student find a job as a training and development specialist. Interested individuals should check classified ads on the Internet and ads in local newspapers for listings under personnel jobs. Candidates can also apply directly to companies that have large personnel departments. Those who are interested in government jobs should apply to take the necessary civil service examination. State and private employment services may also offer job leads.

Advancement Possibilities and Employment Outlook

Trainers can advance by developing expertise in a specialized area, such as marketing or management training. Training and development specialists can also become supervisors, managers, or executives of training programs or organizations. Some training and development specialists establish their own consulting firms. Those with advanced degrees will have the best opportunities.

According to the U.S. Bureau of Labor Statistics, training and development specialists held 216,000 jobs in 2004. Employment of training and development specialists is expected to grow faster than average for all occupations through 2014. Training programs have grown rapidly in recent years as both public- and private-sector employers seek to upgrade the training and productivity of their workers. Growth in the training field is sensitive to the general economic situation, however. Training programs are often among the first areas to be cut during recessionary periods.

Working Conditions

Training and development specialists may work singly or as members of a team of trainers. Their work may involve the use of audiovisual equipment or office machinery. Many trainers travel extensively to conduct training workshops. Because training programs are often scheduled outside normal working hours, trainers frequently work on weekends or in the evening.

Where to Go for More Information

American Society for Training and
   Development
1640 King St., Box 1443
Alexandria, VA 22313
(703) 683-8100
http://www.astd.org

Earnings and Benefits

Earnings of training and development specialists vary according to their education and level of responsibility. The median annual salary for training and development specialists was $44,570 in 2004, according to the Bureau of Labor Statistics. Specialists with salaries in the top 10 percent made more than $74,650 per year. Benefits for salaried trainers generally include health and life insurance, paid holidays and vacations, and pension plans.

Books

Exploring the Working World

American Salaries and Wages Survey, 8th ed., Helen S. Fisher. Farmington Hills, MI: Thomson Gale, 2005.

America's Fastest Growing Jobs: Detailed Information on the 140 Fastest Growing Jobs in Our Economy, 8th ed., Michael Farr. Indianapolis, IN: JIST Publishing, 2004.

America's Top 101 Jobs for College Graduates, 6th ed., Michael Farr. Indianapolis, IN: JIST Publishing, 2005.

America's Top 101 Jobs for People without a Four-Year Degree, 7th ed., Michael Farr. Indianapolis, IN: JIST Publishing, 2004.

America's Top 300 Jobs, 9th ed., U.S. Department of Labor. Indianapolis, IN: JIST Publishing, 2004.

Best Career and Education Web Sites: A Quick Guide to Online Job Search, 4th ed., Rachel Singer Gordon and Anne Wolfinger. Indianapolis, IN: JIST Publishing, 2004.

Best Entry-Level Jobs, Ron Lieber and Tom Meltzer. New York: Princeton Review, 2006.

Best Jobs for the 21st Century, 4th ed., Michael Farr and Laurence Shatkin. Indianapolis, IN: JIST Publishing, 2006.

Big Book of Jobs, 2003–2004, U.S. Department of Labor. New York: McGraw-Hill, 2003.

Career Discovery Encyclopedia, 5th ed., 8 vols. Chicago, IL: Ferguson, 2003.

Enhanced Occupational Outlook Handbook, 5th ed., Indianapolis, IN: JIST Publishing, 2005.

Job Hunter's Sourcebook: A Thomson Gale Career Information Guide. Farmington Hills, MI: Thomson Gale, biennial.

Jobs Rated Almanac, 6th ed., Les Krantz. Fort Lee, NJ: Barricade, 2002.

The National JobBank, 2006. Avon, MA: Adams Media, 2006.

Occupational Outlook Handbook series. Washington, DC: United States Government Printing Office, biennial. Briefs, separately published.

Occupational Outlook Quarterly. Washington, DC: United States Government Printing Office. Quarterly publication.

Professional Careers Sourcebook, 7th ed. Farmington Hills, MI: Thomson Gale, 2002.

200 Best Jobs for College Graduates, 3rd ed., Michael Farr and Laurence Shatkin. Indianapolis, IN: JIST Publishing, 2006.

Recommended

Best Jobs for the 21st Century, 4th ed., Michael Farr and Laurence Shatkin. Indianapolis, IN: JIST Publishing, 2006. Lists five hundred jobs and categorizes them into sixty-five "Best Jobs for…" lists. Organizes jobs by category, education required, best growth potential.

Jobs Rated Almanac, 6th ed., Les Krantz. Fort Lee, NJ: Barricade, 2002. Rates 250 jobs and sorts into "best for" and "worst for" rankings. Factors include salary, benefits, and stress level.

300 Best Jobs without a Four-Year Degree, 2nd ed. Michael Farr and Laurence Shatkin. Indianapolis, IN: JIST Publishing, 2006.

VGM's Career Encyclopedia, 5th ed., New York: McGraw-Hill, 2002.

Vocational Careers Sourcebook, 5th ed., Farmington Hills, MI: Thomson Gale, 2002.

Education and Training Opportunities

Acing the College Application: How to Maximize Your Chances for Admission to the College of Your Choice, Michele Hernandez. New York: Ballantine, 2002.

Admission Matters: What Students and Parents Need to Know about Getting Into College, Sally P. Springer and Marion R. Franck. San Francisco, CA: Jossey-Bass, 2005.

Barron's Guide to Graduate Business Schools, Eugene Miller and Neuman F. Pollack. Hauppauge, NY: Barron's Educational Series, revised regularly.

Barron's Guide to Law Schools. Hauppauge, NY: Barron's Educational Series, revised regularly.

Barron's Guide to Medical and Dental Schools, Sol Wischnitzer and Edith Wischnitzer. Hauppauge, NY: Barron's Educational Series, revised regularly.

Barron's Profiles of American Colleges. Hauppauge, NY: Barron's Educational Series, annual.

Bear's Guide to College Degrees by Mail and Internet, 10th ed., John Bear. Berkeley, CA: Ten Speed Press, 2005.

Best 109 Internships, 9th ed., Mark Oldman and Samer Hamadah. New York: Princeton Review, 2003.

The Best 361 Colleges. New York: Princeton Review, annual.

Chronicle Vocational School Manual. Moravia, NY: Chronicle Guidance Publications, annual.

The College Application Essay, Sarah Myers McGinty. New York: The College Board, 2004.

The College Board Book of Majors, 2nd ed. New York: The College Board, 2006.

The College Board Scholarship Handbook. New York: The College Board, annual.

The College Cost and Financial Aid Handbook. New York: The College Board, annual.

College Financial Aid: How to Get Your Fair Share, 6th ed., Peter V. Laurenzo. Albany, NY: Hudson Financial Press, 2002.

The College Handbook. New York: The College Board, annual.

College Majors Handbook with Real Career Paths and Payoffs, 2nd ed., Neeta P. Fogg. Indianapolis, IN: JIST Publishing, 2004.

College Planning for Gifted Students, 3rd ed., Sandra L. Berger. Waco, TX: Prufrock Press, 2006.

College Success Guide: Top 12 Secrets for Student Success, Karine Blackett and Patricia Weiss. Indianapolis, IN: JIST Publishing, 2005.

Recommended

Acing the College Application: How to Maximize Your Chances for Admission to the College of Your Choice, Michele Hernandez. New York: Ballantine, 2002. Written by former Dartmouth College admissions officer. Frank but reassuring advice on application, essay, and personal interview.

The Insider's Guide to Colleges. New York: St. Martin's Griffin, annual. Surveys students at 320 U.S. and Canadian schools on dorm life, class size, and other campus-related topics.

Vault Guide to Top Internships, Samer Hamadah. New York: Vault, 2005. Provides information on internships offered by 700-plus companies, including Fortune 500 corporations. Nonprofit and government programs also listed.

Complete Book of Colleges. New York: Princeton Review, annual.

Fiske Guide to Colleges, Edmund Fiske. Naperville, IL: Sourcebooks, annual.

The Gourman Report: A Rating of Undergraduate Programs in American and International Universities, Jack Gourman. Los Angeles, CA: National Educational Standards, revised regularly.

Guide to College Majors. New York: Princeton Review, 2006.

Guide to the Most Competitive Colleges. Hauppauge, NY: Barron's Educational Series, revised regularly.

How to Choose a College Major, Linda Landis Andrews. New York: McGraw-Hill, 2006.

How to Write Your College Application Essay, Kenneth Nourse. New York: McGraw-Hill, 2001.

The Insider's Guide to Colleges. New York: St. Martin's Griffin, annual.

The Internship Bible, 10th ed. New York: Princeton Review, 2005.

The National Guide to Educational Credit for Training Programs. Washington, DC: American Council on Education, revised regularly.

100 Successful College Application Essays, 2nd ed. New York: New American Library, 2002.

Peterson's Best College Admission Essays, 3rd ed. Princeton, NJ: Thomson Peterson's, 2004.

Peterson's College Money Handbook. Princeton, NJ: Thomson Peterson's, annual.

Peterson's College and University Almanac. Princeton, NJ: Thomson Peterson's, annual.

Peterson's Competitive Colleges. Princeton, NJ: Thomson Peterson's, annual.

Peterson's Financial Aid Answer Book. Princeton, NJ: Thomson Peterson's, annual.

Peterson's Guide to Four-Year Colleges. Princeton, NJ: Thomson Peterson's, annual.

Peterson's Guide to Two-Year Colleges. Princeton, NJ: Thomson Peterson's, annual.

Peterson's Internships. Princeton, NJ: Thomson Peterson's, annual.

Quick Guide to College Majors and Careers, Laurence Shatkin. Indianapolis, IN: JIST Publishing, 2002.

Rugg's Recommendations on the Colleges, Frederick Rugg. Fallbrook, CA: Rugg's Recommendations, annual.

Students' Guide to Colleges: The Definitive Guide to America's Top 100 Schools Written by the Real Experts—the Students Who Attend Them, Jordan Goldman and Colleen Buyers. New York: Penguin, 2005.

The Truth about Getting In: A Top College Advisor Tells You Everything You Need to Know, Katherine Cohen. New York: Hyperion, 2002.

US News Ultimate College Guide. Naperville, IL: Sourcebooks, annual.

Vault Guide to Top Internships, Samer Hamadah. New York, Vault, 2005.

Career Goals

The Career Adventure: Your Guide to Personal Assessment, Career Exploration, and Decision Making, 4th ed., Susan M. Johnston. Upper Saddle, NJ: Prentice-Hall, 2005.

Career Guide to America's Top Industries, 6th ed., U.S. Department of Labor. Indianapolis, IN: JIST Publishing, 2004.

Career Warfare: 10 Rules for Building a Successful Personal Brand and Fighting to Keep It, David F. D'Alessandro and Michele Owens. New York: McGraw-Hill, 2003.

College Majors and Careers: A Resource Guide for Effective Life Planning, 5th ed., Paul Phifer. Chicago, IL: Ferguson, 2003.

Cool Careers for Dummies, Marty Nemko, Paul Edwards, and Sarah Edwards. Foster City, CA: IDG Books, 2001.

Customize Your Career, Roz Usheroff. New York: McGraw-Hill, 2004.

Do What You Are: Discover the Perfect Career for You Through the Secrets of Personality Type, 3rd ed., Paul D. Tieger and Barbara Barron-Tieger. New York: Little, Brown, 2001.

50 Best Jobs for Your Personality, Michael Farr and Laurence Shatkin. Indianapolis, IN: JIST Publishing, 2005.

Finding a Career That Works for You: A Step-by-Step Guide to Choosing a Career and Finding a Job, Wilma Fellman. Plantation, FL: Specialty Press, 2000.

Finding Your Perfect Work: The New Career Guide to Making a Living, Creating a Life, 2nd ed., Paul Edwards and Susan Edwards. New York: Penguin, 2003.

The 5 Patterns of Extraordinary Careers: The Guide for Achieving Success and Satisfaction, James M. Citrin and Richard Smith. New York: Crown Business, 2003.

The Global Citizen: A Guide to Creating an International Life and Career, Elizabeth Kruempelmann. Berkeley, CA: Ten Speed Press, 2002.

Guide to Your Career, 5th ed., Alan B. Bernstein. New York: Princeton Review, 2004.

How Hard Are You Knocking? The Job Seeker's Guide to Opening Career Doors, Timothy J. Augustine and Rona Curcio. Winchester, VA: Oakhill Press, 2005.

Job Search and Career Checklists: 101 Proven Time-Saving Checklists to Organize and Plan Your Career Search, Arlene S. Hirsch. Indianapolis, IN: JIST Publishing, 2005.

Recommended

Finding Your Perfect Work: The New Career Guide to Making a Living, Creating a Life, 2nd ed., Paul Edwards and Susan Edwards. New York: Penguin, 2003. Lists types of careers, with emphasis on self-employment opportunities.

What Color Is Your Parachute?: A Practical Manual for Job-Hunters and Career-Changers, Richard Nelson Bolles. Berkeley, CA: Ten Speed Press, revised annually. The classic in the genre, and the top-selling career-advice book consistently since the mid-1970s. Updated to reflect twenty-first-century concerns.

Monster Careers: How to Land the Job of Your Life, Jeffrey Taylor and Douglas Hardy. New York: Penguin, 2004.

New Guide for Occupational Exploration: Linking Interests, Learning and Careers, 4th ed., Michael Farr and Laurence Shatkin. Indianapolis, IN: JIST Publishing, 2006.

The Play of Your Life: Your Program for Finding the Career of Your Dreams—And a Step-by-Step Guide to Making It a Reality, Colleen A. Sabatino. New York: Rodale, 2004.

What Color Is Your Parachute?: A Practical Manual for Job-Hunters and Career-Changers, Richard Nelson Bolles. Berkeley, CA: Ten Speed Press, revised annually.

What Should I Do with My Life?: The True Story of People Who Answered the Ultimate Question, Po Brosnan. New York: Random House, 2002.

Where's My Oasis?: The Essential Handbook for Everyone Wanting the Perfect Job, Rowan Manahan. New York: Vermillion, 2004.

Getting the Job and Getting Ahead

Almanac of American Employers, Jack W. Plunkett. Galveston, TX: Plunkett Research Ltd., biennial.

e-Resumes: A Guide to Successful Online Job Hunting, Pat Criscito. Hauppauge, NY: Barron's Educational Series, 2004.

Guide to Internet Job Searching, Margaret Riley Dikel. New York: McGraw-Hill, 2004.

How to Earn What You're Worth: Leveraging Your Goals and Talents to Land Your Dream Job, Sunny Bates. New York: McGraw-Hill, 2004.

How to Get Any Job with Any Major: Career Launch & Re-launch for Everyone Under 30 (or How to Avoid Living in Your Parent's Basement), Donald Asher. Berkeley, CA: Ten Speed Press, 2004.

How to Get Your First Job and Keep It, 2nd ed., Deborah Perlmutter Bloch. New York: McGraw-Hill, 2002.

Insider's Guide to Finding A Job: Expert Advice From America's Top Employers and Recruiters, Wendy S. Enelow and Shelly Goldman. Indianapolis, IN: JIST Publishing, 2004.

International Job Finder: Where the Jobs Are Worldwide, Daniel Lauber and Kraig Rice. River Forest, IL: Planning/Communications, 2002.

International Jobs: Where They Are and How to Get Them, 6th ed., Nina Segal and Eric Kocher. New York: Basic Books, 2003.

Job-Hunting On the Internet, 4th ed., Richard Nelson Bolles and Mark Emery Bolles. Berkeley, CA: Ten Speed Press, 2005.

Job Savvy: How to be Success at Work, 3rd ed., LaVerne L. Ludden. Indianapolis, IN: JIST Publishing, 2002.

Job Search Magic: Insider Secrets from America's Career and Life Coach, Susan Britton Whitcomb. Indianapolis, IN: JIST Publishing, 2006.

The Job Search Solution: The Ultimate System for Finding a Great Job Now!, Tony Bashara. New York: AMACOM, 2005.

Job Seeker's Online Goldmine: A Step-by-Step Guidebook to Government and No-Cost Web Tools, Janet E. Wall. Indianapolis, IN: JIST Publishing, 2006.

Knock 'Em Dead 2006: The Ultimate Job Seekers Guide, Martin Yate. Avon, MA: Adams Media, 2006.

National Job Hotline Directory: The Job Finder's Hot List, 3rd ed., Sue Cubbage and Marcia Williams. River Forest, IL: Planning/Communications, 2003.

1000 Best Job Hunting Secrets, Diane Stafford and Moritza Day. Naperville, IL: Sourcebooks, 2004.

Super Job Search: The Complete Manual for Job-Seekers & Career-Changers, 3rd ed., Peter Studner. Los Angeles, CA: Jamenair Ltd., 2003.

10 Insider Secrets to a Winning Job Search: Everything You Need to Get the Job You Want in 24 Hours—Or Less, Todd Bermont. Franklin Lakes, NJ: Career Press, 2004.

Very Quick Job Search: Get a Better Job in Half the Time, 3rd ed., Michael Farr. Indianapolis, IN: JIST Publishing, 2003.

Recommended

How to Get Any Job with Any Major: Career Launch & Re-launch for Everyone Under 30 (or How to Avoid Living in Your Parent's Basement), Donald Asher. Berkeley, CA: Ten Speed Press, 2004. Counsels liberal-arts degree-holders on how to package their education and strengths to land a high-paying position.

Knock 'Em Dead 2006: The Ultimate Job Seekers Guide, Martin Yate. Avon, MA: Adams Media, 2006. Offers range of advice for job-hunters at all levels, including resume-building, interview strategies, and salary negotiation tips.

Resumes and Interviews

Adams Job Interview Almanac, 2nd ed., Richard Wallace. Avon, MA: Adams Media Corp., 2005.

Adams Resume Almanac, 2nd ed., Richard Wallace. Avon, MA: Adams Media Corp., 2005.

Amazing Resumes: What Employers Want to See—and How to Say It, Jim Bright and Joanne Earl. Indianapolis, IN: JIST Publishing, 2005.

Competency-Based Resumes: How to Bring Your Resume to the Top of the Pile, Robin Kessler and Linda A. Strasburg. Franklin Lakes, NJ: Career Press, 2004.

Cover Letter Magic, 2nd ed., Wendy S. Enelow and Louise Kursmark. Indianapolis, IN: JIST Publishing, 2004.

Cover Letters That Knock 'Em Dead, 6th ed., Martin Yate. Avon, MA: Adams Media, 2004.

The Elements of Resume Style: Essential Rules and Eye-opening Advice for Writing Resumes and Cover Letters That Work, Scott Bennett. New York: AMACOM, 2005.

Expert Resumes for Career Changers, Wendy S. Enelow and Louise M. Kursmark. Indianapolis, IN: JIST Publishing, 2005.

Fearless Interviewing: How to Win the Job by Communicating with Confidence, Marky Stein. New York: McGraw-Hill, 2002.

Ferguson Guide to Resumes and Job-Hunting Skills, Maurene J. Hinds. Chicago, IL: Ferguson, 2005.

Gallery of Best Resumes: A Collection of Quality Resumes by Professional Resume Writers, 3rd ed., David F. Noble, Ph.D. Indianapolis, IN: JIST Publishing, 2004.

Get the Interview Every Time: Fortune 500 Hiring Professionals' Tips for Writing Winning Resumes and Cover Letters, Brenda Greene. Chicago, IL: Dearborn Trade Publishing, 2004.

How to Interview Like a Top MBA: Job-Winning Strategies From Headhunters, Fortune 100 Recruiters, and Career Counselors, Shel Leanne. New York: McGraw-Hill, 2003.

How to Turn an Interview into a Job, Jeffrey G. Allen. New York: Simon and Schuster, 2004.

McGraw-Hill's Big Red Book of Resumes. New York: McGraw-Hill, 2002.

Recommended

Resume Magic: Trade Secrets of a Professional Resume Writer, 2nd ed., Susan Britton Whitcomb. Indianapolis, IN: JIST Publishing, 2003. Before and after resume samples provide a how-to on crafting the perfect resume. Includes tips on e-resumes and tricks for scannable-text submissions.

301 Smart Answers to Tough Interview Questions, Vicky Oliver. Naperville, IL: Sourcebooks, 2005. Advice on how to handle the questions designed to unsettle, from explaining gaps in work history to acing arcane trivia volleys.

Monster Careers: Interviewing—Master the Moment That Gets You the Job, Jeffrey Taylor and Doug Hardy. New York: Penguin Books, 2005.

The Resume.com Guide to Writing Unbeatable Resumes, Warren Simons and Rose Curtis. New York: McGraw-Hill, 2004.

The Resume Handbook: How to Write Outstanding Resumes & Cover Letters for Every Situation, 4th ed., Arthur D. Rosenberg and David V. Hizer. Avon, MA: Adams Media, 2003.

Resume Magic: Trade Secrets of a Professional Resume Writer, 2nd ed., Susan Britton Whitcomb. Indianapolis, IN: JIST Publishing, 2003.

Resumes for Dummies, 4th ed., Joyce Lain Kennedy. Indianapolis, IN: Wiley Publishing, 2003.

Resumes That Knock 'Em Dead, 6th ed., Martin Yate. Avon, MA: Adams Media, 2004.

301 Smart Answers to Tough Interview Questions, Vicky Oliver. Naperville, IL: Sourcebooks, 2005.

201 Best Questions to Ask on Your Interview, John Kador. New York: McGraw-Hill Co., Inc., 2002.

Winning the Interview Game: Everything You Need to Know to Land the Job, Alan H. Nierenberg. New York: AMACOM, 2005.

Mid-Career Options

Change Your Job, Change Your Life: Careering and Re-Careering in the New Boom/Bust Economy, 9th ed., Ron Krannich. Manassas Park, VA: Impact, 2004.

Fearless Career Change, Marky Stein. New York: McGraw-Hill, 2005.

Fire Your Boss, Stephen M. Pollan and Mark Levine. New York: HarperCollins, 2004.

I Don't Know What I Want, But I Know It's Not This: A Step-by-Step Guide to Finding Gratifying Work, Julie Jansen. New York: Penguin Books, 2003.

Over-40 Job Search Guide: 10 Strategies for Making Your Age an Advantage in Your Career, Gail Geary. Indianapolis, IN: JIST Publishing, 2004.

Radical Careering: 100 Truths to Jumpstart Your Job, Your Career, and Your Life, Sally Hogshead. New York: Gotham, 2005.

Second Acts: Creating the Life You Really Want, Building the Career You Truly Desire, Stephen M. Pollan and Mark Levine. New York: HarperCollins, 2003.

Working Identity: Unconventional Strategies for Reinventing Your Career, Hermania Ibarra. Boston, MA: Harvard Business School Press, 2003.

Recommended

I Don't Know What I Want, But I Know It's Not This: A Step-by-Step Guide to Finding Gratifying Work, Julie Jansen. New York: Penguin Books, 2003. Experienced career coach identifies the top six reasons people are dissatisfied with their jobs, and provides a step-by-step process for finding a career that suits the personality.

Working Identity: Unconventional Strategies for Reinventing Your Career, Hermania Ibarra. Boston, MA: Harvard Business School Press, 2003. Help for those considering a mid-career change.

Equality of Opportunity

Dancing on the Glass Ceiling, Nancy Frederick and Candy Deemer. New York: McGraw-Hill, 2004.

Job-Hunting for the So-Called Handicapped or People Who Have Disabilities, 2nd ed., Richard Nelson Bolles and Dale Susan Brown. Berkeley, CA: Ten Speed Press, 2001.

Job Search Handbook for People with Disabilities, 2nd ed., Daniel J. Ryan. Indianapolis, IN: JIST Publishing, 2004.

Lavender Road to Success: The Career Guide for the Gay Community, Kirk Snyder. Berkeley, CA: Ten Speed Press, 2003.

Resources for People with Disabilities, 2nd ed., Shawn Woodyard. Chicago, IL: Ferguson, 2001.

Recommended

Dancing on the Glass Ceiling, Nancy Frederick and Candy Deemer. New York: McGraw-Hill, 2004. A former advertising executive teams with a professional executive coach to provide practical as well as inspirational advice for women in the workplace.

Job-Hunting for the So-Called Handicapped or People Who Have Disabilities, 2nd ed., Richard Nelson Bolles and Dale Susan Brown. Berkeley, CA: Ten Speed Press, 2001. From the author of *What Color Is Your Parachute?* Advice for the physically or mentally challenged on finding a career niche.

Lists and Indexes of Career and Vocational Information

Encyclopedia of Careers and Vocational Guidance, 13th ed., 5 vols. Chicago, IL: Ferguson, 2006.

O*Net Dictionary of Occupational Titles, 3rd ed. Indianapolis, IN: JIST Publishing, 2004.

Internet Sites

Sites with Extensive Links

About.com
http://careerplanning.about.com

Beyond.com
http://www.beyond.com

Jobweb.com
http://www.jobweb.com

JIST Publishing
http://www.jist.com

Job Hunt: Online Job Search Guide and Resource Directory
http://www.job-hunt.org

Vault.com
http://www.vault.com

Vocational Information Center
http://www.khake.com

Career Development Resources

Career Magazine
http://www.careermag.com

Career Resource Homepage
http://www.careerresource.net

Job Hunters Bible
http://www.jobhuntersbible.com

Princeton Review
http://www.princetonreview.com

Quintessential Careers
http://www.quintcareers.com

Online Information and References

AT&T Toll-Free Internet Directory
http://www.tollfree.att.net

The Best Jobs in the USA Today
http://www.bestjobsusa.com

Careers.org
http://www.careers.org

Federal Jobs Digest
http://www.fedworld.gov/jobs/jobsearch.html

Job Finders Online
http://www.planningcommunications.com/jf

Job Safari
http://www.jobsafari.com

Monster Career Center
http://content.monster.com

Occupational Outlook Handbook
http://www.bls.gov/oco

SpherionExchange
http://employee.spherionexchange.com/start.cfm

U.S. Bureau of Labor Statistics Homepage
http://www.bls.gov/home.htm

US News and World Report Career Center
http://www.usnews.com/usnews/biztech/career/career_home.htm

Wall Street Journal Career Journal
http://www.careerjournal.com

Yahoo! Business and Economy
http://dir.yahoo.com/Business_and_Economy

Job Databases and Resume Posting

After College
http://www.aftercollege.com

America's Job Bank
http://www.ajb.org

Career Builder
http://www.careerbuilder.com

Career Mart
http://www.careermart.com

Employment Guide
http://www.employmentguide.com

Yahoo! Hot Jobs
http://hotjobs.yahoo.com

Idealist Nonprofit Career Center
http://www.idealist.org

Job.com
http://www.job.com

JobBank USA
http://www.jobbankusa.com

Job Web
http://www.jobweb.org

Monster Jobs
http://www.monster.com

Monstertrak
http://www.monstertrak.monster.com

NationJob.com
http://www.nationjob.com

Now Hiring
http://www.nowhiring.com

Audiovisual Materials

The following titles include, where possible, the developer's name and location or else the name and location of a distributor. Audiovisual titles may be available through several distributors.

Exploring the Working World

Career Advantage: Strategies for Success series. Video, guide. Princeton, NJ: Films Media Group.

Career Clusters series. Video Charleston, WV: Cambridge Educational.

Career Exploration series. Video. South Charleston, WV: Meridian Education Corp.

Career Guidance Videos series. Video. South Charleston, WV: Meridian Education Corp.

Career S.E.L.F. Assessment: Finding a Career That Works for You. Video. Charleston, WV: Cambridge Educational.

Careers, Careers, Careers! Video, guide. Princeton, NJ: Films Media Group.

Careers for the 21st Century series. Video, guide. South Charleston, WV: Meridian Education Corp.

Careers without College. Video. Charleston, WV: Cambridge Educational.

The Changing Workplace: Technology and Globalization. Video. Princeton, NJ: Films Media Group.

Choices Today for Career Satisfaction Tomorrow. Video, guide. Charleston, WV: Cambridge Educational.

Complete Job Search System. Video. Charleston, WV: Cambridge Educational.

Connect on the Net: Finding a Job on the Internet. Video. Charleston, WV: Cambridge Educational.

Educational Planning for Your Career. Video. South Charleston, WV: Meridian Education Corp.

The 50 Best Jobs for the 21st Century series. Video. Indianapolis, IN: JIST Publishing.

The JIST Video Guide for Occupational Exploration series. Video. Indianapolis, IN: JIST Publishing.

Internet Careers: College Not Required. Video. Charleston, WV: Cambridge Educational.

Introduction to Career and Educational Exploration. Video. Princeton, NJ: Films Media Group.

JIST TV series: The Job Search Channel. Video. Indianapolis, IN: JIST Publishing.

Jobs for the 21st Century. Video. Mt. Kisco, NY: Guidance Associates.

Learning for Earning. Video, guide. South Charleston, WV: Meridian Education Corp.

Log On for Success: Using Internet Job Sites. Video, guide. Charleston, WV: Cambridge Educational.

Researching Career Options: New Technologies and Current Techniques. Video. Princeton, NJ: Films Media Group.

School-to-Work Transition. Video. South Charleston, WV: Meridian Education Corp.

Ten Fastest Growing Careers: Jobs for the Future. Video. Mt. Kisco, NY: Guidance Associates.

What Would I Be Good At? Video. Mt. Kisco, NY: Guidance Associates.

What's Out There: How the World of Work is Organized. Video. Princeton, NJ: Films Media Group.

Your Career Search: Taking the First Step. Video. Mt. Kisco, NY: Guidance Associates.

Your Future: Planning Through Career Exploration. Video. South Charleston, WV: Meridian Education Corp.

Getting the Job and Getting Ahead

Career Evaluation. Video. Charleston, WV: Cambridge Educational.

Common Mistakes People Make in Interviews. Video, guide. Charleston, WV: Cambridge Educational.

Exceptional Employee: A Guide to Success on the Job. Video. Charleston, WV: Cambridge Educational.

Exceptional Interviewing Tips: A View from the Inside. Video, workbook. Charleston, WV: Cambridge Educational.

Extraordinary Answers to Common Interview Questions. Video. Charleston, WV: Cambridge Educational.

Finding a Job. Video. Charleston, WV: Cambridge Educational.

First Impressions: Etiquette and Work Habits for New Employees. Video, guide. Charleston, WV: Cambridge Educational.

From Pinkslip to Paycheck: The Road to Reemployment series. Video. Indianapolis, IN: JIST Publishing.

Getting Good Answers to Tough Interview Questions. Video. Indianapolis, IN: JIST Publishing.

Getting the Job You Really Want series. Video, workbook, guide. Indianapolis, IN: JIST Publishing.

How to Find a Job on the Internet. Video. Indianapolis, IN: JIST Publishing.

How to Be a Success at Work series. Video. Indianapolis, IN: JIST Publishing.

The Ideal Resume. Video. Charleston, WV: Cambridge Educational.

If at First: How to Get a Job and Keep It. Video. Mt. Kisco, NY: Guidance Associates.

Interview to Win Your First Job. Video. Indianapolis, IN: JIST Publishing.

Interviewing for a Job. Video. Charleston, WV: Cambridge Educational.

Job Survival Kit. Video. Charleston, WV: Cambridge Educational.

On-the-Job Success series. Video. Indianapolis, IN: JIST Publishing.

Planning Your Career. Video. Charleston, WV: Cambridge Educational.

The Portfolio Resume series. Video. Charleston, WV: Cambridge Educational.

"Quick" Job Search series. Video. Indianapolis, IN: JIST Publishing.

Succeeding on the Job. Video. Charleston, WV: Cambridge Educational.

Success in the Job World series. Video. Indianapolis, IN: JIST Publishing.

Staying on Track in Your Work Search. Video. Princeton, NJ: Films Media Group.

Power Interviewing Skills: Strategies for the Interviewee. Video. Charleston, WV: Cambridge Educational.

Take This Job and Love It: Keys to Surviving Your New Job. Video. Charleston, WV: Cambridge Educational.

Ten Commandments of Resumes. Video. Charleston, WV: Cambridge Educational.

Tough Times Job Strategies. Video, guide. Charleston, WV: Cambridge Educational.

Understanding and Using the O*NET. Video, guide. Charleston, WV: Cambridge Educational.

The Very Quick Job Search Video. Video. Indianapolis, IN: JIST Publishing.

The Video Guide to JIST's Self-Directed Job Search series. Video. Indianapolis, IN: JIST Publishing.

Web Resumes. Video. Charleston, WV: Cambridge Educational.

Computer Software

The following titles include, where possible, the developer's name and location or else the name and location of a distributor. Software titles may be available through several distributors.

Ace the Interview: The Multimedia Job Interview Guide. CD-ROM. Charleston, WV: Cambridge Educational.

Adams Media JobBank FastResume Suite. CD-ROM for Windows. Avon, MA: Adams Media.

Barron's Profiles of American Colleges on CD-ROM. Windows or Macintosh. Hauppauge, NY: Barron's Educational Series.

Cambridge Career Center. CD-ROM. Charleston, WV: Cambridge Educational.

Career Discovery Encyclopedia. CD-ROM. Chicago, IL: Ferguson.

Career Explorer. CD-ROM for Windows. Indianapolis, IN: JIST Publishing.

Career Finder Plus. CD-ROM. Indianapolis, IN: JIST Publishing.

CareerOINKs on the Web. Network. Indianapolis, IN: JIST Publishing.

Careers without College. CD-ROM. Indianapolis, IN: JIST Publishing.

Complete Resume Designer. CD-ROM. Charleston, WV: Cambridge Educational.

Custom Resume Creator. CD-ROM for Windows. Indianapolis, IN: JIST Publishing.

Decisions. CD-ROM. Indianapolis, IN: JIST Publishing.

Electronic Career Planner. CD-ROM for Windows. Indianapolis, IN: JIST Publishing.

Exploring the World of Work. CD-ROM. New York: McGraw-Hill.

JIST Presents Interview Mastery. CD-ROM. Indianapolis, IN: JIST Publishing.

Job Search series. CD-ROM. Indianapolis, IN: JIST Publishing.

Job Survival series. CD-ROM. Indianapolis, IN: JIST Publishing.

The Keys to Interviewing Success: Unlocking Your Professional Future. CD-ROM. Charleston, WV: Cambridge Educational.

Moving on Up: An Interactive Guide to Finding a Great Job. CD-ROM for Windows. Charleston, WV: Cambridge Educational.

Multimedia Career Center. CD-ROM. Charleston, WV: Cambridge Educational.

The Multimedia Career Path. CD-ROM. Charleston, WV: Cambridge Educational.

The Multimedia Guide to Occupational Exploration. CD-ROM. Charleston, WV: Cambridge Educational.

Multimedia Job Search. CD-ROM for Windows. Charleston, WV: Cambridge Educational.

Multimedia Take This Job and Love It. CD-ROM. Charleston, WV: Cambridge Educational.

OOH Career Center. CD-ROM. Charleston, WV: Cambridge Educational.

School-to Work Career Center. CD-ROM. Charleston, WV: Cambridge Educational.

Success in the World of Work: Succeeding on the Job. CD-ROM. South Charleston, WV: Meridian Education Corp.

Targeting Success. CD-ROM. Indianapolis, IN: JIST Publishing.

General

Books

Careers in International Business, 2nd ed., Edward J. Halloran. New York: McGraw-Hill, 2003.

Complete Book of Business Schools 2004, Nedda Gilbert. Princeton, NJ: Princeton Review, 2003.

The Complete Idiot's Guide to Starting Your Own Business, 4th ed., Edward Paulson. Indianapolis, IN: Alpha Books, 2003.

Encyclopedia of Business Information Sources, Detroit: Gale, updated regularly.

Great Jobs for Business Majors, 2nd ed., Stephen E. Lambert. New York: McGraw-Hill, 2003.

The Harvard Business Review on Managing Your Career, David Baskerville. Boston: Harvard Business School Press, 2003.

How to Get Into the Top MBA Programs, 3rd ed., Richard Mantauk. Englewood Cliffs, NJ: Prentice Hall, 2005.

Leadership 101: What Every Leader Needs to Know, John C. Maxwell. Nashville, TN: Thomas Nelson, 2002.

The Portable MBA, 4th ed., Robert F. Bruner, et al. Hoboken, NJ: John Wiley & Sons, 2002.

Small Business Owner's Manual: Everything You Need to Know to Start Up and Run Your Own Business, Joe Kennedy. Franklin Lakes, NJ: Career Press, 2005.

Standard & Poor's Register of Corporations, Directors and Executives. New York: Standard & Poor's Corporation, annual.

They Don't Teach Corporate in College, Alexandra Levit. Franklin Lakes, NJ: The Career Press, 2004.

Top Careers for Business Majors. New York: Facts on File, 2003.

The Wall Street Journal Guide to the Top Business Schools 2006, Ronald Alsop. New York: Random House, 2005.

Internet Sites

Bloomberg Careers
http://about.bloomberg.com/careers/index.html

Careers in Business
http://www.careers-in-business.com

Careers Inc./bankjobs.com
http://www.bankjobs.com

Computerwork.com
http://www.computerwork.com

Dice Inc.
http://www.dice.com

Information Week
http://www.informationweek.com/career3

International Association of Administrative Professionals
http://www.iaap-hq.org

Internetnews.com
http://www.internetnews.com

Information Technology Management WEB
http://www.itmweb.com

The NonProfit Times
http://www.nptimes.com

Real Estate Jobs
http://www.realestatejobstore.com

SmartPros
http://www.accountingnet.com

TechJobBank
http://www.techjobbank.com

Yahoo! Finance
http://finance.yahoo.com

Computers, Computer Science, and Data Processing

Books

Ace the IT Job Interview!, Paula Moreira. Berkeley, CA: McGraw-Hill Osborne Media, 2003.

Ace the IT Resume!, Paula Moreira. Berkeley, CA: McGraw-Hill Osborne Media, 2001.

Career Guide for the High-Tech Professional, David Perry. Franklin Lakes, NJ: The Career Press, 2004.

Careers for Computer Buffs and Other Technological Types, 3rd ed., Marjorie Eberts and Margaret Gisler. New York: McGraw-Hill, 2006.

Careers for Cybersurfers and Other Online Types, 2nd ed., Marjorie Eberts and Rachel Kelsey. New York: McGraw-Hill, 2003.

Careers in Computers, 3rd ed., Lila B. Stair and Leslie Stair. Chicago: VGM Career Books, 2002.

Careers in Information Technology, 2006. San Francisco, CA: WetFeet, 2005.

Choosing a Career in Computers, Chris Weigant. New York: Rosen Publishing Group, 2001.

Engineering Your Start-Up: A Guide for the High-Tech Entrepreneur, 2nd ed., James A. Swanson and Michael C. Baird. Belmont. CA: Professional Publications, 2003.

Get Your IT Career in Gear!, Leslie Jaye Goff. Berkeley, CA: McGraw-Hill Osborne Media, 2001.

Opportunities in Data and Word Processing Careers, Marianne Forrester Munday. Chicago: VGM Career Books, 2002.

101 Best Tech Resumes, 2nd ed., Jay A. Block. New York: McGraw-Hill, 2002.

Vault Guide to Technology Careers, Evan Koblentz and Tod Emko. New York: Vault, 2005.

Finance and Management

Books

Career Opportunities in Banking, Finance, and Insurance, Thomas P. Fitch. New York: Facts on File, 2002.

Careers in Accounting, 4th ed., Gloria L. Gaylord and Glenda E. Reid. New York: McGraw-Hill, 2006.

Great Jobs for Accounting Majors, 2nd ed., Jan Goldberg. New York: McGraw-Hill, 2005.

Opportunities in Financial Careers, Michael Sumichrast and Martin Sumichrast. New York: McGraw-Hill, 2004.

The Portable MBA in Finance and Accounting, 3rd ed., John Leslie Livingstone and Theodore Grossman, eds. New York: John Wiley & Sons, 2001.

The Portable MBA in Management, 2nd ed., Allen R. Cohen. New York: John Wiley & Sons, 2002.

Office Work and Services

Books

Administrative and Executive Assistant Career Starter, 2nd ed., Shirley Tarbell. New York: LearningExpress, 2002.

Administrative Assistant's and Secretary's Handbook, 2nd ed., James Stroman et al. New York: AMACOM Books, 2004.

Home-Based Business for Dummies, 2nd ed., Paul Edwards, Sarah Edwards, and Peter Economy. Hoboken, NJ: John Wiley & Sons, 2005.

Most Likely to Succeed at Work: How Work Is Just Like High School, Wilma Davidson and Jack Dougherty. New York: St. Martin's Press, 2003.

Real Resumes for Administrative Support, Office and Secretarial Jobs, Anne McKinney. Fayetteville, NC: PREP Publishing, 2004.

The 60-Second Commute: A Guide to Your 24/7 Home Office Life, Erica Orloff. Upper Saddle River, NJ: Pearsons Education, 2003.

The information in this directory was generated from the IPEDS (Integrated Postsecondary Education Data System) database of the U.S. Department of Education. It includes only regionally or nationally accredited institutions offering postsecondary occupational training in computing, business, and office occupations. Because college catalogs and directories of colleges and universities are readily available elsewhere, this directory does not include institutions that offer only bachelor's and advanced degrees.

Accounting

ALABAMA

Bessemer State Technical College
1100 9th Ave
Bessemer 35021

Central Alabama Community College
1675 Cherokee Rd.
Alexander 35010

Chauncey Sparks State Technical
College
Hwy. 431 S
Eufaula 36027

Douglas MacArthur Technical College
1708 North Main St.
Opp 36467

Draughons Junior College
122 Commerce St.
Montgomery 36104

Enterprise State Junior College
600 Plaza Dr.
Enterprise 36330

Gadsden Business College
750 Forrest Ave.
Gadsden 35901

Gadsden Business College, Anniston
P.O. Box 1559
Anniston 36202-1575

George C Wallace State Community
College, Selma
3000 Earl Goodwin Pkwy.
Selma 36702-1049

George C Wallace State Community
College, Dothan
Rte. 6, P.O. Box 62
Dothan 36303-9234

Harry M Ayers State Technical College
1801 Coleman Rd.
Anniston 36202

Jefferson State Community College
2601 Carson Rd.
Birmingham 35215-3098

John C Calhoun State Community
College
Hwy. 31 N
Decatur 35609-2216

New World College of Business
P.O. Box 2287
Anniston 36201

Northwest Shoals Community College
800 George Wallace Blvd.
Muscle Shoals 35662

University of Alabama in Huntsville
301 Sparkman Dr.
Huntsville 35899

ALASKA

Alaska Computer Institute
701 East Tudor Rd.
Anchorage 99503

Charter College
2221 East Northern Lights Blvd., Ste. 120
Anchorage 99508

New Frontier Vocational-Technical
Center
35270 K Bearch Rd., Ste. 37B
Soldotna 99669

People Count, Inc.
P.O. Box 1310
Kenai 99611

University of Alaska, Anchorage
3211 Providence Dr.
Anchorage 99508

ARIZONA

Academy Business College
3320 West Beryl Ave.
Phoenix 85021

Arizona Institute of Business and
Technology
6049 North 43rd Ave.
Phoenix 85019

Central Arizona College
8470 North Overfield Rd.
Coolidge 85228-9778

Glendale Community College
6000 West Olive Ave.
Glendale 85302

Mesa Community College
1833 West Southern Ave.
Mesa 85202

Pima Community College
2202 West Anklam Rd.
Tucson 85709-0001

Tucson College
7302-10 East 22nd St.
Tucson 85710

ARKANSAS

Cossatot Technical College
183 Hwy. 399
De Queen 71832

Foothills Technical Institute
1800 East Moore St.
Searcy 72143

Great Rivers Vocational-Technical
School
P.O. Box 747, Hwy. 1 NE
McGehee 71654

Northwest Technical Institute
709 South Old Missouri Rd.
Springdale 72764

Ouachita Technical College
One College Circle
Malvern 72104

Southeast Arkansas Technical College
1900 Hazel
Pine Bluff 71603

Pulaski Technical College
3000 West Scenic Dr.
North Little Rock 72118

CALIFORNIA

Allan Hancock College
800 South College Dr.
Santa Maria 93454

American River College
4700 College Oak Dr.
Sacramento 95841

Barstow College
2700 Barstow Rd.
Barstow 92311

Cabrillo College
6500 Soquel Dr.
Aptos 95003

Canada College
4200 Farm Hill Blvd.
Redwood City 94061

Career Development Center
255 East Bonita Ave.
Pomona 91767

Center for Employment Training, El
Centro
294 South Third St.
El Centro 92243

Center for Employment Training,
Gilroy
7800 Arroyo Circle
Gilroy 95020

Center for Employment Training, San
Jose-Vine
701 Vine St.
San Jose 95110

Cerritos College
11110 Alondra Blvd.
Norwalk 90650

Chabot College
25555 Hesperian Blvd.
Hayward 94545

Chaffey Community College
5885 Haven Ave.
Rancho Cucamonga 91737-3002

City College of San Francisco
50 Phelan Ave.
San Francisco 94112

College of Alameda
555 Atlantic Ave.
Alameda 94501

Crafton Hills College
11711 Sand Canyon Rd.
Yucaipa 92399-1799

De Anza College
21250 Stevens Creek Blvd.
Cupertino 95014

Diablo Valley College
321 Golf Club Rd.
Pleasant Hill 94523

East Los Angeles Skill Center
3921 Selig Place
Los Angeles 90031

El Camino College
16007 Crenshaw Blvd.
Torrance 90506

Eldorado College
2204 El Camino Real
Oceanside 92054

Eldorado College
1901 Pacific Ave.
West Covina 91790

Empire College School of Business
3033 Cleveland Ave.
Santa Rosa 95403

Evergreen Valley College
3095 Yerba Buena Rd.
San Jose 95135-1598

Foothill College
12345 El Monte Rd.
Los Altos Hills 94022

Fresno City College
1101 East University Ave.
Fresno 93741

Fullerton College
321 East Chapman Ave.
Fullerton 92632-2095

Gavilan College
5055 Santa Teresa Blvd.
Gilroy 95020

Glendale Community College
1500 North Verdugo Rd.
Glendale 91208-2894

Golden West College
15744 Golden W
Huntington Beach 92647

Goodwill Industries of Santa Cruz
350 Encinal St.
Santa Cruz 95060

Grossmont College
8800 Grossmont College Dr.
El Cajon 92020

Hacienda La Puente Unified School
District-Valley Vocational Center
15959 East Gale Ave.
La Puente 91749

Imperial Valley College
P.O. Box 158
Imperial 92251-0158

Laney College
900 Fallon St.
Oakland 94607

Long Beach City College
4901 East Carson St.
Long Beach 90808

Los Angeles City College
855 North Vermont Ave.
Los Angeles 90029

Los Angeles Trade Technical College
400 West Washington Blvd.
Los Angeles 90015-4181

Los Medanos College
2700 East Leland Rd.
Pittsburg 94565

Marin Regional Occupational Program
P.O. Box 4925
San Rafael 94913

Mendocino College
P.O. Box 3000
Ukiah 95482

Merced College
3600 M St.
Merced 95348-2898

Mexican American Opportunity
    Foundation
2001 28th St.
Bakersfield 93301-1924

Mira Costa College
One Barnard Dr.
Oceanside 92056-3899

Mission College
3000 Mission College Blvd.
Santa Clara 95054-1897

Modesto Junior College
435 College Ave.
Modesto 95350-5800

Monterey Peninsula College
980 Fremont Blvd.
Monterey 93940-4799

Moorpark College
7075 Campus Rd.
Moorpark 93021

Mount San Antonio College
1100 North Grand
Walnut 91789

MTI Business College, Inc.
6006 North El Dorado St.
Stockton 95207-4349

MTI Western Business College
5221 Madison Ave.
Sacramento 95841

Napa Valley College
2277 Napa Vallejo Hwy.
Napa 94558

Ohlone College
43600 Mission Blvd.
Fremont 94539

Orange Coast College
2701 Fairview Rd.
Costa Mesa 92626

Orange County Business College
2035 East Ball Rd.
Anaheim 92806

Oxnard College
4000 South Rose Ave.
Oxnard 93033

Palomar College
1140 West Mission
San Marcos 92069-1487

Pasadena City College
1570 East Colorada Blvd.
Pasadena 91106

Rancho Santiago College
1530 West 17th St.
Santa Ana 92706

Rio Hondo College
3600 Workman Mill Rd.
Whittier 90601-1699

Riverside Community College
4800 Magnolia Ave.
Riverside 92506-1299

Sacramento City College
3835 Freeport Blvd.
Sacramento 95822

San Diego City College
1313 12th Ave.
San Diego 92101

San Diego Mesa College
7250 Mesa College Dr.
San Diego 92111-4998

San Joaquin Delta College
5151 Pacific Ave.
Stockton 95207

Santa Barbara Business College
211 South Real Rd.
Bakersfield 93309

Santa Barbara Business College
4333 Hansen Ave.
Fremont 94536

Santa Barbara Business College, Santa
    Maria Branch
303 East Plaza Dr., Ste. 1
Santa Maria 93454

Santa Monica College
1900 Pico Blvd.
Santa Monica 90405-1628

Santa Rosa Junior College
1501 Mendocino Ave.
Santa Rosa 95401-4395

Shasta College
P.O. Box 496006
Redding 96049

Sierra College
5000 Rocklin Rd.
Rocklin 95677

Sierra Valley Business College
4747 North First St., Bldg. D
Fresno 93726

Solano County Community College
    District
4000 Suisun Valley Rd.
Suisun 94585-3197

Southwestern College
900 Otay Lakes Rd.
Chula Vista 92010

Spectrum Community Services, Inc.
1435 Grove Way
Hayward 94546

Ventura College
4667 Telegraph Rd.
Ventura 93003

Yuba College
2088 North Beale Rd.
Marysville 95901

COLORADO

Aims Community College
P.O. Box 69
Greeley 80632

Arapahoe Community College
2500 West College Dr.
Littleton 80160-9002

Blair College
828 Wooten Rd.
Colorado Springs 80915

Boulder Valley Area Vocational-
    Technical Center
6600 East Arapahoe
Boulder 80303

Colorado Mountain College
P.O. Box 10001
Glenwood Springs 81602

Community College of Aurora
16000 East Centre Tech Pkwy.
Aurora 80011-9036

Denver Institute of Technology
7350 North Broadway
Denver 80221

Denver Technical College
925 South Niagara St.
Denver 80224

Front Range Community College
3645 West 112th Ave.
Westminster 80030

Parks College
9065 Grant St.
Denver 80229

Pikes Peak Community College
5675 South Academy Blvd.
Colorado Springs 80906-5498

Red Rocks Community College
13300 West Sixth Ave.
Lakewood 80226

San Luis Valley Area Education Center
1011 Main St.
Alamosa 81101

Technical Trades Institute
772 Horizon Dr.
Grand Junction 81506

CONNECTICUT

Asnuntuck Community Technical
    College
170 Elm St.
Enfield 06082

Branford Hall Career Institute
One Summit Place
Branford 06405

Capital Community Technical College
61 Woodland St.
Hartford 06105-2354

Housatonic Community Technical
    College
900 Lafayette Blvd.
Bridgeport 06604

Manchester Community College
60 Bidwell St.
Manchester 06040-1046

Naugatuck Valley Community
    Technical College
750 Chase Pkwy.
Waterbury 06708

Middlesex Community Technical
    College
100 Training Hill Rd.
Middletown 06457

Northwestern Connecticut Community
    Technical College
Park Place E
Winsted 06098

Norwalk Community Technical College
188 Richards Ave.
Norwalk 06854

Quinebaug Valley Community
    Technical College
742 Upper Maple St.
Danielson 06239

Ridley Lowell Business and Technical
    Institute
470 Bank St.
New London 06320

Stone Academy
1315 Dixwell Ave.
Hamden 06514

Teikyo Post University
800 Country Club Rd.
P.O. Box 2540
Waterbury 06723-2540

Three Rivers Community Technical
    College
Mahan Dr.
Norwich 06360

Tunxis Community Technical College
Rtes. 6 and 177
Farmington 06032

DELAWARE

Delaware Technical and Community
    College, Owens Campus
P.O. Box 610
Georgetown 19947

Delaware Technical and Community
    College, Stanton-Wilmington
400 Stanton-Christiana Rd.
Newark 19702

Delaware Technical and Community
    College, Terry Campus
1832 North Dupont Pkwy.
Dover 19901

Goldey-Beacom College
4701 Limestone Rd.
Wilmington 19808

DISTRICT OF COLUMBIA

Strayer College
1025 15th St. NW
Washington 20005

University of the District of Columbia
4200 Connecticut Ave. NW
Washington 20008

FLORIDA

Atlantic Vocational-Technical Center
4700 Coconut Creek Pkwy.
Coconut Creek 33063

Branell Institute
1700 Halstead Blvd.
Tallahassee 32308

Brevard Community College, Cocoa
    Campus
1519 Clearlake Rd.
Cocoa 32922

Broward Community College
225 East Las Olas Blvd.
Fort Lauderdale 33301

Charlotte Vocational-Technical Center
18300 Toledo Blade Blvd.
Port Charlotte 33948-3399

Daytona Beach Community College
1200 Volusia Ave.
Daytona Beach 32114

Hillsborough Community College
P.O. Box 31127
Tampa 33631-3127

Indian River Community College
3209 Virginia Ave.
Fort Pierce 34981

Jones College Jacksonville
5353 Arlington Expwy.
Jacksonville 32211

Lake County Area Vocational-Technical
    Center
2001 Kurt St.
Eustis 32726

Miami Lakes Technical Education
    Center
5780 Northwest 158th St.
Miami Lakes 33169

North Technical Education Center
7071 Garden Rd.
Riviera Beach 33404

Pensacola Junior College
1000 College Blvd.
Pensacola 32504

Saint Augustine Technical Center
2980 Collins Ave.
Saint Augustine 32095-1919

Saint Petersburg Junior College
8580 66 St. N
Pinellas Park 34665

Santa Fe Community College
3000 Northwest 83rd St.
Gainesville 32606

Sheridan Vocational Center
5400 Sheridan St.
Hollywood 33021

Suwannee-Hamilton Area Vocational
    and Adult Center
415 Southwest Pinewood Dr.
Live Oak 32060

Valencia Community College
P.O. Box 3028
Orlando 32802

Webster College, Inc.
2127 Grand Blvd.
Holiday 34691

GEORGIA

Albany Technical Institute
1021 Lowe Rd.
Albany 31708

Atlanta Area Technical School
1560 Stewart Ave. SW
Atlanta 30310

Augusta Technical Institute
3116 Deans Bridge Rd.
Augusta 30906

East Central Technical Institute
667 Perry Honse Rd.
Fitzgerald 31750

Carroll Technical Institute
997 South Hwy. 16
Carrollton 30117

Chattahoochee Technical Institute
980 South Cobb Dr.
Marietta 30060-3398

Columbus Technical Institute
928 45th St.
Columbus 31904-6572

Coosa Valley Technical Institute
785 Cedar Ave.
Rome 30161

Griffin Technical Institute
501 Varsity Rd.
Griffin 30223

Gwinnett College of Business
4230 Hwy. 29, Ste. 11
Lilburn 30047

Gwinnett Technical Institute
5051 Sugarloaf Pkwy.
Lawrenceville 30043

Kerr Business College
2528 Centerwest Pkwy., Bldg. A
Augusta 30900

Lanier Technical Institute
P.O. Box 58
Oakwood 30566

Macon Technical Institute
3300 Macon Tech Dr.
Macon 31206

Moultrie Area Technical Institute
361 Industrial Dr.
Moultrie 31768

North Georgia Technical Institute
Georgia Hwy. 197, P.O. Box 65
Clarkesville 30523

South College
709 Mall Blvd.
Savannah 31406

Swainsboro Technical Institute
346 Kite Rd.
Swainsboro 30401

Valdosta Technical Institute
4089 Valtech Rd.
Valdosta 31602-9796

Walker Technical Institute
265 Bicentennial Trail
Rock Spring 30739

West Georgia Technical Institute
303 Fort Dr.
La Grange 30240

HAWAII

Heald College School of Business and
Technology
1500 Kapiolani Blvd.
Honolulu 96816

Hawaii Business College
33 South King St., 4th floor, Ste. 405
Honolulu 96817

University of Hawaii at Hilo
200 West Kawili St.
Hilo 96720-4091

Kapiolani Community College
4303 Diamond Head Rd.
Honolulu 96816

Kauai Community College
3-1901 Kaumualii Hwy.
Lihue 96766

Leeward Community College
96-045 Ala Ike
Pearl City 96782

Maui Community College
310 Kaahumanu Ave.
Kahului 96732

IDAHO

College of Southern Idaho
P.O. Box 1238
Twin Falls 83301

ITT Technical Institute
12302 Explorer Dr.
Boise 83713

Ricks College
Rexburg 83460-4107

Shadow Mountain Business Careers
11911 Ustic Rd.
Boise 83713

ILLINOIS

Black Hawk College
6600 34th Ave.
Moline 61265

City College of Chicago, Harold
Washington College
30 East Lake St.
Chicago 60601

City College of Chicago, Olive-Harvey
College
10001 South Woodlawn Ave.
Chicago 60628

City College of Chicago, Richard J
Daley College
7500 South Pulaski Rd.
Chicago 60652

City College of Chicago, Truman
College
1145 Wilson Ave.
Chicago 60640

City College of Chicago, Wilbur Wright
College
4300 North Narragansett
Chicago 60634

College of Du Page
425 22nd St.
Glen Ellyn 60137-6599

College of Lake County
19351 West Washington St.
Grayslake 60030-1198

Danville Area Community College
2000 East Main St.
Danville 61832

Illinois Central College
One College Dr.
East Peoria 61635-0001

Illinois Valley Community College
815 North Orlando Smith Ave.
Oglesby 61348-9692

Joliet Junior College
1215 Houbolt Ave.
Joliet 60431

Kankakee Community College
P.O. Box 888
Kankakee 60901

Kaskaskia College
27210 College Rd.
Centralia 62801

Lake Land College
5001 Lake Land Blvd.
Mattoon 61938

Lincoln Land Community College
Shepherd Rd.
Springfield 62194-9256

MacCormac College
506 South Wabash
Chicago 60605

McHenry County College
8900 U.S. Hwy. 14
Crystal Lake 60012

Northwestern Business College
4829 North Lipps Ave.
Chicago 60630

Northwestern University
633 Clark St.
Evanston 60208

Oakton Community College
1600 East Golf Rd.
Des Plaines 60016

Parkland College
2400 West Bradley Ave.
Champaign 61821

Richland Community College
One College Park
Decatur 62521

Robert Morris College
180 North Lasalle St.
Chicago 60601

Rock Valley College
3301 North Mulford Rd.
Rockford 61114

Rockford Business College
730 North Church St.
Rockford 61103

Saint Augustine College
1333 West Argyle
Chicago 60640

South Suburban College
15800 South State St.
South Holland 60473

Taylor Business Institute
200 North Michigan Ave., Ste. 301
Chicago 60601

Waubonsee Community College
Rte. 47 at Harter Rd.
Sugar Grove 60554-0901

William Rainey Harper College
1200 West Algonquin Rd.
Palatine 60067-7398

INDIANA

Commonwealth Business College, Main
Campus
4200 West 81st Ave.
Merrillville 46410

Davenport College, Merrillville
8200 Georgia St.
Merrillville 46410

Davenport College, South Bend
Mishawaka
7121 Grape Rd.
Granger 46530

Indiana Business College
140 East 53rd St.
Anderson 46013

Indiana Business College
2222 Poshard Dr.
Columbus 47203-9988

Indiana Business College
802 North Meridian St.
Indianapolis 46204

Indiana Business College
2 Executive Dr.
Lafayette 47905

Indiana Business College
830 North Miller Ave.
Marion 46952

Indiana Business College
1809 North Walnut
Muncie 47303

Indiana Business College
3175 South Third Place
Terre Haute 47802

Indiana Business College
1431 Willow St.
Vincennes 47591

Indiana University, Purdue University
at Fort Wayne
2101 Coliseum Blvd. E
Fort Wayne 46805

International Business College
3811 Illinois Rd.
Fort Wayne 46804

International Business College,
Indianapolis Branch
7205 Shadeland Station
Indianapolis 46256

Ivy Tech State College, Central Indiana
One West 26th St.
Indianapolis 46206-1763

Ivy Tech State College, Columbus
4475 Central Ave.
Columbus 47203

Ivy Tech State College, East Central
4301 South Cowan Rd., P.O. Box 3100
Muncie 47302

Ivy Tech State College, Kokomo
1815 East Morgan St.
Kokomo 46901

Ivy Tech State College, Lafayette
3101 South Creasy Lane, P.O. Box 6299
Lafayette 47903

Ivy Tech State College, North Central
1534 West Sample St.
South Bend 46619

Ivy Tech State College, Northeast
3800 North Anthony Blvd.
Fort Wayne 46805

Ivy Tech State College, Northwest
1440 East 35th Ave.
Gary 46409

Ivy Tech State College, South Central
8204 Hwy. 311
Sellersburg 47172

Ivy Tech State College, Southeast
590 Ivy Tech Dr.
Madison 47250

Ivy Tech State College, Southwest
3501 First Ave.
Evansville 47710

Ivy Tech State College, Wabash Valley
7999 U.S. Hwy. 41
Terre Haute 47802-4898

Ivy Tech State College, Whitewater
P.O. Box 1145
Richmond 47374

Michiana College
1030 East Jefferson Blvd.
South Bend 46617

Sawyer College, Hammond
6040 Hohman Ave.
Hammond 46320

Sawyer College, Merrillville Branch
3803 East Lincoln Hwy.
Merrillville 46410

Vincennes University
1002 North First St.
Vincennes 47591

IOWA

American Institute of Business
2500 Fleur Dr.
Des Moines 50321

Des Moines Community College
2006 Ankeny Blvd.
Ankeny 50021

Eastern Iowa Community College
District
306 West River Dr.
Davenport 52801-1221

Hamilton College, Main Campus
1924 D St. SW
Cedar Rapids 52404

Hamilton College, Mason City Branch
100 First St. NW
Mason City 50401

Hawkeye Community College
1501 East Orange Rd.
Waterloo 50704

Indian Hills Community College
525 Grandview
Ottumwa 52501

Iowa Lakes Community College
19 South Seventh St.
Estherville 51334

Iowa Valley Community College
P.O. Box 536
Marshalltown 50158

Kirkwood Community College
P.O. Box 2068
Cedar Rapids 52406

North Iowa Area Community College
500 College Dr.
Mason City 50401

Northeast Iowa Community College,
Calmar
Hwy. 150 S
P.O. Box 400
Calmar 52132-0400

Southeastern Community College
1015 South Gear Ave.
P.O. Drawer F
West Burlington 52655-0605

Southwestern Community College
1501 Townline
Creston 50801

Western Iowa Technical Community
College
4647 Stone Ave., P.O. Box 5199
Sioux City 51102-5199

KANSAS

The Brown Mackie College
126 South Santa Fe St.
Salina 67402-1787

Butler County Community College
901 South Haverhill Rd.
El Dorado 67042

Coffeyville Community College
400 West 11th St.
Coffeyville 67337

Cowley County Community College
125 South Second St.
Arkansas City 67005

Hutchinson Community College
1300 North Plum St.
Hutchinson 67501

Independence Community College
Brookside Dr. and College Ave.
Independence 67301

Kansas City Area Vocational-Technical
School
2220 North 59th St.
Kansas City 66104

Kansas City Kansas Community College
7250 State Ave.
Kansas City 66112

Pratt Community College
348 NE St., Rte. 61
Pratt 67124

KENTUCKY

Ashland Community College
1400 College Dr.
Ashland 41101

Fugazzi College
406 Lafayette Ave.
Lexington 40502

Jefferson Community College
109 East Broadway
Louisville 40202

Kentucky College of Business
628 East Main St.
Lexington 40508

Kentucky Technical-Bowling Green
Regional Technical School
845 Loop Dr.
Bowling Green 42101-3601

West Kentucky Tech
5200 Blandvill Rd.
Paducah 42002

Madisonville Community College
University Dr.
Madisonville 42431

Mayo Regional Technology Center
Third St.
Paintsville 41240

Paducah Community College
P.O. Box 7380
Paducah 42002-7380

Prestonsburg Community College
Bert Combs Dr.
Prestonsburg 41653

Southern Ohio College
309 Buttermilk Pike
Fort Mitchell 41017

Spencerian College
4627 Dixie Hwy.
Louisville 40216

Thomas More College
333 Thomas More Pkwy.
Crestview Hills 41017-3428

LOUISIANA

American School of Business
702 Professional Dr. N
Shreveport 71105

Baton Rouge School of Computers
9255 Interline Dr.
Baton Rouge 70809

Charles B Coreil Technical Institute
Industrial Park Ward I
P.O. Box 296
Ville Platte 70586

Delta School of Business and
Technology
517 Broad St.
Lake Charles 70601

Louisiana Technical College, Baton
Rouge Campus
3250 North Acadian Hwy. E
Baton Rouge 70805

Louisiana Technical College, Gulf Area
Campus
1115 Clover St.
Abbeville 70510

Louisiana Technical College, Jefferson
Campus
5200 Blair Dr.
Metairie 70001

Louisiana Technical College, Lafayette
Campus
1101 Bertrand Dr.
Lafayette 70502-4909

Louisiana Technical College, Lamar
Salter Campus
15014 Lake Charles Hwy.
Leesville 71446

Louisiana Technical College, Mansfield
Campus
943 Oxford Rd.
Mansfield 71052

Louisiana Technical College, Sabine
Valley Campus
1255 Fisher Rd.
Many 71449

Louisiana Technical College, Sullivan
Campus
1710 Sullivan Dr.
Bogalusa 70427

Louisiana Technical College, T.H.
Harris Campus
337 East South St.
Opelousas 70570

Louisiana Technical College, Teche
Area Campus
P.O. Box 11057
New Iberia 70562-1057

Louisiana Technical College, Young
Memorial
900 Youngs Rd.
Morgan City 70380

Louisiana Technical Institute,
Alexandria Campus
4311 South MacArthur Dr.
Alexandria 71302-3137

MAINE

Andover College
901 Washington Ave.
Portland 04103

Beal College
629 Main St.
Bangor 04401

Casco Bay College
477 Congress St.
Portland 04101

Husson College
One College Circle
Bangor 04401

Mid-State College
88 East Hardscrabble Rd.
Auburn 04210

Northern Maine Technical College
33 Edgemont Dr.
Presque Isle 04769

MARYLAND

Abbie Business Institute
5310 Spectrum Dr.
Frederick 21703

Anne Arundel Community College
101 College Pkwy.
Arnold 21012

Baltimore City Community College
2901 Liberty Heights Ave.
Baltimore 21215

Catonsville Community College
800 South Rolling Rd.
Catonsville 21228

Charles County Community College
8730 Mitchell Rd.
La Plata 20646-0910

Essex Community College
7201 Rossville Blvd.
Baltimore 21237

Frederick Community College
7932 Opossumtown Pike
Frederick 21702

Hagerstown Business College
18618 Crestwood Dr.
Hagerstown 21742

Hagerstown Junior College
11400 Robinwood Dr.
Hagerstown 21742-6590

Harford Community College
401 Thomas Run Rd.
Bel Air 21015

Prince Georges Community College
301 Largo Rd.
Largo 20774-2199

University of Baltimore
Charles at Mount Royal
Baltimore 21201

University of Maryland, Baltimore
County Campus
1000 Hilltop Circle
Baltimore 21250

Villa Julie College
Green Spring Valley Rd.
Stevenson 21153

Wor-Wic Community College
32000 Campus Dr.
Salisbury 21801-7131

MASSACHUSETTS

Aquinas College at Milton
303 Adams St.
Milton 02186

Bay State College
122 Commonwealth Ave.
Boston 02116

Bunker Hill Community College
250 New Rutherford Ave.
Boston 02129

Burdett School
745 Boylston St.
Boston 02116

Burdett School
100 Front St.
Worcester 01608

Cape Cod Community College
2240 Iyanough Rd.
West Barnstable 02668-1599

Fisher College
118 Beacon St.
Boston 02116

Greenfield Community College
One College Dr.
Greenfield 01301-9739

Holyoke Community College
303 Homestead Ave.
Holyoke 01040

Katharine Gibbs School
126 Newbury
Boston 02116

Kinyon-Campbell Business School
59 Linden St.
New Bedford 02740

Marian Court College
35 Littles Point Rd.
Swampscott 01907

Massachusetts Bay Community College
50 Oakland St.
Wellesley Hills 02181

Massasoit Community College
One Massasoit Blvd.
Brockton 02402

Mount Wachusett Community College
444 Green St.
Gardner 01440

New England School of Accounting
155 Ararat St.
Worcester 01606

Newbury College, Inc.
129 Fisher Ave.
Brookline 02146

North Shore Community College
One Ferncroft Rd.
Danvers 01923

Northeastern University
360 Huntington Ave.
Boston 02115

Northern Essex Community College
Elliott Way
Haverhill 01830-2399

Skills
150 Fearing St.
Amherst 01002

Springfield Technical Community
College
1 Armory Square
Springfield 01105

MICHIGAN

Alpena Community College
666 Johnson St.
Alpena 49707

Baker College of Flint
G1050 West Bristol Rd.
Flint 48507

Baker College of Muskegon
1903 Marquette Ave.
Muskegon 49442

Baker College of Owosso
1020 South Washington St.
Owosso 48867

Bay De Noc Community College
2001 North Lincoln Rd.
Escanaba 49289

Cleary College
2170 Washtenaw Ave.
Ypsilanti 48197

Davenport College
415 East Fulton
Grand Rapids 49503

Davenport College, Kalamazoo Branch
4123 West Main St.
Kalamazoo 49006-2791

Davenport College, Lansing Branch
220 East Kalamazoo
Lansing 48933

Delta College
University Center 48710

Detroit Business Institute
1249 Washington Blvd., Ste. 1200
Detroit 48226

Detroit Business Institute, Downriver
19100 Fort St.
Riverview 48192

Detroit College of Business
4801 Oakman Blvd.
Dearborn 48126-3799

Detroit College of Business
3488 North Jennings
Flint 48504-1700

Detroit College of Business
27500 Dequindre
Warren 48092-5209

Dorsey Business Schools
30821 Barrington
Madison Heights 48071

Dorsey Business Schools
15755 Northline Rd.
Southgate 48195

The Educational Institute, American
Hotel & Motel Association
2113 North High St.
East Lansing 48906

Glen Oaks Community College
62249 Shimmel Rd.
Centreville 49032

Gogebic Community College
East 4946 Jackson Rd.
Ironwood 49938

Grand Rapids Community College
143 Bostwick Ave. NE
Grand Rapids 49503-3295

Henry Ford Community College
5101 Evergreen Rd.
Dearborn 48128

Kalamazoo Valley Community College
6767 West O Ave.
Kalamazoo 49009

Kellogg Community College
450 North Ave.
Battle Creek 49017

Kirtland Community College
10775 North St. Helen Rd.
Roscommon 48653

Lake Michigan College
2755 East Napier Ave.
Benton Harbor 49022-8099

Lansing Community College
419 North Capitol Ave.
Lansing 48901-7210

Lansing Computer Institute
501 North Marshall St., Ste. 101
Lansing 48912

Macomb Community College
14500 Twelve Mile Rd.
Warren 48093-3896

Mid-Michigan Community College
1375 South Clare Ave.
Harrison 48625

Monroe County Community College
1555 South Raisinville Rd.
Monroe 48161

Montcalm Community College
2800 College Dr.
Sidney 48885

Mott Community College
1401 East Court St.
Flint 48503

Northeastern School of Commerce
701 North Madison Ave.
Bay City 48708

Northwestern Michigan College
1701 East Front St.
Traverse City 49686

Northwood Institute
3225 Cook Rd.
Midland 48640

Oakland Community College
2480 Opdyke Rd.
Bloomfield Hills 48304-2266

Oakland University
Rochester Hills 48309-4401

Payne-Pulliam School of Trade and
Commerce, Inc.
2345 Cass Ave.
Detroit 48201-3305

Ross Business Institute
37065 South Gratiot
Clinton Township 48036

Ross Business Institute
22293 Eureka
Taylor 48180

Schoolcraft College
18600 Haggerty Rd.
Livonia 48152

Southwestern Michigan College
58900 Cherry Grove Rd.
Dowagiac 49047-9793

Washtenaw Community College
P.O. Drawer One
Ann Arbor 48016-1610

Wayne County Community College
801 West Fort St.
Detroit 48226

West Shore Community College
3000 North Stiles Rd.
Scottville 49454

MINNESOTA

Academy Education Center, Inc.
3050 Metro Dr., Ste. 200
Minneapolis 55425

Alexandria Technical College
1601 Jefferson St.
Alexandria 56308

Anoka-Ramsey Community College
11200 Mississippi Blvd.
Coon Rapids 55433-3470

Century Community and Metro
Technical College
3300 Century Ave. N
White Bear Lake 55110

Dakota County Technical College
1300 East 145th St.
Rosemount 55068

Duluth Business University, Inc.
412 West Superior St.
Duluth 55802

Lake Superior College
2101 Trinity Rd.
Duluth 55811

Globe College of Business
175 Fifth St. E, Ste. 201, P.O. Box 60
Saint Paul 55101-2901

Hennepin Technical College
9000 Brooklyn Blvd.
Brooklyn Park 55445

Hibbing Community College
1515 East 25th St.
Hibbing 55746

Inver Hills Community College
2500 80th St. E
Inver Grove Heights 55076

Itasca Community College
1851 Hwy. 169 E
Grand Rapids 55744

Minneapolis Community and Technical
College
1501 Hennepin Ave.
Minneapolis 55403-1799

Minnesota West Community and
Technical College, Canby
1011 First St. W
Canby 56220

Minnesota West Community and
Technical College, Granite Falls
1593 11th Ave.
Granite Falls 56241

Minnesota West Community and
Technical College, Jackson
401 West St.
Jackson 56143

Minnesota West Community and
Technical College, Pipestone
P.O. Box 250
Pipestone 56164

Normandale Community College
9700 France Ave. S
Bloomington 55431

North Hennepin Community College
7411 85th Ave. N
Brooklyn Park 55445

Northland Community and Technical
College
Hwy. 1 E
Thief River Falls 56701

Northwest Technical College, Moorhead
1900 28th Ave. S
Moorhead 56560

Pine Technical College
1000 Fourth St.
Pine City 55063

Rasmussen College
3500 Federal Dr.
Eagan 55122

Rasmussen College
501 Holly Ln.
Mankato 56001

Rasmussen College, Corporate Office
Minnetonka 55305

Ridgewater College, A Community and
Technical College,
P.O. Box 1097
Willmar 56201

Riverland Community College, Albert
Lea
2200 Technical Dr.
Albert Lea 56007

Saint Cloud Technical College
1540 Northway Dr.
Saint Cloud 56303

Saint Paul Technical College
235 Marshall Ave.
Saint Paul 55102

South Central Technical College,
Faribault
1225 Southwest Third St.
Faribault 55021

South Central Technical College,
Mankato
1920 Lee Blvd.
North Mankato 56003

MISSISSIPPI

Mississippi Gulf Coast Community
College
Central Office
P.O. Box 67
Perkinston 39573

Northeast Mississippi Community
College
Cunningham Blvd.
Booneville 38829

Northwest Mississippi Community
College
510 North Panola, Hwy. 51 N
Senatobia 38668

MISSOURI

Drury College
900 North Benton Ave.
Springfield 65802

Jefferson College
1000 Viking Dr.
Hillsboro 63050

Longview Community College
500 Longview Rd.
Lees Summit 64081

Metro Business College
2305 North Bishop Hwy. 63 N
Rolla 65401

Metro Business College of Cape
Girardeau
1732 North Kings Hwy.
Cape Girardeau 63701

Sanford-Brown Business College
12006 Manchester Rd.
Des Peres 63131

Sikeston Area Vocational-Technical
School
1002 Virginia St.
Sikeston 63801

State Fair Community College
3201 West 16th
Sedalia 65301-2199

Three Rivers Community College
Three Rivers Blvd.
Poplar Bluff 63901

MONTANA

Fort Belknap College
P.O. Box 159
Harlem 59526

Helena College of Technology of the
University of Montana
1115 North Roberts St.
Helena 59601

Montana College of Technology,
Billings
3803 Central Ave.
Billings 59102

Montana State University, College of
Technology, Great Falls
2100 16th Ave. S
Great Falls 59405

Montana Tech, College of Technology
25 Basin Creek Rd.
Butte 59701

NEBRASKA

Central Community College Area
P.O. Box 4903
Grand Island 68802

Lincoln School of Commerce
1821 K St.
P.O. Box 82826
Lincoln 68501-2826

Metropolitan Community College Area
5300 North 30th St.
Omaha 68103

Nebraska College of Business
3350 North 90th
Omaha 68134

Northeast Community College
801 East Benjamin
P.O. Box 469
Norfolk 68702-0469

Southeast Community College Area
1111 St., Ste. 111
Lincoln 68520

Western Nebraska Community College
1601 East 27th St. NE
Scottsbluff 69361-1899

NEVADA

Community College of Southern
Nevada
3200 East Cheyenne Ave.
Las Vegas 89030

Morrison College
140 Washington St.
Reno 89503

Western Nevada Community College
2201 West College Pkwy.
Carson City 89703

NEW HAMPSHIRE

Castle College
23 Searles Rd.
Windham 03087-1200

Franklin Pierce College
College Rd.
Rindge 03461

Hesser College
Three Sundial Ave.
Manchester 03103

McIntosh College
23 Cataract Ave.
Dover 03820

New Hampshire College
2500 North River Rd.
Manchester 03106

New Hampshire Community Technical
College at Berlin
2020 Riverside Dr.
Berlin 03570

New Hampshire Community Technical
College at Nashua
505 Amherst St.
Nashua 03061-2052

New Hampshire Technical Institute
11 Institute Dr.
Concord 03301

NEW JERSEY

The Academy of Professional
Development
1075 Easton Ave., Tower 2, Ste. 5
Edison 08837

Atlantic Community College
5100 Black Horse Pike
Mays Landing 08330-2699

Bergen Community College
400 Paramus Rd.
Paramus 07652

Brookdale Community College
765 Newman Springs Rd.
Lincroft 07738-1599

Burlington County College
Rte. 530
Pemberton 08068

Camden County College
P.O. Box 200
Blackwood 08012

Dover Business College
15 East Blackwell St.
Dover 07801

Dover Business College
East 81 Rte. 4 W
Paramus 07652

Drake College of Business
125 Broad St.
Elizabeth 07201

Essex County College
303 University Ave.
Newark 07102

Gloucester County College
1400 Tanyard Rd.
Sewell 08080

Hudson County Community College
25 Journal Square
Jersey City 07306

Katharine Gibbs School
80 Kingsbridge Rd.
Piscataway 08854

Mercer County Community College
1200 Old Trenton Rd.
Trenton 08690

Middlesex County College
155 Mill Rd.
Edison 08818-3050

Raritan Valley Community College
P.O. Box 3300, Lamington Rd.
Somerville 08876

Stuart School of Business
Administration
2400 Belmar Blvd.
Wall 07719

Union County College
1033 Springfield Ave.
Cranford 07016

NEW MEXICO

Albuquerque Technical-Vocational
Institute
525 Buena Vista SE
Albuquerque 87106

International Business College
650 East Montana
Las Cruces 88001

Northern New Mexico Community
College
1002 North Onate St.
Espanola 87532

San Juan College
4601 College Blvd.
Farmington 87402

Santa Fe Community College
6401 Richards Ave.
Santa Fe 87505

Southwestern Indian Polytechnic
Institute
9169 Coors Rd. NW
Albuquerque 87120

University of New Mexico, Gallup
Campus
200 College Rd.
Gallup 87301

University of New Mexico, Main
Campus
Albuquerque 87131

NEW YORK

Adirondack Community College
Bay Rd.
Queensbury 12804

Berkeley College of New York City
Three East 43rd St.
New York 10017

Broome Community College
P.O. Box 1017
Binghamton 13902

Bryant and Stratton Business Institute,
Albany
1259 Central Ave.
Albany 12205

Bryant and Stratton Business Institute,
Buffalo
1028 Main St.
Buffalo 14202

Bryant and Stratton Business Institute,
Rochester
82 Saint Paul St.
Rochester 14604

Bryant and Stratton Business Institute,
Syracuse
953 James St.
Syracuse 13203-2502

Cayuga County Community College
Franklin St.
Auburn 13021

Cazenovia College
Cazenovia 13035

Central City Business Institute
224 Harrison St.
Syracuse 13202

Cheryl Felis School of Business
2541 Military Rd.
Niagara Falls 14304

Corning Community College
Spencer Hill
Corning 14830

CUNY Borough of Manhattan
Community College
199 Chambers St.
New York 10007

CUNY Bronx Community College
West 181st St. & University Ave.
Bronx 10453

CUNY Hostos Community College
500 Grand Concourse
Bronx 10451

CUNY Kingsborough Community
College
2001 Oriental Blvd.
Brooklyn 11235

CUNY La Guardia Community College
31-10 Thomson Ave.
Long Island City 11101

CUNY New York City Technical College
300 Jay St.
Brooklyn 11201

CUNY Queensborough Community
College
56th Ave. & Springfield Blvd.
New York 11364

Dutchess Community College
53 Pendell Rd.
Poughkeepsie 12601

FEGS Trades and Business School
17 Battery Place
New York 10004

Finger Lakes Community College
4355 Lake Shore Dr.
Canandaigua 14424

Fulton-Montgomery Community
College
2805 State Hwy. 67
Johnstown 12095

Genesee Community College
One College Rd.
Batavia 14020

Herkimer County Community College
Reservoir Rd.
Herkimer 13350-1598

Hilbert College
5200 South Park Ave.
Hamburg 14075-1597

Hudson Valley Community College
80 Vandenburgh Ave.
Troy 12180

Hunter Business School
3601 Hempstead Tpke.
Levittown 11756

Interboro Institute
450 West 56th St.
New York 10019

Jefferson Community College
Outer Coffeen St.
Watertown 13601

Katharine Gibbs School, New York City
200 Park Ave.
New York 10166

Long Island Business Institute
6500 Jericho Tpke.
Commack 11725

Maria College of Albany
700 New Scotland Ave.
Albany 12208

Mohawk Valley Community College
1101 Sherman Dr.
Utica 13501

Monroe College, Main Campus
Monroe College Way
Bronx 10468

Monroe Community College
1000 East Henrietta Rd.
Rochester 14623

Nassau Community College
One Education Dr.
Garden City 11530

National Tax Training School
Four Melnick Dr.
Monsey 10952

Niagara County Community College
3111 Saunders Settlement Rd.
Sanborn 14132

Olean Business Institute
301 North Union St.
Olean 14760

Onondaga Community College
4941 Onondaga Rd.
Syracuse 13215

Orange County Community College
115 South St.
Middletown 10940

Plaza Business Institute
74-09 37th Ave.
Jackson Heights 11372

Professional Business Institute
125 Canal St.
New York 10002-5049

Ridley-Lowell School of Business
116 Front St.
Binghamton 13905

Rochester Business Institute
1850 East Ridge Rd.
Irondequort 14622

Rochester Institute of Technology
One Lamb Memorial Dr.
Rochester 14623-5603

Rockland Community College
145 College Rd.
Suffern 10901

Schenectady County Community
College
Washington Ave.
Schenectady 12305

Siena College
515 Loudon Rd.
Loudonville 12211

The Sobelsohn School
370 Seventh Ave.
New York 10001

Suffolk County Community College,
   Ammerman Campus
533 College Rd.
Selden 11784

Suffolk County Community College,
   Eastern Campus
Speonk Riverhead Rd.
Riverhead 11901

Suffolk County Community College,
   Western Campus
Crooked Hill Rd.
Brentwood 11717

Sullivan County Community College
1000 Le Roy Rd.
Loch Sheldrake 12759-4002

SUNY College of Agriculture &
   Technology at Cobleskill
Cobleskill 12043

SUNY College of Technology &
   Agriculture at Morrisville
Morrisville 13408

SUNY College of Technology at Alfred
Alfred 14802

SUNY College of Technology at Canton
Cornell Dr.
Canton 13617

SUNY College of Technology at Delhi
Delhi 13753

SUNY Westchester Commmunity
   College
75 Grasslands Rd.
Valhalla 10595

Syrit Computer School Systems
1760 53rd St.
Brooklyn 11204

Taylor Business Institute
120 West 30th St.
New York 10001

Tompkins-Cortland Community
   College
170 North St.
Dryden 13053

The Westchester Business Institute
325 Central Ave.
White Plains 10606

Wood Tobe-Coburn School
Eight East 40th St.
New York 10016

NORTH CAROLINA

Asheville Buncombe Technical
   Community College
340 Victoria Rd.
Asheville 28801

Beaufort County Community College
P.O. Box 1069
Washington 27889

Brookstone College
8307 University Executive Park Dr., Ste.
240
Charlotte 28262

Cape Fear Community College
411 North Front St.
Wilmington 28401

Catawba Valley Community College
2550 Hwy. 70 SE
Hickory 28602-0699

Central Carolina Community College
1105 Kelly Dr.
Sanford 27330

Central Piedmont Community College
P.O. Box 35009
Charlotte 28235-5009

Coastal Carolina Community College
444 Western Blvd.
Jacksonville 28546-6877

Craven Community College
800 College Ct.
New Bern 28562

Davidson County Community College
297 Davidson Community College Rd.
Lexington 27292

Durham Technical Community College
1637 Lawson St.
Durham 27703

Fayetteville Technical Community
   College
2201 Hull Rd.
Fayetteville 28303-0236

Forsyth Technical Community College
2100 Silas Creek Pkwy.
Winston-Salem 27103

Gaston College
201 Hwy. 321 S
Dallas 28034

Guilford Technical Community College
P.O. Box 309
Jamestown 27282

Johnston Community College
P.O. Box 2350
Smithfield 27577-2350

Mayland Community College
P.O. Box 547
Spruce Pine 28777

Nash Community College
P.O. Box 7488
Rocky Mount 27804

Pitt Community College
Hwy. 11 S, P.O. Drawer 7007
Greenville 27835-7007

Randolph Community College
629 Industrial Park Ave.
Asheboro 27204

Richmond Community College
P.O. Box 1189
Hamlet 28345

Robeson Community College
P.O. Box 1420
Lumberton 28359

Rockingham Community College
P.O. Box 38, Hwy. 65 County Home Rd.
Wentworth 27375-0038

Rowan-Cabarrus Community College
P.O. Box 1595
Salisbury 28145-1595

Sampson Community College
P.O. Box 318
Clinton 28329-0318

Sandhills Community College
2200 Airport Rd.
Pinehurst 28374

Southwestern Community College
447 College Dr.
Sylva 28779

Stanly Community College
141 College Dr.
Albemarle 28001

Surry Community College
P.O. Box 304
Dobson 27017-0304

Vance-Granville Community College
State Rd. 1126
P.O. Box 917
Henderson 27536

Wake Technical Community College
9101 Fayetteville Rd.
Raleigh 27603-5696

Wayne Community College
3000 Wayne Memorial Dr.
Goldsboro 27533-8002

Western Piedmont Community College
1001 Burkemont Ave.
Morganton 28655-9978

Wilson Technical Community College
902 Herring Ave.
Wilson 27893

NORTH DAKOTA

Aakers Business College
201 North Third St.
Grand Forks 58203

Interstate Business College
520 East Main Ave.
Bismarck 58501

Interstate Business College
2720 32nd Ave. SW
Fargo 58103

North Dakota State College of Science
800 North Sixth St.
Wahpeton 58076

OHIO

Akron Adult Vocational Services
147 Park St.
Akron 44308

Ashtabula County Joint Vocational
   School
1565 State Rte. 167
Jefferson 44047

Baldwin-Wallace College
275 Eastland Rd.
Berea 44017

Belmont Technical College
120 Fox Shannon Place
Saint Clairsville 43950

Boheckers Business College
326 East Main St.
Ravenna 44266

Bryant and Stratton College
12955 Snow Rd.
Parma 44130

Butler County JVS District-D Russel Lee
   Career Center
3603 Hamilton Middletown Rd.
Hamilton 45011

Central Ohio Technical College
1179 University Dr.
Newark 43055-1767

Cincinnati State Technical and
   Community College
3520 Central Pkwy.
Cincinnati 45223

Clark State Community College
570 East Leffel Ln.
Springfield 45505

Columbus State Community College
550 East Spring St.
P.O. Box 1609
Columbus 43216

Cuyahoga Community College District
700 Carnegie Ave.
Cleveland 44115-2878

Davis College
4747 Monroe St.
Toledo 43623

Edison State Community College
1973 Edison Dr.
Piqua 45356

Franklin University
201 South Grant Ave.
Columbus 43215-5399

Hocking Technical College
3301 Hocking Pkwy.
Nelsonville 45764

Jefferson Community College
4000 Sunset Blvd.
Steubenville 43952-3598

Kent State University, Trumbull
   Regional Campus
4314 Mahoning Ave. NW
Warren 44483

Kent State University, Tuscaraws
   Regional Campus
University Dr. NE
New Philadelphia 44663

Lakeland Community College
7700 Clocktower Dr.
Kirtland 44094-5198

Lima Technical College
4240 Campus Dr.
Lima 45804

Lorain County Community College
1005 North Abbe Rd.
Elyria 44035

Marion Technical College
1467 Mount Vernon Ave.
Marion 43302-5694

Miami University, Oxford Campus
500 High St.
Oxford 45056

Miami-Jacobs College
400 East Second St.
Dayton 45401

Muskingum Area Technical College
1555 Newark Rd.
Zanesville 43701

North Central Technical College
2441 Kenwood Circle, P.O. Box 698
Mansfield 44901

Northwest State Community College
22-600 South Rte. 34
Archbold 43502-9542

Northwestern College
1441 North Cable Rd.
Lima 45805

Ohio University, Lancaster Branch
1570 Granville Pike
Lancaster 43130

Owens Community College
39335 Oregon Rd.
Toledo 43699-1947

Sawyer College of Business
3150 Mayfield Rd.
Cleveland Heights 44118

Sawyer College of Business, West
13027 Lorain Ave.
Cleveland 44111

Shawnee State University
940 Second St.
Portsmouth 45662

Sinclair Community College
444 West Third St.
Dayton 45402

Southeastern Business College
1855 Western Ave.
Chillicothe 45601

Southeastern Business College
1522 Sheridan Dr.
Lancaster 43130

Southeastern Business College
4020 Milan Rd.
Sandusky 44870-5871

Southeastern Business College, Lorain
1907 North Ridge Rd.
Lorain 44055

Southern Ohio College, Northeast
2791 Mogadore Rd.
Akron 44312

Southern State Community College
100 Hobart Dr.
Hillsboro 45133

Stark State College of Technology
6200 Frank Ave. NW
Canton 44720

Terra State Community College
2830 Napoleon Rd.
Fremont 43420

Tiffin University
155 Miami St.
Tiffin 44883

Tri-County Vocational School
156 75th St. & Rte. 691
Nelsonville 45764

University of Akron, Main Campus
302 Buchtel Common
Akron 44325-4702

University of Cincinnati, Main Campus
P.O. Box 210127
Cincinnati 45221-0127

University of Toledo
2801 West Bancroft
Toledo 43606

Washington State Community College
710 Colegate Dr.
Marietta 45750

Wright State University, Lake Campus
7600 Rte. 703E
Celina 45822

Youngstown State University
One University Plaza
Youngstown 44555

OKLAHOMA

Carl Albert State College
1507 South McKenna
Poteau 74953-5208

Connors State College
Rte. 1, P.O. Box 1000
Warner 74469

Northeastern Oklahoma Agricultural
and Mechanical College
200 I St. NE
Miami 74354

Oklahoma City Community College
7777 South May Ave.
Oklahoma City 73159

Oklahoma State University, Okmulgee
1801 East Fourth St.
Okmulgee 74447-3901

Rogers University, Claremore
1701 West Will Rogers Blvd.
Claremore 74017

Tulsa Community College
6111 East Skelly Dr.
Tulsa 74135

Western Oklahoma State College
2801 North Main St.
Altus 73521-1397

OREGON

Blue Mountain Community College
P.O. Box 100
Pendleton 97801

Chemeketa Community College
4000 Lancaster Dr. NE
Salem 97305

Columbia College
8800 Southeast Sunnyside Rd.
Clackamas 97015

Elliott Bookkeeping School
1225 Northwest Murray Rd., Ste. 112
Portland 97229

Linn-Benton Community College
6500 Southwest Pacific Blvd.
Albany 97321

Mount Hood Community College
26000 Southeast Stark St.
Gresham 97030

Oregon Institute of Technology
3201 Campus Dr.
Klamath Falls 97601-8801

Rogue Community College
3345 Redwood Hwy.
Grants Pass 97527

Southwestern Oregon Community
College
1988 Newmark Ave.
Coos Bay 97420

Western Business College
425 SW Washington
Portland 97204

PENNSYLVANIA

Allentown Business School
1501 Lehigh St.
Allentown 18103

Bucks County Community College
Swamp Rd.
Newtown 18940

Butler County Community College
College Dr. Oak Hills
Butler 16003-1203

Central Pennsylvania Business School
107 College Hill Rd.
Summerdale 17093-0309

Churchman Business School
355 Spring Garden St.
Easton 18042

Community College of Allegheny
County
800 Allegheny Ave.
Pittsburgh 15233-1895

Community College of Beaver County
One Campus Dr.
Monaca 15061

Community College of Philadelphia
1700 Spring Garden St.
Philadelphia 19130

Consolidated School of Business
1605 Clugston Rd.
York 17404

Delaware County Community College
901 South Media Line Rd.
Media 19063-1094

Erie Business Center-1094
246 West Ninth St.
Erie 16501

Franklin and Marshall College
P.O. Box 3003
Lancaster 17604-3003

Garfield Business Institute
709 Third Ave.
New Brighton 15066

ICM School of Business and Medical
Careers
10-14 Wood St.
Pittsburgh 15222

Lackawanna Junior College
501 Vine St.
Scranton 18509

Lansdale School of Business
201 Church Rd.
North Wales 19454

Lehigh Carbon Community College
4525 Education Park Dr.
Schnecksville 18078-2598

Luzerne County Community College
1333 South Prospect St.
Nanticoke 18634

McCann School of Business
Main St. and Pine St.
Mahanoy City 17948

Montgomery County Community
College
340 Dekalb Pike
Blue Bell 19422

Mount Aloysius College
7373 Admiral Pearl Hwy.
Cresson 16630-1999

Northampton County Area Community
College
3835 Green Pond Rd.
Bethlehem 18020-7599

Peirce College
1420 Pine St.
Philadelphia 19102

Pennsylvania State University, Main
Campus
201 Old Main
University Park 16802

The PJA School
7900 West Chester Pike
Upper Darby 19082

Reading Area Community College
P.O. Box 1706
Reading 19603-1706

Sawyer School
717 Liberty Ave.
Pittsburgh 15222

University of Pittsburgh, Main Campus
4200 Fifth Ave.
Pittsburgh 15260

Westmoreland County Community
College
Youngwood 15697-1895

RHODE ISLAND

Community College of Rhode Island
400 East Ave.
Warwick 02886-1807

Johnson and Wales University
8 Abbott Park Place
Providence 02903-3376

Nasson Institute
286 Main St.
Pawtucket 02860

Ocean State Business Institute
140 Point Judith Rd., Unit 3A
Narragansett 02882

SOUTH CAROLINA

Aiken Technical College
P.O. Drawer 696
Aiken 29802

Central Carolina Technical College
506 North Guignard Dr.
Sumter 29150

Florence-Darlington Technical College
P.O. Box 100548
Florence 29501-0548

Greenville Technical College
Station B, P.O. Box 5616
Greenville 29606-5616

Midlands Technical College
P.O. Box 2408
Columbia 29202

Orangeburg-Calhoun Technical College
3250 Saint Matthew's Rd.
Orangeburg 29115

Spartanburg Technical College
Hwy. I-85
Spartanburg 29305

Tri-County Technical College
P.O. Box 587
Pendleton 29670

Trident Technical College
P.O. Box 118067
Charleston 29423-8067

York Technical College
452 South Anderson Rd.
Rock Hill 29730

SOUTH DAKOTA

Lake Area Technical Institute
230 11th St. NE
Watertown 57201

Mitchell Technical Institute
821 North Capital St.
Mitchell 57301

Nettleton Career College
100 South Spring Ave.
Sioux Falls 57104

TENNESSEE

Chattanooga State Technical
Community College
4501 Amnicola Hwy.
Chattanooga 37406

Concorde Career Institute
5100 Poplar Ave., Ste. 132
Memphis 38137

Draughons Junior College of Business
Plus Park at Pavilion Blvd.
Nashville 37217

Jackson State Community College
2046 North Pkwy.
Jackson 38301

Knoxville Business College
720 North Fifth Ave.
Knoxville 37917

Morristown School of Business
400 North Henry St.
Morristown 37814

Nashville State Technical Institute
120 White Bridge Rd.
Nashville 37209

State Technical Institute at Memphis
5983 Macon Cove
Memphis 38134

TEXAS

American Commercial College
2007 34th St.
Lubbock 79411

American Commercial College
3177 Executive Dr.
San Angelo 76904

Austin Community College
5930 Middle Fiskville Rd.
Austin 78752

Central Texas Commercial College
315 North Center St.
P.O. Box 1324
Brownwood 76801

Eastfield College
3737 Motley Dr.
Mesquite 75150

El Paso Community College
P.O. Box 20500
El Paso 79998

Grayson County College
6101 Grayson Dr.
Denison 75020

Hallmark Institute of Technology
8901 Wetmore Rd.
San Antonio 78216

Houston Community College System
22 Waugh Dr.
Houston 77270-7849

International Business College
4121 Montana Ave.
El Paso 79903

Kilgore College
1100 Broadway
Kilgore 75662-3299

Lamar University, Port Arthur
1500 Proctor St.
Port Arthur 77640

Laredo Community College
West End Washington St.
Laredo 78040

McLennan Community College
1400 College Dr.
Waco 76708

Microcomputer Technology Institute
7277 Regency Square Blvd.
Houston 77036

Navarro College
3200 West 7th
Corsicana 75110

North Harris Montgomery Community
College District
250 North Sam Houston Pkwy. E, Ste.
300
Houston 77060

Richland College
12800 Abrams Rd.
Dallas 75243-2199

San Antonio College
1300 San Pedro Ave.
San Antonio 78284

San Jacinto College, Central Campus
8060 Spencer Hwy.
Pasadena 77505

South Plains College
1401 College Ave.
Levelland 79336

Tarrant County Junior College
1500 Houston St.
Fort Worth 76102

Texas School of Business, Inc.
711 Airtex Dr.
Houston 77073

Texas Southmost College
80 Fort Brown
Brownsville 78520

Vernon Regional Junior College
4400 College Dr.
Vernon 76384-4092

Wharton County Junior College
911 Boling Hwy.
Wharton 77488

UTAH

Bridgerland Applied Technology Center
1301 North 600 West
Logan 84321

Dixie College
225 South 700 East
Saint George 84770

Latter Day Saints Business College
411 East South Temple
Salt Lake City 84111-1392

Salt Lake Community College
P.O. Box 30808
Salt Lake City 84129

Sevier Valley Applied Technology
Center
800 West 200 S
Richfield 84701

Stevens-Henager College of Business
2168 Washington Blvd.
Ogden 84401

Stevens-Henager College of Business
25 East 1700 S
Provo 84606-6157

Utah Valley State College
800 West 1200 S
Orem 84058

VERMONT

Champlain College
163 South Willard St.
Burlington 05401

VIRGINIA

Commonwealth College
1120 West Mercury Blvd.
Hampton 23666

Commonwealth College
301 Centre Pointe Dr.
Virginia Beach 23462

National Business College
1813 East Main St.
Salem 24153

WASHINGTON

Bates Technical College
1101 South Yakima Ave.
Tacoma 98405

Bellevue Community College
3000 Landerholm Circle SE
Bellevue 98007-6484

Bellingham Technical College
3028 Lindbergh Ave.
Bellingham 98225

Centralia College
600 West Locust St.
Centralia 98531

Edmonds Community College
20000 68th Ave. W
Lynnwood 98036

Everett Community College
801 Wetmore Ave.
Everett 98201

Grays Harbor College
1620 Edward P Smith Dr.
Aberdeen 98520

Green River Community College
12401 Southeast 320th St.
Auburn 98092

Highline Community College
P.O. Box 98000
Des Moines 98198-9800

Lake Washington Technical College
11605 132nd Ave. NE
Kirkland 98034

Olympic College
1600 Chester Ave.
Bremerton 98310-1699

Seattle Community College, Central
Campus
1701 Broadway
Seattle 98122

Seattle Community College, North
Campus
9600 College Way N
Seattle 98103

Seattle Community College, South
Campus
6000 16th Ave. SW
Seattle 98106

Shoreline Community College
16101 Greenwood Ave. N
Seattle 98133

South Puget Sound Community College
2011 Mottman Rd. SW
Olympia 98512

Spokane Community College
North 1810 Greene Ave.
Spokane 99207

Spokane Falls Community College
West 3410 Fort George Wright Dr.
Spokane 99224

Tacoma Community College
5900 South 12th St.
Tacoma 98465

Walla Walla Community College
500 Tausick Way
Walla Walla 99362

Yakima Valley Community College
P.O. Box 1647
Yakima 98907

WEST VIRGINIA

Huntington Junior College
900 Fifth Ave.
Huntington 25701

Mountain Cap of West Virginia, Inc.
26 North Kanawha St.
Buckhannon 26201

Salem-Teikyo University
223 West Main St.
Salem 26426

Southern West Virginia Community
and Technical College
P.O. Box 2900
Mt. Gay 25637

West Virginia Northern Community
College
1704 Market St.
Wheeling 26003

West Virginia State College
Rte. 25
Institute 25112

WISCONSIN

Blackhawk Technical College
P.O. Box 5009
Janesville 53547

Fox Valley Technical College
1825 North Bluemound Dr.
Appleton 54913-2277

Gateway Technical College
3520 30th Ave.
Kenosha 53144-1690

Lakeshore Technical College
1290 North Ave.
Cleveland 53015

Madison Area Technical College
235 North National Ave.
P.O. Box 1940
Fond Du Lac 54936-1940

Madison Junior College of Business
31 South Henry St.
Madison 53703-3110

MBTI Business Training Institute
606 West Wisconsin Ave.
Milwaukee 53203

Mid-State Technical College
500 32nd St. N
Wisconsin Rapids 54494

Milwaukee Area Technical College
700 West State St.
Milwaukee 53233-1443

Moraine Park Technical College
235 North National Ave.
Fond Du Lac 54936-1904

Nicolet Area Technical College
Hwy. G S
Rhinelander 54501

North Central Technical College
1000 Campus Dr.
Wausau 54401-1899

Northeast Wisconsin Technical College
2740 West Mason St.
P.O. Box 19042
Green Bay 54307-9042

Southwest Wisconsin Technical College
1800 Bronson Blvd.
Fennimore 53809

Waukesha County Technical College
800 Main St.
Pewaukee 53072

Western Wisconsin Technical College
304 North Sixth St.
P.O. Box 908
La Crosse 54602-0908

Wisconsin Area Vocational Training
and Adult Education System,
District Number Four
3550 Anderson St.
Madison 53704

Wisconsin Indianhead Technical
College
505 Pine Ridge Dr.
P.O. Box 10B
Shell Lake 54871

WYOMING

Casper College
125 College Dr.
Casper 82601

Central Wyoming College
2660 Peck Ave.
Riverton 82501

Eastern Wyoming College
3200 West C St.
Torrington 82240

Northwest Community College
231 West Sixth St.
Powell 82435

Western Wyoming Community College
2500 College Dr.
Rock Springs 82902

Banking and Finance

ALABAMA

Chattahoochee Valley Community
College
2602 College Dr.
Phenix City 36869

Community College of the Air Force
130 West Maxwell Blvd.
Montgomery 36112-6613

ARIZONA

Pima Community College
2202 West Anklam Rd.
Tucson 85709-0001

ARKANSAS

Great Rivers Vocational-Technical
School
P.O. Box 747, Hwy. 1 NE
McGehee 71654

CALIFORNIA

East Los Angeles Skill Center
3921 Selig Place
Los Angeles 90031

Marin Regional Occupational Program
P.O. Box 4925
San Rafael 94913

Southwestern College
900 Otay Lakes Rd.
Chula Vista 92010

FLORIDA

Charlotte Vocational-Technical Center
18300 Toledo Blade Blvd.
Port Charlotte 33948-3399

Miami Lakes Technical Education
Center
5780 Northwest 158th St.
Miami Lakes 33169

HAWAII

Hawaii Business College
33 South King St., 4th Floor, Ste. 405
Honolulu 96817

INDIANA

Vincennes University
1002 North First St.
Vincennes 47591

KENTUCKY

Western Kentucky University
One Big Red Way
Bowling Green 42101-3576

MARYLAND

University of Maryland, Baltimore
County Campus
1000 Hilltop Circle
Baltimore 21250

MASSACHUSETTS

Northeastern University
360 Huntington Ave.
Boston 02115

MICHIGAN

Detroit College of Business
4801 Oakman Blvd.
Dearborn 48126-3799

Lansing Community College
419 North Capitol Ave.
Lansing 48901-7210

MINNESOTA

Alexandria Technical College
1601 Jefferson St.
Alexandria 56308

Hennepin Technical College
9000 Brooklyn Blvd.
Brooklyn Park 55445

Saint Cloud Technical College
1540 Northway Dr.
Saint Cloud 56303

NEBRASKA

Southeast Community College Area
111 O St., Ste. 111
Lincoln 68520

NEVADA

Community College of Southern
Nevada
3200 East Cheyenne Ave.
Las Vegas 89030

NEW JERSEY

Bergen Community College
400 Paramus Rd.
Paramus 07652

NEW YORK

CUNY Kingsborough Community
College
2001 Oriental Blvd.
Brooklyn 11235

Hudson Valley Community College
80 Vandenburgh Ave.
Troy 12180

Mohawk Valley Community College
1101 Sherman Dr.
Utica 13501

New York Institute of Credit
71 West 23rd St.
New York 10010

New York University
70 Washington Square S
New York 10012

Pace University, New York
One Pace Plaza
New York 10038

Suffolk County Community College,
Ammerman Campus
533 College Rd.
Selden 11784

NORTH CAROLINA

Fayetteville Technical Community
College
2201 Hull Rd.
Fayetteville 28303-0236

OHIO

Columbus State Community College
550 East Spring St.
P.O. Box 1609
Columbus 43216

Owens Community College
39335 Oregon Rd.
Toledo 43699-1947

Sinclair Community College
444 West Third St.
Dayton 45402

University of Akron, Main Campus
302 Buchtel Common
Akron 44325-4702

OKLAHOMA

Oklahoma City Community College
7777 South May Ave.
Oklahoma City 73159

Tulsa Community College
6111 East Skelly Dr.
Tulsa 74135

PENNSYLVANIA

Lackawanna Junior College
501 Vine St.
Scranton 18509

Reading Area Community College
P.O. Box 1706
Reading 19603-1706

RHODE ISLAND

Johnson and Wales University
8 Abbott Park Place
Providence 02903-3376

SOUTH CAROLINA

Midlands Technical College
P.O. Box 2408
Columbia 29202

TENNESSEE

Cleveland State Community College
P.O. Box 3570
Cleveland 37320-3570

Pellissippi State Technical Community
College
P.O. Box 22990
Knoxville 37933-0990

TEXAS

Austin Institute of Real Estate
7801 North Lamar, Ste. F35
Austin 78752

Bee County College
3800 Charco Rd.
Beeville 78102

Houston Community College System
22 Waugh Dr.
Houston 77270-7849

McLennan Community College
1400 College Dr.
Waco 76708

UTAH

Salt Lake Community College
P.O. Box 30808
Salt Lake City 84129

WASHINGTON

Bellingham Technical College
3028 Lindbergh Ave.
Bellingham 98225

WEST VIRGINIA

West Virginia State College
Rte. 25
Institute 25112

WISCONSIN

Fox Valley Technical College
1825 North Bluemound Dr.
Appleton 54913-2277

Milwaukee Area Technical College
700 West State St.
Milwaukee 53233-1443

Northeast Wisconsin Technical College
2740 West Mason St., P.O. Box 19042
Green Bay 54307-9042

Southwest Wisconsin Technical College
1800 Bronson Blvd.
Fennimore 53809

Western Wisconsin Technical College
304 North Sixth St. P.O. Box 908
La Crosse 54602-0908

Madison Area Technical College
3550 Anderson St.
Madison 53704

Business and Data Processing Machine Maintenance

VIRGINIA

Falwell Aviation, Inc.
4332 Richmond Hwy.
Lynchburg 24501

WISCONSIN

Blackhawk Technical College
P.O. Box 5009
Janesville 53547

Clerical and Secretarial Technology

ALABAMA

Bessemer State Technical College
1100 9th Ave.
Bessemer 35021

Bevill State Community College
100 State St.
Sumiton 35148

Bishop State Community College
351 North Broad St.
Mobile 36608

Chattahoochee Valley Community
College
2602 College Dr.
Phenix City 36869

Chauncey Sparks State Technical
College
Hwy. 431 S
Eufaula 36027

Community College of the Air Force
130 West Maxwell Blvd.
Montgomery 36112-6613

Douglas MacArthur Technical College
1708 North Main St.
Opp 36467

Draughons Junior College
122 Commerce St.
Montgomery 36104

Enterprise State Junior College
600 Plaza Dr.
Enterprise 36330

Gadsden Business College
750 Forrest Ave.
Gadsden 35901

Gadsden Business College, Anniston
P.O. Box 1559
Anniston 36202-1575

Gadsden State Community College
1001 George Wallace Dr.
Gadsden 35902-0227

George C Wallace State Community
College
3000 Earl Goodwin Pkwy.
Selma 36702-1049

George C Wallace State Community
College, Dothan
Rte. 6, P.O. Box 62
Dothan 36303-9234

George C Wallace State Community
College, Hanceville
801 Main St. NW
Hanceville 35077-2000

Harry M Ayers State Technical College
1801 Coleman Rd.
Anniston 36202

Herzing Institutes of Alabama
208 West Valley Ave.
Birmingham 35209

J F Ingram State Technical College
5375 Ingram Rd.
Deatsville 36022

James H. Faulkner State Community
College
1900 U.S. Hwy. 31 S
Bay Minette 36507

Jefferson Davis Community College,
Brewton Campus
Alco Dr.
Brewton 36426

Jefferson State Community College
2601 Carson Rd.
Birmingham 35215-3098

John C Calhoun State Community
College
Hwy. 31 N
Decatur 35602

John M Patterson State Technical
College
3920 Troy Hwy.
Montgomery 36116

Lawson State Community College
3060 Wilson Rd. SW
Birmingham 35221

Lurleen B Wallace State Junior College
Hwy. 84 E
Andalusia 36420

Northeast Alabama State Community
College
Hwy. 35 W
Rainsville 35986

Prince Institute of Professional Studies
7735 Atlanta Hwy.
Montgomery 36117-4231

Reid State Technical College
165 and Hwy. 83
Evergreen 36401

Shelton State Community College
9500 Old Greensboro Rd.
Tuscaloosa 35405

Northwest Shoals Community College
George Wallace Blvd.
Muscle Shoals 35662

Snead State Community College
220 North Walnut St.
Boaz 35957-0734

University of Alabama at Birmingham,
Walker College
1411 Indiana Ave.
Jasper 35501

ALASKA

Alaska Computer Institute of
Technology
701 East Tudor Rd.
Anchorage 99503

Alaska Vocational-Technical Center
809 Second Ave.
Seward 99664

Charter College
2221 East Northern Lights Blvd., Ste. 1
Anchorage 99508

Mila Inc.
3330 Artic Blvd., Ste. 201
Anchorage 99503

New Frontier Vocational-Technical
Center
35207 K Beach Rd., Ste. 37B
Soldotna 99669

People Count, Inc.
P.O. Box 1310
Kenai 99611

University of Alaska, Anchorage
3211 Providence Dr.
Anchorage 99508

ARIZONA

Academy Business College
3320 West Beryl Ave.
Phoenix 85021

Apollo College
3870 North Oracle Rd.
Tucson 85705

Apollo College, Phoenix, Inc.
8503 North 27th Ave.
Phoenix 85051

Apollo College, Tri City, Inc.
630 West Southern Ave.
Mesa 85210

Arizona Institute of Business and
Technology
6049 North 43rd Ave.
Phoenix 85019

Central Arizona College
8470 North Overfield Rd.
Coolidge 85228-9778

Chaparral Career College
4585 East Speedway Blvd., Ste. 204
Tucson 85712

Eastern Arizona College
Church St.
Thatcher 85552-0769

Gateway Community College
108 North 40th St.
Phoenix 85034

Glendale Community College
6000 West Olive Ave.
Glendale 85302

Lamson Junior College
1126 North Scottsdale Rd., Ste. 100
Tempe 82581-1700

Mesa Community College
1833 West Southern Ave.
Mesa 85202

Mohave Community College
1971 Jagerson Ave.
Kingman 86401

Opportunities Industrialization Center,
Phoenix
39 East Jackson St.
Phoenix 85004

Phoenix College
1202 West Thomas Rd.
Phoenix 85013

Pima Community College
2202 West Anklam Rd.
Tucson 85709-0001

Rio Salado Community College
2323 West 14th St.
Tempe 85281

Scottsdale Community College
9000 East Chaparral Rd.
Scottsdale 85253

Yavapai College
1100 East Sheldon St.
Prescott 86301

ARKANSAS

Arkansas Valley Technical Institute
Hwy. 23 N P.O. Box 506
Ozark 72949

Cossatot Technical College
183 Hwy. 399
De Queen 71832

Cotton Boll Technical Institute
155 and Hwy. 148
Burdette 72321

East Arkansas Community College
1700 Newcastle Rd.
Forrest City 72335

Eastern College of Health Vocations
6423 Forbing Rd.
Little Rock 72209

Foothills Technical Institute
1800 East Moore St.
Searcy 72143

Garland County Community College
101 College Dr.
Hot Springs 71913

Great Rivers Vocational-Technical
School
P.O. Box 747, Hwy. 1 NE
McGehee 71654

Northwest Technical Institute
709 South Old Missouri Rd.
Springdale 72764

Ouachita Technical College
One College Circle
Malvern 72104

Petit Jean College of the University of
Arkansas
One Bruce St.
Morrilton 72110

Phillips Community College of the
University of Arkansas
P.O. Box 785
Helena 72342

Pulaski Technical College
3000 West Scenic Dr.
North Little Rock 72118

Quapaw Technical Institute
200 Mid America Blvd.
Hot Springs 71913

Westark College
P.O. Box 3649
Fort Smith 72913

CALIFORNIA

Academy of Court Reporting, Inc.
8376 Hercules St.
La Mesa 91942

American River College
4700 College Oak Dr.
Sacramento 95841

Antelope Valley College
3041 West Ave. K
Lancaster 93536

Barstow College
2700 Barstow Rd.
Barstow 92311

Bryan College of Court Reporting
2511 Beverly Blvd.
Los Angeles 90057

Butte College
3536 Butte Campus Dr.
Oroville 95965

Cabrillo College
6500 Soquel Dr.
Aptos 95003

California Business Institute
3550 Johnson Ave.
El Monte 91731

California Technical College
1203 Main St.
Delano 93215

Canada College
4200 Farm Hill Blvd.
Redwood City 94061

Career Development Center
255 East Bonita Ave.
Pomona 91767

Career Resources Development Center
655 Geary St.
San Francisco 94102

Center for Employment Training, El
Centro
294 South Third St.
El Centro 92243

Center for Employment Training,
Gilroy
7800 Arroyo Circle
Gilroy 95020

Center for Employment Training,
Riverside
1099 West Lacadena Dr.
Riverside 92501

Center for Employment Training,
Salinas
421 Monterey St.
Salinas 93901

Center for Employment Training, San
Diego
3295 Market St.
San Diego 92102

Center for Employment Training, San
Jose-Vine
701 Vine St.
San Jose 95110

Center for Training and Careers
1600 Las Plumas
San Jose 95133

Cerritos College
11110 Alondra Blvd.
Norwalk 90650

Cerro Coso Community College
3000 College Heights Blvd.
Ridgecrest 93555-7777

Chabot College
25555 Hesperian Blvd.
Hayward 94545

Chaffey Community College
5885 Haven Ave.
Rancho Cucamonga 91737-3002

Citrus College
1000 West Foothill Blvd.
Glendora 91741-1899

City College of San Francisco
50 Phelan Ave.
San Francisco 94112

Coastline Community College
11460 Warner Ave.
Fountain Valley 92708

College of Marin
835 College Ave.
Kentfield 94904

College of San Mateo
1700 West Hillsdale Blvd.
San Mateo 94402

College of the Desert
43-500 Monterey St.
Palm Desert 92260

College of the Redwoods
7351 Tompkins Hill Rd.
Eureka 95501-9302

Contra Costa College
2600 Mission Bell Dr.
San Pablo 94806

Cuesta College
P.O. Box 8106
San Luis Obispo 93403-8106

Cypress College
9200 Valley View
Cypress 90630

De Anza College
21250 Stevens Creek Blvd.
Cupertino 95014

East Los Angeles College
1301 Brooklyn Ave.
Monterey Park 91754

East Los Angeles Skill Center
3921 Selig Place
Los Angeles 90031

EBM Business Institute
6024 San Juan Ave., Ste. C
Citrus Heights 95610

El Camino College
16007 Crenshaw Blvd.
Torrance 90506

Eldorado College
2204 El Camino Real
Oceanside 92054

Eldorado College
1901 Pacific Ave.
West Covina 91790

Empire College School of Business
3033 Cleveland Ave.
Santa Rosa 95403

Fil-Am Employment and Training
Center
2940 16th St., Ste. 319
San Francisco 94103

Fresno City College
1101 East University Ave.
Fresno 93741

Fullerton College
321 East Chapman Ave.
Fullerton 92632-2095

Galen College of Medical and Dental
Assistants
3908 West Coldwell, Ste. A
Visalia 93277

Gavilan College
5055 Santa Teresa Blvd.
Gilroy 95020

Glendale Community College
1500 North Verdugo Rd.
Glendale 91208-2894

Golden West College
15744 Golden W
Huntington Beach 92647

Goodwill Industries of Santa Cruz
350 Encinal St.
Santa Cruz 95060

Grossmont College
8800 Grossmont College Dr.
El Cajon 92020

Hartnell College
156 Homestead Ave.
Salinas 93901

Humphreys College
3600 Sisk Rd.
Modesto 95356

Humphreys College
6650 Inglewood St.
Stockton 95207-3896

Imperia Valley College
P.O. Box 158
Imperial 92251-0158

Institute of Computer Technology
3200 Wilshire Blvd.
Los Angeles 90010

Jobs for Progress, Inc.
5161 East Pomona Blvd., Ste. 106
Los Angeles 90022

Kings River Community College
995 North Reed
Reedley 93654

Laney College
900 Fallon St.
Oakland 94607

Lassen College
Hwy. 139
Susanville 96130

Long Beach City College
4901 East Carson St.
Long Beach 90808

Los Angeles City College
855 North Vermont Ave.
Los Angeles 90029

Los Angeles Harbor College
1111 Figueroa Place
Wilmington 90744

Los Angeles Pierce College
6201 Winnetka Ave.
Woodland Hills 91371

Los Angeles Trade Technical College
400 West Washington Blvd.
Los Angeles 90015-4181

Los Angeles Valley College
5800 Fulton Ave.
Van Nuys 91401

Maric College of Medical Careers
3666 Kearny Villa Rd., Ste. 100
San Diego 92123

Marin Regional Occupational Program
P.O. Box 4925
San Rafael 94913

Mendocino College
P.O. Box 3000
Ukiah 95482

Merced College
3600 M St.
Merced 95348-2898

Mexican American Opportunity
Foundation
2001 28th St.
Bakersfield 93301-1924

Mission Lanauage & Vocational School
2929 19th St.
San Francisco 94110

Modesto Junior College
435 College Ave.
Modesto 95350-5800

Monterey Peninsula College
980 Fremont Blvd.
Monterey 93940-4799

Moorpark College
7075 Campus Rd.
Moorpark 93021

Mount San Antonio College
1100 North Grand
Walnut 91789

MTI Business College, Inc.
6006 North El Dorado St.
Stockton 95207-4349

Napa Valley College
2277 Napa Vallejo Hwy.
Napa 94558

Ohlone College
43600 Mission Blvd.
Fremont 94539

Orange County Business College
2035 East Ball Rd.
Anaheim 92806

Oxnard College
4000 South Rose Ave.
Oxnard 93033

Pacific Asian Consortium in
Employment
1541 Wilshire Blvd., Ste. 407
Los Angeles 90017

Palo Verde College
811 West Chanslorway
Blythe 92225

Palomar College
1140 West Mission
San Marcos 92069-1487

Pasadena City College
1570 East Colorada Blvd.
Pasadena 91106

Platt College, San Diego
6250 El Cajon Blvd.
San Diego 92115

Rancho Santiago College
1530 West 17th St.
Santa Ana 92706

Rio Hondo College
3600 Workman Mill Rd.
Whittier 90601-1699

Riverside Community College
4800 Magnolia Ave.
Riverside 92506-1299

Sacramento City College
3835 Freeport Blvd.
Sacramento 95822

San Diego City College
1313 12th Ave.
San Diego 92101

San Diego Mesa College
7250 Mesa College Dr.
San Diego 92111-4998

San Diego Urban League Training
Center
4262 Market St.
San Diego 92102

San Joaquin Delta College
5151 Pacific Ave.
Stockton 95207

San Joaquin Valley College
201 New Stine Rd.
Bakersfield 93309

San Joaquin Valley College
8400 West Mineral King Ave.
Visalia 93291

Santa Barbara Business College
211 South Real Rd.
Bakersfield 93309

Santa Barbara Business College
4333 Hansen Ave.
Fremont 94536

Santa Barbara Business College, Santa
Maria Branch
303 East Plaza Dr., Ste. 1
Santa Maria 93454

Santa Barbara City College
721 Cliff Dr.
Santa Barbara 93109-2394

Santa Rosa Junior College
1501 Mendocino Ave.
Santa Rosa 95401-4395

Shasta College
P.O. Box 496006
Redding 96049

Sierra College
5000 Rocklin Rd.
Rocklin 95677

Sierra Valley Business College
4747 North First St., Bldg. D
Fresno 93726

Skyline College
3300 College Dr.
San Bruno 94066

Solano County Community College
District
4000 Suisun Valley Rd.
Suisun 94585-3197

South Coast College of Court Reporting
1380 South Sanderson Ave.
Anaheim 92806

Southwestern College
900 Otay Lakes Rd.
Chula Vista 92010

Spectrum Community Services, Inc.
1435 Grove Way
Hayward 94546

Taft College
29 Emmons Park Dr.
Taft 93268

United Education Institute
3727 West Sixth St., Ste. 317
Los Angeles 90020

Vallecitos CET, Inc.
597 C St.
Hayward 94541

Valley Commercial College
1207 I St.
Modesto 95354

Ventura College
4667 Telegraph Rd.
Ventura 93003

Victor Valley College
18422 Bear Valley Rd.
Victorville 92392-9699

Watterson College
150 South Los Robles Blvd., Ste. 100
Pasadena 91101

West Hills Community College
300 Cherry Ln.
Coalinga 93210

West Valley College
14000 Fruitvale Ave.
Saratoga 95070

Western Career College
8909 Folsom Blvd.
Sacramento 95826

Yuba College
2088 North Beale Rd.
Marysville 95901

COLORADO

Aims Community College
P.O. Box 69
Greeley 80632

Arapahoe Community College
2500 West College Dr.
Littleton 80160-9002

Blair College
828 Wooten Rd.
Colorado Springs 80915

Community College of Denver
P.O. Box 173363
Denver 80217

Delta-Montrose Area Vocational-
Technical Center
1765 U.S. Hwy. 50
Delta 81416

Denver Academy of Court Reporting
7290 Samuel Dr., Ste. 200
Denver 80221-2792

Denver Institute of Technology
7350 North Broadway
Denver 80221

Front Range Community College
3645 West 112th Ave.
Westminster 80030

Northeastern Junior College
100 College Dr.
Sterling 80751

Otero Junior College
1802 Colorado Ave.
La Junta 81050

Parks College
9065 Grant St.
Denver 80229

Pikes Peak Community College
5675 South Academy Blvd.
Colorado Springs 80906-5498

PPI Health Careers School
2345 North Academy Blvd.
Colorado Springs 80909

Pueblo Community College
900 West Orman Ave.

Pueblo 81004

Red Rocks Community College
13300 West Sixth Ave.
Lakewood 80228

San Juan Basin Area Vocational School
P.O. Box 970
Cortez 81321

T H Pickens Technical Center
500 Airport Blvd.
Aurora 80011

Technical Trades Institute
772 Horizon Dr.
Grand Junction 81506

Trinidad State Junior College
600 Prospect St.
Trinidad 81082

Trinidad State Junior College, San Luis
Valley Education Center
1011 Main St.
Alamosa 81101

CONNECTICUT

Asnuntuck Community Technical
College
170 Elm St.
Enfield 06082

Branford Hall Career Institute
1 Summit Place
Branford 06405

Briarwood College
2279 Mount Vernon Rd.
Southington 06489

Butler Business School, Inc.
2710 North Ave.
Bridgeport 06604

Data Institute
745 Burnside Ave.
East Hartford 06108

Capital Community Technical College
61 Woodland St.
Hartford 06105-2354

Gibbs College
142 East Ave.
Norwalk 06851

Housatonic Community Technical
College
900 Lafayette Blvd.
Bridgeport 06604

Huntington Institute, Inc.
193 Broadway
Norwich 06360

Manchester Community Technical
College
60 Bidwell St.,
P.O. Box 1045
Manchester 06040-1046

Middlesex Community Technical
College
100 Training Hill Rd.
Middletown 06457

Mitchell College
437 Pequot Ave.
New London 06320

Morse School of Business
275 Asylum St.
Hartford 06103

Naugatuck Valley Community
Technical College
750 Chase Pkwy.
Waterbury 06708

Northwestern Connecticut Community
Technical College
Park Place E
Winsted 06098

Norwalk Community Technical College
188 Richards Ave.
Norwalk 06854

Porter and Chester Institute
138 Weymouth Rd.
Enfield 06082

Porter and Chester Institute
670 Lordship Blvd.
Stratford 06497

Porter and Chester Institute
320 Sylvan Lake Rd.
Watertown 06779-1400

Porter and Chester Institute
125 Silas Deane Hwy.
Wethersfield 06109

Quinebaug Valley Community
Technical College
742 Upper Maple St.
Danielson 06239

Sacred Heart University
5151 Park Ave.
Fairfield 06432-1023

Stone Academy
1315 Dixwell Ave.
Hamden 06514

Three Rivers Community Technical
College
Mahan Dr.
Norwich 06360

Tunxis Community Technical College
Rtes. 6 and 177
Farmington 06032

University of New Haven
300 Orange Ave.
West Haven 06516

DELAWARE

Delaware Technical and Community
College, Owens Campus
P.O. Box 610
Georgetown 19947

Delaware Technical and Community
College, Stanton-Wilmington
400 Stanton-Christiana Rd.
Newark 19702

Delaware Technical and Community
College, Terry Campus
1832 North Dupont Pkwy.
Dover 19901

Goldey-Beacom College
4701 Limestone Rd.
Wilmington 19808

DISTRICT OF COLUMBIA

University of the District of Columbia
4200 Connecticut Ave. NW
Washington 20008

FLORIDA

Atlantic Vocational-Technical Center
4700 Coconut Creek Pkwy.
Coconut Creek 33063

Beacon Career Institute, Inc.
2900 Northwest 183rd St.
Miami 33056

Brevard Community College, Cocoa
Campus
1519 Clearlake Rd.
Cocoa 32922

Broward Community College
225 East Las Olas Blvd.
Fort Lauderdale 33301

Central Florida Community College
3001 SW College Rd.
Ocala 34474

Charlotte Vocational-Technical Center
18300 Toledo Blade Blvd.
Port Charlotte 33948-3399

Daytona Beach Community College
1200 Volusia Ave.
Daytona Beach 32114

Florida Community College at
Jacksonville
501 West State St.
Jacksonville 32202

Gulf Coast Community College
5230 West Hwy. 98
Panama City 32401

Hillsborough Community College
P.O. Box 31127
Tampa 33631-3127

Indian River Community College
3209 Virginia Ave.
Fort Pierce 34981

Jones College Jacksonville
5353 Arlington Expwy.
Jacksonville 32211

Lake City Community College
Rte. 19
Box 1030
Lake City 32025

Lake County Area Vocational-Technical
Center
2001 Kurt St.
Eustis 32726

Lee County High-Technical Center,
Central
3800 Michigan Ave.
Fort Myers 33916

Lindsey Hopkins Technical Education
Center
750 Northwest 20th St.
Miami 33127

Lively Technical Center
500 North Appleyard Dr.
Tallahassee 32304

Manatee Vocational-Technical Center
5603 34th St. W
Bradenton 34210

Miami-Dade Community College
300 Northeast Second Ave.
Miami 33132

Miami Lakes Technical Education
Center
5780 Northwest 158th St.
Miami Lakes 33169

Okaloosa-Walton Community College
100 College Blvd.
Niceville 32578

Orlando College
5421 Diplomat Circle
Orlando 32810

Pasco-Hernando Community College
36727 Blanton Rd.
Dade City 33525-7599

Pensacola Junior College
1000 College Blvd.
Pensacola 32504

Pinellas Technical Education Center,
Clearwater Campus
6100 154th Ave. N
Clearwater 34620

Polk Community College
999 Ave. H NE
Winter Haven 33881

Robert Morgan Vocational-Technical
Center
18180 Southwest 122nd Ave.
Miami 33177

Ross Technical Institute
1490 South Military Trail
West Palm Beach 33415-9141

Saint Petersburg Junior College
8580 66 St. N
Pinellas Park 34665

Santa Fe Community College
3000 Northwest 83rd St.
Gainesville 32606

Sarasota County Technical Institute
4748 Beneva Rd.
Sarasota 34233-1798

Seminole Community College
100 Weldon Blvd.
Sanford 32773-6199

Sheridan Vocational Center
5400 Sheridan St.
Hollywood 33021

South Florida Community College
600 West College Dr.
Avon Park 33825

Southern College
5600 Lake Underhill Rd.
Orlando 32807

Stenotype Institute of Jacksonville, Inc.
500 Ninth Ave. N
Jacksonville 32250-4599

Suwannee-Hamilton Area Vocational
and Adult Center
415 Southwest Pinewood Dr.
Live Oak 32060

Valencia Community College
P.O. Box 3028
Orlando 32802

Washington-Holmes Area Vocational-
Technical Center
757 Hoyt St.
Chipley 32428

GEORGIA

Advanced Career Training
One Corporate Square, Ste. 110
Atlanta 30329

Albany Technical Institute
1021 Lowe Rd.
Albany 31708

Atlanta Area Technical School
1560 Stewart Ave. SW
Atlanta 30310

Augusta Technical Institute
3116 Deans Bridge Rd.
Augusta 30906

Bainbridge College
2500 East Shotwell St.
Bainbridge 31717

Brown College of Court Reporting &
Medical Transcription
1740 Peachtree St. NW
Atlanta 30309-2848

Carroll Technical Institute
997 South Hwy. 16
Carrollton 30117

Chattahoochee Technical Institute
980 South Cobb Dr.
Marietta 30060-3398

Clayton College and State University
5900 Lee St.
Morrow 30260

Columbus Technical Institute
928 45th St.
Columbus 31904-6572

Coosa Valley Technical Institute
785 Cedar Ave.
Rome 30161

Dalton College
213 North College Dr.
Dalton 30720

East Central Technical Institute
667 Perry House Rd.
Fitzgerald 31750

Floyd College
P.O. Box 1864
Rome 30162-1864

Georgia Institute of Real Estate
5784 Lake Forest Dr.
Atlanta 30328

Georgia Medical Institute
40 Marietta St., Ste. 1333
Atlanta 30303

Griffin Technical Institute
501 Varsity Rd.
Griffin 30223

Gwinnett Technical Institute
5150 Sugarloaf Pkwy.
P.O. Box 1505
Lawrenceville 30043

Heart of Georgia Technical Institute
560 Pine Hill Rd.
Dublin 31021

Kerr Business College
2528 Centerwest Pkwy., Bldg. A
Augusta 30909

Lanier Technical Institute
P.O. Box 58
Oakwood 30566

Macon Technical Institute
3300 Macon Tech Dr.
Macon 31206

Meadows Junior College
1170 Brown Ave.
Columbus 31906

Moultrie Area Technical Institute
361 Industrial Dr.
Moultrie 31768

North Georgia Technical Institute
Georgia Hwy. 197, P.O. Box 65
Clarkesville 30523

Pickens Technical Institute
100 Pickens Tech Dr.
Jasper 30143

Savannah Technical Institute
5717 White Bluff Rd.
Savannah 31405-5594

South College
709 Mall Blvd.
Savannah 31406

South Georgia College
100 West College Park Dr.
Douglas 31533

Swainsboro Technical Institute
346 Kite Rd.
Swainsboro 30401

Thomas College
1501 Millpond Rd.
Thomasville 31792

Thomas Technical Institute
15689 U.S. Hwy. 19 N
Thomasville 31792

Valdosta Technical Institute
4089 Valtech Rd.
Valdosta 31602-9796

Walker Technical Institute
265 Bicentennial Trail
Rock Spring 30739

HAWAII

Hawaii Business College
33 South King St., Fourth Floor, Ste. 405
Honolulu 96817

Hawaii Pacific University
1164 Bishop St.
Honolulu 96813

Herald College School of Business and
Technology
1500 Kapiolani Blvd.
Honolulu 96816

Kapiolani Community College
4303 Diamond Head Rd.
Honolulu 96816

Leeward Community College
96-045 Ala Ike
Pearl City 96782

Maui Community College
310 Kaahumanu Ave.
Kahului 96732

Medical Assistant School of Hawaii, Inc.
33 South King, Ste. 223
Honolulu 96813

University of Hawaii at Hilo
200 West Kawili St.
Hilo 96720-4091

IDAHO

Boise State University
1910 University Dr.
Boise 83725

College of Southern Idaho
P.O. Box 1238
Twin Falls 83301

Eastern Idaho Technical College
1600 South 2500 East
Idaho Falls 83404

Idaho State University
741 South Seventh Ave.
Pocatello 83209

ITT Technical Institute
12302 Explorer Dr.
Boise 83713

Lewis-Clark State College
500 Eighth Ave.
Lewiston 83501

North Idaho College
1000 West Garden Ave.
Coeur D' Alene 83814

Ricks College
Rexburg 83460-4107

Shadow Mountain Business Careers
11911 Ustic Rd.
Boise 83713

Valley Business College
508 Thain Rd.
Lewiston 83501

ILLINOIS

Belleville Area College
2500 Carlyle Rd.
Belleville 62221

Black Hawk College
6600 34th Ave.
Moline 61265

Carl Sandburg College
2232 South Lake Storey Rd.
Galesburg 61401

Chicago College of Commerce
11 East Adams St.
Chicago 60603-6301

City College of Chicago, Harold
  Washington
30 East Lake St.
Chicago 60601

City College of Chicago, Kennedy-King
6800 South Wentworth Ave.
Chicago 60621

City College of Chicago, Olive-Harvey
  College
10001 South Woodlawn Ave.
Chicago 60628

City College of Chicago, Richard J
  Daley College
7500 South Pulaski Rd.
Chicago 60652

City College of Chicago, Truman
  College
1145 Wilson Ave.
Chicago 60640

City College of Chicago, Wilbur Wright
  College
4300 North Narragansett
Chicago 60634

City Colleges of Chicago, Central Office
226 West Jackson Blvd.
Chicago 60606

City Colleges of Chicago, Malcolm X
1900 West Van Buren
Chicago 60612

College of Du Page
425 22nd St.
Glen Ellyn 60137-6599

College of Lake County
19351 West Washington St.
Grayslake 60030-1198

Danville Area Community College
2000 East Main St.
Danville 61832

Elgin Community College
1700 Spartan Dr.
Elgin 60123

First Institute Inc.
790 McHenry Ave.
Crystal Lake 60014

Fox Secretarial College
4201 West 93rd St.
Oak Lawn 60453

Heartland School of Business
211 West State St.
Jacksonville 62650

Highland Community College
2998 West Pearl City Rd.
Freeport 61032-9341

Illinois Central College
One College Dr.
East Peoria 61635-0001

Illinois Eastern Community Colleges,
  Olney Central College
305 North West St.
Olney 62450

Illinois Valley Community College
815 North Orlando Smith Ave.
Oglesby 61348-9692

John A Logan College
700 Logan College Rd.
Carterville 62918

John Wood Community College
150 South 48th St.
Quincy 62301-9147

Joliet Junior College
1215 Houbolt Ave.
Joliet 60431

Kankakee Community College
P.O. Box 888
Kankakee 60901

Kaskaskia College
27210 College Rd.
Centralia 62801

Kishwaukee College
21193 Malta Rd.
Malta 60150

Lake Land College
5001 Lake Land Blvd.
Mattoon 61938

Lewis and Clark Community College
5800 Godfrey Rd.
Godfrey 62035

Lincoln College
300 Keokuk St.
Lincoln 62656

Lincoln Land Community College
Shepherd Rd.
Springfield 62194-9256

MacCormac College
506 South Wabash
Chicago 60605

MacMurray College
East College Ave.
Jacksonville 62650

Midstate College
244 Southwest Jefferson
Peoria 61602

Moraine Valley Community College
10900 South 88th Ave.
Palos Hills 60465-0937

Morton College
3801 South Central Ave.
Cicero 60650

Northwestern Business College
4829 North Lipps Ave.
Chicago 60630

Oakton Community College
1600 East Golf Rd.
Des Plaines 60016

Operation Uplift Training Resource
  Center, Inc.
104 South Fifth Ave.
Maywood 60153

Parkland College
2400 West Bradley Ave.
Champaign 61821

Prairie State College
202 Halsted St.
Chicago Heights 60411

Rend Lake College
468 North Ken Graz Pkwy.
Ina 62846

Richland Community College
One College Park
Decatur 62521

Robert Morris College
180 North Lasalle St.
Chicago 60601

Rockford Business College
730 North Church St.
Rockford 61103

Rock Valley College
3301 North Mulford Rd.
Rockford 61114

Saint Augustine College
1333 West Argyle
Chicago 60640

Sauk Valley Community College
173 Illinois, Rte. 2
Dixon 61021

Shawnee Community College
8364 Shawnee College Rd.
Ullin 62992

South Suburban College
15800 South State St.
South Holland 60473

Southeastern Illinois College
3575 College Rd.
Harrisburg 62946

Southern Illinois University,
  Carbondale
Faner Hall 2179
Carbondale 62901-4512

Spanish Coalition for Jobs, Inc.
2011 West Pershing Rd.
Chicago 60609

Sparks College
131 South Morgan St.
Shelbyville 62565

Spoon River College
23235 North Co. 22
Canton 61520

Triton College
2000 Fifth Ave.
River Grove 60171

VIP Schools, Inc.
600N McClurg Ct., Ste. 304A
Chicago 60611-3044

Waubonsee Community College
Rte. 47 at Harter Rd.
Sugar Grove 60554-0901

William Rainey Harper College
1200 West Algonquin Rd.
Palatine 60067-7398

INDIANA

Ball State University
2000 University Ave.
Muncie 47306

College of Court Reporting, Inc.
111 West Tenth St., Ste. 111
Hobart 46342

Commonwealth Business College, Main
  Campus
4200 West 81st Ave.
Merrillville 46410

Davenport College, Merrillville
8200 Georgia St.
Merrillville 46410

Davenport College, South Bend,
  Mishawaka
7121 Grape Rd.
Granger 46530

Indiana Business College
140 East 53rd St.
Anderson 46013

Indiana Business College
802 North Meridian St.
Indianapolis 46204

Indiana Business College
2 Executive Dr.
Lafayette 47905

Indiana Business College
830 North Miller Ave.
Marion 46952

Indiana Business College
1809 North Walnut
Muncie 47303

Indiana Business College
3175 South Third Place
Terre Haute 47802

Indiana Business College
1431 Willow St.
Vincennes 47591

Indiana College of Commerce
7147 Kennedy Ave.
Hammond 46323-2226

Indiana State University
210 North Seventh St.
Terre Haute 47809

Indiana University, Purdue University
  at Fort Wayne
2101 Coliseum Blvd. E
Fort Wayne 46805

International Business College
3811 Illinois Rd.
Fort Wayne 46804

International Business College,
  Indianapolis Branch
7205 Shadeland Station
Indianapolis 46256

Ivy Tech State College, Central Indiana
One West 26th St.
Indianapolis 46206-1763

Ivy Tech State College, Columbus
4475 Central Ave.
Columbus 47203

Ivy Tech State College, Kokomo
1815 East Morgan St.
Kokomo 46901

Ivy Tech State College, Lafayette
3101 South Creasy Ln.
P.O. Box 6299
Lafayette 47903

Ivy Tech State College, North Central
1534 West Sample St.
South Bend 46619

Ivy Tech State College, Northeast
3800 North Anthony Blvd.
Fort Wayne 46805

Ivy Tech State College, Northwest
1440 East 35th Ave.
Gary 46409

Ivy Tech State College, South Central
8204 Hwy. 311
Sellersburg 47172

Ivy Tech State College, Southeast
590 Ivy Tech Dr., P.O. Box 209
Madison 47250

Ivy Tech State College, Southwest
3501 First Ave.
Evansville 47710

Ivy Tech State College, Wabash Valley
7999 U.S. Hwy. 41
Terre Haute 47802-4898

Ivy Tech State College, Whitewater
P.O. Box 1145
Richmond 47374

ITT Technical Institute
4919 Coldwater Rd.
Fort Wayne 46825

ITT Technical Institute
9511 Angola Ct.
Indianapolis 46268

Michiana College
1030 East Jefferson Blvd.
South Bend 46617

Purdue University, North Central
Campus
1401 South U.S. Hwy. 421
Westville 46391

Sawyer College, Hammond
6040 Hohman Ave.
Hammond 46320

Sawyer College, Merrillville Branch
3803 East Lincoln Hwy.
Merrillville 46410

University of Southern Indiana
8600 University Blvd.
Evansville 47712

Vincennes University
1002 North First St.
Vincennes 47591

Wilson College
5425 S. East St.
Indianapolis 46227

IOWA

American Institute of Business
2500 Fleur Dr.
Des Moines 50321

Des Moines Community College
2006 Ankeny Blvd.
Ankeny 50021

Dordt College
498 Fourth Ave. NE
Sioux Center 51250

Eastern Iowa Community College
District
306 West River Dr.
Davenport 52801-1221

Hamilton College, Main Campus
1924 D St. SW
Cedar Rapids 52404

Hamilton College, Mason City Branch
100 First St. NW
Mason City 50401

Hawkeye Community College
1501 East Orange Rd.
Waterloo 50704

Indian Hills Community College
525 Grandview
Ottumwa 52501

Iowa Central Community College
330 Ave. M
Fort Dodge 50501

Iowa Lakes Community College
19 South Seventh St.
Estherville 51334

Iowa Western Community College
2700 College Rd.
P.O. Box 4C
Council Bluffs 51502

Kirkwood Community College
P.O. Box 2068
Cedar Rapids 52406

North Iowa Area Community College
500 College Dr.
Mason City 50401

Northeast Iowa Community College,
Calmar
Hwy. 150 S P.O. Box 400
Calmar 52132-0400

Southeastern Community College
1015 South Gear Ave., P.O. Drawer F
West Burlington 52655-0605

Southwestern Community College
1501 Townline
Creston 50801

Western Iowa Technical Community
College
4647 Stone Ave., P.O. Box 5199
Sioux City 51102-5199

KANSAS

Allen County Community College
1801 North Cottonwood
Iola 66749

Barton County Community College
245 NE 30th Rd.
Great Bend 67530

The Brown Mackie College
126 South Santa Fe St.
Salina 67402-1787

Butler County Community College
901 South Haverhill Rd.
El Dorado 67042

Coffeyville Community College
400 West 11th St.
Coffeyville 67337

Cowley County Community College
125 South Second St.
Arkansas City 67005

Dodge City Community College
2501 North 14th Ave.
Dodge City 67801

Flint Hills Technical College
3301 West 18th St.
Emporia 66801

Fort Hays State University
600 Park St.
Hays 67601-4099

Hesston College
P.O. Box 3000
Hesston 67062

Hutchinson Community College
1300 North Plum St.
Hutchinson 67501

Independence Community College
Brookside Dr. and College Ave.
Independence 67301

Johnson County Area Vocational-
Technical School
311 East Park
Olathe 66061

Johnson County Community College
12345 College Blvd.
Overland Park 66210-1299

Kansas City Area Vocational-Technical
School
2220 North 59th St.
Kansas City 66104

Kansas City Kansas Community College
7250 State Ave.
Kansas City 66112

Kaw Area Technical School
5724 Huntoon
Topeka 66604

Labette Community College
200 South 14th
Parsons 67357

Manhattan Area Technical Center
3136 Dickens Ave.
Manhattan 66503

Neosho County Community College
800 West 14th St.
Chanute 66720

North Central Kansas Technical College
Hwy. 24, P.O. Box 507
Beloit 67420

Northeast Kansas Area Vocational-
Technical School
1501 West Riley St., P.O. Box 277
Atchison 66002

Northwest Kansas Area Vocational-
Technical School
P.O. Box 668
Goodland 67735

Pratt Community College
348 NE St., Rte. 61
Pratt 67124

Salina Area Vocational-Technical
School
2562 Scanlan Ave.
Salina 67401

Seward County Community College
P.O. Box 1137
Liberal 67905-1137

Southeast Kansas Area Vocational-
Technical School
600 Roosevelt
Coffeyville 67337

Southwest Kansas Technical School
2215 N Kansas
Liberal 67905-1599

Topeka Technical College
1620 Northwest Gage
Topeka 66618

Wichita Area Technical College
201 North Water
Wichita 67202-1292

KENTUCKY

Ashland Community College
1400 College Dr.
Ashland 41101

Eastern Kentucky University
Lancaster Ave.
Richmond 40475

Elizabethtown Community College
College Street Rd.
Elizabethtown 42701

Fugazzi College
406 Lafayette Ave.
Lexington 40502

Hazard Community College
Hazard 41701

Hopkinsville Community College
North Dr.
Hopkinsville 42240

Jefferson Community College
109 East Broadway
Louisville 40202

Kentucky College of Business
628 East Main St.
Lexington 40508

Kentucky Tech, Ashland Regional
Technology Center
4818 Roberts Dr.
Ashland 41102

Kentucky Tech, Bowling Green
Regional Technical Center
1845 Loop Dr.
Bowling Green 42101-3601

Kentucky Tech, Central Kentucky SVTS
308 Vo Tech Rd.
Lexington 40511-2626

Kentucky Tech, Davies County
Vocational-Technical School
1901 Southeastern Pkwy.
Owensboro 42303

Kentucky Tech, Jefferson State
Vocational-Technical School
727 West Chestnut St.
Louisville 40203-2036

Kentucky Tech, Rowan Regional
Technology Center
600 Viking Dr.
Morehead 40351

Kentucky Tech, Somerset Regional
Technlogy Center
230 Airport Rd.
Somerset 42501

Lexington Community College
Cooper Dr.
Lexington 40506

Madisonville Community College
University Dr.
Madisonville 42431

Maysville Community College
Maysville 41056

Midway College
512 Stephens St.
Midway 40347-1120

Northern Kentucky State Vocational-
Technical School
1025 Amsterdam Rd.
Covington 41011

Owensboro Junior College of Business
1515 East 18th St., P.O. Box 1350
Owensboro 42302

Paducah Community College
P.O. Box 7380
Paducah 42002-7380

Somerset Community College
808 Monticello Rd.
Somerset 42501

Southeast Community College
300 College Rd.
Cumberland 40823

Southern Ohio College, Fort Mitchell
309 Buttermilk Pike
Fort Mitchell 41017

Spencerian College
4627 Dixie Hwy.
Louisville 40216

Sullivan College, Louisville
3101 Bardstown Rd.
Louisville 40205

West Kentucky Tech
5200 Blandville Rd.
Paducah 42002-7408

Western Kentucky University
One Big Red Way
Bowling Green 42101-3576

LOUISIANA

American School of Business
702 Professional Dr. N
Shreveport 71105

Ayers Institute, Inc.
2924 Knight St., Ste. 318
Shreveport 71105

Louisana Technical College, Alexandria
Campus
4311 South MacArthur Dr.
Alexandria 71302-3137

Louisiana Technical College, Ascension
Campus
P.O. Box 38
Sorrento 70778

Louisiana Technical College, Bastrop
Campus
Kammell St.
Bastrop 71221-1120

Baton Rouge School of Computers
9255 Interline Dr.
Baton Rouge 70809

Cameron College
2740 Canal St.
New Orleans 70119

Charles B Coreil Technical Institute
Industrial Park Ward I
Ville Platte 70586

Delgado Community College
501 City Park Ave.
New Orleans 70119

Delta School of Business and
Technology
517 Broad St.
Lake Charles 70601

Grambling State University
100 Main St.
Grambling 71245

Huey P Long Technical Institute
303 South Jones St.
Winnfield 71483

Louisiana Technical College, Claiborne
College
3001 Minden Rd.
Homer 71040

Louisiana Technical College, Florida
Parishes
P.O. Box 130
Greensburg 70441

Louisiana Technical College, Folkes
Campus
3337 Hwy. 10
Jackson 70748

Louisiana Technical College, Gulf Area
Campus
1115 Clover St.
Abbeville 70510

Louisiana Technical College, Lafayette
Campus
1101 Bertrand Dr.
Lafayette 70502-4909

Louisiana Technical College, Lamar
Salter Campus
15014 Lake Charles Hwy.
Leesville 71446

Louisiana Technical College,
Natchitoches Campus
P.O. Box 657
Natchitoches 71458-0657

Louisiana Technical College, Northwest
Louisiana
P.O. Box 835
Minden 71058-0835

Louisiana Technical College, Ruston
Campus
1010 James St.
Ruston 71273-1070

Louisiana Technical College, Sabine
Valley Campus
1255 Fisher Rd.
Many 71449

Louisiana Technical College, Sidney
North Collier Campus
3727 Louisa St.
New Orleans 70126

Louisiana Technical College, Slidell
Campus
1000 Canulette Rd.
Slidell 70459

Louisiana Technical College, Sullivan
Campus
1710 Sullivan Dr.
Bogalusa 70427

Louisiana Technical College, Teche
Area Campus
609 Ember Dr.
New Iberia 70562-1057

Louisiana Technical College, West
Jefferson Campus
475 Manhattan Blvd.
Harvey 70058

Louisiana Technical College, Young
Memorial Campus
900 Youngs Rd.
Morgan City 70380

Louisiana Technical University
Tech Station, P.O. Box 3168
Ruston 71272

McNeese State University
4100 Ryan St.
Lake Charles 70609

Nicholls State University
University Station, LA Hwy. One
Thibodaux 70310

Remington College
303 Rue Louis XIV
Lafayette 70508

Southeastern Louisiana University
100 West Dakota
Hammond 70402

Southern University Shreveport, Bossier
City Campus
3050 Martin L King Dr.
Shreveport 71107

MAINE

Andover College
901 Washington Ave.
Portland 04103

Beal College
629 Main St.
Bangor 04401

Casco Bay College
477 Congress St.
Portland 04101

Husson College
One College Circle
Bangor 04401

Kennebec Valley Technical College
92 Western Ave.
Fairfield 04937-1367

Mid-State College
88 East Hardscrabble Rd.
Auburn 04210

Northern Maine Technical College
33 Edgemont Dr.
Presque Isle 04769

Thomas College
180 West River Rd.
Waterville 04901-5097

Washington County Technical College
RR 1, P.O. Box 22C
Calais 04619

MARYLAND

Abbie Business Institute
5310 Spectrum Dr.
Frederick 21703

Allegany Community College
12401 Willowbrook Rd. SE
Cumberland 21502

Anne Arundel Community College
101 College Pkwy.
Arnold 21012

Baltimore City Community College
2901 Liberty Heights Ave.
Baltimore 21215

Catonsville Community College
800 South Rolling Rd.
Catonsville 21228

Charles County Community College
8730 Mitchell Rd.
La Plata 20646-0910

Chesapeake College
P.O. Box 8
Wye Mills 21679-0008

Dundalk Community College
7200 Sollers Point Rd.
Dundalk 21222

Fleet Business School
2530 Riva Rd., Ste. 201
Annapolis 21401

Frederick Community College
7932 Opossumtown Pike
Frederick 21702

Hagerstown Business College
18618 Crestwood Dr.
Hagerstown 21742

Howard Community College
10901 Little Patuxent Pkwy.
Columbia 21044

Montgomery College of Rockville
51 Mannakee St.
Rockville 20850

Prince Georges Community College
301 Largo Rd.
Largo 20774-2199

Villa Julie College
Green Spring Valley Rd.
Stevenson 21153

Wor-Wic Community College
32000 Campus Dr.
Salisbury 21801-7131

MASSACHUSETTS

Aquinas College at Milton
303 Adams St.
Milton 02186

Aquinas College at Newton
15 Walnut Park
Newton 02158

Bay Path College
588 Longmeadow St.
Longmeadow 01106

Bay State College
122 Commonwealth Ave.
Boston 02116

Becker College, Worcester
61 Sever St.
Worcester 01615-0071

Berkshire Community College
1350 West St.
Pittsfield 01201-5786

Bristol Community College
777 Elsbree St.
Fall River 02720

Bunker Hill Community College
250 New Rutherford Ave.
Boston 02129

Burdett School
745 Boylston St.
Boston 02116

Cape Cod Community College
2240 Iyanough Rd.
West Barnstable 02668-1599

Computer Learning Center of Boston
Five Middlesex Ave.
Somerville 02145

Computer Processing Institute
615 Massachusetts Ave.
Cambridge 02139

Dean College
99 Main St.
Franklin 02038

Endicott College
376 Hale St.
Beverly 01915

Fisher College
118 Beacon St.
Boston 02116

Greenfield Community College
One College Dr.
Greenfield 01301-9739

Hickox School of Information
Technology
200 Tremont St.
Boston 02116

Holyoke Community College
303 Homestead Ave.
Holyoke 01040

Katharine Gibbs School
126 Newbury
Boston 02116

Kinyon-Campbell Business School
59 Linden St.
New Bedford 02740

Marian Court College
35 Littles Point Rd.
Swampscott 01907

Massachusetts Bay Community College
50 Oakland St.
Wellesley Hills 02181

Massasoit Community College
One Massasoit Blvd.
Brockton 02402

Middlesex Community College
Springs Rd.
Bedford 01730

Mount Wachusett Community College
444 Green St.
Gardner 01440

Newbury College, Inc.
129 Fisher Ave.
Brookline 02146

North Shore Community College
One Ferncroft Rd.
Danvers 01923

Northern Essex Community College
Elliott Way
Haverhill 01830-2399

Quincy College
34 Coddington St.
Quincy 02169

Quinsigamond Community College
670 West Boylston St.
Worcester 01606

The Salter School
155 Ararat St.
Worcester 01606

Skills
150 Fearing St.
Amherst 01002

Springfield Technical Community
College
One Armory Square
Springfield 01105

MICHIGAN

Alpena Community College
666 Johnson St.
Alpena 49707

Andrews University
Berrien Springs 49104

Baker College of Flint
G1050 West Bristol Rd.
Flint 48507

Baker College of Muskegon
903 Marquette Ave.
Muskegon 49442

Baker College of Owosso
1020 South Washington St.
Owosso 48867

Bay De Noc Community College
2001 North Lincoln Rd.
Escanaba 49289

Carnegie Institute
550 Stephenson Hwy.
Troy 48083

Cleary College
2170 Washtenaw Ave.
Ypsilanti 48197

Cornerstone College
1001 East Beltline Ave. NE
Grand Rapids 49505-5897

Davenport College
415 East Fulton
Grand Rapids 49503

Davenport College, Kalamazoo Branch
4123 West Main St.
Kalamazoo 49006-2791

Davenport College, Lansing Branch
220 East Kalamazoo
Lansing 48933

Delta College
University Center 48710

Detroit Business Institute
1249 Washington Blvd., Ste. 1200
Detroit 48226

Detroit Business Institute, Downriver
19100 Fort St.
Riverview 48192

Detroit College of Business
4801 Oakman Blvd.
Dearborn 48126-3799

Detroit College of Business
3488 North Jennings
Flint 48504-1700

Detroit College of Business
27500 Dequindre
Warren 48092-5209

Dorsey Business Schools
30821 Barrington
Madison Heights 48071

Dorsey Business Schools
15755 Northline Rd.
Southgate 48195

Elsa Cooper Institute of Court
Reporting
26500 Northwestern Hwy., Ste. 250
Southfield 48076-3752

Ferris State University
901 South State St.
Big Rapids 49307

Glen Oaks Community College
62249 Shimmel Rd.
Centreville 49032

Gogebic Community College
East 4946 Jackson Rd.
Ironwood 49938

Grand Rapids Community College
143 Bostwick Ave. NE
Grand Rapids 49503-3295

Great Lakes Junior College of Business
310 South Washington Ave.
Saginaw 48607

Henry Ford Community College
5101 Evergreen Rd.
Dearborn 48128

Jackson Community College
2111 Emmons Rd.
Jackson 49201-8399

Kalamazoo Valley Community College
6767 West O Ave.
Kalamazoo 49009

Kellogg Community College
450 North Ave.
Battle Creek 49017

Kirtland Community College
10775 North St. Helen Rd.
Roscommon 48653

Lake Michigan College
2755 East Napier Ave.
Benton Harbor 49022-8099

Lake Superior State University
650 West Easterday Ave.
Sault Sainte Marie 49783

Lansing Community College
419 North Capitol Ave.
Lansing 48901-7210

Lewis College of Business
17370 Meyers Rd.
Detroit 48235

Macomb Community College
14500 Twelve Mile Rd.
Warren 48093-3896

Mid Michigan Community College
1375 South Clare Ave.
Harrison 48625

Monroe County Community College
1555 South Raisinville Rd.
Monroe 48161

Montcalm Community College
2800 College Dr.
Sidney 48885

Mott Community College
1401 East Court St.
Flint 48503

Muskegon Community College
221 South Quarterline Rd.
Muskegon 49442

North Central Michigan College
1515 Howard St.
Petoskey 49770

Northern Michigan University
1401 Presque Isle
Marquette 49855

Northwestern Michigan College
1701 East Front St.
Traverse City 49686

Oakland Community College
2480 Opdyke Rd.
Bloomfield Hills 48304-2266

Payne-Pulliam School of Trade and
Commerce, Inc.
2345 Cass Ave.
Detroit 48201-3305

Ross Medical Education Center
1036 Gilbert St.
Flint 48532

Ross Medical Education Center
913 West Holmes, Ste. 260
Lansing 48910

Ross Medical Education Center
26417 Hoover Rd.
Warren 48089

Ross Technical Institute
20820 Greenfield Rd., Ste. 101
Oak Park 48237

Saint Clair County Community College
323 Erie, P.O. Box 5015
Port Huron 48061-5015

Schoolcraft College
18600 Haggerty Rd.
Livonia 48152

Southwestern Michigan College
58900 Cherry Grove Rd.
Dowagiac 49047-9793

Washtenaw Community College
P.O. Drawer 1
Ann Arbor 48016-1610

Wayne County Community College
801 West Fort St.
Detroit 48226

West Shore Community College
3000 North Stiles Rd.
Scottville 49454

MINNESOTA

Alexandria Technical College
1601 Jefferson St.
Alexandria 56308

Anoka-Ramsey Community College
11200 Mississippi Blvd.
Coon Rapids 55433-3470

Central Lakes College, Brainerd
501 West College Dr.
Brainerd 56401

Central Lakes College, Staples Technical
Campus
1830 Airport Rd.
Staples 56479

Century Community and Technical
College
3300 Century Ave. N
White Bear Lake 55110

Dakota County Technical College
1300 East 145th St.
Rosemount 55068

Duluth Business University, Inc.
412 West Superior St.
Duluth 55802

Fergus Falls Community College
1414 College Way
Fergus Falls 56537

Globe College of Business
175 Fifth St. E, Ste. 201, P.O. Box 60
Saint Paul 55101-2901

Hennepin Technical College
9000 Brooklyn Blvd.
Brooklyn Park 55445

Hibbing Community College
1515 East 25th St.
Hibbing 55746

Inver Hills Community College
2500 80th St. E
Inver Grove Heights 55076

Itasca Community College
1851 Hwy. 169 E
Grand Rapids 55744

Lake Superior College
2101 Trinity Rd.
Duluth 55811

Lakeland Medical and Dental Academy
1402 West Lake St.
Minneapolis 55408

Minnesota West Community and
Technical College, Canby
1011 First St. W
Canby 56220

Minnesota West Community and
Technical College, Granite Falls
1593 11th Ave.
Granite Falls 56241

Minnesota West Community and
Technical College, Jackson Campus
401 West St.
Jackson 56143

Minnesota West Community and
Technical College, Pipestone
P.O. Box 250
Pipestone 56164

Normandale Community College
9700 France Ave. S
Bloomington 55431

Northland Community and Technical
College
Hwy. 1 E
Thief River Falls 56701

Northwest Technical College, Moorhead
1900 28th Ave. S
Moorhead 56560

Northwest Technical College, Wadena
405 Southwest Colfax Ave.
P.O. Box 566
Wadena 56482

Pillsbury Baptist Bible College
315 South Grove
Owatonna 55060

Pine Technical College
1000 Fourth St.
Pine City 55063

Rainy River Community College
1501 Hwy. 71
International Falls 56649

Rasmussen College
3500 Federal Dr.
Eagan 55122

Rasmussen College
501 Holly Lane
Mankato 56001

Rasmussen College, Corporate Office
Minnetonka 55305

Red Wing-Winona Technical College,
Red Wing Campus
308 Pioneer Rd.
Red Wing 55066

Red Wing-Winona Technical College,
Winona Campus
1250 Homer Rd. P.O. Box 409
Winona 55987

Ridgewater College, A Community and
Technical College, Hutchinson
Campus
Two Century Ave. SE
Hutchinson 55350

Ridgewater College, A Community and
Technical College, Willmar
P.O. Box 1097
Willmar 56201

Riverland Community College
1900 Eighth Ave. NW
Austin 55912

Riverland Community College, Albert
Lea
2200 Technical Dr.
Albert Lea 56007

Rochester Community and Technical
College
851 30th Ave. SE
Rochester 55904-4999

Saint Cloud Technical College
1540 Northway Dr.
Saint Cloud 56303

Saint Paul Technical College
235 Marshall Ave.
Saint Paul 55102

South Central Technical College,
Mankato
1920 Lee Blvd.
North Mankato 56003

South Central Technical College,
Faribault
1225 Southwest Third St.
Faribault 55021

University of Minnesota Crookston
105 Selvig Hall
Crookston 56716

Vermilion Community College
1900 East Camp
Ely 55731

MISSISSIPPI

Coahoma Community College
3240 Friars Point Rd.
Clarksdale 38614

Copiah-Lincoln Community College
P.O. Box 457
Wesson 39191

Copiah-Lincoln Community College,
Natchez Campus
11 Co-Lin Circle
Natchez 39120

East Mississippi Community College
P.O. Box 158
Scooba 39358

Hinds Community College, Raymond
Campus
Raymond 39154

Holmes Community College
Hill St.
Goodman 39079

Itawamba Community College
602 West Hill St.
Fulton 38843

Jones County Junior College
900 South Court St.
Ellisville 39437

Meridian Community College
910 Hwy. 19 N
Meridian 39307

Mississippi Delta Community College
P.O. Box 668
Moorhead 38761

Mississippi Gulf Coast Community
College
Central Office, P.O. Box 67
Perkinston 39573

Northeast Mississippi Community
College
Cunningham Blvd.
Booneville 38829

Northwest Mississippi Community
College
Hwy. 51 North Panola
Senatobia 38668

Pearl River Community College
Station A
Poplarville 39470

Southwest Mississippi Community
College
College Dr.
Summit 39666

MISSOURI

Baptist Bible College
628 East Kearney
Springfield 65803

Cape Girardeau Area Vocational-
Technical School
301 North Clark Ave.
Cape Girardeau 63701

Central Missouri State University
Warrensburg 64093

Columbia Area Vocational-Technical
School
4203 South Providence Rd.
Columbia 65203

Crowder College
601 Laclede
Neosho 64850

East Central College
P.O. Box 529
Union 63084

Grand River Vocational Technical
School
1200 Fair St.
Chillicothe 64601

Jefferson College
1000 Viking Dr.
Hillsboro 63050

Linn Technical College
One Technology Dr.
Linn 65051

Longview Community College
500 Longview Rd.
Lees Summit 64081

Maple Woods Community College
2601 Northeast Barry Rd.
Kansas City 64156

Metro Business College of Cape
Girardeau
1732 North Kings Hwy.
Cape Girardeau 63701

Mineral Area College
P.O. Box 1000
Park Hills 63601-1000

Miss Vanderschmidts Secretarial School
4625 Lindell Blvd.
Saint Louis 63108

Missouri College
10121 Manchester Rd.
Saint Louis 63122

Missouri Western State College
4525 Downs Dr.
Saint Joseph 64507

Moberly Area Community College
101 College Ave.
Moberly 65270

Nichols Career Center
609 Union
Jefferson City 65101

North Central Missouri College
1301 Main St.
Trenton 64683

Northwest Missouri State University
800 University Dr.
Maryville 64468

Penn Valley Community College
3201 Southwest Trafficway
Kansas City 64111

Rolla Technical Institute
1304 East Tenth St.
Rolla 65401

Saint Louis Community College, Forest
Park
5600 Oakland Ave.
Saint Louis 63110

Sikeston Area Vocational-Technical
School
1002 Virginia St.
Sikeston 63801

Southeast Missouri State University
One University Plaza
Cape Girardeau 63701

Southwest Missouri State University
901 South National
Springfield 65804

State Fair Community College
3201 West 16th
Sedalia 65301-2199

Three Rivers Community College
Three Rivers Blvd.
Poplar Bluff 63901

Tri County Technical School
Second and Pine
Eldon 65026

MONTANA

Blackfeet Community College
Hwy. 2 and 89
Browning 59417-0819

Flathead Valley Community College
777 Grandview Dr.
Kalispell 59901

Helena College of Technology of the
University of Montana
1115 North Roberts St.
Helena 59601

May Technical College
1306 Central Ave.
Billings 59103

Miles Community College
2715 Dickinson
Miles City 59301

Montana State University, College of
Technology, Billings
3803 Central Ave.
Billings 59102

Montana State University, College of
Technology, Great Falls
2100 16th Ave. S
Great Falls 59405

Montana Tech, College of Technology
25 Basin Creek Rd.
Butte 59701

Salish Kootenai College
P.O. Box 117
Pablo 59855

NEBRASKA

Central Community College Area
P.O. Box 4903
Grand Island 68802

Lincoln School of Commerce
1821 K St.
P.O. Box 82826
Lincoln 68501-2826

Metropolitan Community College Area
5300 North 30th St.
Omaha 68103

Mid Plains Community College
416 North Jeffers
North Platte 69101

Nebraska College of Business
3350 North 90th
Omaha 68134

Nebraska School of Real Estate
225 North Cotner, Ste. 106
Lincoln 68505

Northeast Community College
801 East Benjamin
P.O. Box 469
Norfolk 68702-0469

Opportunity Industrialization Center
Omaha
2725 North 24th St.
Omaha 68110

Southeast Community College Area
1111 O St., Ste. 111
Lincoln 68520

Western Nebraska Community College
1601 East 27th St. NE
Scottsbluff 69361-1899

NEVADA

Career College of Northern Nevada
1195 A Corporate Blvd.
Reno 89502

Community College of Southern
Nevada
3200 East Cheyenne Ave.
Las Vegas 89030

Morrison College
140 Washington St.
Reno 89503

Nevada Training Corporation
2215c Renaissance Dr.
Las Vegas 89119

Truckee Meadows Community College
7000 Dandini Blvd.
Reno 89512

NEW HAMPSHIRE

Castle College
23 Searles Rd.
Windham 03087-1200

Hesser College
Three Sundial Ave.
Manchester 03103

New Hampshire Technical College at
Berlin
2020 Riverside Dr.
Berlin 03570

New Hampshire Technical College at
Manchester
1066 Front St.
Manchester 03102

NEW JERSEY

The Academy of Professional
Development
1075 Easton Ave., Tower 2, Ste. 5
Edison 08837

American Business Academy
66 Moore St.
Hackensack 07601

Bergen Community College
400 Paramus Rd.
Paramus 07652

Berkeley College
44 Rifle Camp Rd.
West Paterson 07424

Brookdale Community College
765 Newman Springs Rd.
Lincroft 07738-1599

Burlington County College
Rte. 530
Pemberton 08068

Business Training Institute
Four Forest Ave.
Paramus 07652

Camden County College
P.O. Box 200
Blackwood 08012

The Chubb Institute
Eight Sylvan Way
Parsipanny 07054

Cittone Institute
1697 Oak Tree Rd.
Edison 08820-2896

County College of Morris
214 Center Grove Rd.
Randolph 07869

Dover Business College
15 East Blackwell St.
Dover 07801

Dover Business College
East 81 Rte. 4 W
Paramus 07652

Drake College of Business
125 Broad St.
Elizabeth 07201

Empire Technical School of New Jersey
576 Central Ave.
East Orange 07018

Essex County College
303 University Ave.
Newark 07102

Gloucester County College
1400 Tanyard Rd.
Sewell 08080

Harris School of Business
654 Longwood Ave. at Rte. 38
Cherry Hill 08002

Ho-Ho-Kus School
50 South Franklin Tpke.
Ramsey 07446

Katharine Gibbs School
33 Plymouth St.
Montclair 07042

Katharine Gibbs School
80 Kingsbridge Rd.
Piscataway 08854

Mercer County Community College
1200 Old Trenton Rd.
Trenton 08690

Middlesex County College
155 Mill Rd., P.O. Box 3050
Edison 08818-3050

Ocean County College
College Dr.
Toms River 08753

Passaic County Community College
One College Blvd.
Paterson 07505-1179

Pennco Technical
Erial Rd., P.O. Box 1427
Blackwood 08012

The Plaza School of Technology
Bergen Mall
Paramus 07652

PTC Career Institute, University
Heights
200 Washington St.
Newark 07102

Raritan Valley Community College
P.O. Box 3300, Lamington Rd.
Somerville 08876

Salem Community College
460 Hollywood Ave.
Carneys Point 08069

South Jersey Professional School of
Business
Marlton Square Shopping Center Rte. 70
and Cropwell Rd.
Marlton 08053

Stuart School of Business
Administration
2400 Belmar Blvd.
Wall 07719

Thomas A Edison State College
101 West State St.
Trenton 08608-1176

Union County College
1033 Springfield Ave.
Cranford 07016

NEW MEXICO

Albuquerque Technical-Vocational
Institute
525 Buena Vista SE
Albuquerque 87106

Clovis Community College
417 Schepps Blvd.
Clovis 88101

Crownpoint Institute of Technology
P.O. Box 849
Crownpoint 87313

Eastern New Mexico University, Roswell
Campus
52 University Blvd., Administrative
Center
Roswell 88202

International Business College
650 East Montana
Las Cruces 88001

New Mexico Junior College
5317 Lovington Hwy.
Hobbs 88240

New Mexico State University,
Alamogordo
P.O. Box 477, 2400 North Senic Dr.
Alamogordo 88310

New Mexico State University, Carlsbad
1500 University Dr.
Carlsbad 88220

New Mexico State University, Grants
1500 Third St.
Grants 87020

New Mexico State University, Main
Campus
P.O. Box 30001, Dept. 3Z Weddell Dr.
Las Cruces 88003-0105

Northern New Mexico Community
College
1002 North Onate St.
Espanola 87532

San Juan College
4601 College Blvd.
Farmington 87402

Santa Fe Community College
6401 Richards Ave.
Santa Fe 87505

Southwestern Indian Polytechnic
Institute
9169 Coors Rd. NW
Albuquerque 87120

University of New Mexico, Gallup
200 College Rd.
Gallup 87301

University of New Mexico, Valencia
280 La Entrada
Los Lunas 87031

Western New Mexico University
1000 College Ave.
Silver City 88061

NEW YORK STATE:

Adirondack Community College
Bay Rd.
Queensbury 12804

Berkeley College
West Red Oak Ln.
White Plains 10604

Berkeley College of New York City
Three East 43rd St.
New York 10017

Broome Community College
P.O. Box 1017
Binghamton 13902

Bryant and Stratton Business Institute,
Albany
1259 Central Ave.
Albany 12205

Bryant and Stratton Business Institute,
Buffalo
1028 Main St.
Buffalo 14202

Bryant and Stratton Business Institute,
Rochester
82 Saint Paul St.
Rochester 14604

Bryant and Stratton Business Institute,
Syracuse
953 James St.
Syracuse 13203

Business Informatics Center, Inc.
134 South Central Ave.
Valley Stream 11580

Cayuga County Community College
Franklin St.
Auburn 13021

Cazenovia College
Cazenovia 13035

Central City Business Institute
224 Harrison St.
Syracuse 13202

Cheryl Fells School of Business
2541 Military Rd.
Niagara Falls 14304

Clinton Community College
136 Clinton Pt. Dr.
Plattsburgh 12901

Columbia-Greene Community College
4400 Rte. 23
Hudson 12534

Cope Institute
84 William St.
New York 10038

Corning Community College
Spencer Hill
Corning 14830

CUNY Borough of Manhattan
Community College
199 Chambers St.
New York 10007

CUNY Bronx Community College
West 181st St. & University Ave.
Bronx 10453

CUNY Kingsborough Community
College
2001 Oriental Blvd.
Brooklyn 11235

CUNY La Guardia Community College
31-10 Thomson Ave.
Long Island City 11101

CUNY New York City Technical College
300 Jay St.
Brooklyn 11201

CUNY Queensborough Community
College
56th Ave. & Springfield Blvd.
New York 11364

Drake Business School
225 Broadway
New York 10007

Dutchess Community College
53 Pendell Rd.
Poughkeepsie 12601

Elmira Business Institute
180 Clemens Center Pkwy.
Elmira 14901

Erie Community College, City Campus
121 Ellicott St.
Buffalo 14203

Erie Community College, North
Campus
Main St. and Youngs Rd.
Williamsville 14221

Erie Community College, South
Campus
4140 Southwestern Blvd.
Orchard Park 14127

Finger Lakes Community College
4355 Lake Shore Dr.
Canandaigua 14424

Fulton-Montgomery Community
College
2805 State Hwy. 67
Johnstown 12095

Genesee Community College
One College Rd.
Batavia 14020

Global Business Institute
1931 Mott Ave.
Far Rockaway 11691

Global Business Institute
209 West 125th St.
New York 10027

Herkimer County Community College
Reservoir Rd.
Herkimer 13350-1598

Hilbert College
5200 South Park Ave.
Hamburg 14075-1597

Hudson Valley Community College
80 Vandenburgh Ave.
Troy 12180

Hunter Business School
3601 Hempstead Tpke.
Levittown 11756

Interboro Institute
450 West 56th St.
New York 10019

Iona College
715 North Ave.
New Rochelle 10801

Island Drafting and Technical Institute
128 Broadway Rte. 110
Amityville 11701

Jamestown Business College
Seven Fairmount Ave.
Jamestown 14701

Jefferson Community College
Outer Coffeen St.
Watertown 13601

Katharine Gibbs School, Melville
320 South Service Rd.
Melville 11747

Katharine Gibbs School, New York City
200 Park Ave.
New York 10166

Krissler Business Institute
166 Mansion Square Pk.
Poughkeepsie 12601

Long Island Business Institute
6500 Jericho Tpke.
Commack 11725

Marist College
290 North Rd.
Poughkeepsie 12601

Massena School of Business
22 Main St.
Massena 13662-1994

Mater Dei College
5428 St. Hwy. 37
Ogdensburg 13669

Mohawk Valley Community College
1101 Sherman Dr.
Utica 13501

Monroe College, Main Campus
Monroe College Way
Bronx 10468

Monroe Community College
1000 East Henrietta Rd.
Rochester 14623

Nassau Community College
One Education Dr.
Garden City 11530

New York Institute of Credit
71 West 23rd St.
New York 10010

New York School for Medical and
Dental Assistants
116-16 Queens Blvd.
Forest Hills 11375

New York University
70 Washington Square S
New York 10012

Niagara County Community College
3111 Saunders Settlement Rd.
Sanborn 14132

North Country Community College
20 Winona Ave., P.O. Box 89
Saranac Lake 12983

Olean Business Institute
301 North Union St.
Olean 14760

Onondaga Community College
4941 Onondaga Rd.
Syracuse 13215

Orange County Community College
115 South St.
Middletown 10940

Pace University, New York
One Pace Plaza
New York 10038

Plaza Business Institute
74-09 37th Ave.
Jackson Heights 11372

Professional Business Institute
125 Canal St.
New York 10002-5049

Ridley-Lowell School of Business
116 Front St.
Binghamton 13905

Rochester Business Institute
1850 East Ridge Rd.
Irondequort 14622

Rochester Institute of Technology
One Lamb Memorial Dr.
Rochester 14623-5603

Rockland Community College
145 College Rd.
Suffern 10901

Russell Sage College, Main Campus
45 Ferry St.
Troy 12180

Saint John's University, New York
8000 Utopia Pkwy.
Jamaica 11439

Schenectady County Community
College
Washington Ave.
Schenectady 12305

Spencer Business and Technical
Institute
200 State St.
Schenectady 12305

Stenotype Academy
15 Park Row
New York 10038

Suffolk County Community College,
Ammerman Campus
533 College Rd.
Selden 11784

Suffolk County Community College,
Eastern Campus
Speonk Riverhead Rd.
Riverhead 11901

Suffolk County Community College,
    Western Campus
Crooked Hill Rd.
Brentwood 11717

SUNY at Buffalo
Capen Hall
Buffalo 14260

SUNY College of Agriculture &
    Technology at Cobleskill
Cobleskill 12043

SUNY College of Technology &
    Agriculture at Morrisville
Morrisville 13408

SUNY College of Technology at Alfred
Alfred 14802

SUNY College of Technology at Canton
Cornell Dr.
Canton 13617

SUNY College of Technology at Delhi
Delhi 13753

SUNY College of Technology at
    Farmingdale
Melville Rd.
Farmingdale 11735-1021

SUNY Ulster County Community
    College
Cottekill Rd.
Stone Ridge 12484

SUNY Westchester Commmunity
    College
75 Grasslands Rd.
Valhalla 10595

Superior Career Institute, Inc.
254 West 29th St. 3rd Floor
New York 10011

Taylor Business Institute
120 West 30th St.
New York 10001

Technical Career Institutes
320 West 31st St.
New York 10001

Wood Tobe-Coburn School
Eight East 40th St.
New York 10016

Tompkins-Cortland Community
    College
170 North St.
Dryden 13053

Utica School of Commerce
201 Bleecker St.
Utica 13501

The Westchester Business Institute
325 Central Ave.
White Plains 10606

NORTH CAROLINA

American Business and Fashion
    Institute
1515 Mockingbird Ln., Ste. 600
Charlotte 28209

Anson Community College
P.O. Box 126
Polkton 28135

Asheville Buncombe Technical
    Community College
340 Victoria Rd.
Asheville 28801

Brookstone College
8307 University Executive Park Dr., Ste.
    240
Charlotte 28262

Brunswick Community College
P.O. Box 30
Supply 28462

Caldwell Community College and
    Technical Institute
P.O. Box 600
Lenoir 28645

Cape Fear Community College
411 North Front St.
Wilmington 28401

Carteret Community College
3505 Arendell St.
Morehead City 28557

Catawba Valley Community College
2550 Hwy. 70 SE
Hickory 28602-0699

Central Carolina Community College
1105 Kelly Dr.
Sanford 27330

Central Piedmont Community College
P.O. Box 35009
Charlotte 28235-5009

Cleveland Community College
137 South Post Rd.
Shelby 28152

Coastal Carolina Community College
444 Western Blvd.
Jacksonville 28546-6877

Craven Community College
800 College Ct.
New Bern 28562

Davidson County Community College
297 Davidson Community College Rd.
Lexington 27293

Fayetteville Technical Community
    College
2201 Hull Rd.
Fayetteville 28303-0236

Forsyth Technical Community College
2100 Silas Creek Pkwy.
Winston-Salem 27103

Gaston College
201 Hwy. 321 S
Dallas 28034

Guilford Technical Community College
P.O. Box 309
Jamestown 27282

Halifax Community College
P.O. Drawer 809
Weldon 27890

Isothermal Community College
P.O. Box 804
Spindale 28160

James Sprunt Community College
P.O. Box 398
Kenansville 28349

Johnston Community College
P.O. Box 2350
Smithfield 27577-2350

Lenoir Community College
P.O. Box 188
Kinston 28502-0188

Martin Community College
1161 Kehukee Park Rd.
Williamston 27892-9988

Mayland Community College
P.O. Box 547
Spruce Pine 28777

McDowell Technical Community
    College
Rte. 1, P.O. Box 170
Marion 28752

Mitchell Community College
500 West Broad
Statesville 28677

Nash Community College
P.O. Box 7488
Rocky Mount 27804

Pitt Community College
Hwy. 11 S, P.O. Drawer 7007
Greenville 27835-7007

Randolph Community College
629 Industrial Park Ave.
Asheboro 27204

Richmond Community College
P.O. Box 1189
Hamlet 28345

Roanoke-Chowan Community College
Rte. 2, P.O. Box 46A
Ahoskie 27910

Robeson Community College
P.O. Box 1420
Lumberton 28359

Rockingham Community College
P.O. Box 38, Hwy. 65 West County Home
    Rd.
Wentworth 27375-0038

Rowan-Cabarrus Community College
P.O. Box 1595
Salisbury 28145-1595

Salisbury Business College
1400 Jake Alexander Blvd. W
Salisbury 28147

Sampson Community College
P.O. Box 318
Clinton 28328

Sandhills Community College
2200 Airport Rd.
Pinehurst 28374

Stanly Community College
141 College Dr.
Albemarle 28001

Surry Community College
P.O. Box 304
Dobson 27017-0304

Vance-Granville Community College
State Rd. 1126, P.O. Box 917
Henderson 27536

Wake Technical Community College
9101 Fayetteville Rd.
Raleigh 27603-5696

Wayne Community College
3000 Wayne Memorial Dr.
Goldsboro 27533-8002

Western Piedmont Community College
1001 Burkemont Ave.
Morganton 28655-9978

Wilkes Community College
Collegiate Dr.
Wilkesboro 28697

Wilson Technical Community College
902 Herring Ave.
Wilson 27893

NORTH DAKOTA

Aakers Business College
201 North Third St.
Grand Forks 58203

Bismarck State College
P.O. Box 5587
Bismarck 58506-5587

Dickinson State University
Third St. and Eighth Ave. W
Dickinson 58601

Interstate Business College
520 East Main Ave.
Bismarck 58501

Interstate Business College
2720 32nd Ave. SW
Fargo 58103

Mayville State University
330 Third St. NE
Mayville 58257

Minot State University
500 University Ave. W
Minot 58707

North Dakota State College of Science
800 North Sixth St.
Wahpeton 58076

Sitting Bull College
1341 92nd St.
Fort Yates 58538

United Tribes Technical College
3315 University Dr.
Bismarck 58501

University of North Dakota, Lake
    Region
1801 North College Dr.
Devils Lake 58301

University of North Dakota, Williston
1410 University Ave.
Williston 58801

Valley City State University
101 Southwest College St.
Valley City 58072

OHIO

Academy of Court Reporting
614 Superior Ave. NW
Cleveland 44113

Akron Adult Vocational Services
147 Park St.
Akron 44308

Ashtabula County Joint Vocational
    School
1565 State Rte. 167
Jefferson 44047

Auburn Career Center
8140 Auburn Rd.
Painesville 44077

Belmont Technical College
120 Fox Shannon Place
Saint Clairsville 43950

Boheckers Business College
326 East Main St.
Ravenna 44266

Bryant and Stratton Business Institute
12955 Snow Rd.
Parma 44130

Butler County JVS District-D Russel Lee
    Career Center
3603 Hamilton Middletown Rd.
Hamilton 45011

Central Ohio Technical College
1179 University Dr.
Newark 43055-1767

Choffin Career Center
200 East Wood St.
Youngstown 44503

Cincinnati State Technical and
    Community College
3520 Central Pkwy.
Cincinnati 45223

Clark State Community College
570 East Leffel Ln.
Springfield 45505

Columbus State Community College
550 East Spring St. P.O. Box 1609
Columbus 43216

Cuyahoga Community College District
700 Carnegie Ave.
Cleveland 44115-2878

Davis College
4747 Monroe St.
Toledo 43623

Edison State Community College
1973 Edison Dr.
Piqua 45356

Ehove Career Center
316 West Mason Rd.
Milan 44846

ETI Technical College
2076 Youngstown Warren Rd.
Niles 44446-4398

Finishing Touches Secretarial School
37 West Seventh St., Ste. 701
Cincinnati 45201-1016

Hocking Technical College
3301 Hocking Pkwy.
Nelsonville 45764

ITT Technical Institute
1030 Meridan Rd.
Youngstown 44509

ITT Technical Institute
3325 Stop Eight Rd.
Dayton 45414

Jefferson Community College
4000 Sunset Blvd.
Steubenville 43952-3598

Kent State University, Trumbull
Regional Campus
4314 Mahoning Ave. NW
Warren 44483

Lakeland Community College
7700 Clocktower Dr.
Kirkland 44094-5198

Lima Technical College
4240 Campus Dr.
Lima 45804

Lorain County Community College
1005 North Abbe Rd.
Elyria 44035

Marion Technical College
1467 Mount Vernon Ave.
Marion 43302-5694

Medina County Career Center
1101 West Liberty St.
Medina 44256

Miami-Jacobs College
400 East Second St.
Dayton 45401

Miami University, Oxford Campus
500 High St.
Oxford 45056

Muskingum Area Technical College
1555 Newark Rd.
Zanesville 43701

North Central Technical College
2441 Kenwood Circle
P.O. Box 698
Mansfield 44901

Northwest State Community College
22-600 South Rte. 34
Archbold 43502-9542

Northwestern College
1441 North Cable Rd.
Lima 45805

Ohio University, Chillicothe
571 West Fifth St.
Chillicothe 45601

Ohio University, Lancaster Branch
1570 Granville Pike
Lancaster 43130

Ohio University, Main Campus
Athens 45701

Ohio University, Southern Campus
1804 Liberty Ave.
Ironton 45638

Ohio Valley Business College, Inc.
500 Maryland Ave., P.O. Box 7000
East Liverpool 43920

Owens Community College
39335 Oregon Rd.
Toledo 43699-1947

Owens Community College, Findlay
Campus
300 Davis St.
Findlay 45840

Professional Skills Institute
20 Arco Dr.
Toledo 43607

Raedel College and Industrial Welding
School
14 Lincoln Way W
Massilon 44647

RETS Technical Center
116 Westpark Rd.
Centerville 45459

Sawyer College of Business, West
13027 Lorain Ave.
Cleveland 44111

Shawnee State University
940 Second St.
Portsmouth 45662

Sinclair Community College
444 West Third St.
Dayton 45402

Southeastern Business College
1855 Western Ave.
Chillicothe 45601

Southeastern Business College
1522 Sheridan Dr.
Lancaster 43130

Southeastern Business College
3879 Rhodes Ave.
New Boston 45662

Southeastern Business College
4020 Milan Rd.
Sandusky 44870-5871

Southeastern Business College, Lorain
1907 North Ridge Rd.
Lorain 44055

Southern Ohio College
1011 Glendale Milford Rd.
Cincinnati 45215

Southern Ohio College, Northeast
2791 Mogadore Rd.
Akron 44312

Southern State Community College
100 Hobart Dr.
Hillsboro 45133

Stark State College of Technology
6200 Frank Ave. NW
Canton 44720

Stautzenberger College
5355 Southwyck Blvd.
Toledo 43614

Terra State Community College
2830 Napoleon Rd.
Fremont 43420

Tiffin University
155 Miami St.
Tiffin 44883

Tri-County Vocational School
156 75th St. & Rte. 691
Nelsonville 45764

University of Akron, Main Campus
302 Buchtel Common
Akron 44325-4702

University of Akron, Wayne College
1901 Smucker Rd.
Orrville 44667

University of Cincinnati, Main Campus
P.O. Box 210127
Cincinnati 45221-0127

University of Rio Grande
North College St.
Rio Grande 45674

University of Toledo
2801 West Bancroft
Toledo 43606

Upper Valley Joint Vocational School
8811 Career Dr.
Piqua 45356

Washington State Community College
710 Colegate Dr.
Marietta 45750

Youngstown State University
One University Plaza
Youngstown 44555

OKLAHOMA

Eastern Oklahoma State College
1301 West Main St.
Wilburton 74578

Northeastern Oklahoma Agricultural
and Mechanical College
200 Eye St. NE
Miami 74354

Northern Oklahoma College
P.O. Box 310, Tonkawa
Tonkawa 74653

Oklahoma City Community College
7777 South May Ave.
Oklahoma City 73159

Oklahoma State University, Okmulgee
1801 East Fourth St.
Okmulgee 74447-3901

Redland Community College
1300 South Country Club Rd.
El Reno 73036-5304

Rogers University, Claremore
1701 West Will Rogers Blvd.
Claremore 74017

Rose State College
6420 Southeast 15th
Midwest City 73110

Southwestern Oklahoma State
University
100 Campus Dr.
Weatherford 73096-3098

Tulsa Community College
6111 East Skelly Dr.
Tulsa 74135

Western Oklahoma State College
2801 North Main St.
Altus 73521-1397

OREGON

Blue Mountain Community College
P.O. Box 100
Pendleton 97801

Central Oregon Community College
2600 Northwest College Way
Bend 97701

Chemeketa Community College
4000 Lancaster Dr. NE
Salem 97305

Clackamas Community College
19600 Molalla Ave.
Oregon City 97045

College of Legal Arts
527 Southwest Hall
Portland 97201

Columbia College
8800 SE Sunnyside Rd.
Clackamas 97015

Lane Community College
4000 East 30th Ave.
Eugene 97405

Linn-Benton Community College
6500 Southwest Pacific Blvd.
Albany 97321

Mount Hood Community College
26000 Southeast Stark St.
Gresham 97030

Oregon Institute of Technology
3201 Campus Dr.
Klamath Falls 97601-8801

Pioneer Pacific College
25195 Southwest Parkway Ave.
Wilsonville 97070

Portland Community College
P.O. Box 19000
Portland 97280-0990

Southwestern Oregon Community
College
1988 Newmark Ave.
Coos Bay 97420

Treasure Valley Community College
650 College Blvd.
Ontario 97914

Trend Business College
400 Earhart St.
Medford 97501

Umpqua Community College
P.O. Box 967
Roseburg 97470

Western Business College
425 Southwest Washington
Portland 97204

PENNSYLVANIA

Academy of Medical Arts and Business
2301 Academy Dr.
Harrisburg 17112

Allentown Business School
1501 Lehigh St.
Allentown 18103

Altoona School of Commerce
508 58th St.
Altoona 16602

American Center of Technical Arts
1930 Chestnut St.
Philadelphia 19103

Baptist Bible College and Seminary
538 Venard Rd.
Clarks Summit 18411

Berean Institute
1901 West Girard Ave.
Philadelphia 19130

Bidwell Training Center, Inc.
1815 Metropolitan St.
Pittsburgh 15233

Bucks County Community College
Swamp Rd.
Newtown 18940

Business Institute of Pennsylvania
335 Boyd Dr.
Sharon 16146

Butler County Community College
College Dr. Oak Hills
Butler 16003-1203

Cambria Rowe Business College
221 Central Ave.
Johnstown 15902

Career Training Academy
703 Fifth Ave.
New Kensington 15068

Center for Innovative Training and
Education
841 Chestnut St., Ste. 30
Philadelphia 19107

Central Pennsylvania Business School
107 College Hill Rd.
Summerdale 17093-0309

Churchman Business School
355 Spring Garden St.
Easton 18042

Community College of Allegheny
County
800 Allegheny Ave.
Pittsburgh 15233-1895

Community College of Beaver County
One Campus Dr.
Monaca 15061

Community College of Philadelphia
1700 Spring Garden St.
Philadelphia 19130

Computer Learning Network, Resident
School
1110 Fernwood Ave.
Camp Hill 17011

Consolidated School of Business
1605 Clugston Rd.
York 17404

Delaware County Community College
901 South Media Line Rd.
Media 19063-1094

Douglas School of Business
130 Seventh St.
Monessen 15062

Du Bois Business College
One Beaver Dr.
Du Bois 15801

Duffs Business Institute
110 Ninth St.
Pittsburgh 15222

Erie Business Center
246 West Ninth St.
Erie 16501

Garfield Business Institute
709 Third Ave.
New Brighton 15066

Harcum College
750 Montgomery Ave.
Bryn Mawr 19010

Harrisburg Area Community College,
 Harrisburg Campus
One Hacc Dr.
Harrisburg 17110

ICM School of Business and Medical
 Careers
10-14 Wood St.
Pittsburgh 15222

J H Thompson Academies
2910 State St.
Erie 16508

Lackawanna Junior College
501 Vine St.
Scranton 18509

Lansdale School of Business
201 Church Rd.
North Wales 19454

Lehigh Carbon Community College
4525 Education Park Dr.
Schnecksville 18078-2598

Luzerne County Community College
1333 South Prospect St.
Nanticoke 18634

Manor Junior College
700 Fox Chase Rd.
Jenkintown 19046

Martin School of Business
2417 Welsh Rd.
Philadelphia 19114

McCann School of Business
Main St. and Pine St.
Mahanoy City 17948

Mercyhurst College
501 East 38th St.
Erie 16546

Montgomery County Community
 College
340 Dekalb Pike
Blue Bell 19422

Newport Business Institute
941 West Third St.
Williamsport 17701

Northampton County Area Community
 College
3835 Green Pond Rd.
Bethlehem 18020-7599

Orleans Technical Institute
1330 Rhawn St.
Philadelphia 19111-2899

Pace Institute
606 Court St.
Reading 19601

Peirce College
1420 Pine St.
Philadelphia 19102

Pennco Technical
3815 Otter St.
Bristol 19007

Pennsylvania Commercial Inc.
82 South Main St.
Washington 15301

Pennsylvania Institute of Technology
800 Manchester Ave.
Media 19063

Pennsylvania State University, Main
 Campus
201 Old Main
University Park 16802

Point Park College
201 Wood St.
Pittsburgh 15222

Reading Area Community College
P.O. Box 1706
Reading 19603-1706

Robert Morris College
881 Narrows Run Rd.
Moon Township 15108-1189

Sawyer School
717 Liberty Ave.
Pittsburgh 15222

Schuylkill Business Institute
2400 West End Ave.
Pottsville 17901

South Hills School of Business and
 Technology
480 Waupelani Dr.
State College 16801

Waynesburg College
51 West College St.
Waynesburg 15370

Westmoreland County Community
 College
Youngwood 15697-1895

York College Pennsylvania
Country Club Rd.
York 17405-7199

Yorktowne Business Institute
West Seventh Ave.
York 17404

RHODE ISLAND

Community College of Rhode Island
400 East Ave.
Warwick 02886-1807

Johnson and Wales University
8 Abbott Park Place
Providence 02903-3376

Katharine Gibbs School
178 Butler Ave.
Providence 02906

Nasson Institute
286 Main St.
Pawtucket 02860

New England Institute of Technology
2500 Post Rd.
Warwick 02886

Ocean State Business Institute
140 Point Judith Rd., Unit 3A
Narragansett 02882

Sawyer School
101 Main St.
Pawtucket 02860

School of Medical and Legal Secretarial
 Sciences
60 South Angell St.
Providence 02906

SOUTH CAROLINA

Aiken Technical College
P.O. Drawer 696
Aiken 29802

Denmark Technical College
P.O. Box 327, Solomon Blatt Blvd.
Denmark 29042

Florence-Darlington Technical College
P.O. Box 100548
Florence 29501-0548

Greenville Technical College
Station B, P.O. Box 5616
Greenville 29606-5616

Horry-Georgetown Technical College
P.O. Box 1966
Conway 29526

Midlands Technical College
P.O. Box 2408
Columbia 29202

Orangeburg-Calhoun Technical College
3250 Saint Matthew's Rd.
Orangeburg 29115

Piedmont Technical College
P.O. Drawer 1467
Greenwood 29648

Spartanburg Technical College
Hwy. I-85, P.O. Drawer 4386
Spartanburg 29305

Technical College of the Low Country
100 Ribaut Rd.
Beaufort 29902

Tri-County Technical College
P.O. Box 587
Pendleton 29670

Trident Technical College
P.O. Box 118067
Charleston 29423-8067

Williamsburg Technical College
601 Martin Luther King Jr. Ave.
Kingstree 29556

York Technical College
452 South Anderson Rd.
Rock Hill 29730

SOUTH DAKOTA

Lake Area Technical Institute
230 11th St. NE
Watertown 57201

Mitchell Technical Institute
821 North Capital St.
Mitchell 57301

National American University
321 Kansas City St.
Rapid City 57701

Nettleton Career College
100 South Spring Ave.
Sioux Falls 57104

Northern State University
1200 South Jay St.
Aberdeen 57401-7198

Presentation College
1500 North Main
Aberdeen 57401

Southeast Technical Institute
2301 Career Place
Sioux Falls 57107

Western Dakota Vocational-Technical
 Institute
800 Mickelson Dr.
Rapid City 57701

TENNESSEE

Chattanooga State Technical
 Community College
4501 Amnicola Hwy.
Chattanooga 37406

Cleveland State Community College
P.O. Box 3570
Cleveland 37320-3570

Columbia State Community College
P.O. Box 1315
Columbia 38402

Draughons Junior College of Business
Plus Park at Pavilion Blvd.
Nashville 37217

Dyersburg State Community College
1510 Lake Rd.
Dyersburg 38024

Jackson State Community College
2046 North Pkwy.
Jackson 38301

Knoxville Business College
720 North Fifth Ave.
Knoxville 37917

Middle Tennessee State University
Murfreesboro 37132

Morristown School of Business
400 North Henry St.
Morristown 37814

Nashville College
400-402 Plaza Professional Building S
Madison 37115

Nashville State Technical Institute
120 White Bridge Rd.
Nashville 37209

Pellissippi State Technical Community
 College
P.O. Box 22990
Knoxville 37933-0990

Roane State Community College
276 Patton Ln.
Harriman 37748

Shelby State Community College
P.O. Box 40568
Memphis 38174-0568

State Technical Institute at Memphis
5983 Macon Cove
Memphis 38134

Tennessee Technology Center at Athens
1635 Vo Tech Dr.
Athens 37371-0848

Tennessee Technology Center at
 Covington
P.O. Box 249
Covington 38019

Tennessee Technology Center at
 Elizabethton
1500 Arney St.
Elizabethton 37643

Tennessee Technology Center at
 Harriman
P.O. Box 1109
Harriman 37748

Tennessee Technology Center at
 Hartsville
Hwy. 25 & 716 McMurry Blvd.
Hartsville 37074

Tennessee Technology Center at
 Hohenwald
813 West Main
Hohenwald 38462-2201

Tennessee Technology Center at
 Jacksboro
Rte. 1
Jacksboro 37757

Tennessee Technology Center at
 Livingston
740 High Tech Dr.
Livingston 38570

Tennessee Technology Center at
 Murfreesboro
1303 Old Fort Pkwy.
Murfreesboro 37129

Tennessee Technology Center at
 Newbern
340 Washington St.
Newbern 38059

Tennessee Technology Center at Pulaski
1233 East College St.
Pulaski 38478

Tennessee Technology Center at Ripley
South Industrial Park
Ripley 38063

Tennessee Technology Center at
 Shelbyville
1405 Madison St.
Shelbyville 37160

Walters State Community College
500 South Davy Crockett Pkwy.
Morristown 37813-6899

TEXAS

Alvin Community College
3110 Mustang Rd.
Alvin 77511

Amarillo College
P.O. Box 447
Amarillo 79178

American Commercial College
2007 34th St.
Lubbock 79411

American Commercial College
3177 Executive Dr.
San Angelo 76904

Austin Community College
5930 Middle Fiskville Rd.
Austin 78752

Austin Institute of Real Estate
7801 North Lamar, Ste. F35
Austin 78752

Bee County College
3800 Charco Rd.
Beeville 78102

Blinn College
902 College Ave.
Brenham 77833

Bradford School of Business
4669 Southwest Fwy., Ste. 300
Houston 77027

Brazosport College
500 College Dr.
Lake Jackson 77566

Brookhaven College
3939 Valley View Ln.
Farmers Branch 75244-4997

Cedar Valley College
3030 North Dallas Ave.
Lancaster 75134

Central Texas College
P.O. Box 1800
Killeen 76540-1800

Central Texas Commercial College
315 North Center St.
P.O. Box 1324
Brownwood 76801

Cisco Junior College
Rte. 3, P.O. Box 3
Cisco 76437

Clarendon College
P.O. Box 968
Clarendon 79226

Clerical Art School
6420 Richmond, Ste. 120
Houston 77057

College of the Mainland
1200 Amburn Rd.
Texas City 77591

Court Reporting Institute, Wheeler
Institute of Texas
8585 Stemmons, Ste. 200N
Dallas 75247

Del Mar College
101 Baldwin
Corpus Christi 78404-3897

Eastfield College
3737 Motley Dr.
Mesquite 75150

El Centro College
Main and Lamar
Dallas 75202

El Paso Community College
P.O. Box 20500
El Paso 79998

Executive Secretarial School of Texas
4849 Greenville Ave., Ste. 200
Dallas 75206

Galveston College
4015 Ave. Q
Galveston 77550

Grayson County College
6101 Grayson Dr.
Denison 75020

Hallmark Institute of Technology
8901 Wetmore Rd.
San Antonio 78216

Hill College
P.O. Box 619
Hillsboro 76645

Houston Community College System
22 Waugh Dr.
Houston 77270-7849

Howard County Junior College District
1001 Birdwell Ln.
Big Spring 79720

International Business College
4121 Montana Ave.
El Paso 79903

International Business College, Bond
Office
1030 North Zaragosa Rd.
El Paso 79907

ITT Technical Institute
2201 Arlington Downs Rd.
Arlington 76011

ITT Technical Institute
2950 South Gessner
Houston 77063

Kilgore College
1100 Broadway
Kilgore 75662-3299

Lamar University, Orange
410 Front St.
Orange 77630-5899

Lamar University, Port Arthur
1500 Proctor St.
Port Arthur 77640

Laredo Community College
West End Washington St.
Laredo 78040

Lee College
200 Lee Dr.
Baytown 77520-4703

McLennan Community College
1400 College Dr.
Waco 76708

Midland College
3600 North Garfield
Midland 79705

Mountain View College
4849 West Illinois
Dallas 75211

Navarro College
3200 West 7th
Corsicana 75110

North Harris Montgomery Community
College District
250 North Sam Houston Pkwy. E, Ste.
300
Houston 77060

North Lake College
5001 North MacArthur Blvd.
Irving 75038-3899

Northeast Texas Community College
FM 1735
Mount Pleasant 75456

Odessa College
201 West University
Odessa 79764

Paris Junior College
2400 Clarksville St.
Paris 75460

Professional Court Reporting, Inc.
1401 North Central Expwy.
Richardson 75080

Ranger College
College Circle
Ranger 76470

Richland College
12800 Abrams Rd.
Dallas 75243-2199

Saint Philip's College
1801 Martin Luther King Dr.
San Antonio 78203

San Antonio College
1300 San Pedro Ave.
San Antonio 78284

San Jacinto College, Central Campus
8060 Spencer Hwy.
Pasadena 77505

San Jacinto College, South Campus
13735 Beamer Rd.
Houston 77089-6009

South Plains College
1401 College Ave.
Levelland 79336

South Texas Vocational-Technical
Institute, McAllen Branch
2901 North 23rd St.
McAllen 78501

Southern Career Institute, Inc.
2301 South Congress
Austin 78704

Southwest School of Business and
Technical Careers
602 West South Cross
San Antonio 78221

Southwest Texas Junior College
2401 Garner Field Rd.
Uvalde 78801

Stenograph Institute of Texas
202 Pine St.
Abilene 79601

Tarrant County Junior College
1500 Houston St.
Fort Worth 76102

Temple College
2600 South First St.
Temple 76504-7435

Texarkana College
2500 North Robison Rd.
Texarkana 75599

Texas School of Business, Inc.
711 Airtex Dr.
Houston 77073

Texas Southmost College
80 Fort Brown
Brownsville 78520

Texas State Technical College,
Harlingen Campus
2424 Boxwood
Harlingen 78550-3697

Texas State Technical College,
Sweetwater Campus
300 College Dr.
Sweetwater 79556

Trinity Valley Community College
500 South Prairieville
Athens 75751

Tyler Junior College
1327 South Baxter Ave.
Tyler 75711

Vernon Regional Junior College
4400 College Dr.
Vernon 76384-4092

Victoria College
2200 East Red River
Victoria 77901

Wayland Baptist University
1900 West 7th
Plainview 79072

Weatherford College
308 East Park Ave.
Weatherford 76086

UTAH

American Institute of Medical-Dental
Technology
1675 North 200 West, Bldg. 4
Provo 84604

Bridgerland Applied Technology Center
1301 North 600 West
Logan 84321

Davis Applied Technology Center
550 East 300 S
Kaysville 84037

Dixie College
225 South 700 East
Saint George 84770

Intermountain College of Court
Reporting
5980 South Fashion Blvd.
Murray 84107

Latter Day Saints Business College
411 East South Temple
Salt Lake City 84111-1392

Odgen-Weber Applied Technology
Center
559 East AVC Ln.
Ogden 84404-6704

Salt Lake Community College
P.O. Box 30808
Salt Lake City 84130

Salt Lake Community College, Skills
Center, South City Campus
1575 South State St.
Salt Lake City 84115

Snow College
150 East College Ave.
Ephraim 84627

Southern Utah University
351 West Center
Cedar City 84720

Stevens-Henager College of Business
2168 Washington Blvd.
Ogden 84401

Stevens-Henager College of Business
25 East 1700 S
Provo 84606-6157

Uintah Basin Applied Technology
Center
1100 East Lagoon St.
Roosevelt 84066

Utah State University
UMC 1480
Logan 84322

Utah Valley State College
800 West 1200 S
Orem 84058

Weber State University
3750 Harrison Blvd.
Ogden 84408

VERMONT

Champlain College
163 South Willard St.
Burlington 05401

Vermont Technical College
P.O. Box 500
Randolph Center 05061

VIRGINIA

Blue Ridge Community College
P.O. Box 80
Weyers Cave 24486

Braxton School of Business
4917 Augusta Ave.
Richmond 23230-3601

Central Virginia Community College
3506 Wards Rd.
Lynchburg 24502

Commonwealth College
301 Centre Pointe Dr.
Virginia Beach 23462

Danville Community College
1008 South Main St.
Danville 24541

Dominion Business School
4142-1 Melrose Ave.
Roanoke 24017

J Sargeant Reynolds Community
College
P.O. Box 85622
Richmond 23285-5622

John Tyler Community College
13101 Jefferson Davis Hwy.
Chester 23831-5399

Kee Business College
803 Diligence Dr.
Newport News 23606

Lord Fairfax Community College
173 Skirmisher Ln.
Middletown 22645

Mountain Empire Community College
P.O. Drawer 700
Big Stone Gap 24219

New River Community College
P.O. Drawer 1127
Dublin 24084-1127

Northern Virginia Community College
4001 Wakefield Chapel Rd.
Annandale 22003

Patrick Henry Community College
P.O. Box 5311
Martinsville 24115-5311

Paul D Camp Community College
100 North College Dr., P.O. Box 737
Franklin 23851

Rappahannock Community College,
Glenns Campus
12745 College Rd.
Glenns 23149

Reporting Academy of Virginia
Pembroke Three, Ste. 300
Virginia Beach 23462

Southside Training Skill Center,
Nottoway County
P.O. Box 258
Crewe 23930

Southside Virginia Community College
109 Campus Dr.
Alberta 23821

Southwest Virginia Community College
P.O. Box SVCC
Richlands 24641

Thomas Nelson Community College
P.O. Box 9407
Hampton 23670

Virginia Highlands Community College
P.O. Box 828
Abingdon 24212-0828

Virginia Western Community College
3095 Colonial Ave.
Roanoke 24015

Washinton County Adult Skill Center
848 Thompson Dr.
Abingdon 24210

Washington Business School of North
Virginia
1980 Gallows Rd.
Vienna 22182

Wise Skills Center
515 Hurricane Rd. N
Wise 24293

Wytheville Community College
1000 East Main St.
Wytheville 24382

WASHINGTON

Bates Technical College
1101 South Yakima Ave.
Tacoma 98405

Bellingham Technical College
3028 Lindbergh Ave.
Bellingham 98225

Centralia College
600 West Locust St.
Centralia 98531

Clark College
1800 East McLoughlin Blvd.
Vancouver 98663-3598

Eton Technical Institute
3649 Frontage Rd.
Port Orchard 98366

Grays Harbor College
1620 Edward P Smith Dr.
Aberdeen 98520

Highline Community College
P.O. Box 98000
Des Moines 98198-9800

Interface Computer School
9921 Nevada
Spokane 99205

Lake Washington Technical College
11605 132nd Ave. NE
Kirkland 98034

Lower Columbia College
P.O. Box 3010
Longview 98632

Olympic College
1600 Chester Ave.
Bremerton 98310-1699

Seattle Community College, Central
Campus
1701 Broadway
Seattle 98122

Seattle Community College, North
Campus
9600 College Way N
Seattle 98103

Seattle Community College, South
Campus
6000 16th Ave. SW
Seattle 98106

South Puget Sound Community College
2011 Mottman Rd. SW
Olympia 98512

Spokane Community College
North 1810 Greene Ave.
Spokane 99207

Spokane Falls Community College
West 3410 Fort George Wright Dr.
Spokane 99224

Tacoma Community College
5900 South 12th St.
Tacoma 98465

Walla Walla College
204 South College Ave.
College Place 99324

Walla Walla Community College
500 Tausick Way
Walla Walla 99362

Wenatchee Valley College
1300 Fifth St.
Wenatchee 98801

Yakima Valley Community College
P.O. Box 1647
Yakima 98907

WEST VIRGINIA

Bluefield State College
219 Rock St.
Bluefield 24701

Cabell County Vocational-Technical
Center
1035 Norway Ave.
Huntington 25705

Fairmont State College
1201 Locust Ave.
Fairmont 26554

Glenville State College
200 High St.
Glenville 26351

Huntington Junior College
900 Fifth Ave.
Huntington 25701

Marshall University
400 Hal Greer Blvd.
Huntington 25755

Mercer County Technical Education
Center
1397 Stafford Dr.
Princeton 24740

Mountain Cap of West Virginia, Inc.
26 North Kanawha St.
Buckhannon 26201

Shepherd College
King St., Ikenberry Hall
Shepherdstown 25443

Southern West Virginia Community
and Technical College
P.O. Box 2900
Mt. Gay 25637

West Virginia Northern Community
College
1704 Market St.
Wheeling 26003

West Virginia State College
Rte. 25
Institute 25112

West Virginia University at Parkersburg
300 Campus Dr.
Parkersburg 26101

WISCONSIN

Blackhawk Technical College
P.O. Box 5009
Janesville 53547

Concordia University, Wisconsin
12800 North Lake Shore Dr., Ste. 9W
Mequon 53097-2402

Fox Valley Technical College
1825 North Bluemound Dr.
Appleton 54913-2277

Gateway Technical College
3520 30th Ave.
Kenosha 53144-1690

Lakeshore Technical College
1290 North Ave.
Cleveland 53015

Madison Area Technical College
3550 Anderson St.
Madison 53704

Madison Junior College of Business
31 South Henry St.
Madison 53703-3110

MBTI Business Training Institute
606 West Wisconsin Ave.
Milwaukee 53203

Mid-State Technical College
500 32nd St. N
Wisconsin Rapids 54494

Milwaukee Area Technical College
700 West State St.
Milwaukee 53233-1443

Moraine Park Technical College
235 North National Ave.
P.O. Box 1940
Fond Du Lac 54936-1940

Nicolet Area Technical College
Hwy. G South
Rhinelander 54501

North Central Technical College
1000 Campus Dr.
Wausau 54401-1899

Northeast Wisconsin Technical College
2740 West Mason St.
P.O. Box 19042
Green Bay 54307-9042

Southwest Wisconsin Technical College
1800 Bronson Blvd.
Fennimore 53809

Waukesha County Technical College
800 Main St.
Pewaukee 53072

Western Wisconsin Technical College
304 North Sixth St.
P.O. Box 908
La Crosse 54602-0908

Wisconsin Indianhead Technical
College
505 Pine Ridge Dr.
P.O. Box 10B
Shell Lake 54871

WYOMING

Casper College
125 College Dr.
Casper 82601

Central Wyoming College
2660 Peck Ave.
Riverton 82501

Eastern Wyoming College
3200 West C St.
Torrington 82240

Sheridan College
3059 Coffeen Ave.
Sheridan 82801

Western Wyoming Community College
2500 College Dr.
Rock Springs 82902

Computer and Peripheral Equipment Operation

ARIZONA

Central Arizona College
8470 North Overfield Rd.
Coolidge 85228-9778

ARKANSAS

Northwest Technical Institute
709 South Missouri Rd.
Springdale 72764

CALIFORNIA

San Joaquin Valley College
8400 West Mineral King Ave.
Visalia 93291

FLORIDA

Lee County High Technical Center,
Central
3800 Michigan Ave.
Fort Myers 33916

Saint Augustine Technical Center
2980 Collins Ave.
Saint Augustine 32095-1919

GEORGIA

Gwinnett College of Business
4230 Hwy. 29, Ste. 11
Lilburn 30047

Savannah Technical Institute
5717 White Bluff Rd.
Savannah 31405-5594

ILLINOIS

City College of Chicago, Truman
College
1145 Wilson Ave.
Chicago 60640

College of Lake County
19351 West Washington St.
Grayslake 60030-1198

Danville Area Community College
2000 East Main St.
Danville 61832

INDIANA

Professional Career Institute
2611 Waterfront Pkwy. & East Dr.
Indianapolis 46214-2028

IOWA

Indian Hills Community College
525 Grandview
Ottumwa 52501

Kirkwood Community College
P.O. Box 2068
Cedar Rapids 52406

KANSAS

Butler County Community College
901 South Haverhill Rd.
El Dorado 67042

Johnson County Community College
12345 College Blvd.
Overland Park 66210-1299

Kaw Area Technical School
5724 Huntoon
Topeka 66604

Manhattan Area Technical Center
3136 Dickens Ave.
Manhattan 66503

Northeast Kansas Area Vocational-
Technical School
1501 West Riley St.
P.O. Box 277
Atchison 66002

KENTUCKY

Kentucky Tech, Laurel County State
Vocational-Technical School
235 South Laurel Rd.
London 40741

LOUISIANA

American School of Business
702 Professional Dr. N
Shreveport 71105

Louisiana Technical College, Sullivan
Campus
1710 Sullivan Dr.
Bogalusa 70427

Louisiana Technical College, T H Harris
Campus
337 East South St.
P.O. Box 713
Opelousas 70570

MARYLAND

Fleet Business School
2530 Riva Rd., Ste. 201
Annapolis 21401

MASSACHUSETTS

Computer Processing Institute
615 Massachusetts Ave.
Cambridge 02139

MICHIGAN

Washtenaw Community College
P.O. Drawer 1
Ann Arbor 48016-1610

West Shore Community College
3000 North Stiles Rd.
Scottville 49454

MISSOURI

Saint Louis Community College, Forest
Park
5600 Oakland Ave.
Saint Louis 63110

TAD Technical Institute
7910 Troost Ave.
Kansas City 64131

NEW JERSEY

The Chubb Institute
Eight Sylvan Way
Parsippany 07054

NEW YORK

CUNY Borough of Manhattan
Community College
199 Chambers St.
New York 10007

CUNY Medgar Evers College
1650 Bedford Ave.
Brooklyn 11225

Rockland Community College
145 College Rd.
Suffern 10901

Sullivan County Community College
1000 Le Roy Rd.
Loch Sheldrake 12759-4002

NORTH CAROLINA

Blue Ridge Community College
College Dr.
Flat Rock 28731-9624

Central Piedmont Community College
P.O. Box 35009
Charlotte 28235-5009

Lenoir Community College
P.O. Box 188
Kinston 28502-0188

Piedmont Community College
P.O. Box 1197
Roxboro 27573

Wake Technical Community College
9101 Fayetteville Rd.
Raleigh 27603-5696

NORTH DAKOTA

North Dakota State College of Science
800 North Sixth St.
Wahpeton 58076

OHIO

Cincinnati State Technical and
Community College
3520 Central Pkwy.
Cincinnati 45223

PENNSYLVANIA

Community College of Philadelphia
1700 Spring Garden St.
Philadelphia 19130

TENNESSEE

State Technical Institute at Memphis
5983 Macon Cove
Memphis 38134

Tennessee Technology Center at
Murfreesboro
1303 Old Fort Pkwy.
Murfreesboro 37129

TEXAS

Del Mar College
101 Baldwin
Corpus Christi 78404-3897

Laredo Junior College
West End Washington St.
Laredo 78040

Microcomputer Technology Institute
7277 Regency Square Blvd.
Houston 77036

San Antonio College
1300 San Pedro Ave.
San Antonio 78284

WEST VIRGINIA

Huntington Junior College
900 Fifth Ave.
Huntington 25701

WISCONSIN

Fox Valley Technical College
1825 North Bluemound Dr.
Appleton 54913-2277

Western Wisconsin Technical College
304 North Sixth St.
P.O. Box 908
La Crosse 54602-0908

Computer Programming

ALABAMA

Bessemer State Technical College
1100 9th Ave.
Bessemer 35021

Bevill State Community College
100 State St.
Sumiton 35148

Bishop State Community College
351 North Broad St.
Mobile 36608

Central Alabama Community College
1675 Cherokee Rd.
Alexander 35010

Community College of the Air Force
120 West Maxwell Blvd.
Montgomery 36112-6613

Douglas MacArthur Technical College
1708 North Main St.
Opp 36467

Enterprise State Junior College
600 Plaza Dr.
Enterprise 36330

Gadsden Business College
750 Forrest Ave.
Gadsden 35901

George C Wallace State Community
College
3000 Earl Goodwin Pkwy.
Selma 36702

Harry M Ayers State Technical College
1801 Coleman Rd.
Anniston 36202

John C Calhoun State Community
College
Hwy. 31
Decatur 35602

John M Patterson State Technical
College
3920 Troy Hwy.
Montgomery 36116

Lawson State Community College
3060 Wilson Rd. SW
Birmingham 35221

North West Shoals Community College
800 George Wallace Blvd.
Muscle Shoals 35662

Northeast Alabama State Community
College
Hwy. 35 W
Rainsville 35986

Snead State Community College
220 North Walnut St.
Boaz 35957-0734

University of Alabama at Birmingham,
Walker College
1411 Indiana Ave.
Jasper 35501

ALASKA

Charter College
2221 East Northern Lights Blvd.
Anchorage 99508

New Frontier Vocational-Technical
Center
35270 K Beach Rd., Ste. 37B
Soldotna 99669

ARIZONA

Central Arizona College
8470 North Overfield Rd.
Coolidge 85228-9778

Chaparral Career College
4585 East Speedway Blvd., Ste. 204
Tucson 85712

Cochise College
4190 West Hwy. 80
Douglas 85607-9724

Eastern Arizona College
Church St.
Thatcher 85552-0769

Glendale Community College
6000 West Olive Ave.
Glendale 85302

High-Technical Institute
1515 East Indian School Rd.
Phoenix 85014

ITT Technical Institute
4837 East McDowell Rd.
Phoenix 85008-4292

ITT Technical Institute
1840 East Benson Hwy.
Tucson 85714

Lamson Junior College
1126 North Scottsdale Rd., Ste. 17
Tempe 85281-1700

Mesa Community College
1833 West Southern Ave.
Mesa 85202

Mohave Community College
1971 Jagerson Ave.
Kingman 86401

Pima Community College
2202 West Anklam Rd.
Tucson 85709-0001

Rio Salado Community College
2323 West 14th St.
Tempe 85281

Yavapai College
1100 East Sheldon St.
Prescott 86301

ARKANSAS

Arkansas State University, Main
Campus
P.O. Box 790
State University 72467

Arkansas Valley Technical Institute
Hwy. 23 N
P.O. Box 506
Ozark 72949

Cossatot Technical College
183 Hwy. 399
De Queen 71832

Crowley's Ridge Technical School
140 Crowley's Ridge Rd.
Forrest City 72336-0925

Garland County Community College
101 College Dr.
Hot Springs 71913

Mississippi County Community College
P.O. Box 1109
Blytheville 72316-1109

Northwest Technical Institute
709 South Missouri Rd.
Springdale 72764

Ouachita Technical College
One College Circle
Malvern 72104

Quapaw Technical Institute
200 Mid America Blvd.
Hot Springs 71913

CALIFORNIA

Allan Hancock College
800 South College Dr.
Santa Maria 93454

Ameritech Colleges
5445 Lankershim Blvd.
North Hollywood 91601

Associated Technical College
1475 Sixth Ave.
San Diego 92101

Associated Technical College, Anaheim
1177 North Magnolia Ave.
Anaheim 92801

Bakersfield College
1801 Panorama Dr.
Bakersfield 93305-1299

Cabrillo College
6500 Soquel Dr.
Aptos 95003

California Paramedical and Technical College
4550 La Sierra Ave.
Riverside 92505

Chabot College
25555 Hesperian Blvd.
Hayward 94545

Chaffey Community College
5885 Haven Ave.
Rancho Cucamonga 91737-3002

Citrus College
1000 West Foothill Blvd.
Glendora 91741-1899

City College of San Francisco
50 Phelan Ave.
San Francisco 94112

Coleman College
7380 Parkway Dr.
La Mesa 91942-1532

Computer Learning Center
3580 Wilshire Blvd., Ste. 100
Los Angeles 90010

Computer Learning Center
111 North Market St., Ste. 105
San Jose 95113-1109

Computer Learning Center of Anaheim
222 South Harbor Blvd.
Anaheim 92805

Cosumnes River College
8401 Center Pkwy.
Sacramento 95823-5799

De Anza College
21250 Stevens Creek Blvd.
Cupertino 95014

East Los Angeles Skill Center
3921 Selig Place
Los Angeles 90031

El Camino College
16007 Crenshaw Blvd.
Torrance 90506

Foothill-Deanza Community College, District Office
12345 El Monte Rd.
Los Altos Hills 94022-4599

Fullerton College
321 East Chapman Ave.
Fullerton 92632-2095

Glendale Community College
1500 North Verdugo Rd.
Glendale 91208-2894

Hartnell College
156 Homestead Ave.
Salinas 93901

Imperial Valley College
P.O. Box 158
Imperial 92251-0158

ITT Technical Institute of West Covina
1530 West Cameron Ave.
West Covina 91790

Lassen College
Hwy. 139
Susanville 96130

Long Beach City College
4901 East Carson St.
Long Beach 90808

Los Angeles City College
855 North Vermont Ave.
Los Angeles 90029

Los Angeles Harbor College
1111 Figueroa Place
Wilmington 90744

Los Angeles Pierce College
6201 Winnetka Ave.
Woodland Hills 91371

Los Angeles Trade Technical College
400 West Washington Blvd.
Los Angeles 90015-4181

Los Angeles Valley College
5800 Fulton Ave.
Van Nuys 91401

Merced College
3600 M St.
Merced 95348-2898

Modesto Junior College
435 College Ave.
Modesto 95350-5800

Monterey Peninsula College
980 Fremont St.
Monterey 93940-4799

MTI Business College, Inc.
6006 North El Dorado St.
Stockton 95207-4349

Napa Valley College
2277 Napa Vallejo Hwy.
Napa 94558

Orange Coast College
2701 Fairview Rd.
Costa Mesa 92626

Orange County Business College
2035 East Ball Rd.
Anaheim 92806

Oxnard College
4000 South Rose Ave.
Oxnard 93033

Palomar College
1140 West Mission
San Marcos 92069-1487

Pasadena City College
1570 East Colorada Blvd.
Pasadena 91106

Phillips Junior College
8520 Balboa Blvd.
Northridge 91325

Rancho Santiago College
1530 West 17th St.
Santa Ana 92706

Riverside Community College
4800 Magnolia Ave.
Riverside 92506-1299

Sacramento City College
3835 Freeport Blvd.
Sacramento 95822

San Diego City College
1313 12th Ave.
San Diego 92101

San Diego Mesa College
7250 Mesa College Dr.
San Diego 92111-4998

San Diego Miramar College
10440 Black Mountain Rd.
San Diego 92126-2999

San Joaquin Delta College
5151 Pacific Ave.
Stockton 95207

San Joaquin Valley College
201 New Stine Rd.
Bakersfield 93309

Santa Monica College
1900 Pico Blvd.
Santa Monica 90405-1628

Santa Rosa Junior College
1501 Mendocino Ave.
Santa Rosa 95401-4395

Sierra College
5000 Rocklin Rd.
Rocklin 95677

Solano County Community College District
4000 Suisun Valley Rd.
Suisun 94585-3197

Southwestern College
900 Otay Lakes Rd.
Chula Vista 92010

Travel and Trade Career Institute
3635 Atlantic Ave.
Long Beach 90807

Victor Valley College
18422 Bear Valley Rd.
Victorville 92392-9699

WCIL Computer Training Project
11201 La Cienega Blvd.
Los Angeles 90045

Yuba College
2088 North Beale Rd.
Marysville 95901

COLORADO

Aims Community College
P.O. Box 69
Greeley 80632

Arapahoe Community College
2500 West College Dr.
Littleton 80160-9002

Blair College
828 Wooten Rd.
Colorado Springs 80915

College America, Denver
1385 South Colorado Blvd., Ste. A512
Denver 80222

Colorado Technical University
4435 North Chestnut
Colorado Springs 80907-3896

Community College of Aurora
16000 East Centre Tech Pkwy.
Aurora 80011-9036

Denver Technical College
925 South Niagara St.
Denver 80224

Front Range Community College
3645 West 112th Ave.
Westminster 80030

Otero Junior College
1802 Colorado Ave.
La Junta 81050

Parks College
9065 Grant St.
Denver 80229

Pikes Peak Community College
5675 South Academy Blvd.
Colorado Springs 80906-5498

Pueblo Community College
900 West Orman Ave.
Pueblo 81004

Red Rocks Community College
13300 West Sixth Ave.
Lakewood 80228

CONNECTICUT

Asnuntuck Community Technical College
170 Elm St.
Enfield 06082

Data Institute
745 Burnside Ave.
East Hartford 06108

Capital Community Technical College
61 Woodland St.
Hartford 06105-2354

Lift Programming Institute
37 Bliss Memorial Rd.
Unionville 06085

Manchester Community Technical College
60 Bidwell St.
Manchester 06040-1046

Middlesex Community Technical College
100 Training Hill Rd.
Middletown 06457

Norwalk Community Technical College
188 Richards Ave.
Norwalk 06854

DELAWARE

Delaware Technical and Community College, Owens Campus
P.O. Box 610
Georgetown 19947

Delaware Technical and Community College, Terry Campus
1832 North Dupont Pkwy.
Dover 19901

Goldey-Beacom College
4701 Limestone Rd.
Wilmington 19808

DISTRICT OF COLUMBIA

Sanz School
1511 K St. NW
Washington 20005

Strayer College
1025 15th St. NW
Washington 20005

University of the District of Columbia
4200 Connecticut Ave. NW
Washington 20008

FLORIDA

Atlantic Vocational-Technical Center
4700 Coconut Creek Pkwy.
Coconut Creek 33063

Education America, Tampa Technical Institute
2410 East Busch Blvd.
Tampa 33612

Florida Computer and Business School, Inc.
8300 West Flagler St., Ste. 200
Miami 33144

Florida Metropolitan University, Tampa College
3319 West Hillsborough Ave.
Tampa 33614

Florida Metropolitan University, Tampa College, Pinellas
2471 McMullen Booth Rd.
Clearwater 33759

Florida Technical College
1819 North Semoran Blvd.
Orlando 32807

Florida Technical College of Jacksonville, Inc.
8711 Lone Star Rd.
Jacksonville 32211

Hialeah Technical Center
1780 East Fourth Ave.
Hialeah 33102

Keiser College
1500 Northwest 49th St.
Fort Lauderdale 33309

Lake County Area Vocational-Technical
Center
2001 Kurt St.
Eustis 32726

Lindsey Hopkins Technical Education
Center
750 Northwest 20th St.
Miami 33127

Lively Technical Center
500 North Appleyard Dr.
Tallahassee 32304

Miami Lakes Technical Education
Center
5780 Northwest 158th St.
Miami Lakes 33169

Miami Technical College
14701 Northwest Seventh Ave.
North Miami 33168

Miriam Vocational School, Inc.
135 SW 57th Ave.
Miami 33144

National School of Technology, Inc.
4410 West 16th Ave., Ste. 52
Hialeah 33012

National School of Technology, Inc.
16150 Northeast 17th Ave.
North Miami Beach 33162

North Technical Education Center
7071 Garden Rd.
Riviera Beach 33404

Orlando College
5421 Diplomat Circle
Orlando 32810

Robert Morgan Vocational-Technical
Center
18180 Southwest 122nd Ave.
Miami 33177

Sarasota County Technical Institute
4748 Beneva Rd.
Sarasota 34233-1798

Sheridan Vocational Center
5400 Sheridan St.
Hollywood 33021

Southern College
5600 Lake Underhill Rd.
Orlando 32807

Suwannee-Hamilton Area Vocational
and Adult Center
415 Southwest Pinewood Dr.
Live Oak 32060

Valencia Community College
P.O. Box 3028
Orlando 32802

GEORGIA

Clayton College and State University
5900 Lee St.
Morrow 30260

Meadows Junior College
1170 Brown Ave.
Columbus 31906

South College
709 Mall Blvd.
Savannah 31406

HAWAII

Electronics Institute
1270 Queen Emma St., Rm. 108
Honolulu 96813

Hawaii Business College
33 South King St., 4th Floor, Ste. 405
Honolulu 96817

Heald College School of Business and
Technology
1500 Kapiolani Blvd.
Honolulu 96816

Kapiolani Community College
4303 Diamond Head Rd.
Honolulu 96816

University of Hawaii at Hilo
200 West Kawili St.
Hilo 96720-4091

IDAHO

College of Southern Idaho
P.O. Box 1238
Twin Falls 83301

Idaho State University
741 South Seventh Ave.
Pocatello 83209

North Idaho College
1000 West Garden Ave.
Coeur D'Alene 83814

Northwest Nazarene College
623 Holly St.
Nampa 83686-5897

Ricks College
Rexburg 83460-4107

ILLINOIS

Computer Learning Center
200 South Michigan Ave.
Chicago 60604-2404

MacMurray College
East College Ave.
Jacksonville 62650

Northwestern Business College
4829 North Lipps Ave.
Chicago 60630

Northwestern University
633 Clark St.
Evanston 60208

Rend Lake College
468 North Ken Graz Pkwy.
Ina 62846

INDIANA

Indiana University, Purdue University
at Fort Wayne
2101 Coliseum Blvd. E
Fort Wayne 46805

Indiana University Southeast
4201 Grant Line Rd.
New Albany 47150

Ivy Tech State College, Central Indiana
One West 26th St.
Indianapolis 46206-1763

Ivy Tech State College, Columbus
4475 Central Ave.
Columbus 47203

Ivy Tech State College, East Central
4301 South Cowan Rd., P.O. Box 3100
Muncie 47302

Ivy Tech State College, Kokomo
1815 East Morgan St.
Kokomo 46901

Ivy Tech State College, Lafayette
3101 South Creasy Ln.
P.O. Box 6299
Lafayette 47903

Ivy Tech State College, North Central
1534 West Sample St.
South Bend 46619

Ivy Tech State College, Northeast
3800 North Anthony Blvd.
Fort Wayne 46805

Ivy Tech State College, Northwest
1440 East 35th Ave.
Gary 46409

Ivy Tech State College, South Central
8204 Hwy. 311
Sellersburg 47172

Ivy Tech State College, Southeast
590 Ivy Tech Dr.
Madison 47250

Ivy Tech State College, Southwest
3501 First Ave.
Evansville 47710

Ivy Tech State College, Wabash Valley
7999 U.S. Hwy. 41
Terre Haute 47802-4898

Ivy Tech State College, Whitewater
P.O. Box 1145
Richmond 47374

Professional Career Institute
2611 Waterfront Pkwy. & East Dr.
Indianapolis 46214-2028

Sawyer College, Hammond
6040 Hohman Ave.
Hammond 46320

Vincennes University
1002 North First St.
Vincennes 47591

IOWA

American Institute of Business
2500 Fleur Dr.
Des Moines 50321

Iowa Western Community College
2700 College Rd. P.O. Box 4C
Council Bluffs 51502

Southwestern Community College
1501 Townline
Creston 50801

Western Iowa Technical Community
College
4647 Stone Ave. P.O. Box 5199
Sioux City 51102-5199

KANSAS

Coffeyville Community College
400 West 11th St.
Coffeyville 67337

Dodge City Community College
2501 North 14th Ave.
Dodge City 67801

Hutchinson Community College
1300 North Plum St.
Hutchinson 67501

Kansas City Kansas Community College
7250 State Ave.
Kansas City 66112

Kansas State University
Anderson Hall
Manhattan 66506

North Central Kansas Technical College
Hwy. 24 P.O. Box 507
Beloit 67420

Northwest Kansas Area Vocational-
Technical School
P.O. Box 668
Goodland 67735

Seward County Community College
P.O. Box 1137
Liberal 67905-1137

Washburn University of Topeka
1700 College Ave.
Topeka 66621

KENTUCKY

The Computer School
820 Lane Allen Rd.
Lexington 40504

Fugazzi College
406 Lafayette Ave.
Lexington 40502

Kentucky College of Business
628 East Main St.
Lexington 40508

Kentucky Tech, Jefferson State
Vocational-Technical School
727 West Chestnut
Louisville 40203-2036

Louisville Technical Institute
3901 Atkinson Dr.
Louisville 40218

Southern Ohio College, Fort Mitchell
309 Buttermilk Pike
Fort Mitchell 41017

LOUISIANA

Cameron College
2740 Canal St.
New Orleans 70119

Delta School of Business and
Technology
517 Broad St.
Lake Charles 70601

Louisiana Technical College, Lafayette
Campus
1101 Bertrand Dr.
Lafayette 70502-4909

RETS Training Center
3321 Hessmer Ave.
Metairie 70002

Tulane University of Louisiana
6823 Saint Charles Ave.
New Orleans 70118

MAINE

Andover College
901 Washington Ave.
Portland 04103

Northern Maine Technical College
33 Edgemont Dr.
Presque Isle 04769

MARYLAND

Allegany Community College
12401 Willowbrook Rd. SE
Cumberland 21502

Anne Arundel Community College
101 College Pkwy.
Arnold 21012

Catonsville Community College
800 South Rolling Rd.
Catonsville 21228

Frederick Community College
7932 Opossumtown Pike
Frederick 21702

Hagerstown Junior College
11400 Robinwood Dr.
Hagerstown 21742-6590

Harford Community College
401 Thomas Run Rd.
Bel Air 21015

Howard Community College
10901 Little Patuxent Pkwy.
Columbia 21044

Montgomery College of Germantown
20200 Observation Dr.
Germantown 20874

Montgomery College of Rockville
51 Mannakee St.
Rockville 20850

Montgomery College of Takoma Park
Takoma Ave. and Fenton St.
Takoma Park 20912

Prince Georges Community College
301 Largo Rd.
Largo 20774-2199

The Radio Electronic Television
Schools, Inc.
1520 South Caton Ave.
Baltimore 21227-1063

Technical Education Center
12500 Ardennes Ave.
Rockville 20852

Tesst Technology Institute
5122 Baltimore Ave.
Hyattsville 20781

MASSACHUSETTS

Berkshire Community College
1350 West St.
Pittsfield 01201-5786

Bristol Community College
777 Elsbree St.
Fall River 02720

Computer Learning Center of Boston
Five Middlesex Ave.
Somerville 02145

Computer Processing Institute
615 Massachusetts Ave.
Cambridge 02139

Dean College
99 Main St.
Franklin 02038

Fisher College
118 Beacon St.
Boston 02116

Greenfield Community College
One College Dr.
Greenfield 01301-9739

Holyoke Community College
303 Homestead Ave.
Holyoke 01040

Massasoit Community College
One Massasoit Blvd.
Brockton 02402

Merrimack College
315 Turpike St.
North Andover 01845

Middlesex Community College
Springs Rd.
Bedford 01730

Mount Wachusett Community College
444 Green St.
Gardner 01440

Newbury College, Inc.
129 Fisher Ave.
Brookline 02146

North Shore Community College
One Ferncroft Rd.
Danvers 01923

Northeastern University
360 Huntington Ave.
Boston 02115

Northern Essex Community College
Elliott Way
Haverhill 01830-2399

Quincy College
34 Coddington St.
Quincy 02169

Wentworth Institute of Technology
550 Huntington Ave.
Boston 02115

MICHIGAN

Baker College of Flint
G1050 West Bristol Rd.
Flint 48507

Baker College of Muskegon
903 Marquette Ave.
Muskegon 49442

Davenport College
415 East Fulton
Grand Rapids 49503

Davenport College, Lansing Branch
220 East Kalamazoo
Lansing 48933

Delta College
University Center 48710

Detroit College of Business
4801 Oakman Blvd.
Dearborn 48126-3799

Detroit College of Business
3488 North Jennings
Flint 48504-1700

Dorsey Business Schools
30821 Barrington
Madison Heights 48071

Dorsey Business Schools
15755 Northline Rd.
Southgate 48195

Glen Oaks Community College
62249 Shimmel Rd.
Centreville 49032

Gogebic Community College
East 4946 Jackson Rd.
Ironwood 49938

Grand Rapids Community College
143 Bostwick Ave. NE
Grand Rapids 49503-3295

Henry Ford Community College
5101 Evergreen Rd.
Dearborn 48128

Kalamazoo Valley Community College
6767 West O Ave.
Kalamazoo 49009

Kellogg Community College
450 North Ave.
Battle Creek 49017

Lake Superior State University
650 West Easterday Ave.
Sault Sainte Marie 49783

Lansing Community College
419 North Capitol Ave.
Lansing 48901-7210

Lansing Computer Institute
501 North Marshall St., Ste. 101
Lansing 48912

Macomb Community College
14500 Twelve Mile Rd.
Warren 48093-3896

Mott Community College
1401 East Court St.
Flint 48503

Muskegon Community College
221 South Quarterline Rd.
Muskegon 49442

National Institute of Technology
2620 Remico St. SW
Wyoming 49509

Northwestern Michigan College
1701 East Front St.
Traverse City 49686

Oakland Community College
2480 Opdyke Rd.
Bloomfield Hills 48304-2266

Ross Business Institute
37065 South Gratiot
Clinton Township 48036

Ross Business Institute
22293 Eureka
Taylor 48180

Ross Technical Institute
20820 Greenfield Rd.
Oak Park 48237

Schoolcraft College
18600 Haggerty Rd.
Livonia 48152

Southwestern Michigan College
58900 Cherry Grove Rd.
Dowagiac 49047-9793

Specs Howard School of Broadcast Arts, Inc.
16900 West Nine Mile Rd.
Southfield 48075

Washtenaw Community College
P.O. Drawer 1
Ann Arbor 48016-1610

MINNESOTA

Alexandria Technical College
1601 Jefferson St.
Alexandria 56308

Brown Institute, Ltd.
2225 East Lake St.
Minneapolis 55407

Dakota County Technical College
1300 East 145th St.
Rosemount 55068

Hennepin Technical College
9000 Brooklyn Blvd.
Brooklyn Park 55445

Hibbing Community College
1515 East 25th St.
Hibbing 55746

Lake Superior College
2101 Trinity Rd.
Duluth 55811

Northwest Technical College, Moorhead
1900 28th Ave. S
Moorhead 56560

Riverland Community College, Albert Lea
1920 Lee Blvd.
North Mankato 56003

Saint Paul Technical College
235 Marshall Ave.
Saint Paul 55102

The School of Communication Arts
5051 Hwy. 7
Minneapolis 55416

University of Minnesota Twin Cities
100 Church St. SE
Minneapolis 55455

MISSISSIPPI

Copiah-Lincoln Community College
P.O. Box 457
Wesson 39191

East Mississippi Community College
P.O. Box 158
Scooba 39358

Hinds Community College, Raymond Campus
Raymond 39154

Mary Holmes College
Hwy. 50 W
West Point 39773

Meridian Community College
910 Hwy. 19 N
Meridian 39307

Mississippi Delta Community College
P.O. Box 668
Moorhead 38761

Mississippi Gulf Coast Community College
Central Office
P.O. Box 67
Perkinston 39573

Northeast Mississippi Community College
Cunningham Blvd.
Booneville 38829

Northwest Mississippi Community College
510 North Panola, Hwy. 51 N
Senatobia 38668

MISSOURI

Columbia College
1001 Rogers
Columbia 65216

Lincoln University
820 Chestnut
Jefferson City 65102-0029

Linn Technical College
One Technology Dr.
Linn 65051

Longview Community College
500 Longview Rd.
Lees Summit 64081

Park College
8700 River Park Dr.
Parkville 64152-3795

Ranken Technical College
4431 Finney Ave.
Saint Louis 63113

Saint Louis Community College, Forest Park
5600 Oakland Ave.
Saint Louis 63110

Sanford-Brown College
12006 Manchester Rd.
Des Peres 63131

Sikeston Area Vocational-Technical School
1002 Virginia St.
Sikeston 63801

TAD Technical Institute
7910 Troost Ave.
Kansas City 64131

Three Rivers Community College
Three Rivers Blvd.
Poplar Bluff 63901

MONTANA

Helena College of Technology of the University of Montana
1115 North Roberts St.
Helena 59601

University of Great Falls
1301 Twentieth St. S
Great Falls 59405-4996

NEBRASKA

Central Community College Area
P.O. Box 4903
Grand Island 68802

Lincoln School of Commerce
1821 K St. P.O. Box 82826
Lincoln 68501-2826

Metropolitan Community College Area
5300 North 30th St.
Omaha 68103

Northeast Community College
801 East Benjamin, P.O. Box 469
Norfolk 68702-0469

Southeast Community College Area
1111 O St., Ste. 111
Lincoln 68520

Union College
3800 South 48th
Lincoln 68506

NEVADA

Community College of Southern Nevada
3200 East Cheyenne Ave.
Las Vegas 89030

Western Business Academy
1055 East Tropicana
Las Vegas 89119

Western Nevada Community College
2201 West College Pkwy.
Carson City 89703

NEW HAMPSHIRE

Franklin Pierce College
College Rd.
Rindge 03461

Hesser College
Three Sundial Ave.
Manchester 03103

Keene State College
229 Main
Keene 03431

McIntosh College
23 Cataract Ave.
Dover 03820

New Hampshire Technical Institute
11 Institute Dr.
Concord 03301

Rivier College
429 Main St.
Nashua 03060

NEW JERSEY

Atlantic Community College
5100 Black Horse Pike
Mays Landing 08330-2699

Brick Computer Science Institute
515 Hwy. 70
Brick 08723

Brookdale Community College
765 Newman Springs Rd.
Lincroft 07738-1599

Burlington County College
Rte. 530
Pemberton 08068

Camden County College
P.O. Box 200
Blackwood 08012

Cittone Institute
1697 Oak Tree Rd.
Edison 08820-2896

County College of Morris
214 Center Grove Rd.
Randolph 07869

Dover Business College
East 81 Rte. 4 W
Paramus 07652

Drake College of Business
125 Broad St.
Elizabeth 07201

Empire Technical School of New Jersey
576 Central Ave.
East Orange 07018

Essex County College
303 University Ave.
Newark 07102

Gloucester County College
1400 Tanyard Rd.
Sewell 08080

Hudson County Community College
25 Journal Square
Jersey City 07306

Mercer County Community College
1200 Old Trenton Rd.
Trenton 08690

Middlesex County College
155 Mill Rd., P.O. Box 3050
Edison 08818-3050

Ocean County College
College Dr.
Toms River 08753

Passaic County Community College
One College Blvd.
Paterson 07505-1179

Raritan Valley Community College
P.O. Box 3300, Lamington Rd.
Somerville 08876

Star Technical Institute
4313 RR 130 S
Edgewater Park 08010

Star Technical Institute
1386 South Delsea Dr.
Vineland 08360

Union County College
1033 Springfield Ave.
Cranford 07016

NEW MEXICO

Crownpoint Institute of Technology
P.O. Box 849
Crownpoint 87313

Santa Fe Community College
6401 Richards Ave.
Santa Fe 87505

University of New Mexico, Gallup
Campus
200 College Rd.
Gallup 87301

University of New Mexico, Los Alamos
4000 University Dr.
Los Alamos 87544

University of New Mexico, Main
Campus
Albuquerque 87131

University of New Mexico, Valencia
Campus
280 La Entrada
Los Lunas 87031

NEW YORK

Broome Community College
P.O. Box 1017
Binghamton 13902

Bryant and Stratton Business Institute,
Albany
1259 Central Ave.
Albany 12205

Bryant and Stratton Business Institute,
Buffalo
1028 Main St.
Buffalo 14202

Bryant and Stratton Business Institute,
Rochester
82 Saint Paul St.
Rochester 14604

Bryant and Stratton Business Institute,
Syracuse
953 James St.
Syracuse 13203

Careers Blazers Learning Center
290 Madison Ave.
New York 10017

Cayuga County Community College
Franklin St.
Auburn 13021

Columbia-Greene Community College
4400 Rte. 23
Hudson 12534

Cope Institute
84 William St.
New York 10038

Corning Community College
Spencer Hill
Corning 14830

CUNY Borough of Manhattan
Community College
199 Chambers St.
New York 10007

CUNY Bronx Community College
West 181st St. & University Ave.
Bronx 10453

CUNY College of Staten Island
2800 Victory Blvd.
Staten Island 10314

CUNY La Guardia Community College
31-10 Thomson Ave.
Long Island City 11101

Dutchess Community College
53 Pendell Rd.
Poughkeepsie 12601

Erie Community College, North
Campus
Main St. and Youngs Rd.
Williamsville 14221

Finger Lakes Community College
4355 Lake Shore Dr.
Canandaigua 14424

Fulton-Montgomery Community
College
2805 State Hwy. 67
Johnstown 12095

Hudson Valley Community College
80 Vandenburgh Ave.
Troy 12180

Jamestown Community College
525 Falconer St.
Jamestown 14701

Jefferson Community College
Outer Coffeen St.
Watertown 13601

Mohawk Valley Community College
1101 Sherman Dr.
Utica 13501

Monroe Community College
1000 East Henrietta Rd.
Rochester 14623

Nassau Community College
One Education Dr.
Garden City 11530

Onondaga Community College
4941 Onondaga Rd.
Syracuse 13215

Orange County Community College
115 South St.
Middletown 10940

Schenectady County Community
College
Washington Ave.
Schenectady 12305

Spencer Business and Technical
Institute
200 State St.
Schenectady 12305

Suffolk County Community College,
Ammerman Campus
533 College Rd.
Selden 11784

Suffolk County Community College,
Western Campus
Crooked Hill Rd.
Brentwood 11717

Sullivan County Community College
1000 Le Roy Rd.
Loch Sheldrake 12759-4002

SUNY College of Agriculture &
Technology at Cobleskill
Cobleskill 12043

SUNY College of Technology &
Agriculture at Morrisville
Morrisville 13408

SUNY College of Technology at Alfred
Alfred 14802

SUNY College of Technology at Canton
Cornell Dr.
Canton 13617

SUNY College of Technology at Delhi
Delhi 13753

SUNY College of Technology at
Farmingdale
Melville Rd.
Farmingdale 11735-1021

SUNY Ulster County Community
College
Cottekill Rd.
Stone Ridge 12484

SUNY Westchester Commmunity
College
75 Grasslands Rd.
Valhalla 10595

Superior Career Institute, Inc.
254 West 29th St., 3rd Floor
New York 10011

Syrit College
1760 53rd St.
Brooklyn 11204

Tompkins-Cortland Community
College
170 North St.
Dryden 13053

The Westchester Business Institute
325 Central Ave.
White Plains 10606

NORTH CAROLINA

Carteret Community College
3505 Arendell St.
Morehead City 28557

Cleveland Community College
137 South Post Rd.
Shelby 28152

Edgecombe Community College
2009 West Wilson St.
Tarboro 27886

Guilford Technical Community College
P.O. Box 309
Jamestown 27282

Randolph Community College
629 Industrial Park Ave.
Asheboro 27204

NORTH DAKOTA

Interstate Business College
2720 32nd Ave. SW
Fargo 58103

North Dakota State College of Science
800 North Sixth St.
Wahpeton 58076

University of North Dakota, Lake
Region
1801 North College Dr.
Devils Lake 58301

OHIO

Akron Adult Vocational Services
147 Park St.
Akron 44308

Belmont Technical College
120 Fox Shannon Place
Saint Clairsville 43950

Central Ohio Technical College
1179 University Dr.
Newark 43055-1767

Cincinnati State Technical and
Community College
3520 Central Pkwy.
Cincinnati 45223

Clark State Community College
570 East Leffel Ln.
Springfield 45505

Columbus State Community College
550 East Spring St. P.O. Box 1609
Columbus 43216

Cuyahoga Community College District
700 Carnegie Ave.
Cleveland 44115-2878

Edison State Community College
1973 Edison Dr.
Piqua 45356

Franklin University
201 South Grant Ave.
Columbus 43215-5399

Lakeland Community College
7700 Clocktower Dr.
Kirkland 44094-5198

Mahoning County Joint Vocational
School District
7300 North Palmyra Rd.
Canfield 44406

Medina County Career Center
1101 West Liberty St.
Medina 44256

Miami University, Oxford Campus
500 High St.
Oxford 45056

Muskingum Area Technical College
1555 Newark Rd.
Zanesville 43701

North Central Technical College
2441 Kenwood Circle, P.O. Box 698
Mansfield 44901

Northwestern College
1441 North Cable Rd.
Lima 45805

Ohio University, Lancaster Branch
1570 Granville Pike
Lancaster 43130

Ohio University, Main Campus
Athens 45701

Owens Community College
39335 Oregon Rd.
Toledo 43699-1947

Queen City Vocational Center
425 Ezzard Charles Dr.
Cincinnati 45203

RETS Technical Center
116 Westpark Rd.
Centerville 45459

Sawyer College of Business
3150 Mayfield Rd.
Cleveland Heights 44118

Sawyer College of Business, West
13027 Lorain Ave.
Cleveland 44111

Sinclair Community College
444 West Third St.
Dayton 45402

Southeastern Business College
1855 Western Ave.
Chillicothe 45601

Southeastern Business College
1176 Jackson Pike
Gallipolis 45631

Southeastern Business College
1522 Sheridan Dr.
Lancaster 43130

Southeastern Business College
3879 Rhodes Ave.
New Boston 45662

Southern Ohio College, Northeast
2791 Mogadore Rd.
Akron 44312

Southern Ohio College
1011 Glendale Milford Rd.
Cincinnati 45215

Stark State College of Technology
6200 Frank Ave. NW
Canton 44720

Stautzenberger College
5355 Southwyck Blvd.
Toledo 43614

Terra State Community College
2830 Napoleon Rd.
Fremont 43420

University of Akron, Main Campus
302 Buchtel Common
Akron 44325-4702

University of Cincinati, Clermont
College
College Dr.
Batavia 45103

University of Cincinnati, Main Campus
P.O. Box 210127
Cincinnati 45221-0127

Upper Valley Joint Vocational School
8811 Career Dr.
Piqua 45356

Youngstown State University
One University Plaza
Youngstown 44555

OKLAHOMA

Cameron University
2800 Gore Blvd.
Lawton 73505

Connors State College
Rte. 1, P.O. Box 1000
Warner 74469

Northeastern Oklahoma Agricultural
and Mechanical College
200 I St. NE
Miami 74354

Oklahoma State University, Okmulgee
1801 East Fourth St.
Okmulgee 74447-3901

Rose State College
6420 Southeast 15th
Midwest City 73110

OREGON

Blue Mountain Community College
P.O. Box 100
Pendleton 97801

Columbia College
8800 SE Sunnyside Rd.
Clackamas 97015

Oregon Institute of Technology
3201 Campus Dr.
Klamath Falls 97601-8801

Pioneer Pacific College
25195 Southwest Parkway Ave.
Wilsonville 97070

Rogue Community College
3345 Redwood Hwy.
Grants Pass 97527

PENNSYLVANIA

Academy of Medical Arts and Business
2301 Academy Dr.
Harrisburg 17112

Bidwell Training Center, Inc.
1815 Metropolitan St.
Pittsburgh 15233

Bucks County Community College
Swamp Rd.
Newtown 18940

Business Institute of Pennsylvania
335 Boyd Dr.
Sharon 16146

Center for Innovative Training and
Education
841 Chestnut St., Ste. 30
Philadelphia 19107

CHI Institute
520 Street Rd.
Southampton 18966

The Chubb Institute Keystone School
965 Baltimore Pike
Springfield 19064

Community College of Allegheny
County
800 Allegheny Ave.
Pittsburgh 15233-1895

Community College of Philadelphia
1700 Spring Garden St.
Philadelphia 19130

Computer Learning Center, Inc.
3600 Market St.
Philadelphia 19104-2684

Computer Learning Network, Resident
School
1110 Fernwood Ave.
Camp Hill 17011

Consolidated School of Business
1605 Clugston Rd.
York 17404

Delaware County Community College
901 South Media Line Rd.
Media 19063-1094

Du Bois Business College
One Beaver Dr., P.O. Box O
Du Bois 15801

Erie Business Center
246 West Ninth St.
Erie 16501

Garfield Business Institute
709 Third Ave.
New Brighton 15066

Harrisburg Area Community College,
Harrisburg Campus
One Hacc Dr.
Harrisburg 17110

ICM School of Business and Medical
Careers
10-14 Wood St.
Pittsburgh 15222

Information Computer Systems
Institute
2201 Hangar Place
Allentown 18103

J H Thompson Academies
2910 State St.
Erie 16508

Lackawanna Junior College
501 Vine St.
Scranton 18509

Lehigh Carbon Community College
4525 Education Park Dr.
Schnecksville 18078-2598

Lincoln Technical Institute
5151 Tilghman St.
Allentown 18104

Luzerne County Community College
1333 South Prospect St.
Nanticoke 18634

McCann School of Business
Main St. and Pine St.
Mahanoy City 17948

Montgomery County Community
College
340 Dekalb Pike
Blue Bell 19422

Mount Aloysius College
7373 Admiral Pearl Hwy.
Cresson 16630-1999

Northampton County Area Community
College
3835 Green Pond Rd.
Bethlehem 18020-7599

Pennco Technical
3815 Otter St.
Bristol 19007

Pennsylvania State University, Main
Campus
201 Old Main
University Park 16802

Pennsylvania State University,
Schuylkill Campus
200 University Dr.
Schuylkill Haven 17972-2208

South Hills School of Business and
Technology
480 Waupelani Dr.
State College 16801

Tri-State Business Institute
5757 West 26th St.
Erie 16506-1013

Westmoreland County Community
College
Youngwood 15697-1895

RHODE ISLAND

Community College of Rhode Island
400 East Ave.
Warwick 02886-1807

Johnson and Wales University
8 Abbott Park Place
Providence 02903-3376

New England Institute of Technology
2500 Post Rd.
Warwick 02886

SOUTH CAROLINA

Aiken Technical College
P.O. Drawer 696
Aiken 29802

Midlands Technical College
P.O. Box 2408
Columbia 29202

York Technical College
452 South Anderson Rd.
Rock Hill 29730

SOUTH DAKOTA

National American University
321 Kansas City St.
Rapid City 57701

National American University
3109 South Kiwanis Ave.
Sioux Falls 57105

Southeast Technical Institute
2301 Career Place
Sioux Falls 57107

TENNESSEE

Chattanooga State Technical
Community College
4501 Amnicola Hwy.
Chattanooga 37406

Draughons Junior College of Business
Plus Park at Pavilion Blvd.
Nashville 37217

Electronic Computer Program Institute
of Chattanooga
3805 Brainerd Rd.
Chattanooga 37411

Knoxville Business College
720 North Fifth Ave.
Knoxville 37917

Nashville State Technical Institute
120 White Bridge Rd.
Nashville 37209

Pellissippi State Technical Community
College
P.O. Box 22990
Knoxville 37933-0990

State Technical Institute at Memphis
5983 Macon Cove
Memphis 38134

TEXAS

Alvin Community College
3110 Mustang Rd.
Alvin 77511

Amarillo College
P.O. Box 447
Amarillo 79178

American Commercial College
3177 Executive Dr.
San Angelo 76904

Austin Community College
5930 Middle Fiskville Rd.
Austin 78752

Bee County College
3800 Charco Rd.
Beeville 78102

Blinn College
902 College Ave.
Brenham 77833

Brookhaven College
3939 Valley View Ln.
Farmers Branch 75244-4997

Central Texas College
P.O. Box 1800
Killeen 76540-1800

College of the Mainland
1200 Amburn Rd.
Texas City 77591

Del Mar College
101 Baldwin
Corpus Christi 78404-3897

Eastfield College
3737 Motley Dr.
Mesquite 75150

El Centro College
Main and Lamar
Dallas 75202

El Paso Community College
P.O. Box 20500
El Paso 79998

Galveston College
4015 Ave. Q
Galveston 77550

Houston Community College System
22 Waugh Dr.
Houston 77270-7849

Kilgore College
1100 Broadway
Kilgore 75662-3299

Lamar University, Beaumont
P.O. Box 10001, 4400 Mlk
Beaumont 77710

Lamar University, Orange
410 Front St.
Orange 77630-5899

Lamar University, Port Arthur
1500 Proctor St.
Port Arthur 77640

Laredo Community College
West End Washington St.
Laredo 78040

Lee College
200 Lee Dr.
Baytown 77520-4703

McLennan Community College
1400 College Dr.
Waco 76708

Navarro College
3200 West 7th
Corsicana 75110

North Harris Montgomery Community
College District
250 North Sam Houston Pkwy. E, Ste.
300
Houston 77060

Richland College
12800 Abrams Rd.
Dallas 75243-2199

San Antonio College
1300 San Pedro Ave.
San Antonio 78284

San Jacinto College Central Campus
8060 Spencer Hwy.
Pasadena 77505

San Jacinto College North Campus
5800 Uvalde
Houston 77049

San Jacinto College, South Campus
13735 Beamer Rd.
Houston 77089-6009

South Plains College
1401 College Ave.
Levelland 79336

Southwest School of Business and
Technical Careers
602 West South Cross
San Antonio 78221

Tarrant County Junior College
1500 Houston St.
Fort Worth 76102

Temple College
2600 South First St.
Temple 76504-7435

Texas Southmost College
80 Fort Brown
Brownsville 78520

Texas State Technical College,
Harlingen Campus
2424 Boxwood
Harlingen 78550-3697

Texas State Technical College,
Sweetwater Campus
300 College Dr.
Sweetwater 79556

Tyler Junior College
1327 South Baxter Ave.
Tyler 75711

Vernon Regional Junior College
4400 College Dr.
Vernon 76384-4092

Weatherford College
308 East Park Ave.
Weatherford 76086

Wharton County Junior College
911 Boling Hwy.
Wharton 77488

UTAH

Certified Careers Institute
1455 West 2200 S, Ste. 200
Salt Lake City 84119

Dixie College
225 South 700 East
Saint George 84770

Salt Lake Community College
P.O. Box 30808
Salt Lake City 84130

Sevier Valley Applied Technology
Center
800 West 200 S
Richfield 84701

Utah Valley State College
800 West 1200 S
Orem 84058

Weber State University
3750 Harrison Blvd.
Ogden 84408

VERMONT

Vermont Technical College
P.O. Box 500
Randolph Center 05061

VIRGINIA

Central Virginia Community College
3506 Wards Rd.
Lynchburg 24502

Commonwealth College
1120 West Mercury Blvd.
Hampton 23666

Commonwealth College
8141 Hull Street Rd.
Richmond 23235

Commonwealth College
301 Centre Pointe Dr.
Virginia Beach 23462

Computer Learning Center
6295 Edsall Rd., Ste. 210
Alexandria 22312

Danville Community College
1008 South Main St.
Danville 24541

Germanna Community College
2130 Germanna Hwy.
Locust Grove 24501

J Sargeant Reynolds Community
College
P.O. Box 85622
Richmond 23285-5622

Kee Business College
803 Diligence Dr.
Newport News 23606

National Business College
1813 East Main St.
Salem 24153

New River Community College
P.O. Drawer 1127
Dublin 24084-1127

Northern Virginia Community College
4001 Wakefield Chapel Rd.
Annandale 22003

Patrick Henry Community College
P.O. Box 5311
Martinsville 24115-5311

Southside Virginia Community College
109 Campus Dr.
Alberta 23821

Southwest Virginia Community College
P.O. Box SVCC
Richlands 24641

Thomas Nelson Community College
P.O. Box 9407
Hampton 23670

Virginia Highlands Community College
P.O. Box 828
Abingdon 24212-0828

Virginia Western Community College
3095 Colonial Ave.
Roanoke 24015

Washington Business School of North
Virginia
1980 Gallows Rd.
Vienna 22182

WASHINGTON

Bates Technical College
1101 South Yakima Ave.
Tacoma 98405

Big Bend Community College
7662 Chanute St.
Moses Lake 98837

Centralia College
600 West Locust St.
Centralia 98531

Green River Community College
12401 Southeast 320th St.
Auburn 98092

Highline Community College
P.O. Box 98000
Des Moines 98198-9800

Interface Computer School
9921 Nevada
Spokane 99205

Spokane Community College
North 1810 Greene Ave.
Spokane 99207

Spokane Falls Community College
West 3410 Fort George Wright Dr.
Spokane 99224

Walla Walla Community College
500 Tausick Way
Walla Walla 99362

WEST VIRGINIA

Bluefield State College
219 Rock St.
Bluefield 24701

Marshall University
400 Hal Greer Blvd.
Huntington 25755

Potomac State College of West Virginia
University
Fort Ave.
Keyser 26726

Southern West Virginia Community
and Technical College
P.O. Box 2900
Mt. Gay 25637

West Virginia University at Parkersburg
300 Campus Dr.
Parkersburg 26101

WISCONSIN

Fox Valley Technical College
1825 North Bluemound Dr.
Appleton 54913-2277

Gateway Technical College
3520 30th Ave.
Kenosha 53144-1690

Madison Area Technical College
3550 Anderson St.
Madison 53704

Milwaukee Area Technical College
700 West State St.
Milwaukee 53233-1443

Northeast Wisconsin Technical College
2740 West Mason St., P.O. Box 19042
Green Bay 54307-9042

Western Wisconsin Technical College
304 North Sixth St., P.O. Box 908
La Crosse 54602-0908

WYOMING

Casper College
125 College Dr.
Casper 82601

Western Wyoming Community College
2500 College Dr.
Rock Springs 82902

Data Processing

ALABAMA

Bessemer State Technical College
1100 9th Ave.
Bessemer 35021

Bevill State Community College
100 State St.
Sumiton 35148

Community College of the Air Force
130 West Maxwell Blvd.
Montgomery 36112-6613

Gadsden Business College
750 Forrest Ave.
Gadsden 35901

Gadsden Business College, Anniston
P.O. Box 1559
Anniston 36202-1575

Gadsden State Community College
1001 George Wallace Dr.
Gadsden 35902-0227

George C Wallace State Community
College, Dothan
Rte. 6, P.O. Box 62
Dothan 36303-9234

J F Ingram State Technical College
5375 Ingram Rd.
Deatsville 36022

John M Patterson State Technical
College
3920 Troy Hwy.
Montgomery 36116

North West Shoals Community College
800 George Wallace Blvd.
Muscle Shoals 35662

University of Alabama at Birmingham,
Walker College
1411 Indiana Ave.
Jasper 35501

ALASKA

Mila, Inc.
3330 Artic Blvd., Ste. 201
Anchorage 99503

ARIZONA

Arizona Institute of Business and
Technology
6049 North 43rd Ave.
Phoenix 85019

Central Arizona College
8470 North Overfield Rd.
Coolidge 85228-9778

Glendale Community College
6000 West Olive Ave.
Glendale 85302

Mesa Community College
1833 West Southern Ave.
Mesa 85202

Pima Community College
2202 West Anklam Rd.
Tucson 85709-0001

Rio Salado Community College
2323 West 14th St.
Tempe 85281

ARKANSAS

Arkansas State University, Main
 Campus
P.O. Box 790
State University 72467

Arkansas Valley Technical Institute
Hwy. 23 N
P.O. Box 506
Ozark 72949

Cossatot Technical College
183 Hwy. 399
De Queen 71832

Crowley's Ridge Technical School
140 Crowley's Ridge Rd.
Forrest City 72336-0925

Garland County Community College
101 College Dr.
Hot Springs 71913

Great Rivers Vocational-Technical
 School
P.O. Box 747, Hwy. 1 NE
McGehee 71654

Mississippi County Community College
P.O. Box 1109
Blytheville 72316-1109

Northwest Technical Institute
709 South Old Missouri Rd.
Springdale 72764

Ouachita Technical College
One College Circle
Malvern 72104

Ozarka Technical College
P.O. Box 10, 218 South Dr.
Melbourne 72556-0010

Phillips County Community College
P.O. Box 785
Helena 72342

Southern Arkansas University
 Technical
SAU Technical Station
Camden 71701

University of Arkansas Community
 College
P.O. Box 3350
Batesville 72503

CALIFORNIA

Allan Hancock College
800 South College Dr.
Santa Maria 93454

Antelope Valley College
3041 West Ave. K
Lancaster 93536

Career Development Center
255 East Bonita Ave.
Pomona 91767

Center for Employment Training,
 Salinas
421 Monterey St.
Salinas 93901

Cerritos College
11110 Alondra Blvd.
Norwalk 90650

Chabot College
25555 Hesperian Blvd.
Hayward 94545

Chaffey Community College
5885 Haven Ave.
Rancho Cucamonga 91737-3002

Citrus College
1000 West Foothill Blvd.
Glendora 91741-1899

Coleman College
7380 Parkway Dr.
La Mesa 91942-1532

College of San Mateo
1700 West Hillsdale Blvd.
San Mateo 94402

Computer Learning Center
3580 Wilshire Blvd., Ste. 100
Los Angeles 90010

Contra Costa College
2600 Mission Bell Dr.
San Pablo 94806

Cosumnes River College
8401 Center Pkwy.
Sacramento 95823-5799

De Anza College
21250 Stevens Creek Blvd.
Cupertino 95014

EBM Business Institute
6024 San Juan Ave., Ste. C
Citrus Heights 95610

Eldorado College
1901 Pacific Ave.
West Covina 91790

Fresno City College
1101 East University Ave.
Fresno 93741

Grossmont College
8800 Grossmont College Dr.
El Cajon 92020

Imperial Valley College
P.O. Box 158
Imperial 92251-0158

Institute for Business and Technology
2550 Scott Blvd.
Santa Clara 95050

Institute of Computer Technology
3200 Wilshire Blvd.
Los Angeles 90010

Laney College
900 Fallon St.
Oakland 94607

Marin Regional Occupational Program
P.O. Box 4925
San Rafael 94913

Merritt College
12500 Campus Dr.
Oakland 94619

Monterey Peninsula College
980 Fremont Blvd.
Monterey 93940-4799

Moorpark College
7075 Campus Rd.
Moorpark 93021

Mount San Antonio College
1100 North Grand
Walnut 91789

Napa Valley College
2277 Napa Vallejo Hwy.
Napa 94558

Orange County Business College
2035 East Ball Rd.
Anaheim 92806

Pasadena City College
1570 East Colorada Blvd.
Pasadena 91106

San Joaquin Delta College
5151 Pacific Ave.
Stockton 95207

San Joaquin Valley College
201 New Stine Rd.
Bakersfield 93309

Santa Barbara City College
721 Cliff Dr.
Santa Barbara 93109-2394

Santa Rosa Junior College
1501 Mendocino Ave.
Santa Rosa 95401-4395

Sawyer College, A Corinthian School
8475 Jackson Rd.
Sacramento 95826

Solano County Community College
 District
4000 Suisun Valley Rd.
Suisun 94585-3197

Travel and Trade Career Institute
3635 Atlantic Ave.
Long Beach 90807

Vallecitos CET, Inc.
597 C St.
Hayward 94541

Yuba College
2088 North Beale Rd.
Marysville 95901

COLORADO

Aims Community College
P.O. Box 69
Greeley 80632

Arapahoe Community College
2500 West College Dr.
Littleton 80160-9002

Colorado Mountain College
P.O. Box 10001
Glenwood Springs 81602

Community College of Aurora
16000 East Centre Tech Pkwy.
Aurora 80011-9036

Community College of Denver
P.O. Box 173363
Denver 80217

Front Range Community College
3645 West 112th Ave.
Westminster 80030

Morgan Community College
17800 County Rd. 20
Fort Morgan 80701

Otero Junior College
1802 Colorado Ave.
La Junta 81050

Pikes Peak Community College
5675 South Academy Blvd.
Colorado Springs 80906-5498

Pueblo Community College
900 West Orman Ave.
Pueblo 81004

Red Rocks Community College
13300 West Sixth Ave.
Lakewood 80228

CONNECTICUT

Asnuntuck Community Technical
 College
170 Elm St.
Enfield 06082

Data Institute
745 Burnside Ave.
East Hartford 06108

Capital Community Technical College
61 Woodland St.
Hartford 06105-2354

Manchester Community Technical
 College
60 Bidwell St., P.O. Box 1045
Manchester 06040-1046

Middlesex Community Technical
 College
100 Training Hill Rd.
Middletown 06457

Norwalk Community Technical College
188 Richards Ave.
Norwalk 06854

Ridley Lowell Business and Technical
 Institute
470 Bank St.
New London 06320

Stone Academy
1315 Dixwell Ave.
Hamden 06514

DELAWARE

Delaware Technical and Community
 College, Owens Campus
P.O. Box 610
Georgetown 19947

Delaware Technical and Community
 College Stanton, Wilmington
400 Stanton-Christiana Rd.
Newark 19702

DISTRICT OF COLUMBIA

Sanz School
1511 K St. NW
Washington 20005

FLORIDA

Atlantic Vocational-Technical Center
4700 Coconut Creek Pkwy.
Coconut Creek 33063

Brevard Community College, Cocoa
 Campus
1519 Clearlake Rd.
Cocoa 32922

Broward Community College
225 East Las Olas Blvd.
Fort Lauderdale 33301

Career Training Institute
3326 Edgewater Dr.
Orlando 32804

Charlotte Vocational-Technical Center
18300 Toledo Blade Blvd.
Port Charlotte 33948-3399

Daytona Beach Community College
1200 Volusia Ave.
Daytona Beach 32114

Edison Community College
8099 College Pkwy. SW
Fort Myers 33906-6210

Florida Community College at
 Jacksonville
501 West State St.
Jacksonville 32202

Hillsborough Community College
P.O. Box 31127
Tampa 33631-3127

Indian River Community College
3209 Virginia Ave.
Fort Pierce 34981

Lake County Area Vocational-Technical
 Center
2001 Kurt St.
Eustis 32726

Lee County High Technical Center,
 Central
3800 Michigan Ave.
Fort Myers 33916

Lindsey Hopkins Technical Education
 Center
750 Northwest 20th St.
Miami 33127

Miami Lakes Technical Education
 Center
5780 Northwest 158th St.
Miami Lakes 33169

Orlando College
5421 Diplomat Circle
Orlando 32810

Pensacola Junior College
1000 College Blvd.
Pensacola 32504

Phillips Junior College
2401 North Harbor City Blvd.
Melbourne 32935

Pinellas Technical Education Center,
  Clearwater Campus
6100 154th Ave. N
Clearwater 34620

Prospect Hall School of Business
2620 Hollywood Blvd.
Hollywood 33020

Radford M Locklin Technical Center
5330 Berryhill Rd.
Milton 32570

Robert Morgan Vocational-Technical
  Center
18180 Southwest 122nd Ave.
Miami 33177

Saint Augustine Technical Center
2980 Collins Ave.
Saint Augustine 32095

Saint Petersburg Junior College
8580 66th St. N
Pinellas Park 34665

Santa Fe Community College
3000 Northwest 83rd St.
Gainesville 32606

Taylor Technical Institute
3233 Hwy. 19 S
Perry 32347

Valencia Community College
P.O. Box 3028
Orlando 32802

Washington-Holmes Area Vocational-
  Technical Center
757 Hoyt St.
Chipley 32428

GEORGIA

Albany Technical Institute
1021 Lowe Rd.
Albany 31708

Atlanta Area Technical School
1560 Stewart Ave. SW
Atlanta 30310

Augusta Technical Institute
3116 Deans Bridge Rd.
Augusta 30906

Carroll Technical Institute
997 South Hwy. 16
Carrollton 30117

Chattahoochee Technical Institute
980 South Cobb Dr.
Marietta 30060-3398

Clayton College and State University
5900 Lee St., P.O. Box 285
Morrow 30260

Columbus Technical Institute
928 45th St.
Columbus 31904-6572

Coosa Valley Technical Institute
785 Cedar Ave.
Rome 30161

Griffin Technical Institute
501 Varsity Rd.
Griffin 30223

Gwinnett Technical Institute
5150 Sugarloaf Pkwy.
Lawrenceville 30043

Lanier Technical Institute
P.O. Box 58
Oakwood 30566

Macon Technical Institute
3300 Macon Tech Dr.
Macon 31206

Moultrie Area Technical Institute
361 Industrial Dr.
Moultrie 31768

Pickens Technical Institute
100 Pickens Tech Dr.
Jasper 30143

South Georgia Technical Institute
1583 Souther Field Rd.
Americus 31709

Swainsboro Technical Institute
346 Kite Rd.
Swainsboro 30401

Thomas Technical Institute
15689 U.S. Hwy. 19 N
Thomasville 31792

Valdosta Technical Institute
4089 Valtech Rd.
Valdosta 31602-9796

Walker Technical Institute
265 Bicentennial Trail
Rock Spring 30739

West Georgia Technical Institute
303 Fort Dr.
La Grange 30240

HAWAII

Hawaii Pacific University
1164 Bishop St.
Honolulu 96813

Heald College School of Business
  Technology
1500 Kapiolani Blvd.
Honolulu 96816

Kapiolani Community College
4303 Diamond Head Rd.
Honolulu 96816

Leeward Community College
96-045 Ala Ike
Pearl City 96782

University of Hawaii at Hilo
200 West Kawili St.
Hilo 96720-4091

IDAHO

College of Southern Idaho
P.O. Box 1238
Twin Falls 83301

Idaho State University
741 South Seventh Ave.
Pocatello 83209

Shadow Mountain Business Careers
5200 Fairview
Boise 83706

ILLINOIS

Belleville Area College
2500 Carlyle Rd.
Belleville 62221

Black Hawk College
6600 34th Ave.
Moline 61265

Carl Sandburg College
2232 South Lake Storey Rd.
Galesburg 61401

City College of Chicago, Harold
  Washington
30 East Lake St.
Chicago 60601

City College of Chicago, Olive-Harvey
  College
10001 South Woodlawn Ave.
Chicago 60628

City College of Chicago, Richard J
  Daley College
7500 South Pulaski Rd.
Chicago 60652

City College of Chicago, Harry S.
  Truman College
1145 Wilson Ave.
Chicago 60640

City College of Chicago, Wilbur Wright
  College
4300 North Narragansett
Chicago 60634

College of Du Page
425 22nd St.
Glen Ellyn 60137-6599

College of Lake County
19351 West Washington St.
Grayslake 60030-1198

Computer Learning Center
200 South Michigan Ave.
Chicago 60604-2404

Danville Area Community College
2000 East Main St.
Danville 61832

Elgin Community College
1700 Spartan Dr.
Elgin 60123

Illinois Central College
One College Dr.
East Peoria 61635-0001

Illinois Eastern Community Colleges,
  Olney Central College
305 North West St.
Olney 62450

Illinois Valley Community College
815 North Orlando Smith Ave.
Oglesby 61348-9692

John A Logan College
700 Logan College Rd.
Carterville 62918

Joliet Junior College
1215 Houbolt Ave.
Joliet 60431

Kankakee Community College
P.O. Box 888
Kankakee 60901

Kaskaskia College
27210 College Rd.
Centralia 62801

Lake Land College
5001 Lake Land Blvd.
Mattoon 61938

Lewis and Clark Community College
5800 Godfrey Rd.
Godfrey 62035

Lincoln Land Community College
Shepherd Rd.
Springfield 62194-9256

McHenry County College
8900 U.S. Hwy. 14
Crystal Lake 60012

Midstate College
244 Southwest Jefferson
Peoria 61602

Moraine Valley Community College
10900 South 88th Ave.
Palos Hills 60465-0937

Morton College
3801 South Central Ave.
Cicero 60804

Oakton Community College
1600 East Golf Rd.
Des Plaines 60016

Parkland College
2400 West Bradley Ave.
Champaign 61821

Prairie State College
202 Halsted St.
Chicago Heights 60411

Richland Community College
One College Park
Decatur 62521

Robert Morris College
180 North Lasalle St.
Chicago 60601

Rock Valley College
3301 North Mulford Rd.
Rockford 61114

Rockford Business College
730 North Church St.
Rockford 61103

Saint Augustine College
1333 West Argyle
Chicago 60640

Sauk Valley Community College
173 Illinois Rte. 2
Dixon 61021

Southeastern Illinois College
3575 College Rd.
Harrisburg 62946

South Suburban College
15800 South State St.
South Holland 60473

Spoon River College
23235 North Co. 22
Canton 61520

Triton College
2000 Fifth Ave.
River Grove 60171

William Rainey Harper College
1200 West Algonquin Rd.
Palatine 60067-7398

INDIANA

Commonwealth Business College, Main
  Campus
4200 West 81st Ave.
Merrillville 46410

Indiana Business College
802 North Meridian St.
Indianapolis 46204

Indiana University, Purdue University
  at Fort Wayne
2101 Coliseum Blvd. E
Fort Wayne 46805

Indiana University, Purdue University
  at Indianapolis
355 North Lansing
Indianapolis 46202

Indiana Vocational-Technical College,
  Columbus
4475 Central Ave.
Columbus 47203

Ivy Tech State College, Central Indiana
One West 26th St.
Indianapolis 46206-1763

Ivy Tech State College, East Central
4301 South Cowan Rd., P.O. Box 3100
Muncie 47302

Ivy Tech State College, Kokomo
1815 East Morgan St.
Kokomo 46901

Ivy Tech State College, North Central
1534 West Sample St.
South Bend 46619

Ivy Tech State College, Northeast
3800 North Anthony Blvd.
Fort Wayne 46805

Ivy Tech State College, Northwest
1440 East 35th Ave.
Gary 46409

Ivy Tech State College, Southeast
590 Ivy Tech Dr., P.O. Box 209
Madison 47250

Ivy Tech State College, Wabash Valley
7999 U.S. Hwy. 41
Terre Haute 47802-4898

Ivy Tech State College, Whitewater
P.O. Box 1145
Richmond 47374

Purdue University, Calumet Campus
2233 171st St.
Hammond 46323

IOWA

Des Moines Community College
2006 Ankeny Blvd.
Ankeny 50021

Hamilton College, Mason City Branch
100 First St. NW
Mason City 50401

Hawkeye Community College
1501 East Orange Rd.
Waterloo 50704

Kirkwood Community College
P.O. Box 2068
Cedar Rapids 52406

Southeastern Community College
1015 South Gear Ave., P.O. Drawer F
West Burlington 52655-0605

Western Iowa Technical Community
College
4647 Stone Ave., P.O. Box 5199
Sioux City 51102-5199

KANSAS

Colby Community College
1255 South Range
Colby 67701

Dodge City Community College
2501 North 14th Ave.
Dodge City 67801

Flint Hills Technical College
3301 West 18th St.
Emporia 66801

Johnson County Community College
12345 College Blvd.
Overland Park 66210-1299

Kansas City Area Vocational-Technical
School
2220 North 59th St.
Kansas City 66104

Kaw Area Technical School
5724 Huntoon
Topeka 66604

North Central Kansas Technical College
Hwy. 24, P.O. Box 507
Beloit 67420

Northwest Kansas Area Vocational-
Technical School
P.O. Box 668
Goodland 67735

KENTUCKY

Ashland Community College
1400 College Dr.
Ashland 41101

Elizabethtown Community College
College Street Rd.
Elizabethtown 42701

Jefferson Community College
109 East Broadway
Louisville 40202

Kentucky College of Business
628 East Main St.
Lexington 40508

Kentucky Tech, Hazard Regional
Technology Center
101 Tech Dr.
Hazard 41701

Kentucky Tech, Jefferson State
Vocational-Technical School
727 West Chestnut St.
Louisville 40203-2036

Lexington Community College
Cooper Dr.
Lexington 40506

Northern Kentucky State Vocational-
Technical School
1025 Amsterdam Rd.
Covington 41011

Owensboro Junior College of Business
1515 East 18th St.
P.O. Box 1350
Owensboro 42302

Paducah Community College
P.O. Box 7380
Paducah 42002-7380

Sullivan College, Louisville
3101 Bardstown Rd.
Louisville 40205

University of Louisville
2301 South Third St.
Louisville 40292-0001

Western Kentucky University
One Big Red Way
Bowling Green 42101-3576

LOUISIANA

Ayers Institute, Inc.
2924 Knight St., Ste. 318
Shreveport 71105

Baton Rouge School of Computers
9255 Interline Dr.
Baton Rouge 70809

Delgado Community College
501 City Park Ave.
New Orleans 70119

Louisiana Technical College
1710 Warren St.
Winnsboro 71295

Louisiana Technical College, Acadian
Campus
1933 West Hutchinson Ave.
Crowley 70526

Louisiana Technical College, Baton
Rouge Campus
3250 North Acadian Hwy. E
Baton Rouge 70805

Louisiana Technical College, Jefferson
Davis Campus
P.O. Box 1327
Jennings 70546

Louisiana Technical College, Jefferson
Campus
5200 Blair Dr.
Metairie 70001

Louisiana Technical College, Oakdale
Campus
Old Pelican Hwy., P.O. Drawer M
Oakdale 71463

Louisiana Technical College,
Shreveport-Bossier Campus
2010 North Market St.
Shreveport 71137-8527

Louisiana Technical College, Slidell
Campus
1000 Canulette Rd.
Slidell 70459

Louisiana Technical College, South
Louisiana Campus
201 St. Charles St.
P.O. Box 5033
Houma 70361-5033

Louisiana Technical College, Sowela
Campus
3820 J. Bennett Johnston Ave.
Lake Charles 70615

Louisiana Technical College, Sullivan
Campus
1710 Sullivan Dr.
Bogalusa 70427

Louisiana Technical College, T H Harris
Campus
337 East South St., P.O. Box 713
Opelousas 70570

MAINE

Andover College
901 Washington Ave.
Portland 04103

Northern Maine Technical College
33 Edgemont Dr.
Presque Isle 04769

MARYLAND

Abbie Business Institute
5310 Spectrum Dr.
Frederick 21703

Allegany Community College
12401 Willowbrook Rd. SE
Cumberland 21502

Anne Arundel Community College
101 College Pkwy.
Arnold 21012

Baltimore City Community College
2901 Liberty Heights Ave.
Baltimore 21215

Catonsville Community College
800 South Rolling Rd.
Catonsville 21228

Charles County Community College
8730 Mitchell Rd.
La Plata 20646-0910

Chesapeake College
P.O. Box 8
Wye Mills 21679-0008

Dundalk Community College
7200 Sollers Point Rd.
Dundalk 21222

Essex Community College
7201 Rossville Blvd.
Baltimore 21237

Frederick Community College
7932 Opossumtown Pike
Frederick 21702

Hagerstown Business College
18618 Crestwood Dr.
Hagerstown 21742

Hagerstown Junior College
11400 Robinwood Dr.
Hagerstown 21742-6590

Harford Community College
401 Thomas Run Rd.
Bel Air 21015

Howard Community College
10901 Little Patuxent Pkwy.
Columbia 21044

Montgomery College of Germantown
20200 Observation Dr.
Germantown 20874

Montgomery College of Rockville
51 Mannakee St.
Rockville 20850

Montgomery College of Takoma Park
Takoma Ave. and Fenton St.
Takoma Park 20912

Prince Georges Community College
301 Largo Rd.
Largo 20774-2199

Villa Julie College
Green Spring Valley Rd.
Stevenson 21153

MASSACHUSETTS

Bunker Hill Community College
250 New Rutherford Ave.
Boston 02129

Fisher College
118 Beacon St.
Boston 02116

Greenfield Community College
One College Dr.
Greenfield 01301-9739

Holyoke Community College
303 Homestead Ave.
Holyoke 01040

Katharine Gibbs School
126 Newbury
Boston 02116

North Shore Community College
One Ferncroft Rd.
Danvers 01923

Northeastern University
360 Huntington Ave.
Boston 02115

Northern Essex Community College
Elliott Way
Haverhill 01830-2399

Quinsigamond Community College
670 West Boylston St.
Worcester 01606

Springfield Technical Community
College
One Armory Square
Springfield 01105

MICHIGAN

Baker College of Muskegon
903 Marquette Ave.
Muskegon 49442

Davenport College, Kalamazoo Branch
4123 West Main St.
Kalamazoo 49006-2791

Delta College
University Center 48710

Detroit College of Business
3488 North Jennings
Flint 48504-1700

Grand Rapids Community College
143 Bostwick Ave. NE
Grand Rapids 49503-3295

Kalamazoo Valley Community College
6767 West O Ave.
Kalamazoo 49009

Lansing Community College
419 North Capitol Ave.
Lansing 48901-7210

Lansing Computer Institute
501 North Marshall St., Ste. 101
Lansing 48912

Mott Community College
1401 East Court St.
Flint 48503

Muskegon Community College
221 South Quarterline Rd.
Muskegon 49442

Northwestern Michigan College
1701 East Front St.
Traverse City 49684

Oakland Community College
2480 Opdyke Rd.
Bloomfield Hills 48304-2266

Payne-Pulliam School of Trade and
Commerce, Inc.
2345 Cass Ave.
Detroit 48201-3305

MINNESOTA

Brown Institute, Ltd.
2225 East Lake St.
Minneapolis 55407

Globe College of Business
175 Fifth St. E, Ste. 201, P.O. Box 60
Saint Paul 55101-2901

Lake Superior College
2101 Trinity Rd.
Duluth 55811

Saint Paul Technical College
235 Marshall Ave.
Saint Paul 55102

South Central Technical College,
   Mankato
1920 Lee Blvd.
North Mankato 56003

MISSISSIPPI

Copiah-Lincoln Community College
P.O. Box 457
Wesson 39191

East Central Community College
Decatur 39327

Hinds Community College, Raymond
   Campus
Raymond 39154

Itawamba Community College
602 West Hill St.
Fulton 38843

Jones County Junior College
900 South Court St.
Ellisville 39437

Meridian Community College
910 Hwy. 19 N
Meridian 39307

Mississippi Delta Community College
P.O. Box 668
Moorhead 38761

Mississippi Gulf Coast Community
   College
Central Office
P.O. Box 67
Perkinston 39573

Northeast Mississippi Community
   College
Cunningham Blvd.
Booneville 38829

Northwest Mississippi Community
   College
510 North Panola, Hwy. 51 N
Senatobia 38668

Pearl River Community College
Station A
Poplarville 39470

MISSOURI

East Central College
P.O. Box 529
Union 63084

Jefferson College
1000 Viking Dr.
Hillsboro 63050

Longview Community College
500 Longview Rd.
Lees Summit 64081

Maple Woods Community College
2601 Northeast Barry Rd.
Kansas City 64156

Metro Business College of Cape
   Girardeau
1732 North Kings Hwy.
Cape Girardeau 63701

Moberly Area Community College
101 College Ave.
Moberly 65270

Penn Valley Community College
3201 Southwest Trafficway
Kansas City 64111

Saint Louis Community College, Forest
   Park
5600 Oakland Ave.
Saint Louis 63110

Sanford-Brown College
12006 Manchester Rd.
Des Peres 63131

TAD Technical Institute
7910 Troost Ave.
Kansas City 64131

MONTANA

May Technical College
1306 Central Ave.
Billings 59103

Montana State University College of
   Technology, Billings
3803 Central Ave.
Billings 59102

NEBRASKA

Central Community College Area
P.O. Box 4903
Grand Island 68802

Northeast Community College
801 East Benjamin, P.O. Box 469
Norfolk 68702-0469

NEW HAMPSHIRE

Castle College
23 Searles Rd.
Windham 03087-1200

New Hampshire College
2500 North River Rd.
Manchester 03106

NEW JERSEY

Atlantic Community College
5100 Black Horse Pike
Mays Landing 08330-2699

Bergen Community College
400 Paramus Rd.
Paramus 07652

Berkeley College of Business
44 Rifle Camp Rd.
West Paterson 07424

Burlington County College
Rte. 530
Pemberton 08068

Business Training Institute
Four Forest Ave.
Paramus 07652

Camden County College
P.O. Box 200
Blackwood 08012

The Chubb Institute
Eight Sylvan Way
Parsippany 07054

County College of Morris
214 Center Grove Rd.
Randolph 07869

Dover Business College
15 East Blackwell St.
Dover 07801

Drake College of Business
125 Broad St.
Elizabeth 07201

Essex County College
303 University Ave.
Newark 07102

Gloucester County College
1400 Tanyard Rd.
P.O. Box 203
Sewell 08080

Hudson County Community College
25 Journal Square
Jersey City 07306

Mercer County Community College
1200 Old Trenton Rd.
Trenton 08690

Passaic County Community College
One College Blvd.
Paterson 07505-1179

Raritan Valley Community College
P.O. Box 3300, Lamington Rd.
Somerville 08876

Stuart School of Business
   Administration
2400 Belmar Blvd.
Wall 07719

Union County College
1033 Springfield Ave.
Cranford 07016

NEW MEXICO

Albuquerque Technical-Vocational
   Institute
525 Buena Vista SE
Albuquerque 87106

Southwestern Indian Polytechnic
   Institute
9169 Coors Rd. NW
Albuquerque 87120

NEW YORK

Adirondack Community College
Bay Rd.
Queensbury 12804

Bryant and Stratton Business Institute,
   Rochester
82 Saint Paul St.
Rochester 14604

Bryant and Stratton Business Institute,
   Syracuse
953 James St.
Syracuse 13203

CUNY Borough of Manhattan
   Community College
199 Chambers St.
New York 10007

CUNY Hostos Community College
500 Grand Concourse
Bronx 10451

CUNY Kingsborough Community
   College
2001 Oriental Blvd.
Brooklyn 11235

CUNY New York City Technical College
300 Jay St.
Brooklyn 11201

CUNY Queensborough Community
   College
56th Ave. & Springfield Blvd.
New York 11364

FEGS Trades and Business School
17 Battery Place
New York 10004

Herkimer County Community College
Reservoir Rd.
Herkimer 13350-1598

Hunter Business School
3601 Hempstead Tpke.
Levittown 11756

Long Island Business Institute
6500 Jericho Tpke.
Commack 11725

Monroe College, Main Campus
Monroe College Way
Bronx 10468

Nassau Community College
One Education Dr.
Garden City 11530

New York University
70 Washington Square S
New York 10012

Niagara County Community College
3111 Saunders Settlement Rd.
Sanborn 14132

Onondaga Community College
4941 Onondaga Rd.
Syracuse 13215

Ridley-Lowell School of Business
116 Front St.
Binghamton 13905

Rochester Business Institute
1850 East Ridge Rd.
Irondequoit 14622

Rochester Institute of Technology
One Lomb Memorial Dr.
Rochester 14623-5603

Suburban Technical School
175 Fulton Ave.
Hempstead 11550

SUNY College of Technology at
   Farmingdale
Melville Rd.
Farmingdale 11735-1021

Utica School of Commerce
201 Bleecker St.
Utica 13501

NORTH CAROLINA

Asheville Buncombe Technical
   Community College
340 Victoria Rd.
Asheville 28801

Beaufort County Community College
P.O. Box 1069
Washington 27889

Brunswick Community College
P.O. Box 30
Supply 28462

Caldwell Community College and
   Technical Institute
P.O. Box 600
Lenoir 28645

Carteret Community College
3505 Arendell St.
Morehead City 28557

Catawba Valley Community College
2550 Hwy. 70 SE
Hickory 28602-0699

Central Carolina Community College
1105 Kelly Dr.
Sanford 27330

Central Piedmont Community College
P.O. Box 35009
Charlotte 28235-5009

Cleveland Community College
137 South Post Rd.
Shelby 28152

Coastal Carolina Community College
444 Western Blvd.
Jacksonville 28546-6877

Craven Community College
800 College Ct.
New Bern 28562

Davidson County Community College
297 Davidson Community College Way
Lexington 27292

Durham Technical Community College
1637 Lawson St.
Durham 27703

Edgecombe Community College
2009 West Wilson St.
Tarboro 27886

Fayetteville Technical Community
   College
2201 Hull Rd.
Fayetteville 28303-0236

Forsyth Technical Community College
2100 Silas Creek Pkwy.
Winston-Salem 27103

Gaston College
201 Hwy. 321 S
Dallas 28034

Guilford Technical Community College
P.O. Box 309
Jamestown 27282

Haywood Community College
Freedlander Dr.
Clyde 28721

Isothermal Community College
P.O. Box 804
Spindale 28160

James Sprunt Community College
P.O. Box 398
Kenansville 28349

Martin Community College
1161 Kehukee Park Rd.
Williamston 27892-9988

Mitchell Community College
500 West Broad
Statesville 28677

Nash Community College
P.O. Box 7488
Rocky Mount 27804

Piedmont Community College
P.O. Box 1197
Roxboro 27573

Pitt Community College
Hwy. 11 S P.O. Drawer 7007
Greenville 27835-7007

Randolph Community College
629 Industrial Park Ave.
Asheboro 27204

Richmond Community College
P.O. Box 1189
Hamlet 28345

Robeson Community College
P.O. Box 1420
Lumberton 28359

Rockingham Community College
P.O. Box 38, Hwy. 65 West County Home Rd.
Wentworth 27375-0038

Rowan-Cabarrus Community College
P.O. Box 1595
Salisbury 28145-1595

Sampson Community College
P.O. Box 318
Clinton 28328

Sandhills Community College
2200 Airport Rd.
Pinehurst 28374

Stanly Community College
141 College Dr.
Albemarle 28001

Surry Community College
P.O. Box 304
Dobson 27017-0304

Tri-County Community College
2300 Hwy. 64 E
Murphy 28906

Vance-Granville Community College
State Rd. 1126, P.O. Box 917
Henderson 27536

Wake Technical Community College
9101 Fayetteville Rd.
Raleigh 27603-5696

Western Piedmont Community College
1001 Burkemont Ave.
Morganton 28655-9978

Wilson Technical Community College
902 Herring Ave.
Wilson 27893

NORTH DAKOTA

Interstate Business College
520 East Main Ave.
Bismarck 58501

North Dakota State College of Science
800 North Sixth St.
Wahpeton 58076

University of North Dakota, Lake Region
1801 North College Dr.
Devils Lake 58301

OHIO

Cincinnati State Technical and Community College
3520 Central Pkwy.
Cincinnati 45223

Davis College
4747 Monroe St.
Toledo 43623

Hocking Technical College
3301 Hocking Pkwy.
Nelsonville 45764

Jefferson Community College
4000 Sunset Blvd.
Steubenville 43952-3598

Kent State University, Tuscarawas Regional Campus
University Dr. NE
New Philadelphia 44663

Lakeland Community College
7700 Clocktower Dr.
Kirkland 44094-5198

Lima Technical College
4240 Campus Dr.
Lima 45804

Southeastern Business College, Lorain
1907 North Ridge Rd.
Lorain 44055

Southeastern Business College
4020 Milan Rd.
Sandusky 44870-5871

Marion Technical College
1467 Mount Vernon Ave.
Marion 43302-5694

Miami-Jacobs College
400 East Second St.
Dayton 45401

Miami University, Oxford Campus
Oxford 45056

North Central Technical College
2441 Kenwood Circle
P.O. Box 698
Mansfield 44901

Northwestern College
1441 North Cable Rd.
Lima 45805

Ohio University, Lancaster Branch
1570 Granville Pike
Lancaster 43130

Ohio University, Main Campus
Athens 45701

Owens Community College
30335 Oregon Rd.
Toledo 43699-1947

Owens Community College, Findlay Campus
300 Davis St.
Findlay 45840

Sawyer College of Business, West
13027 Lorain Ave.
Cleveland 44111

Shawnee State University
940 Second St.
Portsmouth 45662

Southern State Community College
100 Hobart Dr.
Hillsboro 45133

University of Akron, Main Campus
302 Buchtel Common
Akron 44325-4702

University of Akron, Wayne College
10470 Smucker Rd.
Orrville 44667

University of Cincinnati, Main Campus
P.O. Box 210127
Cincinnati 45221-0127

University of Cincinnati, Raymond Walters College
9555 Plainfield Rd.
Blue Ash 45236

University of Toledo
2801 West Bancroft
Toledo 43606

Upper Valley Joint Vocational School
8811 Career Dr.
Piqua 45356

OKLAHOMA

Cameron University
2800 Gore Blvd.
Lawton 73505

Connors State College
Rte. 1
P.O. Box 1000
Warner 74469

Oklahoma City Community College
7777 South May Ave.
Oklahoma City 73159

Oklahoma State University, Oklahoma City
900 North Portland
Oklahoma City 73107

Oklahoma State University Okmulgee
1801 East Fourth St.
Okmulgee 74447-3901

Rose State College
6420 Southeast 15th
Midwest City 73110

Tulsa Community College
6111 East Skelly Dr.
Tulsa 74135

OREGON

Blue Mountain Community College
P.O. Box 100
Pendleton 97801

Chemeketa Community College
4000 Lancaster Dr. NE
Salem 97305

Lane Community College
4000 East 30th Ave.
Eugene 97405

Linn-Benton Community College
6500 Southwest Pacific Blvd.
Albany 97321

Pioneer Pacific College
25195 Southwest Parkway Ave.
Wilsonville 97070

Portland Community College
P.O. Box 19000
Portland 97280-0990

PENNSYLVANIA

Academy of Medical Arts and Business
2301 Academy Dr.
Harrisburg 17112

Bucks County Community College
Swamp Rd.
Newtown 18940

Community College of Allegheny County
800 Allegheny Ave.
Pittsburgh 15233-1895

Community College of Beaver County
One Campus Dr.
Monaca 15061

Community College of Philadelphia
1700 Spring Garden St.
Philadelphia 19130

Delaware County Community College
901 South Media Line Rd.
Media 19063-1094

Harrisburg Area Community College, Harrisburg Campus
One Hacc Dr.
Harrisburg 17110

Information Computer Systems Institute
2201 Hangar Place
Allentown 18103

Lackawanna Junior College
501 Vine St.
Scranton 18509

Luzerne County Community College
1333 South Prospect St.
Nanticoke 18634

Montgomery County Community College
340 Dekalb Pike
Blue Bell 19422

Northwest Institute of Research
652 West 17th St.
Erie 16502

Peirce College
1420 Pine St.
Philadelphia 19102

Pennsylvania State University, Main Campus
201 Old Main
University Park 16802

Thompson Institute
3440 Market St.
Philadelphia 19104

RHODE ISLAND

Nasson Institute
286 Main St.
Pawtucket 02860

Ocean State Business Institute
140 Point Judith Rd., Unit 3A
Narragansett 02882

Sawyer School
101 Main St.
Pawtucket 02860

SOUTH CAROLINA

Aiken Technical College
P.O. Drawer 696
Aiken 29802

Central Carolina Technical College
506 North Guignard Dr.
Sumter 29150

Denmark Technical College
P.O. Box 327, Solomon Blatt Blvd.
Denmark 29042

Florence-Darlington Technical College
P.O. Box 100548
Florence 29501-0548

Greenville Technical College
Station B
P.O. Box 5616
Greenville 29606-5616

Horry-Georgetown Technical College
P.O. Box 1966
Conway 29526

Midlands Technical College
P.O. Box 2408
Columbia 29202

Orangeburg-Calhoun Technical College
3250 Saint Matthew's Rd.
Orangeburg 29115

Piedmont Technical College
P.O. Drawer 1467
Greenwood 29648

Spartanburg Technical College
Hwy. I-85, P.O. Drawer 4386
Spartanburg 29305

Technical College of the Low Country
921 Ribaut Rd.
Beaufort 29902

Tri-County Technical College
P.O. Box 587
Pendleton 29670

Trident Technical College
P.O. Box 118067
Charleston 29423-8067

York Technical College
452 South Anderson Rd.
Rock Hill 29730

TENNESSEE

Chattanooga State Technical Community College
4501 Amnicola Hwy.
Chattanooga 37406

Draughons College
3200 Elvis Presley Blvd.
Memphis 38116

Jackson State Community College
2046 North Pkwy.
Jackson 38301

Morristown School of Business
400 North Henry St.
Morristown 37814

Motlow State Community College
P.O. Box 88100, Ledford Mill Rd.
Tullahoma 37388-8100

Nashville State Technical Institute
120 White Bridge Rd.
Nashville 37209

Northeast State Technical Community
College
P.O. Box 246
Blountville 37617

State Technical Institute at Memphis
5983 Macon Cove
Memphis 38134

Tennessee Technology Center at
Jackson
2468 Westover Rd.
Jackson 38301

Tennessee Technology Center at
Knoxville
1100 Liberty St.
Knoxville 37919

Tennessee Technology Center at
McKenzie
16940 Highland Dr. N, P.O. Box 427
McKenzie 38201

TEXAS

Bradford School of Business
4669 Southwest Fwy., Ste. 300
Houston 77027

Brazosport College
500 College Dr.
Lake Jackson 77566

College of the Mainland
1200 Amburn Rd.
Texas City 77591

El Paso Community College
P.O. Box 20500
El Paso 79998

Executive Secretarial School of Texas
4849 Greenville Ave., Ste. 200
Dallas 75206

Grayson County College
6101 Grayson Dr.
Denison 75020

International Business College
4121 Montana Ave.
El Paso 79903

International Business College, Bond
Office
1030 North Zaragosa Rd.
El Paso 79907

Lamar University, Beaumont
P.O. Box 10001 4400 Mlk
Beaumont 77710

Lamar University, Orange
410 Front St.
Orange 77630-5899

Lamar University, Port Arthur
1500 Proctor St.
Port Arthur 77640

Laredo Community College
West End Washington St.
Laredo 78040

Lee College
200 Lee Dr.
Baytown 77520-4703

McLennan Community College
1400 College Dr.
Waco 76708

Microcomputer Technology Institute
7277 Regency Square Blvd.
Houston 77036

North Harris Montgomery Community
College District
250 North Sam Houston Pkwy. E, Ste.
300
Houston 77060

Ranger College
College Circle
Ranger 76470

Richland College
12800 Abrams Rd.
Dallas 75243-2199

San Antonio College
1300 San Pedro Ave.
San Antonio 78284

San Jacinto College, South Campus
13735 Beamer Rd.
Houston 77089-6009

South Texas Vocational-Technical
Institute
2255 North Coria
Brownsville 78520

South Texas Vocational-Technical
Institute
2419 East Haggar Ave.
P.O. Box 629
Weslaco 78596

Texas State Technical College,
Harlingen Campus
2424 Boxwood
Harlingen 78550-3697

Texas State Technical College,
Sweetwater Campus
300 College Dr.
Sweetwater 79556

Trinity Valley Community College
500 South Prairieville
Athens 75751

UTAH

Bridgerland Applied Technology Center
1301 North 600 West
Logan 84321

Certified Careers Institute
1455 West 2200 S, Ste. 200
Salt Lake City 84119

Davis Applied Technology Center
550 East 300 S
Kaysville 84037

Latter Day Saints Business College
411 East South Temple
Salt Lake City 84111-1392

Salt Lake Community College
P.O. Box 30808
Salt Lake City 84130

Sevier Valley Applied Technology
Center
800 West 200 S
Richfield 84701

VERMONT

Champlain College
163 South Willard St.
Burlington 05401

VIRGINIA

Braxton School of Business
4917 Augusta Ave.
Richmond 23230-3601

Central Virginia Community College
3506 Wards Rd.
Lynchburg 24502

Computer Learning Center
6295 Edsall Rd., Ste. 210
Alexandria 22312

Danville Community College
1008 South Main St.
Danville 24541

Germanna Community College
2130 Germanna Hwy.
Locust Grove 24501

J Sargeant Reynolds Community
College
P.O. Box 85622
Richmond 23285-5622

Kee Business College
803 Diligence Dr.
Newport News 23606

New River Community College
P.O. Drawer 1127
Dublin 24084-1127

Northern Virginia Community College
4001 Wakefield Chapel Rd.
Annandale 22003

Patrick Henry Community College
P.O. Box 5311
Martinsville 24115-5311

Phillips Business College
1912 Memorial Ave.
Lynchburg 24505-0169

Southside Virginia Community College
109 Campus Dr.
Alberta 23821

Southwest Virginia Community College
P.O. Box SVCC
Richlands 24641

Thomas Nelson Community College
P.O. Box 9407
Hampton 23670

Virginia Highlands Community College
P.O. Box 828
Abingdon 24210

Virginia Western Community College
3095 Colonial Ave.
Roanoke 24015

WASHINGTON

Bates Technical College
1101 South Yakima Ave.
Tacoma 98405

Bellevue Community College
3000 Landerholm Circle SE
Bellevue 98007-6484

Bellingham Technical College
3028 Lindbergh Ave.
Bellingham 98225

Columbia Basin College
2600 North 20th Ave.
Pasco 99301

Edmonds Community College
20000 68th Ave. W
Lynnwood 98036

ITT Technical Institute
12720 Gateway Dr., Ste. 100
Seattle 98168

Lake Washington Technical College
11605 132nd Ave. NE
Kirkland 98034

Lower Columbia College
P.O. Box 3010
Longview 98632

Olympic College
1600 Chester Ave.
Bremerton 98310-1699

Seattle Community College, North
Campus
9600 College Way N
Seattle 98103

Skagit Valley College
2405 College Way
Mount Vernon 98273

South Puget Sound Community College
2011 Mottman Rd. SW
Olympia 98512

Spokane Community College
North 1810 Greene Ave.
Spokane 99207

Yakima Valley Community College
P.O. Box 1647
Yakima 98907

WEST VIRGINIA

Cabell County Vocational-Technical
Center
1035 Norway Ave.
Huntington 25705

Southern West Virginia Community
and Technical College
P.O. Box 2900
Mt. Gay 25637

Valley Training Centers
330 Harper Park Dr.
Beckley 25801

West Virginia Northern Community
College
1704 Market St.
Wheeling 26003

WISCONSIN

Gateway Technical College
3520 30th Ave.
Kenosha 53144-1690

Madison Area Technical College
3550 Anderson St.
Madison 53704

MBTI Business Training Institute
606 West Wisconsin Ave.
Milwaukee 53203

Mid-State Technical College
500 32nd St. N
Wisconsin Rapids 54494

Milwaukee Area Technical College
700 West State St.
Milwaukee 53233-1443

Moraine Park Technical College
235 North National Ave., P.O. Box 1940
Fond Du Lac 54936-1940

Nicolet Area Technical College
Hwy. G S
Rhinelander 54501

North Central Technical College
1000 Campus Dr.
Wausau 54401-1899

Northeast Wisconsin Technical College
2740 West Mason St.
P.O. Box 19042
Green Bay 54307-9042

Southwest Wisconsin Technical College
1800 Bronson Blvd.
Fennimore 53809

Waukesha County Technical College
800 Main St.
Pewaukee 53072

Western Wisconsin Technical College
304 North Sixth St.
P.O. Box 908
La Crosse 54602-0908

Wisconsin Indianhead Technical
College
505 Pine Ridge Dr., P.O. Box 10B
Shell Lake 54871

WYOMING

Western Wyoming Community College
2500 College Dr.
Rock Springs 82902

Office Management and Supervision

ALABAMA

Bessemer State Technical College
1100 9th Ave.
Bessemer 35021

Bevill State Community College
100 State St.
Sumiton 35148

Bishop State Community College
351 North Broad St.
Mobile 36608

Chattahoochee Valley Community
College
2602 College Dr.
Phenix City 36869

Community College of the Air Force
130 West Maxwell Blvd.
Montgomery 36112-6613

Enterprise State Junior College
600 Plaza Dr.
Enterprise 36330

Gadsden Business College
750 Forrest Ave.
Gadsden 35901

Gadsden State Community College
1001 George Wallace Dr.
Gadsden 35902-0227

George C Wallace State Community
College
3000 Earl Goodwin Pkwy.
Selma 36702

George C Wallace State Community
College, Hanceville
801 Main St. NW
Hanceville 35077-2000

Jefferson State Community College
2601 Carson Rd.
Birmingham 35215-3098

John C Calhoun State Community
College
Hwy. 31 North
Decatur 35602

John M Patterson State Technical
College
3920 Troy Hwy.
Montgomery 36116

Lawson State Community College
3060 Wilson Rd. SW
Birmingham 35221

Shelton State Community College
9500 Old Greensboro Rd.
Tuscaloosa 35405

Northwest Shoals Community College
800 George Wallace Blvd.
Muscle Shoals 35662

Snead State Community College
220 North Walnut St.
Boaz 35957-0734

Troy State University in Montgomery
231 Montgomery St.
Montgomery 36103-4419

ALASKA

Alaska Computer Institute of
Technology
701 East Tudor Rd.
Anchorage 99503

University of Alaska, Anchorage
3211 Providence Dr.
Anchorage 99508

ARIZONA

Arizona Institute of Business and
Technology
6049 North 43rd Ave.
Phoenix 85019

Arizona Western College
P.O. Box 929
Yuma 85366

Central Arizona College
8470 North Overfield Rd.
Coolidge 85228-9778

Chaparral Career College
4585 East Speedway Blvd., Ste. 204
Tucson 85712

Cochise College
4190 West Hwy. 80
Douglas 85607-9724

Eastern Arizona College
Church St.
Thatcher 85552-0769

Gateway Community College
108 North 40th St.
Phoenix 85034

Glendale Community College
6000 West Olive Ave.
Glendale 85302

Lamson Junior College
1126 North Scottsdale Rd., Ste. 17
Tempe 85281-1700

Mesa Community College
1833 West Southern Ave.
Mesa 85202

Northland Pioneer College
103 First Ave.
Holbrook 86025

Phoenix College
1202 West Thomas Rd.
Phoenix 85013

Pima Community College
2202 West Anklam Rd.
Tucson 85709-0001

Rio Salado Community College
2323 West 14th St.
Tempe 85281

Scottsdale Community College
9000 East Chaparral Rd.
Scottsdale 85253

South Mountain Community College
7050 South 24th St.
Phoenix 85040

Yavapai College
1100 East Sheldon St.
Prescott 86301

ARKANSAS

Arkansas State University, Main
Campus
P.O. Box 790
State University 72467

Arkansas Valley Technical Institute
Hwy. 23 N, P.O. Box 506
Ozark 72949

Cossatot Technical College
183 Hwy. 399
De Queen 71832

Crowley's Ridge Technical School
140 Crowley's Ridge Rd.
Forrest City 72336-0925

East Arkansas Community College
1700 Newcastle Rd.
Forrest City 72335

Garland County Community College
101 College Dr.
Hot Springs 71913

Mississippi County Community College
P.O. Box 1109
Blytheville 72316-1109

Northwest Technical Institute
709 South Old Misouri Rd.
Springdale 72764

Ouachita Technical College
One College Circle
Malvern 72104

Southern Arkansas University
Technical
SAU Technical Station
Camden 71701

CALIFORNIA

Allan Hancock College
800 South College Dr.
Santa Maria 93454

American River College
4700 College Oak Dr.
Sacramento 95841

Antelope Valley College
3041 West Ave. K
Lancaster 93536

Bakersfield College
1801 Panorama Dr.
Bakersfield 93305-1299

Bryman College, A Corinthian School
3505 North Hart Ave.
Rosemead 91770

Butte College
3536 Butte Campus Dr.
Oroville 95965

Cabrillo College
6500 Soquel Dr.
Aptos 95003

Canada College
4200 Farm Hill Blvd.
Redwood City 94061

Center for Employment Training,
Riverside
1099 West Lacadena Dr.
Riverside 92501

Center for Employment Training, San
Jose-Vine
701 Vine St.
San Jose 95110

Cerritos College
11110 Alondra Blvd.
Norwalk 90650

Chabot College
25555 Hesperian Blvd.
Hayward 94545

Chaffey Community College
5885 Haven Ave.
Rancho Cucamonga 91737-3002

Citrus College
1000 West Foothill Blvd.
Glendora 91741-1899

City College of San Francisco
50 Phelan Ave.
San Francisco 94112

Clovis Adult Education
1452 David E. Cook Way
Clovis 93611

Coastline Community College
11460 Warner Ave.
Fountain Valley 92708

College of Alameda
555 Atlantic Ave.
Alameda 94501

College of Marin
835 College Ave.
Kentfield 94904

College of San Mateo
1700 West Hillsdale Blvd.
San Mateo 94402

College of the Canyons
26455 North Rockwell Canyon Rd.
Santa Clarita 91355

College of the Desert
43-500 Monterey St.
Palm Desert 92260

College of the Sequoias
915 South Mooney Blvd.
Visalia 93277

College of the Siskiyous
800 College Ave.
Weed 96094-2899

Computer Learning Center
3580 Wilshire Blvd., Ste. 100
Los Angeles 90010

Contra Costa College
2600 Mission Bell Dr.
San Pablo 94806

Cosumnes River College
8401 Center Pkwy.
Sacramento 95823-5799

Crafton Hills College
11711 Sand Canyon Rd.
Yucaipa 92399-1799

Cuesta College
P.O. Box 8106
San Luis Obispo 93403-8106

Cuyamaca College
900 Rancho San Diego Pkwy.
El Cajon 92019

De Anza College
21250 Stevens Creek Blvd.
Cupertino 95014

East Los Angeles College
1301 Brooklyn Ave.
Monterey Park 91754

EBM Business Institute
6024 San Juan Ave., Ste. C
Citrus Heights 95610

El Camino College
16007 Crenshaw Blvd.
Torrance 90506

Evergreen Valley College
3095 Yerba Buena Rd.
San Jose 95135-1598

Feather River Community College
District
570 Golden Eagle Ave.
Quincy 95971-6023

Foothill-Deanza Community College,
District Office
12345 El Monte Rd.
Los Altos Hills 94022-4599

Fresno City College
1101 East University Ave.
Fresno 93741

Fullerton College
321 East Chapman Ave.
Fullerton 92632-2095

Gavilan College
5055 Santa Teresa Blvd.
Gilroy 95020

Glendale Community College
1500 North Verdugo Rd.
Glendale 91208-2894

Golden West College
15744 Golden W
Huntington Beach 92647

Grossmont College
8800 Grossmont College Dr.
El Cajon 92020

Hartnell College
156 Homestead Ave.
Salinas 93901

Imperial Valley College
P.O. Box 158
Imperial 92251-0158

Institute of Computer Technology
3200 Wilshire Blvd.
Los Angeles 90010

Kings River Community College
995 North Reed
Reedley 93654

Lake Tahoe Community College
One College Dr.
South Lake Tahoe 96150

Laney College
900 Fallon St.
Oakland 94607

Long Beach City College
4901 East Carson St.
Long Beach 90808

Los Angeles City College
855 North Vermont Ave.
Los Angeles 90029

Los Angeles Mission College
1310 San Fernando Rd.
San Fernando 91340

Los Angeles Pierce College
6201 Winnetka Ave.
Woodland Hills 91371

Los Angeles Trade Technical College
400 West Washington Blvd.
Los Angeles 90015-4181

Los Angeles Valley College
5800 Fulton Ave.
Van Nuys 91401

Los Medanos College
2700 East Leland Rd.
Pittsburg 94565

Mendocino College
P.O. Box 3000
Ukiah 95482

Merced College
3600 M St.
Merced 95348-2898

Merritt College
12500 Campus Dr.
Oakland 94619

Mike Russ Financial Training Centers
3140 De La Cruz Blvd., Ste. 110
Santa clara 95054

Mira Costa College
One Barnard Dr.
Oceanside 92056-3899

Mission College
3000 Mission College Blvd.
Santa Clara 95054-1897

Modesto Junior College
435 College Ave.
Modesto 95350-5800

Monterey Peninsula College
980 Fremont Blvd.
Monterey 93940-4799

Moorpark College
7075 Campus Rd.
Moorpark 93021

Mount Saint Mary's College
12001 Chalon Rd.
Los Angeles 90049

Mount San Antonio College
1100 North Grand
Walnut 91789

Mount San Jacinto College
1499 North State St.
San Jacinto 92383

Napa Valley College
2277 Napa Vallejo Hwy.
Napa 94558

Ohlone College
43600 Mission Blvd.
Fremont 94539

Orange Coast College
2701 Fairview Rd.
Costa Mesa 92626

Orange County Business College
2035 East Ball Rd.
Anaheim 92806

Oxnard College
4000 South Rose Ave.
Oxnard 93033

Pacoima Skills Center, Los Angeles
Unified School District
13545 Van Nuys Blvd.
Pacoima 91331

Palo Verde College
811 West Chanslorway
Blythe 92225

Palomar College
1140 West Mission
San Marcos 92069-1487

Pasadena City College
1570 East Colorada Blvd.
Pasadena 91106

Porterville College
100 East College Ave.
Porterville 93257

Rancho Santiago College
1530 West 17th St.
Santa Ana 92706

Rio Hondo College
3600 Workman Mill Rd.
Whittier 90601-1699

Riverside Community College
4800 Magnolia Ave.
Riverside 92506-1299

Sacramento City College
3835 Freeport Blvd.
Sacramento 95822

San Diego City College
1313 12th Ave.
San Diego 92101

San Diego Mesa College
7250 Mesa College Dr.
San Diego 92111-4998

San Diego Miramar College
10440 Black Mountain Rd.
San Diego 92126-2999

San Joaquin Delta College
5151 Pacific Ave.
Stockton 95207

San Joaquin Valley College
201 New Stine Rd.
Bakersfield 93309

Santa Barbara Business College
211 South Real Rd.
Bakersfield 93309

Santa Barbara Business College
4333 Hansen Ave.
Fremont 94536

Santa Barbara Business College, Santa
Maria Branch
303 East Plaza Dr., Ste. One
Santa Maria 93454

Santa Barbara City College
721 Cliff Dr.
Santa Barbara 93109-2394

Santa Monica College
1900 Pico Blvd.
Santa Monica 90405-1628

Santa Rosa Junior College
1501 Mendocino Ave.
Santa Rosa 95401-4395

Shasta College
P.O. Box 496006
Redding 96049

Sierra College
5000 Rocklin Rd.
Rocklin 95677

Skyline College
3300 College Dr.
San Bruno 94066

Solano County Community College
District
4000 Suisun Valley Rd.
Suisun 94585-3197

Southwestern College
900 Otay Lakes Rd.
Chula Vista 92010

Ventura College
4667 Telegraph Rd.
Ventura 93003

Victor Valley College
18422 Bear Valley Rd.
Victorville 92392-9699

West Hills Community College
300 Cherry Ln.
Coalinga 93210

West Los Angeles College
4800 Freshman Dr.
Culver 90230

West Valley College
14000 Fruitvale Ave.
Saratoga 95070

Yuba College
2088 North Beale Rd.
Marysville 95901

COLORADO

Aims Community College
P.O. Box 69
Greeley 80632

Arapahoe Community College
2500 West College Dr.
Littleton 80160-9002

Blair College
828 Wooten Rd.
Colorado Springs 80915

Colorado Northwestern Community
College
500 Kennedy Dr.
Rangely 81648-3598

Community College of Aurora
16000 East Centre Tech Pkwy.
Aurora 80011-9036

Community College of Denver
P.O. Box 173363
Denver 80217

Denver Academy of Court Reporting
7290 Samuel Dr., Ste. A512
Denver 80221-2792

Denver Institute of Technology
7350 North Broadway
Denver 80221

Denver Technical College
925 South Niagara St.
Denver 80224

Front Range Community College
3645 West 112th Ave.
Westminster 80030

Mesa State College
P.O. Box 2647
Grand Junction 81502

Otero Junior College
1802 Colorado Ave.
La Junta 81050

Parks College
9065 Grant St.
Denver 80229

Pikes Peak Community College
5675 South Academy Blvd.
Colorado Springs 80906-5498

Pueblo Community College
900 West Orman Ave.
Pueblo 81004

Red Rocks Community College
13300 West Sixth Ave.
Lakewood 80228

Regis University
3333 Regis Blvd.
Denver 80221-1099

CONNECTICUT

Asnuntuck Community College
170 Elm St.
Enfield 06082

Data Institute
745 Burnside Ave.
East Hartford 06108

Capital Community Technical College
61 Woodland St.
Hartford 06105-2354

Housatonic Community Technical
College
900 Lafayette Blvd.
Bridgeport 06604

Manchester Community Technical
College
60 Bidwell St.
Manchester 06040-1046

Naugatuck Valley Community
Technical College
750 Chase Pkwy.
Waterbury 06708

Middlesex Community Technical
College
100 Training Hill Rd.
Middletown 06457

Mitchell College
437 Pequot Ave.
New London 06320

Morse School of Business
275 Asylum St.
Hartford 06103

Northwestern Connecticut Community
Technical College
Park Place E
Winsted 06098

Norwalk Community Technical College
188 Richards Ave.
Norwalk 06854

Quinebaug Valley Community
Technical College
742 Upper Maple St.
Danielson 06239

Sacred Heart University
5151 Park Ave.
Fairfield 06432-1023

Stone Academy
1315 Dixwell Ave.
Hamden 06514

Teikyo Post University
800 Country Club Rd., P.O. Box 2540
Waterbury 06723-2540

Three Rivers Community Technical
College
Mahan Dr.
Norwich 06360

Tunxis Community Technical College
Rtes. 6 and 177
Farmington 06032

University of New Haven
300 Orange Ave.
West Haven 06516

DELAWARE

Delaware Technical and Community
College, Owens Campus
P.O. Box 610
Georgetown 19947

Delaware Technical and Community
College, Stanton-Wilmington
400 Stanton-Christiana Rd.
Newark 19702

Goldey-Beacom College
4701 Limestone Rd.
Wilmington 19808

Wesley College
120 North State St.
Dover 19901

DISTRICT OF COLUMBIA

Strayer College, Washington Campus
1025 15th St. NW
Washington 20005

FLORIDA

Brevard Community College, Cocoa
Campus
1519 Clearlake Rd.
Cocoa 32922

Broward Community College
225 East Las Olas Blvd.
Fort Lauderdale 33301

Central Florida Community College
3001 SW College Rd.
Ocala 34474

Daytona Beach Community College
1200 Volusia Ave.
Daytona Beach 32114

Edison Community College
8099 College Pkwy. SW
Fort Myers 33906-6210

Embry-Riddle Aeronautical University
600 South Clyde Morris Blvd.
Daytona Beach 32114-3900

Florida Community College at
    Jacksonville
501 West State St.
Jacksonville 32202

Florida Keys Community College
5901 West College Rd.
Key West 33040

Florida Metropolitan University, Tampa
College
3319 West Hillsborough Ave.
Tampa 33614

Hillsborough Community College
P.O. Box 31127
Tampa 33631-3127

Indian River Community College
3209 Virginia Ave.
Fort Pierce 34981

Jones College Jacksonville
5353 Arlington Expwy.
Jacksonville 32211

Lake City Community College
Rt. 19, Box 1030
Lake City 32025

Lake County Area Vocational-Technical
    Center
2001 Kurt St.
Eustis 32726

Lake-Sumter Community College
9501 U.S. Hwy. 441
Leesburg 34788-8751

Manatee Community College
5840 26th St. W
Bradenton 34207

Miami-Dade Community College
300 Northeast Second Ave.
Miami 33132

Northwood University, Florida
    Education Center
2600 North Military Trail
West Palm Beach 33409

Okaloosa-Walton Community College
100 College Blvd.
Niceville 32578

Orlando College
5421 Diplomat Circle
Orlando 32810

Palm Beach Community College
4200 Congress Ave.
Lake Worth 33461

Pasco-Hernando Community College
36727 Blanton Rd.
Dade City 33525-7599

Pensacola Junior College
1000 College Blvd.
Pensacola 32504

Polk Community College
999 Ave. H NE
Winter Haven 33881

Prospect Hall School of Business
2620 Hollywood Blvd.
Hollywood 33020

Robert Morgan Vocational-Technical
    Center
18180 Southwest 122nd Ave.
Miami 33177

Rollins College
1000 Holt Ave.
Winter Park 32789-4499

Saint Augustine Technical Center
2980 Collins Ave.
Saint Augustine 32095

Saint Petersburg Junior College
8580 66 St. N
Pinellas Park 34665

Santa Fe Community College
3000 Northwest 83rd St.
Gainesville 32606

South Florida Community College
600 West College Dr.
Avon Park 33825

Southern College
5600 Lake Underhill Rd.
Orlando 32807

Tallahassee Community College
444 Appleyard Dr.
Tallahassee 32304-2895

Valencia Community College
P.O. Box 3028
Orlando 32802

GEORGIA

Abraham Baldwin Agricultural College
ABAC 9 2802 Moore Hwy.
Tifton 31794-2601

Atlanta Metropolitan College
1630 Stewart Ave. SW
Atlanta 30310-4498

Clayton College and State University
5900 Lee St.
Morrow 30260

Dalton College
213 North College Dr.
Dalton 30720

Emmanuel College
181 Spring St.
Franklin Springs 30639

Floyd College
P.O. Box 1864
Rome 30162-1864

Gainesville College
3820 Mundy Mill Rd.
Oakwood 30566

Georgia Institute of Real Estate
5784 Lake Forest Dr.
Atlanta 30328

Georgia Military College, Main Campus
201 East Greene St.
Milledgeville 31061-3398

Gordon College
419 College Dr.
Barnesville 30204

Gwinnett College of Business
4230 Hwy. 29, Ste. 11
Lilburn 30047

Gwinnett Technical Institute
5150 Sugarloaf Pkwy.
Lawrenceville 30043

Kennesaw State College
1000 Chastain Rd.
Marietta 30061

Kerr Business College
2528 Centerwest Pkwy., Bldg. A
Augusta 30909

South College
709 Mall Blvd.
Savannah 31406

Thomas College
1501 Millpond Rd.
Thomasville 31792

Truett-McConnell College
100 Alumni Dr.
Cleveland 30528

HAWAII

Hawaii Business College
33 South King St., 4th Floor, Ste. 405
Honolulu 96817

Hawaii Pacific University
1164 Bishop St.
Honolulu 96813

Heald College School of Business and
    Technology
1500 Kapiolani Blvd.
Honolulu 96816

Kapiolani Community College
4303 Diamond Head Rd.
Honolulu 96816

Leeward Community College
96-045 Ala Ike
Pearl City 96782

University of Hawaii at Hilo
200 West Kawili St.
Hilo 96720-4091

IDAHO

College of Southern Idaho
P.O. Box 1238
Twin Falls 83301

Idaho State University
741 South Seventh Ave.
Pocatello 83209

Lewis-Clark State College
500 Eighth Ave.
Lewiston 83501

Ricks College
Rexburg 83460-4107

ILLINOIS

Belleville Area College
2500 Carlyle Rd.
Belleville 62221

Benedictine University
5700 College Rd.
Lisle 60532

Black Hawk College
6600 34th Ave.
Moline 61265

City College of Chicago, Harry S.
    Truman College
1145 Wilson Ave.
Chicago 60640

City College of Chicago, Richard J
    Daley College
7500 South Pulaski Rd.
Chicago 60652

City College of Chicago, Wilbur Wright
    College
4300 North Narragansett
Chicago 60634

College of Du Page
425 22nd St.
Glen Ellyn 60137-6599

College of Lake County
19351 West Washington St.
Grayslake 60030-1198

Elgin Community College
1700 Spartan Dr.
Elgin 60123

Highland Community College
2998 West Pearl City Rd.
Freeport 61032-9341

Illinois Central College
One College Dr.
East Peoria 61635-0001

Illinois Valley Community College
815 North Orlando Smith Ave.
Oglesby 61348-9692

John A Logan College
700 Logan College Rd.
Carterville 62918

John Wood Community College
150 South 48th St.
Quincy 62301-9147

Joliet Junior College
1215 Houbolt Ave.
Joliet 60431

Kankakee Community College
P.O. Box 888
Kankakee 60901

Kaskaskia College
27210 College Rd.
Centralia 62801

Kishwaukee College
21193 Malta Rd.
Malta 60150

Lewis and Clark Community College
5800 Godfrey Rd.
Godfrey 62035

Lincoln College
300 Keokuk St.
Lincoln 62656

Lincoln Land Community College
Shepherd Rd.
Springfield 62194-9256

MacCormac College
506 South Wabash
Chicago 60605

McHenry County College
8900 U.S. Hwy. 14
Crystal Lake 60012

Moraine Valley Community College
10900 South 88th Ave.
Palos Hills 60465-0937

Morton College
3801 South Central Ave.
Cicero 60804

Northwestern Business College
4829 North Lipps Ave.
Chicago 60630

Northwestern University
633 Clark St.
Evanston 60208

Oakton Community College
1600 East Golf Rd.
Des Plaines 60016

Parkland College
2400 West Bradley Ave.
Champaign 61821

Prairie State College
202 Halsted St.
Chicago Heights 60411

Rend Lake College
648 North Ken Graz Pkwy.
Ina 62846

Richland Community College
One College Park
Decatur 62521

Robert Morris College
180 North Lasalle St.
Chicago 60601

Rock Valley College
3301 North Mulford Rd.
Rockford 61114

Saint Augustine College
1333 West Argyle
Chicago 60640

Sauk Valley Community College
173 Illinois Rte. 2
Dixon 61021

South Suburban College
15800 South State St.
South Holland 60473

Southeastern Illinois College
3575 College Rd.
Harrisburg 62946

Triton College
2000 Fifth Ave.
River Grove 60171

Waubonsee Community College
Rte. 47 at Harter Rd.
Sugar Grove 60554-0901

William Rainey Harper College
1200 West Algonquin Rd.
Palatine 60067-7398

INDIANA

Ancilla Domini College
P.O. Box 1
Donaldson 46513

Ball State University
2000 University Ave.
Muncie 47306

Calumet College of Saint Joseph
2400 New York Ave.
Whiting 46394

Commonwealth Business College, Main
Campus
4200 West 81st Ave.
Merrillville 46410

Indiana Business College
140 East 53rd St.
Anderson 46013

Indiana Business College
222 Poshard Dr.
Columbus 47203-9988

Indiana Business College
802 North Meridian St.
Indianapolis 46204

Indiana Business College
2 Executive Dr.
Lafayette 47905

Indiana Business College
830 North Miller Ave.
Marion 46952

Indiana Business College
1809 North Walnut
Muncie 47303

Indiana Business College
3175 South Third Place
Terre Haute 47802

Indiana Business College
1431 Willow St.
Vincennes 47591

Indiana University Bloomington
Bryan Hall
Bloomington 47405

Indiana University East
2325 Chester Blvd.
Richmond 47374

Indiana University Kokomo
2300 South Washington
Kokomo 46902

Indiana University Northwest
3400 Broadway
Gary 46408

Indiana University South Bend
1700 Mishawaka Ave.
South Bend 46615

Indiana University Southeast
4201 Grant Line Rd.
New Albany 47150

Indiana University, Purdue University
at Fort Wayne
2101 Coliseum Blvd. E
Fort Wayne 46805

Indiana University, Purdue University
at Indianapolis
355 North Lansing
Indianapolis 46202

Indiana Wesleyan University
4201 South Washington St.
Marion 46953

International Business College
3811 Illinois Rd.
Fort Wayne 46804

ITT Technical Institute
9511 Angola Ct.
Indianapolis 46268

Ivy Tech State College, Central Indiana
One West 26th St.
Indianapolis 46206-1763

Ivy Tech State College, Columbus
4475 Central Ave.
Columbus 47203

Ivy Tech State College, East Central
4301 South Cowan Rd.
P.O. Box 3100
Muncie 47302

Ivy Tech State College, Kokomo
1815 East Morgan St.
Kokomo 46901

Ivy Tech State College, Lafayette
3101 South Creasy Lane, P.O. Box 6299
Lafayette 47903

Ivy Tech State College, North Central
1534 West Sample St.
South Bend 46619

Ivy Tech State College, Northeast
3800 North Anthony Blvd.
Fort Wayne 46805

Ivy Tech State College, Northwest
1440 East 35th Ave.
Gary 46409

Ivy Tech State College, South Central
8204 Hwy. 311
Sellersburg 47172

Ivy Tech State College, Southeast
590 Ivy Tech Dr., P.O. Box 209
Madison 47250

Ivy Tech State College, Southwest
3501 First Ave.
Evansville 47710

Ivy Tech State College, Wabash Valley
7999 U.S. Hwy. 41
Terre Haute 47802-4898

Ivy Tech State College, Whitewater
P.O. Box 1145
Richmond 47374

Purdue University, Calumet Campus
2233 171st St.
Hammond 46323

Purdue University, North Central
Campus
1401 South U.S. Hwy. 421
Westville 46391

University of Indianapolis
1400 East Hanna Ave.
Indianapolis 46227

University of Southern Indiana
8600 University Blvd.
Evansville 47712

Vincennes University
1002 North First St.
Vincennes 47591

IOWA

American Institute of Business
2500 Fleur Dr.
Des Moines 50321

Des Moines Community College
2006 Ankeny Blvd.
Ankeny 50021

Eastern Iowa Community College
District
306 West River Dr.
Davenport 52801-1221

Indian Hills Community College
525 Grandview
Ottumwa 52501

Iowa Valley Community College
P.O. Box 536
Marshalltown 50158

Kirkwood Community College
P.O. Box 2068
Cedar Rapids 52406

Northeast Iowa Community College,
Calmar
Hwy. 150 S, P.O. Box 400
Calmar 52132-0400

Northwestern College
101 Seventh St. SW
Orange City 51041

Spencer School of Business
217 West Fifth St., P.O. Box 5065
Spencer 51301

Western Iowa Technical Community
College
4647 Stone Ave., P.O. Box 265
Sioux City 51102-0265

KANSAS

Allen County Community College
1801 North Cottonwood
Iola 66749

Barton County Community College
245 NE 30th Rd.
Great Bend 67530

The Brown Mackie College
126 South Santa Fe St.
Salina 67402-1787

Butler County Community College
901 South Haverhill Rd.
El Dorado 67042

Cloud County Community College
2221 Campus Dr., P.O. Box 1002
Concordia 66901-1002

Coffeyville Community College
400 West 11th St.
Coffeyville 67337

Colby Community College
1255 South Range
Colby 67701

Cowley County Community College
125 South Second St.
Arkansas City 67005

Dodge City Community College
2501 North 14th Ave.
Dodge City 67801

Fort Scott Community College
2108 South Horton
Fort Scott 66701

Garden City Community College
801 Campus Dr.
Garden City 67846

Haskell Indian Nations University
155 Indian Ave.
Lawrence 66046-4800

Hesston College
P.O. Box 3000
Hesston 67062

Highland Community College
P.O. Box 68
Highland 66035-0068

Hutchinson Community College
1300 North Plum St.
Hutchinson 67501

Independence Community College
Brookside Dr. and College Ave.
Independence 67301

Johnson County Community College
12345 College Blvd.
Overland Park 66210-1299

Kansas City Kansas Community College
7250 State Ave.
Kansas City 66112

Labette Community College
200 South 14th
Parsons 67357

North Central Kansas Technical College
Hwy. 24
P.O. Box 507
Beloit 67420

Northwest Kansas Area Vocational-
Technical School
P.O. Box 668
Goodland 67735

Pratt Community College
348 NE St. Rte. 61
Pratt 67124

Seward County Community College
P.O. Box 1137
Liberal 67905-1137

Washburn University of Topeka
1700 College Ave.
Topeka 66621

KENTUCKY

Ashland Community College
1400 College Dr.
Ashland 41101

Brescia College
717 Frederica St.
Owensboro 42301-3023

Elizabethtown Community College
College Street Rd.
Elizabethtown 42701

Hazard Community College
Hazard 41701

Henderson Community College
2660 South Green St.
Henderson 42420

Hopkinsville Community College
North Dr.
Hopkinsville 42240

Jefferson Community College
109 East Broadway
Louisville 40202

Kentucky College of Business
628 East Main St.
Lexington 40508

Kentucky Tech, Somerset Regional
Technology Center
230 Airport Rd.
Somerset 42501

Lexington Community College
Cooper Dr.
Lexington 40506

Lindsey Wilson College
210 Lindsey Wilson St.
Columbia 42728

Madisonville Community College
University Dr.
Madisonville 42431

Mayo Regional Technology Center
Third St.
Paintsville 41240

Maysville Community College
Maysville 41056

Midway College
512 Stephens St.
Midway 40347-1120

Northern Kentucky University
University Dr.
Highland Heights 41099

Paducah Community College
P.O. Box 7380
Paducah 42002-7380

Prestonsburg Community College
Bert Combs Dr.
Prestonsburg 41653

Saint Catharine College
2735 Bardstown Rd.
Saint Catharine 40061

Somerset Community College
808 Monticello Rd.
Somerset 42501

Southeast Community College
300 College Rd.
Cumberland 40823

Southern Ohio College, Fort Mitchell
309 Buttermilk Pike
Fort Mitchell 41017

Sue Bennett College
151 College St.
London 40741

Sullivan College, Louisville
3101 Bardstown Rd.
Louisville 40205

Thomas More College
333 Thomas More Pkwy.
Crestview Hills 41017-3428

University of Louisville
2301 South Third St.
Louisville 40292-0001

Western Kentucky University
One Big Red Way
Bowling Green 42101-3576

LOUISIANA

Bossier Parish Community College
2719 Airline Dr. N
Bossier City 71111

Delgado Community College
501 City Park Ave.
New Orleans 70119

Delta School of Business and
    Technology
517 Broad St.
Lake Charles 70601

Elaine P Nunez Community College
3701 Paris Rd.
Chalmette 70043

Louisiana State University Eunice
P.O. Box 1129
Eunice 70535

Louisiana Technical College, Sewela
    Campus
3820 J. Bennett Johnston Ave.
Lake Charles 70615

Nicholls State University
University Station, LA Hwy. One
Thibodaux 70310

Southern University Shreveport, Bossier
    City Campus
3050 Martin L King Dr.
Shreveport 71107

MAINE

Andover College
901 Washington Ave.
Portland 04103

Beal College
629 Main St.
Bangor 04401

Casco Bay College
477 Congress St.
Portland 04101

Eastern Maine Technical College
354 Hogan Rd.
Bangor 04401

Husson College
One College Circle
Bangor 04401

Kennebec Valley Technical College
92 Western Ave.
Fairfield 04937-1367

Maine Maritime Academy
Pleasant St.
Castine 04420

Mid-State College
88 East Hardscrabble Rd.
Auburn 04210

Northern Maine Technical College
33 Edgemont Dr.
Presque Isle 04769

Southern Maine Technical College
Fort Rd.
South Portland 04106

Thomas College
180 West River Rd.
Waterville 04901-5097

University of Maine
Office of Institutional Studies
Orono 04469

University of Maine at Augusta
46 University Dr.
Augusta 04330-9410

University of Southern Maine
96 Falmouth St.
Portland 04103

MARYLAND

Allegany Community College
12401 Willowbrook Rd. SE
Cumberland 21502

Anne Arundel Community College
101 College Pkwy.
Arnold 21012

Baltimore City Community College
2901 Liberty Heights Ave.
Baltimore 21215

Catonsville Community College
800 South Rolling Rd.
Catonsville 21228

Cecil Community College
1000 North East Rd.
North East 21901-1999

Charles County Community College
8730 Mitchell Rd.
La Plata 20646-0910

Chesapeake College
P.O. Box 8
Wye Mills 21679-0008

Dundalk Community College
7200 Sollers Point Rd.
Dundalk 21222

Essex Community College
7201 Rossville Blvd.
Baltimore 21237

Fleet Business School
2530 Riva Rd., Ste. 201
Annapolis 21401

Frederick Community College
7932 Opossumtown Pike
Frederick 21702

Garrett Community College
687 Mosser Rd.
McHenry 21541

Hagerstown Business College
18618 Crestwood Dr.
Hagerstown 21742

Hagerstown Junior College
11400 Robinwood Dr.
Hagerstown 21742-6590

Harford Community College
401 Thomas Run Rd.
Bel Air 21015

Howard Community College
10901 Little Patuxent Pkwy.
Columbia 21044

Montgomery College of Germantown
20200 Observation Dr.
Germantown 20874

Montgomery College of Rockville
51 Mannakee St.
Rockville 20850

Montgomery College of Takoma Park
Takoma Ave. and Fenton St.
Takoma Park 20912

Prince Georges Community College
301 Largo Rd.
Largo 20774-2199

University of Maryland, Baltimore
    County Campus
1000 Hilltop Circle
Baltimore 21250

University of Maryland, College Park
    Campus
College Park 20742

Villa Julie College
Green Spring Valley Rd.
Stevenson 21153

Wor-Wic Community College
32000 Campus Dr.
Salisbury 21801-7131

MASSACHUSETTS

Aquinas College at Milton
303 Adams St.
Milton 02186

Aquinas College at Newton
15 Walnut Park
Newton 02158

Bay Path College
588 Longmeadow St.
Longmeadow 01106

Bay State College
122 Commonwealth Ave.
Boston 02116

Becker College, Leicester
Three Paxton St.
Leicester 01524

Becker College, Worcester
61 Sever St.
Worcester 01615-0071

Bentley College
175 Forest St.
Waltham 02154-4705

Berkshire Community College
1350 West St.
Pittsfield 01201-5786

Bristol Community College
777 Elsbree St.
Fall River 02720

Bunker Hill Community College
250 New Rutherford Ave.
Boston 02129

Burdett School
100 Front St.
Worcester 01608

Cape Cod Community College
2240 Iyanough Rd.
West Barnstable 02668-1599

Dean College
99 Main St.
Franklin 02038

Endicott College
376 Hale St.
Beverly 01915

Fisher College
118 Beacon St.
Boston 02116

Greenfield Community College
One College Dr.
Greenfield 01301-9739

Holyoke Community College
303 Homestead Ave.
Holyoke 01040

Lasell College
1844 Commonwealth Ave.
Newton 02166

Massachusetts Bay Community College
50 Oakland St.
Wellesley Hills 02181

Massasoit Community College
One Massasoit Blvd.
Brockton 02402

Merrimack College
315 Turpike St.
North Andover 01845

Middlesex Community College
Springs Rd.
Bedford 01730

Mount Ida College
777 Dedham St.
Newton Centre 02159

Mount Wachusett Community College
444 Green St.
Gardner 01440

Newbury College, Inc.
129 Fisher Ave.
Brookline 02146

Nichols College
Center Rd.
Dudley 01571

North Shore Community College
One Ferncroft Rd.
Danvers 01923

Northeastern University
360 Huntington Ave.
Boston 02115

Northern Essex Community College
Elliott Way
Haverhill 01830-2399

Quincy College
34 Coddington St.
Quincy 02169

Quinsigamond Community College
670 West Boylston St.
Worcester 01606

Springfield Technical Community
    College
One Armory Square
Springfield 01105

Stonehill College
Washington St.
North Easton 02357

University of Massachusetts at Lowell
One University Ave.
Lowell 01854

MICHIGAN

Alpena Community College
666 Johnson St.
Alpena 49707

Baker College of Flint
G1050 West Bristol Rd.
Flint 48507

Baker College of Muskegon
903 Marquette Ave.
Muskegon 49442

Baker College of Owosso
1020 South Washington St.
Owosso 48867

Bay De Noc Community College
2001 North Lincoln Rd.
Escanaba 49289

Cleary College
2170 Washtenaw Ave.
Ypsilanti 48197

Davenport College
415 East Fulton
Grand Rapids 49503

Davenport College, Kalamazoo Branch
4123 West Main St.
Kalamazoo 49006-2791

Davenport College, Lansing Branch
220 East Kalamazoo
Lansing 48933

Delta College
University Center 48710

Detroit College of Business
4801 Oakman Blvd.
Dearborn 48126-3799

Detroit College of Business
2488 North Jennings
Flint 48504-1700

Detroit College of Business
27500 Dequindre
Warren 48092-5209

Ferris State University
901 South State St.
Big Rapids 49307

Glen Oaks Community College
62249 Shimmel Rd.
Centreville 49032

Gogebic Community College
East 4946 Jackson Rd.
Ironwood 49938

Grand Rapids Community College
143 Bostwick Ave. NE
Grand Rapids 49503-3295

Henry Ford Community College
5101 Evergreen Rd.
Dearborn 48128

Jackson Community College
2111 Emmons Rd.
Jackson 49201-8399

Kalamazoo Valley Community College
6767 West O Ave.
Kalamazoo 49009

Kellogg Community College
450 North Ave.
Battle Creek 49017

Kirtland Community College
10775 North St. Helen Rd.
Roscommon 48653

Lake Michigan College
2755 East Napier Ave.
Benton Harbor 49022-8099

Lake Superior State University
650 West Easterday Ave.
Sault Sainte Marie 49783

Lansing Community College
419 North Capitol Ave.
Lansing 48901-7210

Lewis College of Business
17370 Meyers Rd.
Detroit 48235

Macomb Community College
14500 Twelve Mile Rd.
Warren 48093-3896

Madonna University
36600 Schoolcraft Rd.
Livonia 48150

Mid Michigan Community College
1375 South Clare Ave.
Harrison 48625

Monroe County Community College
1555 South Raisinville Rd.
Monroe 48161

Montcalm Community College
2800 College Dr.
Sidney 48885

Mott Community College
1401 East Court St.
Flint 48503

Muskegon Community College
221 South Quarterline Rd.
Muskegon 49442

North Central Michigan College
1515 Howard St.
Petoskey 49770

Northern Michigan University
1401 Presque Isle
Marquette 49855

Northwestern Michigan College
1701 East Front St.
Traverse City 49686

Northwood Institute
3225 Cook Rd.
Midland 48640

Oakland Community College
2480 Opdyke Rd.
Bloomfield Hills 48304-2266

Saint Clair County Community College
323 Erie, P.O. Box 5015
Port Huron 48061-5015

Schoolcraft College
18600 Haggerty Rd.
Livonia 48152

Siena Heights College
1247 Siena Heights Dr.
Adrian 49221

Southwestern Michigan College
58900 Cherry Grove Rd.
Dowagiac 49047-9793

Washtenaw Community College
P.O. Drawer 1
Ann Arbor 48016-1610

Wayne County Community College
801 West Fort St.
Detroit 48226

MINNESOTA

Alexandria Technical College
1601 Jefferson St.
Alexandria 56308

Anoka-Ramsey Community College
11200 Mississippi Blvd.
Coon Rapids 55433-3470

Brown Institute, Ltd.
2225 East Lake St.
Minneapolis 55407

Central Lakes College, Brainerd
501 West College Dr.
Brainerd 56401

Dakota County Technical College
1300 East 145th St.
Rosemount 55068

Globe College of Business
175 Fifth St. E, Ste. 201, P.O. Box 60
Saint Paul 55101-2901

Inver Hills Community College
2500 80th St. E
Inver Grove Heights 55076

Minneapolis Community and Technical
College
1501 Hennepin Ave.
Minneapolis 55403

Minnesota West Community and
Technical College, Canby Campus
1011 First St. W
Canby 56220

National American University
1380 Energy Ln., Ste. 13
Saint Paul 55108

Normandale Community College
9700 France Ave. S
Bloomington 55431

Northwest Technical College, East
Grand Forks
Hwy. 220 N
East Grand Forks 56721

Rasmussen Business College,
Minneapolis
12450 Wayzata Blvd.
Minnetonka 55305

Rasmussen College
3500 Federal Dr.
Eagan 55122

Rasmussen College Corporate Office
Good Counsel Dr.
Mankato 56001

Red Wing-Winona Technical College,
Red Wing Campus
380 Pioneer Rd.
Red Wing 55066

Ridgewater College, A Community and
Technical College, Hutchinson
Campus
Two Century Ave. SE
Hutchinson 55350

Rochester Community and Technical
College
851 30th Ave. SE
Rochester 55904-4999

Saint Paul Technical College
235 Marshall Ave.
Saint Paul 55102

Southwest State University
1501 State St.
Marshall 56258

University of Minnesota Crookston
105 Selvig Hall
Crookston 56716

University of Minnesota Twin Cities
100 Church St. SE
Minneapolis 55455

MISSISSIPPI

Coahoma Community College
3240 Friars Point Rd.
Clarksdale 38614

Copiah-Lincoln Community College
P.O. Box 457
Wesson 39191

Hinds Community College, Raymond
Campus
Raymond 39154

Jones County Junior College
900 South Court St.
Ellisville 39437

Mary Holmes College
Hwy. 50 W
West Point 39773

Meridian Community College
910 Hwy. 19 N
Meridian 39307

Mississippi Delta Community College
P.O. Box 668
Moorhead 38761

Mississippi Gulf Coast Community
College
Central Office, P.O. Box 67
Perkinston 39573

Northeast Mississippi Community
College
Cunningham Blvd.
Booneville 38829

Northwest Mississippi Community
College
510 North Panola, Hwy. 51 N
Senatobia 38668

MISSOURI

Columbia College
1001 Rogers
Columbia 65216

Crowder College
601 Laclede
Neosho 64850

Drury College
900 North Benton Ave.
Springfield 65802

Jefferson College
1000 Viking Dr.
Hillsboro 63050

Longview Community College
500 Longview Rd.
Lees Summit 64081

Maple Woods Community College
2601 Northeast Barry Rd.
Kansas City 64156

Metro Business College of Cape
Girardeau
1732 North Kings Hwy.
Cape Girardeau 63701

Missouri Baptist College
One College Park Dr.
Saint Louis 63141

Park College
8700 River Park Dr.
Parkville 64152-3795

Penn Valley Community College
3201 Southwest Trafficway
Kansas City 64111

Saint Louis Community College, Forest
Park
5600 Oakland Ave.
Saint Louis 63110

Saint Louis University, Main Campus
221 North Grand Blvd.
Saint Louis 63103

State Fair Community College
3201 West 16th
Sedalia 65301-2199

TAD Technical Institute
7910 Troost Ave.
Kansas City 64131

Three Rivers Community College
Three Rivers Blvd.
Poplar Bluff 63901

MONTANA

Dull Knife Memorial College
P.O. Box 98
Lame Deer 59043

Flathead Valley Community College
777 Grandview Dr.
Kalispell 59901

Montana State University, Northern
300 West 11th St.
Havre 59501

Western Montana College University of
Montana
710 South Atlantic
Dillon 59725-3598

NEBRASKA

Central Community College Area
P.O. Box 4903
Grand Island 68802

College of Saint Mary
1901 South 72nd St.
Omaha 68124

Lincoln School of Commerce
1821 K St.
P.O. Box 82826
Lincoln 68501-2826

Metropolitan Community College Area
5300 North 30th St.
Omaha 68103

Nebraska School of Real Estate
225 North Cotner, Ste. 106
Lincoln 68505

Northeast Community College
801 East Benjamin
P.O. Box 469
Norfolk 68702-0469

Southeast Community College Area
111 O St., Ste. 111
Lincoln 68520

Union College
3800 South 48th
Lincoln 68506

NEVADA

Career College of Northern Nevada
1195 A Corporate Blvd.
Reno 89502

Community College of Southern
Nevada
3200 East Cheyenne Ave.
Las Vegas 89030

Morrison College
140 Washington St.
Reno 89503

Truckee Meadows Community College
7000 Dandini Blvd.
Reno 89512

Western Nevada Community College
2201 West College Pkwy.
Carson City 89703

NEW HAMPSHIRE

Castle College
23 Searles Rd.
Windham 03087-1200

Daniel Webster College
20 University Dr.
Nashua 03063-1300

Franklin Pierce College
College Rd.
Rindge 03461

Hesser College
Three Sundial Ave.
Manchester 03103

McIntosh College
23 Cataract Ave.
Dover 03820

New Hampshire College
2500 North River Rd.
Manchester 03106

New Hampshire Technical College at
Nashua
505 Amherst St.
Nashua 03061-2052

New Hampshire Technical Institute
11 Institute Dr.
Concord 03301

Rivier College
429 Main St.
Nashua 03060

University of New Hampshire at
Manchester
220 Hackett Hill Rd.
Manchester 03102-8597

University of New Hampshire, Main
Campus
Thompson Hall
Durham 03824

NEW JERSEY

The Academy of Professional
Development
1075 Easton Ave., Tower 2, Ste. 5
Edison 08837

Atlantic Community College
5100 Black Horse Pike
Mays Landing 08330-2699

Berkeley College
44 Rifle Camp Rd.
West Paterson 07424

Brookdale Community College
765 Newman Springs Rd.
Lincroft 07738-1599

Burlington County College
Rte. 530
Pemberton 08068

Camden County College
P.O. Box 200
Blackwood 08012

College of Saint Elizabeth
Two Convent Rd.
Morristown 07960-6989

County College of Morris
214 Center Grove Rd.
Randolph 07869

Cumberland County College
College Dr., P.O. Box 517
Vineland 08360

Drake College of Business
125 Broad St.
Elizabeth 07201

Essex County College
303 University Ave.
Newark 07102

Gloucester County College
1400 Tanyard Rd.
Sewell 08080

Hudson County Community College
25 Journal Square
Jersey City 07306

Mercer County Community College
1200 Old Trenton Rd.
Trenton 08690

Middlesex County College
155 Mill Rd., P.O. Box 3050
Edison 08818-3050

RETS Institute
103 Park Ave.
Nutley 07110

Ocean County College
College Dr.
Toms River 08753

Passaic County Community College
One College Blvd.
Paterson 07505-1179

Raritan Valley Community College
P.O. Box 3300, Lamington Rd.
Somerville 08876

Rider University
2083 Lawrenceville Rd.
Lawrenceville 08648-3099

Saint Peter's College
2641 Kennedy Blvd.
Jersey City 07306-5997

Salem Community College
460 Hollywood Ave.
Carneys Point 08069

South Jersey Professional School of
Business
Marlton Square Shopping Center Rte. 70
and Cropwell Rd.
Marlton 08053

Thomas A Edison State College
101 West State St.
Trenton 08608-1176

Union County College
1033 Springfield Ave.
Cranford 07016

NEW MEXICO

Albuquerque Technical-Vocational
Institute
525 Buena Vista SE
Albuquerque 87106

Clovis Community College
417 Schepps Blvd.
Clovis 88101

Eastern New Mexico University, Roswell
Campus
52 University Blvd., Administrative
Center
Roswell 88202

New Mexico Junior College
5317 Lovington Hwy.
Hobbs 88240

New Mexico State University,
Alamogordo
P.O. Box 477, 2400 North Senic Dr.
Alamogordo 88310

New Mexico State University, Carlsbad
1500 University Dr.
Carlsbad 88220

New Mexico State University, Main
Campus
P.O. Box 30001, Dept. 3Z, Weddell Dr.
Las Cruces 88003

Northern New Mexico Community
College
1002 North Onate St.
Espanola 87532

San Juan College
4601 College Blvd.
Farmington 87402

Santa Fe Community College
6401 Richards Ave.
P.O. Box 4187
Santa Fe 87505

Southwestern Indian Polytechnic
Institute
9169 Coors Rd. NW
Albuquerque 87120

University of New Mexico, Valencia
280 La Entrada
Los Lunas 87031

NEW YORK

Adirondack Community College
Bay Rd.
Queensbury 12804

Berkeley College
West Red Oak Ln.
White Plains 10604

Berkeley College of New York City
Three East 43rd St.
New York 10017

Broome Community College
P.O. Box 1017
Binghamton 13902

Bryant and Stratton Business Institute,
Albany
1259 Central Ave.
Albany 12205

Bryant and Stratton Business Institute,
Buffalo
1028 Main St.
Buffalo 14202

Bryant and Stratton Business Institute,
Rochester
82 Saint Paul St.
Rochester 14604

Bryant and Stratton Business Institute,
Syracuse
953 James St.
Syracuse 13203

Cayuga County Community College
Franklin St.
Auburn 13021

Cazenovia College
Cazenovia 13035

Central City Business Institute
224 Harrison St.
Syracuse 13202

Clinton Community College
136 Clinton Point Dr.
Plattsburgh 12901

Columbia-Greene Community College
4400 Rte. 23
Hudson 12534

Corning Community College
Spencer Hill
Corning 14830

CUNY Borough of Manhattan
Community College
199 Chambers St.
New York 10007

CUNY Bronx Community College
West 181st St. & University Ave.
Bronx 10453

CUNY College of Staten Island
2800 Victory Blvd.
Staten Island 10314

CUNY Hostos Community College
500 Grand Concourse
Bronx 10451

CUNY Kingsborough Community
College
2001 Oriental Blvd.
Brooklyn 11235

CUNY La Guardia Community College
31-10 Thomson Ave.
Long Island City 11101

CUNY Medgar Evers College
1650 Bedford Ave.
Brooklyn 11225

CUNY New York City Technical College
300 Jay St.
Brooklyn 11201

CUNY Queensborough Community
College
56th Ave. & Springfield Blvd.
New York 11364

Dutchess Community College
53 Pendell Rd.
Poughkeepsie 12601

Elmira Business Institute
180 Clemens Center Pkwy.
Elmira 14901

Erie Community College, City Campus
121 Ellicott St.
Buffalo 14203

Erie Community College, North
Campus
Main St. and Youngs Rd.
Williamsville 14221

Erie Community College, South
Campus
4140 Southwestern Blvd.
Orchard Park 14127

Finger Lakes Community College
4355 Lake Shore Dr.
Canandaigua 14424

Five Towns College
305 North Service Rd.
Dix Hills 11746-6055

Fulton-Montgomery Community
College
2805 State Hwy. 67
Johnstown 12095

Genesee Community College
One College Rd.
Batavia 14020

Herkimer County Community College
Reservoir Rd.
Herkimer 13350-1598

Hilbert College
5200 South Park Ave.
Hamburg 14075-1597

Hudson Valley Community College
80 Vandenburgh Ave.
Troy 12180

Interboro Institute
450 West 56th St.
New York 10019

Iona College
715 North Ave.
New Rochelle 10801

Jamestown Business College
Seven Fairmount Ave.
Jamestown 14701

Jamestown Community College
525 Falconer St.
Jamestown 14701

Jefferson Community College
Outer Coffeen St.
Watertown 13601

Katharine Gibbs School, New York City
200 Park Ave.
New York 10166

Laboratory Institute of Merchandising
12 East 53rd St.
New York 10022

Maria College of Albany
700 New Scotland Ave.
Albany 12208

Marist College
290 North Rd.
Poughkeepsie 12601

Mater Dei College
5428 St. Hwy. 37
Ogdensburg 13669

Medaille College
18 Agassiz Circle
Buffalo 14214

Mercy College, Main Campus
555 Broadway
Dobbs Ferry 10522

Mohawk Valley Community College
1101 Sherman Dr.
Utica 13501

Monroe College, Main Campus
Monroe College Way
Bronx 10468

Monroe Community College
1000 East Henrietta Rd.
Rochester 14623

Nassau Community College
One Education Dr.
Garden City 11530

New York University
70 Washington Square S
New York 10012

Niagara County Community College
3111 Saunders Settlement Rd.
Sanborn 14132

North Country Community College
20 Winona Ave.
P.O. Box 89
Saranac Lake 12983

Olean Business Institute
301 North Union St.
Olean 14760

Onondaga Community College
4941 Onondaga Rd.
Syracuse 13215

Orange County Community College
115 South St.
Middletown 10940

Pace University-New York
One Pace Plaza
New York 10038

Plaza Business Institute
74-09 37th Ave.
Jackson Heights 11372

Regents College, University of the State
of New York
7 Columbia Circle
Albany 12203

Rochester Business Institute
1850 East Ridge Rd.
Irondequoit 14622

Rochester Institute of Technology
One Lamb Memorial Dr.
Rochester 14623-5603

Rockland Community College
145 College Rd.
Suffern 10901

Russell Sage College, Main Campus
45 Ferry St.
Troy 12180

Saint John's University New York
8000 Utopia Pkwy.
Jamaica 11439

Saint Joseph's College, Main Campus
245 Clinton Ave.
Brooklyn 11205-3688

Saint Joseph's College, Suffolk Campus
155 Roe Blvd.
Patchogue 11772-2399

Schenectady County Community
College
Washington Ave.
Schenectady 12305

Suffolk County Community College,
Ammerman Campus
533 College Rd.
Selden 11784

Suffolk County Community College,
Eastern Campus
Speonk Riverhead Rd.
Riverhead 11901

Suffolk County Community College,
Western Campus
Crooked Hill Rd.
Brentwood 11717

Sullivan County Community College
1000 Le Roy Rd.
Loch Sheldrake 12759-4002

SUNY at Buffalo
Capen Hall
Buffalo 14260

SUNY College of Agriculture &
Technology at Cobleskill
Cobleskill 12043

SUNY College of Technology &
Agriculture at Morrisville
Morrisville 13408

SUNY College of Technology at Alfred
Alfred 14802

SUNY College of Technology at Canton
Cornell Dr.
Canton 13617

SUNY College of Technology at Delhi
Delhi 13753

SUNY College of Technology at
Farmingdale
Melville Rd.
Farmingdale 11735-1021

SUNY Empire State College
Two Union Ave.
Saratoga Springs 12866

SUNY Ulster County Community
College
Cottekill Rd.
Stone Ridge 12484

SUNY Westchester Commmunity
College
75 Grasslands Rd.
Valhalla 10595

Taylor Business Institute
120 West 30th St.
New York 10001

Tompkins-Cortland Community
College
170 North St.
Dryden 13053

Touro College
27-33 West 23rd St.
New York 10010

Utica School of Commerce
201 Bleecker St.
Utica 13501

The Westchester Business Institute
325 Central Ave.
White Plains 10606

Workshop in Business Opportunities
Inc.
23 Gramercy Park
New York 10003

NORTH CAROLINA

Asheville Buncombe Technical
Community College
340 Victoria Rd.
Asheville 28801

Beaufort County Community College
P.O. Box 1069
Washington 27889

Blue Ridge Community College
College Dr.
Flat Rock 28731-9624

Brunswick Community College
P.O. Box 30
Supply 28462

Caldwell Community College and
Technical Institute
P.O. Box 600
Lenoir 28645

Cape Fear Community College
411 North Front St.
Wilmington 28401

Carteret Community College
3505 Arendell St.
Morehead City 28557

Catawba Valley Community College
2550 Hwy. 70 SE
Hickory 28602-0699

Central Carolina Community College
1105 Kelly Dr.
Sanford 27330

Central Piedmont Community College
P.O. Box 35009
Charlotte 28235-5009

Chowan College
Murfreesboro 27855

Cleveland Community College
137 South Post Rd.
Shelby 28152

Coastal Carolina Community College
444 Western Blvd.
Jacksonville 28546-6877

Craven Community College
800 College Ct.
New Bern 28562

Davidson County Community College
297 Davidson Community College Rd.
Lexington 27293

Durham Technical Community College
1637 Lawson St.
Durham 27703

Edgecombe Community College
2009 West Wilson St.
Tarboro 27886

Fayetteville Technical Community
College
2201 Hull Rd.
Fayetteville 28303-0236

Forsyth Technical Community College
2100 Silas Creek Pkwy.
Winston-Salem 27103

Gaston College
201 Hwy. 321 S
Dallas 28034

Guilford Technical Community College
P.O. Box 309
Jamestown 27282

Haywood Community College
Freedlander Dr.
Clyde 28721

Isothermal Community College
P.O. Box 804
Spindale 28160

James Sprunt Community College
P.O. Box 398
Kenansville 28349

Johnston Community College
P.O. Box 2350
Smithfield 27577-2350

Lenoir Community College
P.O. Box 188
Kinston 28502-0188

Louisburg College
501 North Main St.
Louisburg 27549

Martin Community College
1161 Kehukee Park Rd.
Williamston 27892-9988

Mayland Community College
P.O. Box 547
Spruce Pine 28777

Mitchell Community College
500 West Broad
Statesville 28677

Montgomery Community College
P.O. Box 787
Troy 27371

Nash Community College
P.O. Box 7488
Rocky Mount 27804

Piedmont Community College
P.O. Box 1197
Roxboro 27573

Pitt Community College
Hwy. 11 S
P.O. Drawer 7007
Greenville 27835-7007

Randolph Community College
629 Industrial Park Way
Asheboro 27204

Richmond Community College
P.O. Box 1189
Hamlet 28345

Roanoke-Chowan Community College
Rte. 2, P.O. Box 46A
Ahoskie 27910

Robeson Community College
P.O. Box 1420
Lumberton 28359

Rockingham Community College
P.O. Box 38, Hwy. 65 West County Home
Rd.
Wentworth 27375-0038

Rowan-Cabarrus Community College
P.O. Box 1595
Salisbury 28145-1595

Salisbury Business College
1400 Jake Alexander Blvd. W
Salisbury 28147

Sampson Community College
P.O. Box 318
Clinton 28328

Sandhills Community College
2200 Airport Rd.
Pinehurst 28374

Shaw University
118 East South St.
Raleigh 27601

Southwestern Community College
447 College Dr.
Sylva 28779

Stanly Community College
141 College Dr.
Albemarle 28001

Surry Community College
P.O. Box 304
Dobson 27017-0304

Tri-County Community College
2300 Hwy. 64 E
Murphy 28906

Vance-Granville Community College
State Rd. 1126, P.O. Box 917
Henderson 27536

Wake Technical Community College
9101 Fayetteville Rd.
Raleigh 27603-5696

Wayne Community College
3000 Wayne Memorial Dr.
Goldsboro 27533-8002

Western Piedmont Community College
1001 Burkemont Ave.
Morganton 28655-9978

Wilkes Community College
Collegiate Dr.
Wilkesboro 28697

Wilson Technical Community College
902 Herring Ave.
Wilson 27893

NORTH DAKOTA

Interstate Business College
520 East Main Ave.
Bismarck 58501

Interstate Business College
2720 32nd Ave. SW
Fargo 58103

North Dakota State College of Science
800 North Sixth St.
Wahpeton 58076

Turtle Mountain Community College
P.O. Box 340
Belcourt 58316

University of North Dakota, Lake
Region
1801 North College Dr.
Devils Lake 58301

OHIO

Akron Adult Vocational Services
147 Park St.
Akron 44308

Ashland County-West Home Joint Vocational School
1783 Rte. 60 & RD 6
Ashland 44805-9377

Baldwin-Wallace College
275 Eastland Rd.
Berea 44017

Belmont Technical College
120 Fox Shannon Place
Saint Clairsville 43950

Bowling Green State University, Firelands
901 Rye Beach Rd.
Huron 44839

Bryant and Stratton College
12955 Snow Rd.
Parma 44130

Central Ohio Technical College
1179 University Dr.
Newark 43055-1767

Cincinnati State Technical and Community College
3520 Central Pkwy.
Cincinnati 45223

Clark State Community College
570 East Leffel Ln.
Springfield 45505

Columbus State Community College
550 East Spring St.
P.O. Box 1609
Columbus 43216

Cuyahoga Community College District
700 Carnegie Ave.
Cleveland 44115-2878

Davis College
4747 Monroe St.
Toledo 43623

Edison State Community College
1973 Edison Dr.
Piqua 45356

Franklin University
201 South Grant Ave.
Columbus 43215-5399

Hocking Technical College
3301 Hocking Pkwy.
Nelsonville 45764

ITT Technical Institute
1030 North Meridan Rd.
Youngstown 44509

Jefferson Community College
4000 Sunset Blvd.
Steubenville 43952-3598

Kent State University, Ashtabula Regional Campus
3325 West 13th St.
Ashtabula 44004

Kent State University, East Liverpool Regional Campus
400 East Fourth St.
East Liverpool 43920

Kent State University, Salem Regional Campus
2491 South Rte. 45 S
Salem 44460

Kent State University, Trumbull Regional Campus
4314 Mahoning Ave. NW
Warren 44483

Kent State University, Tuscarus Regional Campus
University Dr. NE
New Philadelphia 44663

Lakeland Community College
7700 Clocktower Dr.
Kirkland 44094-5198

Lima Technical College
4240 Campus Dr.
Lima 45804

Lorain County Community College
1005 North Abbe Rd.
Elyria 44035

Marion Technical College
1467 Mount Vernon Ave.
Marion 43302-5694

Miami University, Oxford Campus
500 High St.
Oxford 45056

Miami-Jacobs College
400 East Second St.
Dayton 45401

Muskingum Area Technical College
1555 Newark Rd.
Zanesville 43701

North Central Technical College
2441 Kenwood Circle, P.O. Box 698
Mansfield 44901

Northwest State Community College
22-600 South Rte. 34
Archbold 43502-9990

Northwestern College
1441 North Cable Rd.
Lima 45805

Ohio University, Chillicothe Branch
571 West Fifth St.
Chillicothe 45601

Ohio University, Lancaster Branch
1570 Granville Pike
Lancaster 43130

Ohio University, Main Campus
Athens 45701

Owens Community College
39335 Oregon Rd.
Toledo 43699-1947

Sawyer College of Business
3150 Mayfield Rd.
Cleveland Heights 44118

Sawyer College of Business, West
13027 Lorain Ave.
Cleveland 44111

Shawnee State University
940 Second St.
Portsmouth 45662

Sinclair Community College
444 West Third St.
Dayton 45402

Southeastern Business College
1855 Western Ave.
Chillicothe 45601

Southeastern Business College
1176 Jackson Pike
Gallipolis 45631

Southeastern Business College
1522 Sheridan Dr.
Lancaster 43130

Southeastern Business College
4020 Milan Rd.
Sandusky 44870-5871

Southeastern Business College, Lorain
1907 North Ridge Rd.
Lorain 44055

Southern Ohio College, Northeast
2791 Mogadore Rd.
Akron 44312

Southern Ohio College
1011 Glendale Milford Rd.
Cincinnati 45237

Southern State Community College
200 Hobart Dr.
Hillsboro 45133

Southwestern College of Business
632 Vine St.
Cincinnati 45202

Southwestern College of Business
225 West First St.
Dayton 45402

Stark State College of Technology
6200 Frank Ave. NW
Canton 44720

Stautzenberger College
5355 Southwyck Blvd.
Toledo 43614

Terra State Community College
2830 Napoleon Rd.
Fremont 43420

Tiffin University
155 Miami St.
Tiffin 44883

University of Akron, Main Campus
302 Buchtel Common
Akron 44325-4702

University of Akron, Wayne College
1901 Smucker Rd.
Orrville 44667

University of Cincinnati, Clermont College
College Dr.
Batavia 45103

University of Cincinnati, Main Campus
P.O. Box 210127
Cincinnati 45221-0127

University of Cincinnati, Raymond Walters College
9555 Plainfield Rd.
Blue Ash 45236

University of Toledo
2801 West Bancroft
Toledo 43606

Upper Valley Joint Vocational School
8811 Career Dr.
Piqua 45356

Urbana University
College Way
Urbana 43078

Washington State Community College
710 Colegate Dr.
Marietta 45750

Wilmington College
251 Ludovic St.
Wilmington 45177

Wright State University, Lake Campus
7600 State Rte. 703 E
Celina 45822

Youngstown State University
One University Plaza
Youngstown 44555

OKLAHOMA

Bacone College
2299 Old Bacome Rd.
Muskogee 74403-1597

Bartlesville Wesleyan College
2201 Silver Lake Rd.
Bartlesville 74006-6299

Cameron University
2800 Gore Blvd.
Lawton 73505

Carl Albert State College
1507 South McKenna
Poteau 74953-5208

Connors State College
Rte. 1, P.O. Box 1000
Warner 74469

Eastern Oklahoma State College
1301 West Main St.
Wilburton 74578

Murray State College
One Murray Campus
Tishomingo 73460

Northeastern Oklahoma Agricultural and Mechanical College
200 I St. NE
Miami 74354

Northern Oklahoma College
P.O. Box 310, Tonkawa
Tonkawa 74653

Oklahoma City Community College
7777 South May Ave.
Oklahoma City 73159

Oklahoma State University, Oklahoma City
900 North Portland
Oklahoma City 73107

Oklahoma State University, Okmulgee
1801 East Fourth St.
Okmulgee 74447-3901

Rogers University, Claremore
Will Rogers and College Hill
Claremore 74017

Rose State College
6420 Southeast 15th
Midwest City 73110

Seminole State College
2701 Boren Blvd.
Seminole 74868

Tulsa Community College
6111 East Skelly Dr.
Tulsa 74135

Tulsa County Area Vocational-Technical School District 18
3805 North Peoria
Tulsa 74106

Western Oklahoma State College
2801 North Main St.
Altus 73521-1397

OREGON

Blue Mountain Community College
P.O. Box 100
Pendleton 97801

Central Oregon Community College
2600 Northwest College Way
Bend 97701

Chemeketa Community College
4000 Lancaster Dr. NE
Salem 97305

Clackamas Community College
19600 Molalla Ave.
Oregon City 97045

Lane Community College
4000 East 30th Ave.
Eugene 97405

Linn-Benton Community College
6500 Southwest Pacific Blvd.
Albany 97321

Mount Hood Community College
26000 Southeast Stark St.
Gresham 97030

Pioneer Pacific College
25195 Southwest Parkway Ave.
Wilsonville 97070

Portland Community College
P.O. Box 19000
Portland 97280-0990

Rogue Community College
3345 Redwood Hwy.
Grants Pass 97527

Southern Oregon University
1250 Siskiyou Bld
Ashland 97520

Southwestern Oregon Community College
1988 Newmark Ave.
Coos Bay 97420

Umpqua Community College
P.O. Box 967
Roseburg 97470

PENNSYLVANIA

Allentown Business School
1501 Lehigh St.
Allentown 18103

Altoona School of Commerce
508 58th St.
Altoona 16602

Alvernia College
400 Bernardine St.
Reading 19607

Beaver College
450 South Easton Rds.
Glenside 19038-3295

Berean Institute
1901 West Girard Ave.
Philadelphia 19130

Bucks County Community College
Swamp Rd.
Newtown 18940

Business Institute of Pennsylvania
335 Boyd Dr.
Sharon 16146

Butler County Community College
College Dr. Oak Hills
Butler 16003-1203

California University of Pennsylvania
250 University Ave.
California 15419-1394

Cambria Rowe Business College
221 Central Ave.
Johnstown 15902

Central Pennsylvania Business School
107 College Hill Rd.
Summerdale 17093-0309

The Chubb Institute, Keystone School
965 Baltimore Pike
Springfield 19064

Churchman Business School
355 Spring Garden St.
Easton 18042

Clarion University of Pennsylvania
Wood St.
Clarion 16214

Community College of Allegheny
County
800 Allegheny Ave.
Pittsburgh 15233-1895

Community College of Beaver County
One Campus Dr.
Monaca 15061

Community College of Philadelphia
1700 Spring Garden St.
Philadelphia 19130

Delaware County Community College
901 South Media Line Rd.
Media 19063-1094

Douglas School of Business
130 Seventh St.
Monessen 15062

Du Bois Business College
One Beaver Dr.
Du Bois 15801

Duffs Business Institute
110 Ninth St.
Pittsburgh 15222

Edinboro University of Pennsylvania
Edinboro 16444

Erie Business Center
246 West Ninth St.
Erie 16501

Franklin and Marshall College
P.O. Box 3003
Lancaster 17604-3003

Gannon University
109 West Sixth St.
Erie 16541

Harrisburg Area Community College,
Harrisburg Campus
One Hacc Dr.
Harrisburg 17110

ICM School of Business and Medical
Career
10-14 Wood St.
Pittsburgh 15222

Immaculata College
Immaculata 19345

Indiana University of Pennsylvania
201 Sutton Hall
Indiana 15705

Information Computer Systems
Institute
2201 Hangar Place
Allentown 18103

Keystone College
P.O. Box 50
La Plume 18440-0200

Lackawanna Junior College
501 Vine St.
Scranton 18509

Lansdale School of Business
201 Church Rd.
North Wales 19454

Lebanon Valley College
101 North College Ave.
Annville 17003

Lehigh Carbon Community College
4525 Education Park Dr.
Schnecksville 18078-2598

Luzerne County Community College
1333 South Prospect St.
Nanticoke 18634

Mercyhurst College
501 East 38th St.
Erie 16546

Montgomery County Community
College
340 Dekalb Pike
Blue Bell 19422

Mount Aloysius College
7373 Admiral Pearl Hwy.
Cresson 16630-1999

Newport Business Institute
941 West Third St.
Williamsport 17701

Northampton County Area Community
College
3835 Green Pond Rd.
Bethlehem 18020-7599

Pace Institute
606 Court St.
Reading 19601

Peirce College
1420 Pine St.
Philadelphia 19102

Pennsylvania Commercial Inc.
82 South Main St.
Washington 15301

Pennsylvania State University,
Abington Campus
1600 Woodland Rd.
Abington 19001

Pennsylvania State University, Altoona
Campus
3000 Ivyside Park
Altoona 16601-3760

Pennsylvania State University, Beaver
Campus
Brodhead Rd.
Monaca 15061

Pennsylvania State University, Berks
Campus
Tulpehocken Rd., P.O. Box 7009
Reading 19610-6009

Pennsylvania State University,
Delaware Campus
25 Yearsley Mill Rd.
Media 19063

Pennsylvania State University, Du Bois
Campus
College Place
Du Bois 15801

Pennsylvania State University, Fayette
Campus
One University Dr.
Uniontown 15401

Pennsylvania State University, Hazleton
Campus
Highacres
Hazleton 18201

Pennsylvania State University, Main
Campus
201 Old Main
University Park 16802

Pennsylvania State University, New
Kensington Campus
3550 Seventh St. Rd.
New Kensington 15068

Pennsylvania State University,
Schuylkill Campus
200 University Dr.
Schuylkill Haven 17972-2208

Pennsylvania State University,
Shenango Campus
147 Shenango Ave.
Sharon 16146

Pennsylvania State University,
Worthington Scranton Campus
120 Ridge View Dr.
Dunmore 18512

Pennsylvania State University, York
Campus
1031 Edgecomb Ave.
York 17403

Point Park College
201 Wood St.
Pittsburgh 15222

Reading Area Community College
P.O. Box 1706
Reading 19603-1706

Robert Morris College
881 Narrows Run Rd.
Moon Township 15108-1189

Saint Francis College
P.O. Box 600
Loretto 15940

Sawyer School
717 Liberty Ave.
Pittsburgh 15222

Schuylkill Business Institute
2400 West End Ave.
Pottsville 17901

Seton Hill College
Seton Hill Dr.
Greensburg 15601

South Hills School of Business and
Technology
480 Waupelani Dr.
State College 16801

Thompson Institute
5650 Derry St.
Harrisburg 17111

Thompson Institute
3440 Market St.
Philadelphia 19104

University of Pennsylvania
One College Hall
34th and Spruce Sts.
Philadelphia 19104

University of Pittsburgh at Titusville
504 East Main St.
Titusville 16354

University of Pittsburgh, Main Campus
4200 Fifth Ave.
Pittsburgh 15260

Ursinus College
Main St.
Collegeville 19426

Valley Forge Military College
1001 Eagle Rd. Sorley House
Wayne 19087

Westmoreland County Community
College
Youngwood 15697-1895

Wilson College
1015 Philadelphia Ave.
Chambersburg 17201-1285

York College Pennsylvania
Country Club Rd.
York 17405-7199

Yorktowne Business Institute
West Seventh Ave.
York 17404

RHODE ISLAND

Bryant College
1150 Douglas Pike
Smithfield 02917-1284

Community College of Rhode Island
400 East Ave.
Warwick 02886-1807

Johnson and Wales University
8 Abbott Park Place
Providence 02903-3376

Katharine Gibbs School
178 Butler Ave.
Providence 02906

Roger Williams University
One Old Ferry Rd.
Bristol 02809-2923

SOUTH CAROLINA

Aiken Technical College
P.O. Drawer 696
Aiken 29802

Bob Jones University
Greenville 29614

Chesterfield-Marlboro Technical
College
1201 Chesterfield Hwy.
P.O. Drawer 1007
Cheraw 29520

Clinton Junior College
1029 Crawford Rd.
Rock Hill 29730

Forrest Junior College
601 East River St.
Anderson 29624

Greenville Technical College
Station B, P.O. Box 5616
Greenville 29606-5616

Horry-Georgetown Technical College
P.O. Box 1966
Conway 29526

Limestone College
1115 College Dr.
Gaffney 29340

Midlands Technical College
P.O. Box 2408
Columbia 29202

North Greenville College
P.O. Box 1892
Tigerville 29688-1892

Orangeburg-Calhoun Technical College
3250 Saint Matthew's Rd.
Orangeburg 29115

Piedmont Technical College
P.O. Drawer 1467
Greenwood 29648

Southern Wesleyan University
P.O. Box 1020
Central 29630

Spartanburg Technical College
Hwy. I-85, P.O. Drawer 4386
Spartanburg 29305

Tri-County Technical College
P.O. Box 587
Pendleton 29670

Trident Technical College
P.O. Box 118067
Charleston 29423-8067

York Technical College
452 South Anderson Rd.
Rock Hill 29730

SOUTH DAKOTA

Dakota State University
820 North Washington
Madison 57042

Huron University
333 Ninth St. SW
Huron 57350

Mount Marty College
1105 West 8th
Yankton 57078

National American University
321 Kansas City St.
Rapid City 57701

National American University
3109 South Kiwanis Ave.
Sioux Falls 57105

Nettleton Career College
100 South Spring Ave.
Sioux Falls 57104

Northern State University
1200 South Jay St.
Aberdeen 57401-7198

Southeast Technical Institute
2301 Career Place
Sioux Falls 57107

TENNESSEE

Austin Peay State University
601 College St.
Clarksville 37044

Chattanooga State Technical
    Community College
4501 Amnicola Hwy.
Chattanooga 37406

Cleveland State Community College
P.O. Box 3570
Cleveland 37320-3570

Draughons Junior College of Business
Plus Park at Pavilion Blvd.
P.O. Box 17386
Nashville 37217

Dyersburg State Community College
1510 Lake Rd.
Dyersburg 38024

Hiwassee College
225 Hiwassee College Dr.
Madisonville 37354

Jackson State Community College
2046 North Pkwy.
Jackson 38301

Knoxville Business College
720 North Fifth Ave.
Knoxville 37917

Lincoln Memorial University
Cumberland Gap Pkwy.
Harrogate 37752

Middle Tennessee State University
Murfreesboro 37132

Motlow State Community College
P.O. Box 88100, Ledford Mill Rd.
Tullahoma 37388-8100

Nashville State Technical Institute
120 White Bridge Rd.
Nashville 37209

Northeast State Technical Community
    College
P.O. Box 246
Blountville 37617

Pellissippi State Technical Community
    College
P.O. Box 22990
Knoxville 37933-0990

Roane State Community College
276 Patton Ln.
Harriman 37748

Shelby State Community College
P.O. Box 40568
Memphis 38174-0568

State Technical Institute at Memphis
5983 Macon Cove
Memphis 38134

Tennessee Technology Center at Crump
Hwy. 64 W, P.O. Box 89
Crump 38327

Tennessee Technology Center at
    Dickson
740 Hwy. 46
Dickson 37055

Tennessee Technology Center at
    Elizabethton
1500 Arney St.
P.O. Box 789
Elizabethton 37643

Tennessee Technology Center at
    Harriman
P.O. Box 1109
Harriman 37748

Tennessee Technology Center at
    Hartsville
Hwy. 25 & 716 McMurry Blvd.
Hartsville 37074

Tennessee Technology Center at
    Hohenwald
813 West Main
Hohenwald 38462-2201

Tennessee Technology Center at
    Knoxville
1100 Liberty St.
Knoxville 37919

Tennessee Technology Center at
    Livingston
740 High Tech Dr.
Livingston 38570

Tennessee Technology Center at
    Memphis
550 Alabama Ave.
Memphis 38105-3604

Tennessee Technology Center at Pulaski
1233 East College St.
Pulaski 38478

Tennessee Technology Center at Ripley
South Industrial Park
Ripley 38063

Volunteer State Community College
1480 Nashville Pike
Gallatin 37066-3188

Walters State Community College
500 South Davy Crockett Pkwy.
Morristown 37813-6899

TEXAS

Alvin Community College
3110 Mustang Rd.
Alvin 77511

Amarillo College
P.O. Box 447
Amarillo 79178

Angelina College
P.O. Box 1768
Lufkin 75902-1768

Austin Community College
5930 Middle Fiskville Rd.
Austin 78752

Bee County College
3800 Charco Rd.
Beeville 78102

Brookhaven College
3939 Valley View Ln.
Farmers Branch 75244-4997

Cedar Valley College
3030 North Dallas Ave.
Lancaster 75134

Central Texas College
P.O. Box 1800
Killeen 76540-1800

Cisco Junior College
Rte. 3, P.O. Box 3
Cisco 76437

Clarendon College
P.O. Box 968
Clarendon 79226

College of the Mainland
1200 Amburn Rd.
Texas City 77591

Del Mar College
101 Baldwin
Corpus Christi 78404-3897

Eastfield College
3737 Motley Dr.
Mesquite 75150

El Centro College
Main and Lamar
Dallas 75202

El Paso Community College
P.O. Box 20500
El Paso 79998

Frank Phillips College
P.O. Box 5118
Borger 79008-5118

Grayson County College
6101 Grayson Dr.
Denison 75020

Hill College
P.O. Box 619
Hillsboro 76645

Houston Community College System
22 Waugh Dr.
Houston 77270-7849

Howard County Junior College District
1001 Birdwell Ln.
Big Spring 79720

International Business College, Bond
Office
1030 North Zaragosa Rd.
El Paso 79907

Kilgore College
1100 Broadway
Kilgore 75662-3299

Lamar University, Beaumont
P.O. Box 10001 4400 Mlk
Beaumont 77710

Lamar University, Orange
410 Front St.
Orange 77630-5899

Lamar University, Port Arthur
1500 Proctor St.
Port Arthur 77640

Lee College
200 Lee Dr.
Baytown 77520-4703

McLennan Community College
1400 College Dr.
Waco 76708

Midland College
3600 North Garfield
Midland 79705

Mountain View College
4849 West Illinois
Dallas 75211

Navarro College
3200 West 7th
Corsicana 75110

North Harris Montgomery Community
College District
250 North Sam Houston Pkwy. E., Ste.
300
Houston 77060

North Lake College
5001 North MacArthur Blvd.
Irving 75038-3899

Odessa College
201 West University
Odessa 79764

Panola College
1109 West Panola St.
Carthage 75633

Richland College
12800 Abrams Rd.
Dallas 75243-2199

Saint Philip's College
1801 Martin Luther King Dr.
San Antonio 78203

San Antonio College
1300 San Pedro Ave.
San Antonio 78284

San Jacinto College, Central Campus
8060 Spencer Hwy.
Pasadena 77505-6009

San Jacinto College, North Campus
5800 Uvalde
Houston 77049

San Jacinto College, South Campus
13735 Beamer Rd.
Houston 77089-6009

South Plains College
1401 College Ave.
Levelland 79336

Tarrant County Junior College
1500 Houston St.
Fort Worth 76102

Temple College
2600 South First St.
Temple 76504-7435

Texarkana College
2500 North Robison Rd.
Texarkana 75599

Texas Southmost College
80 Fort Brown
Brownsville 78520

Trinity Valley Community College
500 South Prairieville
Athens 75751

Tyler Junior College
1327 South Baxter Ave.
Tyler 75711

Vernon Regional Junior College
4400 College Dr.
Vernon 76384-4092

Victoria College
2200 East Red River
Victoria 77901

Weatherford College
308 East Park Ave.
Weatherford 76086

Wharton County Junior College
911 Boling Hwy.
Wharton 77488

UTAH

Bridgerland Applied Technology Center
1301 North 600 West
Logan 84321

College of Eastern Utah
400 East 400 N
Price 84501

Dixie College
225 South 700 East
Saint George 84770

Latter Day Saints Business College
411 East South Temple
Salt Lake City 84111-1392

Salt Lake Community College
P.O. Box 30808
Salt Lake City 84130

Sevier Valley Applied Technology
    Center
800 West 200 S
Richfield 84701

Utah Valley State College
800 West 1200 S
Orem 84058

VERMONT

Castleton State College
Castleton 05735

Champlain College
163 South Willard St.
Burlington 05401

College of Saint Joseph
71 Clement Rd.
Rutland 05701-3899

Community College of Vermont
P.O. Box 120
Waterbury 05676

Johnson State College
Johnson 05656

Lyndon State College
Lyndonville 05851

Southern Vermont College
Monument Rd.
Bennington 05201

Trinity College of Vermont
208 Colchester Ave.
Burlington 05401

Vermont Technical College
P.O. Box 500
Randolph Center 05061

VIRGINIA

Blue Ridge Community College
P.O. Box 80
Weyers Cave 24486

Central Virginia Community College
3506 Wards Rd.
Lynchburg 24502

Commonwealth College
1120 West Mercury Blvd.
Hampton 23666

Commonwealth College
301 Centre Pointe Dr.
Norfolk 23462

Dabney South Lancaster Community
College
P.O. Box 1000
Clifton Forge 24422-1000

Danville Community College
1008 South Main St.
Danville 24541

Dominion Business School
4142-1 Melrose Ave.
Roanoke 24017

Eastern Shore Community College
29300 Lankford Hwy.
Melfa 23410

Germanna Community College
2130 Germanna Hwy.
Locust Grove 22508

J Sargeant Reynolds Community
College
P.O. Box 85622
Richmond 23285-5622

John Tyler Community College
13101 Jefferson Davis Hwy.
Chester 23831-5399

Lord Fairfax Community College
173 Skirmisher Ln. P.O. Box 47
Middletown 22645

Mountain Empire Community College
P.O. Drawer 700
Big Stone Gap 24219

National Business College
1813 East Main St.
Salem 24153

New River Community College
P.O. Drawer 1127
Dublin 24084-1127

Northern Virginia Community College
4001 Wakefield Chapel Rd.
Annandale 22003

Patrick Henry Community College
P.O. Box 5311
Martinsville 24115-5311

Paul D Camp Community College
100 North College Dr., P.O. Box 737
Franklin 23851

Phillips Business College
1912 Memorial Ave.
Lynchburg 24505-0169

Piedmont Virginia Community College
501 College Dr.
Charlottesville 22902

Rappahannock Community College,
Glenns Campus
12745 College Dr.
Glenns 23149

Richard Bland College of William and
Mary
11301 Johnson Rd.
Petersburg 23805

Southside Virginia Community College
109 Campus Dr.
Alberta 23821

Southwest Virginia Community College
P.O. Box SVCC
Richlands 24641

Thomas Nelson Community College
P.O. Box 9407
Hampton 23670

University of Richmond
28 Westhampton Way
Richmond 23173

Virginia Highlands Community College
P.O. Box 828
Abingdon 24210

Virginia Western Community College
3095 Colonial Ave.
Roanoke 24015

Wytheville Community College
1000 East Main St.
Wytheville 24382

WASHINGTON

Bellevue Community College
3000 Landerholm Circle SE
Bellevue 98007-6484

Big Bend Community College
7662 Chanute St.
Moses Lake 98837

Clark College
1800 East McLoughlin Blvd.
Vancouver 98663-3598

Columbia Basin College
2600 North 20th Ave.
Pasco 99301

Edmonds Community College
20000 68th Ave. W
Lynnwood 98036

Everett Community College
801 Wetmore Ave.
Everett 98201

Grays Harbor College
1620 Edward P Smith Dr.
Aberdeen 98520

Green River Community College
12401 Southeast 320th St.
Auburn 98092

Heritage College
3240 Fort Rd.
Toppenish 98948

Highline Community College
P.O. Box 98000
Des Moines 98198-9800

Lower Columbia College
P.O. Box 3010
Longview 98632

Olympic College
1600 Chester Ave.
Bremerton 98310-1699

Peninsula College
1502 East Lauridsen Blvd.
Port Angeles 98362

Seattle Community College, Central
Campus
1701 Broadway
Seattle 98122

Seattle Community College, North
Campus
9600 College Way N
Seattle 98103

Seattle Community College, South
Campus
6000 16th Ave. SW
Seattle 98106

Shoreline Community College
16101 Greenwood Ave. N
Seattle 98133

Skagit Valley College
2405 College Way
Mount Vernon 98273

Spokane Community College
North 1810 Greene Ave.
Spokane 99207

Spokane Falls Community College
West 3410 Fort George Wright Dr.
Spokane 99224

Tacoma Community College
5900 South 12th St.
Tacoma 98465

Wenatchee Valley College
1300 Fifth St.
Wenatchee 98801

Whatcom Community College
237 West Kellogg Rd.
Bellingham 98226

WEST VIRGINIA

Bluefield State College
219 Rock St.
Bluefield 24701

Boone County Career & Technical
Center
H.C. 81, P.O. Box 50B
Danville 25053

The College of West Virginia
609 South Kanawha St.
Beckley 25801

Fairmont State College
1201 Locust Ave.
Fairmont 26554

Glenville State College
200 High St.
Glenville 26351

Huntington Junior College
900 Fifth Ave.
Huntington 25701

Marshall University
400 Hal Greer Blvd.
Huntington 25755

Mountain Cap of West Virginia, Inc.
26 North Kanawha St.
Buckhannon 26201

National Institute of Technology, A
Corinthian School
5514 Big Tyler Rd.
Cross Lanes 25313

Opportunities Industrialization Center,
North Central West Virginia
120 Jackson St.
Fairmont 26554

Potomac State College of West Virginia
University
Fort Ave.
Keyser 26726

Southern West Virginia Community
and Technical College
P.O. Box 2900
Mt. Gay 25637

West Virginia Career College
148 Willey St.
Morgantown 26505

West Virginia Institute of Technology
Montgomery 25136

West Virginia Northern Community
College
1704 Market St.
Wheeling 26003

West Virginia State College
Rte. 25
Institute 25112

West Virginia University at Parkersburg
Rte. 5, 300 Campus Dr.
Parkersburg 26101

WISCONSIN

Gateway Technical College
3520 30th Ave.
Kenosha 53144-1690

Lakeshore Technical College
1290 North Ave.
Cleveland 53015

Madison Area Technical College
3550 Anderson St.
Madison 53704

Madison Junior College of Business
31 South Henry St.
Madison 53703-3110

Mid-State Technical College
500 32nd St. N
Wisconsin Rapids 54494

Milwaukee Area Technical College
700 West State St.
Milwaukee 53233-1443

Moraine Park Technical College
235 North National Ave.
P.O. Box 1940
Fond Du Lac 54936-1940

Mount Senario College
1500 College Ave. W
Ladysmith 54848

North Central Technical College
1000 Campus Dr.
Wausau 54401-1899

Northeast Wisconsin Technical College
2740 West Mason St., P.O. Box 19042
Green Bay 54307-9042

Southwest Wisconsin Technical College
1800 Bronson Blvd.
Fennimore 53809

Waukesha County Technical College
800 Main St.
Pewaukee 53072

Western Wisconsin Technical College
304 North Sixth St.
P.O. Box 908
La Crosse 54602-0908

WYOMING

Casper College
125 College Dr.
Casper 82601

Central Wyoming College
2660 Peck Ave.
Riverton 82501

Eastern Wyoming College
3200 West C St.
Torrington 82240

Laramie County Community College
1400 East College Dr.
Cheyenne 82007

Northwest Community College
231 West Sixth St.
Powell 82435

Sheridan College
3059 Coffeen Ave.
Sheridan 82801

Western Wyoming Community College
2500 College Dr.
Rock Springs 82902

Index

All jobs mentioned in this volume are listed and cross-referenced in the index. Entries that appear in all capital letters have occupational profiles. For example, ACTUARY, BILLING CLERK, CLAIMS ADJUSTER and so on are profiles in this volume. Entries that are not capitalized refer to jobs that do not have a separate profile but for which information is given.

Under some capitalized entries there is a section titled "Profile includes." This lists jobs that are mentioned in the profile. For example, in the case of AUDITOR, jobs that are described in the profile are External Auditor and Internal Auditor.

Some entries are followed by a job title in parentheses after the page number on which it can be found. This job title is the occupational profile in which the entry is discussed. For instance, the Registrar entry is followed by the profile title (College/university administrator).